S0-AZY-169

WARIO WORLD™

Prima's Official Strategy Guide

Steve Stratton

Prima Games
A Division of Random House, Inc.

3000 Lava Ridge Court
Roseville, CA 95661
1-800-733-3000
www.primagames.com

The Prima Games logo is a registered trademark of Random House, Inc., registered in the United States and other countries. Primagames.com is a registered trademark of Random House, Inc., registered in the United States.

Product Manager: Sara E. Wilson
Project Editor: Michelle Trujillo
Design & Layout: Derek Hocking, Simon Olney

Wario World © 2003 Nintendo. TM, ®, and the Nintendo GameCube logo are trademarks of Nintendo.

ISBN: 0-7615-4323-6
Library of Congress Catalog Card Number: 2003105567
Printed in the United States of America

03 04 05 06 GG 10 9 8 7 6 5 4 3 2 1

Contents

Welcome to Wario World

Thank you for purchasing *Wario World™: Prima's Official Strategy Guide*. You've made a wise decision, for the pages of this guide are filled with awesome tips, in-depth strategies, and step-by-step walkthroughs for every stage of the game. And although he'd never admit it, Wario thanks you, too. He knows that there's nothing to stop him from reclaiming all his lost treasure now!

It's Not the Wanting, It's the Having

Wario's a material guy, and the one material he values more than anything else is gold. After much effort, he's achieved his innermost desire: a giant castle, built in honor of his unending greed. Wario's mighty stronghold also serves an important purpose—it keeps his ill-gotten wealth safe from prying eyes. He'd never let anyone take so much as a peek at his vast fortune. His most precious gems, jewels, and objects of pure gold lay hidden away in the depths of his castle's basement.

However, Wario could not have foreseen the terrible evil that his own greed would bring to pass. Amid his hoard of treasure, a cursed jewel—black as midnight—awakens with the desire to build a kingdom of its own. Finding itself surrounded by the rest of Wario's riches, the evil black jewel uses the full power of its dreadful curse to change all the pieces of Wario's treasure into horrible monsters.

By the time Wario realizes what's happening, it's too late to put a stop to it. Nearly all his treasure has been transformed into vicious minions of the cursed black jewel. It seems that no greedy deed goes unpunished.

After much loathing and self-pity, Wario finally does the one thing that the black jewel hadn't counted on—he gets very angry! Never one to be outdone by anyone or anything, Wario decides to reclaim all the treasure he'd rightfully stolen in the first place. And once Wario gets really mad, there's no telling what he's capable of doing.

Wario World Basics

This section deals with the larger aspects of *Wario World*, such as the overall layout and object of the game, and includes general tips to keep in mind as you play through each area. All this good stuff helps you out, so read on.

The Objective of the Game

The most basic objective of *Wario World* is to progress through each stage of the game, collecting the four Giant Treasure Chest Keys from the four stage bosses. Once you collect all four Giant Treasure Chest Keys, you unlock the final boss fight against the mysterious black jewel itself. Defeat the black jewel and your job is done.

True *Wario World* fanatics, however, search high and low for every missing treasure, Red Diamond, and trapped Spriteling in the eight areas of the game. You can view your treasure-collecting progress at any time via the in-game Pause screen. Build the Gold Statues of Wario by collecting the eight parts hidden in each area. When you complete a Gold Statue, Wario's Heart Meter increases by half a heart.

An Outline of Wario World

Wario World is made up of four stages, each containing two areas to explore and a stage boss at the end. The stages are all accessed from Treasure Square, the hub of the game. Each time you defeat a stage boss, you get one of the four Giant Treasure Chest Keys, and the next stage's gate opens. Defeat all four stage bosses and use their Giant Treasure Chest Keys to put the hurt on that evil black jewel.

Wario's Tips

The following tips come straight from the man with the zany moustache. Keep these little nuggets of advice in mind as you play through the game, and you're on the same page as Wario, working together in perfect harmony.

Grab the Gold

It's true that Wario loves few things as much as he loves gold, but there's an even better reason to collect those loose coins. Gold coins are used to purchase Heart Meter-restoring Garlic from the Garlic Dispensers in each area. Should Wario's Heart Meter ever become empty, you need a certain number of gold coins to continue.

Build Gold Statues

Combining his two most favorite things, himself and gold, Wario had eight Gold Statues cast in his image when he built his castle. When the black jewel awoke and started working its curse, each Gold Statue was broken into eight parts and scattered throughout each area of Wario World. Collecting all eight Gold Statue parts from an area permanently extends your Heart Meter by half a heart, so be on the lookout for them.

If you listen closely, you sometimes hear a gentle ringing sound as Wario explores an area. Get familiar with that sound—it's the sound of a nearby Gold Statue part. Even if you can't see the part, you know that Wario is standing close to one when you hear that unique sound.

TIP

Use Wario's handy Hyper Suction move to collect gold coins quickly. Press and hold L, and Wario inhales any nearby coins. Check the next section for even more information on Wario's awesome moves and attacks.

Rescue the Spritelings

Spritelings are good-natured and helpful creatures that have been imprisoned by the evil black jewel. Wario can free each Spriteling by breaking open its small, prison-like box. Each time he rescues a Spriteling, Wario receives a helpful hint as a reward.

Five of these tiny little guys are trapped in each area of Wario World. Wario is mainly focused on getting his treasure back (and teaching that nasty black jewel a lesson), but make sure he also stops to rescue the unfortunate Spritelings. Their insightful information helps him overcome many difficult obstacles.

Explore Trapdoors

Trapdoors are all over the place. Wario enters a trapdoor by performing either a Ground Pound or Piledriver move on it. Explore each trapdoor and grab the goodies from the short puzzle areas within.

Each level has at least eight trapdoors, so it's easy to lose track of which ones you've cleared and which ones you haven't. Here's a sneaky hint: Look for faint rays of light shining up through the cracks of a trapdoor. If you see the light, valuable items are to be found inside. After you've collected all the important stuff beneath a trapdoor and returned to the surface, the shining light fades away.

Know Your Enemies, Know Yourself

After fighting a monster, you get a good understanding of its strengths, weaknesses, and attack patterns. Keep all that in mind as you play through the game, and use your head when you encounter a new group of enemies. There's always a (fairly) painless way to maneuver through even the tightest of tight spots. Something—a certain attack or even a nearby object—can give you an edge over the black jewel's evil horde of foes.

It's equally important to get familiar with Wario's assortment of attacks. Become comfortable at executing each of Wario's moves, so that you can quickly assess and deal with any sort of monster encounter. Most of Wario's enemies continually respawn in the same locations, so practice all his moves and attacks in the early stages of the game before you advance too far.

Garlic Dispensers Rule!

Garlic Dispensers are Wario's best friends when the chips are down. Keep a mental note of Garlic Dispenser locations so you can find one quickly if needed (or pause the game and refer to the walkthrough map for the area you're in). Garlic Dispensers can get expensive, but they're much cheaper than continuing.

Read the Next Section

Here's Wario's best tip: Read the entire next section before you begin playing *Wario World*. It's full of vital strategy and detailed information on all the items, objects, and enemies in the game. If you're *that* impatient to start playing, you can just skim it.

Training Time

Wario World is full of items and objects, and it's important to become familiar with each one. This section deals first with all of Wario's basic and advanced attacks and moves, allowing you to control him masterfully. It then goes on to cover every item and object in the game, giving you the edge over Wario's tricky environments. That's right, friends. It's Training Time!

Wario's Basic Moves

Other than moving Wario around with ◎, there are some basic controls and movements to learn. Once you know the basics by heart you're ready to move on to Wario's advanced stuff, but get the basics down first.

Jump

For such a hefty guy, Wario sure can get some air. Press Ⓐ to make Wario jump. If you hold down Ⓐ, Wario jumps a little higher for more hang time.

Hyper Suction

Wario loves his gold coins so much, he inhales them. Press and hold Ⓛ when there are loose coins about. Wario opens wide and sucks them up, adding them to his total. Wario cannot attack or move quickly while Hyper Suction is being used.

Rotate Camera

It's often helpful to get a good view of Wario's surroundings. Use Ⓒ to change the camera angle in the desired direction. This is especially useful when navigating those tricky areas below trapdoors.

Wario's Basic Attacks

The primary focus of *Wario World* is fighting enemies, so you have to know Wario's basic fighting techniques. There's no teacher like experience, so test these attacks early in the game. Practice until you become comfortable with each attack, then move on to the advanced stuff.

Dash Attack

Press Ⓡ until it clicks, and Wario performs a Dash Attack. Wario plows ahead at full steam, ramming anything in his path. This is absolutely the only time Wario can be described as dashing.

Punch

Punching is Wario's main attack method. The guy just likes hitting things. Throw a punch by pressing Ⓑ. If you press Ⓑ rapidly and repeatedly, Wario throws a one-two punch combination. If Wario is beating on an enemy during a punch combo, every third punch becomes an extremely powerful blow.

Wario can also perform another type of punch combo. Press Ⓑ once and hold it down. Wario throws a punch, then quickly initiates his powerful Dash Attack, punishing his opponent.

NOTE

Check out Wario's Advanced Attacks below to find details on the Corkscrew Conk, which is performed by pressing Ⓐ during a Dash Attack. Wario can punch, Dash Attack, and then Corkscrew Conk his opponent in one fluid combo.

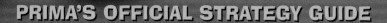
Finally, Wario can punch while jumping through the air. This allows him to attack flying enemies or elevated objects. Press Ⓐ to jump, then Ⓑ to punch.

Ground Pound

The Ground Pound is a versatile attack. It's used to enter trapdoors, bounce off Bunny Springs, and more. First, Wario must be in the air. Press Ⓐ to jump, and while Wario is airborne, press Ⓡ until it clicks. Wario flips gracefully in midair and then plummets down at full force, booty first. Anything beneath a Ground Pound is in for a big, round, purple surprise!

Wario's Advanced Attacks

Now that you have a firm handle on Wario's basic moves and attacks, learn the advanced stuff. Without a well-rounded knowledge of Wario's advanced attacks, you have a hard time dealing with powerful monsters. As always, it pays to practice these moves early so you're comfortable with them when the going gets tough.

Throws

The weakest of Wario's enemies can be bested by a single punch, but it takes more effort to get rid of the rest. Rather than being defeated outright, most enemies first become stunned. You can identify a stunned enemy by the yellow chicks that circle its head.

Once you've beaten an enemy into a stunned state, press Ⓑ and Wario lifts the dazed creature over his head. In this position, you can use a variety of devastating attacks.

NOTE

Wario can also perform any of the following moves with other objects he is able to lift, such as Columns and Sculptures.

Throw

After Wario has stunned and picked up an enemy, press Ⓑ again to have him throw the creature. You can even throw one monster into another. This is a weak throw attack, and defeats only weaker enemies—stronger ones need more impact to finish off.

Power Throw

With an enemy raised over his head, Wario can perform a more powerful throwing attack. Press and hold Ⓑ to power up Wario, using ◎ to take aim in the meantime. After a few seconds, Wario begins to flash. Release Ⓑ and Wario hurls the monster straight ahead with incredible force. This move can defeat just about any enemy.

TIP

The Power Throw is great for hitting distant targets, because Wario throws whatever he's holding in a straight line. Line up your target and whack it with a fully charged Power Throw.

The Piledriver

The Piledriver is the ultimate Ground Pound. Wario must first stun a monster and lift it over his head (or simply pick up a nearby Column). From there, press Ⓐ to make Wario jump, then press Ⓡ all the way in until it clicks. Wario spins in midair, flashes, then comes crashing down with his unfortunate enemy's head stuck between his legs. So powerful is the Piledriver that its wide shock wave inflicts damage on all nearby monsters.

The Wild Swing-Ding

The Wild Swing-Ding is Wario's best attack when monsters swarm in. While carrying a creature (or an object, such as a Column), rotate ◎ clockwise or counterclockwise. As you do, Wario begins to spin, swinging the enemy or object he's carrying. This crazy spinning attack nails anything that comes too close.

The longer you rotate ◎, the longer Wario spins. After a bit of spinning, Wario may flash, indicating that Autospin has taken over. Autospin lets you move Wario as he continues the Wild Swing-Ding attack. Press Ⓑ to throw the enemy when you want to stop swinging. This is one of Wario's more difficult moves to pull off, because you must be able to rotate ◎ quickly and consistently. When you get good at controlling the Wild Swing-Ding, Wario becomes a whirling force to be reckoned with!

TIP

To get large sums of gold coins, use the Wild Swing-Ding attack whenever you face a 60-second battle against waves of monsters.

The Corkscrew Conk

The Corkscrew Conk allows Wario to inflict multiple hits on flying enemies. Begin by pressing Ⓡ (or press and hold Ⓑ) to make Wario perform a Dash Attack. Press Ⓐ during a Dash Attack and Wario leaps, flipping through the air at high speed. This move is great against tough flying enemies, but be careful—Wario can easily Corkscrew Conk himself right off a cliff.

TIP

Use the Corkscrew Conk to make Wario jump across wide gaps.

Items

Wario World has many items for you to collect. Only a few items are absolutely necessary to beat the game (such as the Red Diamonds and Giant Treasure Chest Keys), but you miss out on a whole lot of cool stuff if you don't grab everything else. Besides, Wario won't be satisfied getting just *some* of his missing treasure back. He wants *all* his stuff.

NOTE

Pressing (START) at any time brings up the Item screen. Use this handy feature to keep track of your treasure-collecting progress. Press Ⓛ or Ⓡ at the Item screen to flip the page in either direction, allowing you to view all the treasures you've collected from each area.

Garlic

Garlic can be found inside Wooden Chests, and can also be purchased from Garlic Dispensers, using gold coins. When consumed, each clove refills one heart in Wario's Heart Meter. These items are used immediately, so they're not listed on the Item screen.

TIP

Garlic moves about. Use Hyper Suction to have Wario quickly gobble it up.

Giant Treasure Chest Keys

After working its vile curse, the evil black jewel locked itself inside the Giant Treasure Chest in Treasure Square. Wario must collect four keys to unlock the Giant Treasure Chest. These important items are known as Giant Treasure Chest Keys.

Each time Wario defeats a big, bad stage boss, he collects the Giant Treasure Chest Key that the stage boss was guarding. After clearing all four stages and defeating their respective bosses, Wario can unlock the Giant Treasure Chest and take his revenge against the evil black jewel.

Gold Coins

Money makes the world go round, and nobody knows that better than Wario. Gold coins are found nearly everywhere, but if you're running low, you can always get them by beating up on monsters. Collect every gold coin you see, as they're used to purchase Garlic from Garlic Dispensers. You also need gold coins to continue the game, should Wario's Heart Meter ever become empty.

Gold coins come in two sizes, small and large. The small ones are worth one coin; the large ones are worth ten. Press ⒧ to use Wario's Hyper Suction move and quickly collect nearby loose coins.

NOTE

Wario gets bonus coins for defeating monsters efficiently. For example, using a Wild Swing-Ding to clear out a swarm of enemies often yields extra gold. Experiment with this and use it to fatten your coin purse.

Gold Statues

Each of the eight areas in Wario World contains eight parts to a Gold Statue of the big man himself. That makes 64 Gold Statue parts in all to find and collect. Looks like Wario's got his work cut out for him.

When you collect all eight Gold Statue parts from an area, you complete a Gold Statue of Wario. Each completed statue adds half a heart to Wario's Heart Meter. Find all 64 parts, complete all eight Gold Statues, and increase Wario's Heart Meter by four whole hearts.

TIP

Gold Statue parts make a distinct, gentle ringing sound. If you hear that sound, you know that Wario is close to a Gold Statue part.

Red Diamonds

Red Diamonds are always hidden inside trapdoors, and each of the game's eight areas has eight Red Diamonds to collect. That's right—64 Red Diamonds to find! Each trapdoor's puzzling underground area hides one Red Diamond, so Wario must explore them thoroughly.

Wario must collect a certain number of Red Diamonds to unlock the Goal Trapdoor at the end of each area. Beneath the Goal Trapdoor, the area's boss awaits! It's always wise for Wario to fill up on Garlic before he Ground Pounds his way into an area boss's lair, because they can be pretty tough customers.

NOTE

You may need to collect only a few Red Diamonds to unlock the Goal Trapdoor, but Wario says you should try to find all eight from every area in the game. Why? Because they're his!

Spritelings

Technically speaking, these little guys aren't items, but they *do* appear on the Item screen if you press ⓢⓣⓐⓡⓣ during the game. Each game area has five Spritelings trapped inside small, distinct-looking wooden boxes. That means 40 Spritelings to find in all.

Although Wario doesn't really see the use of rescuing these small, colorful folk, you certainly do. Every time Wario smashes open a Spriteling box, he receives a helpful hint. Rescue all the Spritelings—you're their only hope.

Treasures

Now we're talking Wario's kind of talk! Each of the eight game areas contains eight of Wario's missing treasures—64 missing treasures to collect in all. It seems that Wario was doing all right for himself until that rotten black jewel decided to spoil everything.

To find a treasure, Wario must first locate a large, colorful Button with a big "W" printed on top. These big and brightly colored Buttons are easy to spot. Each area has eight Buttons to activate. Make sure Wario punches or attacks every one.

Once a colored Button has been activated, a big Treasure Chest appears on a platform of matching color. Sometimes the platform is a way off, so don't expect always to find it right away. Once you locate the Treasure Chest, punch it to claim one of Wario's lost treasures.

Objects

When he's not beating the stuffing out of monsters or sucking up gold coins by the chest-load, Wario must occasionally interact with various objects in his environment. This next section deals with every type of block, switch, trapdoor, and every other sort of object found in *Wario World*.

Did we mention that Wario can use a few of these objects to help him pound on monsters, too?

Blocks

Besides the normal, stationary sort, *Wario World* has several other types of blocks. Some blocks can be manipulated, while others move and even disappear. Wario spends a fair amount of time traversing these tricky blocks, so be familiar with each type.

Arrow Blocks

These distinctive blocks are dark gray and feature red arrows on all six sides. Wario can move Arrow Blocks by punching or otherwise attacking them. Arrow Blocks always move straight ahead in the direction they're hit until they run into something that stops them. For example, performing a Ground Pound on an Arrow Block moves it downward until it hits something solid.

When one Arrow Block bumps into another, both blocks move in opposite directions. If Wario punches one Arrow Block into another, the one he punched comes flying back toward him, while the other continues onward in the direction it was hit by the first. Arrow Blocks are usually found in the small puzzle areas beneath trapdoors, and Wario must manipulate them to reach the trapdoor's goodies.

Drop Blocks

Drop Blocks are usually found in the short puzzle areas accessed via trapdoors. These blocks seem stable enough at a glance, but when Wario's ample bulk lands on top of them, they give way and plummet downward. Get familiar with Drop Blocks so that their sudden descent doesn't catch you off guard.

Marshmallow Blocks

Marshmallow Blocks may not have a very threatening name, but they're probably the trickiest blocks to cross in the game. When Wario steps onto a Marshmallow Block, it disappears. Fortunately, their distinctive look makes them easy to spot. Wario can jump across a line of Marshmallow Blocks if he's quick. Otherwise, he's in for a long drop.

Rock Blocks

Rock Blocks are the most common type of block—Wario runs into these things everywhere. As their name implies, Rock Blocks are solid and cannot be moved. Each has a weak side, however, which is taped in an "X" design. Wario can smash any Rock Block into bits by punching or otherwise attacking its weak side. Be on the lookout for Rock Blocks, as they may be hiding something valuable.

Bunny Springs

A Bunny Spring looks like a little bunny rabbit with a coiled spring underneath. When Wario jumps onto one, he begins to hop up and down. By performing a Ground Pound onto a Bunny Spring, Wario can leap and soar over obstacles.

Buttons

Each area in *Wario World* contains eight large, colorful Buttons. Every Button has a distinctive color, making it easy to tell them apart.

When Wario punches or otherwise attacks a colored Button, a Treasure Chest appears on a nearby platform of matching color. Once the Treasure Chest has been opened and the treasure taken, the Button and its matching platform turn into a dull shade of gray, indicating that they're of no further use.

ByeBye Balloons

ByeBye Balloons appear near each area's Goal Trapdoor. They look like a bunch of colored balloons attached to a single Glue Globe. When Wario jumps and grabs a ByeBye Balloon's Glue Globe, he returns to the beginning of the area. This allows you to make a second run through an area, collecting any items you may have missed on your first attempt.

NOTE

The ByeBye Balloon also appears at the beginning of an area after you defeat the area's boss, allowing you to quickly reach the last segment of the area if you need to.

Columns

Columns are tall pillars made of solid stone, commonly found near large groups of monsters. That's because Wario is strong enough to pick up a Column and use it as a weapon.

Wario can throw or perform a Piledriver or Wild Swing-Ding attack when he's carrying a Column. Keep your eyes peeled for these helpful objects, and use them to ease the more difficult battles.

Escape Springs

Escape Springs allow Wario to return to the main area whenever he enters an outside location. In other words, you find Escape Springs in the Unithorn's Lair and inside every trapdoor area. Move Wario into an Escape Spring to bounce him back up to the main area.

Garlic Dispensers

Several Garlic Dispensers are found in every area. These handy objects work just like vending machines: Coins go in, Garlic comes out. The cost of using a Garlic Dispenser varies depending on which area you're in, and the price goes up by 10 coins with each use. Using Garlic Dispensers too often can get expensive, but they're your best bet when Wario's Heart Meter runs low.

Glue Globes

Glue Globes are common objects that help Wario progress through each area. When Wario touches one of these yellow balls, he latches onto it like a magnet. Make Wario shimmy around a Glue Globe by moving ◎ in the desired direction.

Wario can also jump off Glue Globes; press Ⓐ to make him jump. In some areas, Wario must jump from Glue Globe to Glue Globe to reach his destination, so brush up on this skill early.

Old Red-Mug

Old Red-Mug is found only in certain areas of *Wario World*. It looks like a tall brick wall with arms, legs, and a bright red face. When Wario jumps up and punches Old Red-Mug in its face, it teeters backward. After a few more punches, Old Red-Mug falls flat on its back, bridging a gap to a new section of the area.

Sculptures

Sculptures are works of art, but these have to be an exception! Many of the game's areas feature giant Sculptures in the form of Wario's jumbo, mustachioed melon. These

objects are used exactly like Columns. Wario can pick one up and put it to use against unsuspecting monsters. Throw it or use it to execute a Piledriver or Wild Swing-Ding.

Swirly Slabs

Swirly Slabs appear in certain areas. Their appearance changes slightly to match the surrounding area, but you can easily identify one by its swirl-pattern top.

These objects help Wario reach high platforms and items. A Swirly Slab rises like an elevator when Wario stands atop it and executes a Wild Swing-Ding. Jump off the Swirly Slab once it has gone all the way up, as it soon begins to wind back down again.

Swirly Spinners

Swirly Spinners open tall gates in certain areas of *Wario World*. They look like thick yellow disks sticking out from walls. Along their sides are red arrows that point in a certain direction.

To activate a Swirly Spinner and open its gate, Wario must attack it with a Wild Swing-Ding, spinning in the direction that the Swirly Spinner's arrows indicate. Continue to attack the Swirly Spinner until the nearby gate retracts into the wall. Once the gate has opened, run through before it closes again.

Trapdoors

Trapdoors come in three flavors: wooden, steel, and goal. Each one is slightly different from the others, but every trapdoor is similar in that they all bring Wario to a small place set apart from the current area. Wario's new surroundings vary depending on the type of trapdoor he entered. Explore every trapdoor thoroughly.

Wooden Trapdoors

Wooden Trapdoors are the most common and easy to access of the three types. Wario needs only to perform a Ground Pound on any Wooden Trapdoor to enter and explore it.

Wario always finds himself in a small room after entering a Wooden Trapdoor. There he must solve a puzzle to collect the Red Diamond and any other treasure beneath the trapdoor. Once all the goodies have been collected, use the resident Escape Spring to return to the normal area.

Steel Trapdoors

Steel Trapdoors are the second most common, but they're a bit more difficult to enter. Instead of a Ground Pound, Wario must execute a Piledriver to enter a Steel Trapdoor. Grab a nearby enemy or object and have at it!

Steel Trapdoors lead to wide-open outdoor areas that seem to have no ground at all. From his starting point, Wario must find a way to cross the tricky pathway ahead and reach the Red Diamond and Escape Spring on the platform at the other side. These areas get tricky in the later stages of the game.

Goal Trapdoors

There's only one Goal Trapdoor per area in *Wario World*, and at first it's always sealed and guarded

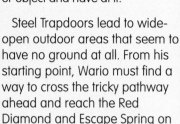

by a stone statue. These trapdoors lead to the area boss's lair, so be prepared for a fight when you enter.

To unseal a Goal Trapdoor, you must collect enough Red Diamonds to get rid of the large stone statue that stands guard atop it. The amount of Red Diamonds required varies from area to area, increasing as you progress through the game. Once you've unsealed a Goal Trapdoor, Wario can Ground Pound his way in and face the area's boss.

TIP

It's easy to tell a fully explored trapdoor from one that hasn't yet been cleared. If you see faint shafts of light shining up through the cracks of a trapdoor, there are goodies inside.

Treasure Chests

Each area of *Wario World* has eight Treasure Chests, and each one holds one of Wario's beloved treasures. There's a catch, though—the Treasure Chests are all invisible. To make a Treasure Chest appear, Wario must first activate a nearby colored Button.

Once Wario has activated a colored Button by attacking it, a Treasure Chest appears on a distinctive-looking platform of the same color. Attack the Treasure Chest to open it, and Wario claims one of his long-lost treasures. Collect every one of Wario's 64 missing treasures for special rewards.

Wooden Chests

These are common objects found in every area of *Wario World*. Wooden Chests always contain either a large quantity of gold coins or a clove of that smelly Garlic. Wario loves to punch things, so have him smash open every Wooden Chest you see and grab the goods from inside.

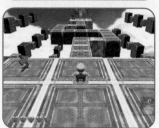

Wario's Enemies

Being a greedy and spiteful man hasn't made Wario a lot of friends. In fact, he's made plenty of enemies, and the Evil Black Jewel hasn't helped the situation by turning all of Wario's ill-gotten treasures into monsters. All in all, Wario has a lot of reasons to look over his shoulder. Fortunately, this section gives you all the information you need to handle even the toughest of Wario's foes.

The Little Ones

Not all of Wario's enemies pose a serious threat—many are mere annoyances. These weak monsters aren't very bright and often run in terror from Wario. Wario can easily stun or defeat these monsters with only a few punches. Sometimes just one punch does the trick! These enemies include Magons, Zombie Magons, Clowns, Snowmen, Wolves, and Mummies.

The Ones with Sticks

Then again, not all of Wario's enemies are weaklings. Wario faces many strong monsters on his jaunt to defeat the Evil Black Jewel. These monsters can only be defeated with a powerful move such as a Piledriver or Wild Swing-Ding. And because they wield clubs and the like, Wario must attack them from behind. Watch out for their charging attack when they flash—they're invincible and most dangerous during a charge. Examples of these monsters are Clubosaurs, Skelosaurs, Gatorbabies, Polar Bears, Grizzlies, Masked Clubbers, and Club Mummies.

The Ones with Guns

Other than bosses, these are the strongest monsters Wario faces. These enemies are so huge all they can do is turn around. They also have a tight defensive shell. Punch them

rapidly and repeatedly to stun them. Examples of these massive monsters are Ankirons, Skeletal Ankirons, Circus Ankirons, Ice Ankirons, Rhino Ankirons, Stuffed Ankirons, and Mummy Ankirons. Notice a pattern?

The Ones That Fly

Now *these* enemies just make Wario mad. They fly about, staying just out of reach, forcing the portly Wario to jump to hit them. If he didn't enjoy hitting things so much, maybe he wouldn't bother. These flying monsters like to swoop down and snatch Wario up in their claws. If one catches you, wiggle ◎ from side to side to drop down. Some flying enemies also enjoy dropping bombs, spiked balls, and such. Flying monsters include Cractyls, Bone Cractyls, Pigeons, Snow Bombers, and Hawks.

Crystal Entities

Crystal Entities are found in many areas of *Wario World*. They like to surprise Wario by dropping in from above or popping up from the ground. Crystal Entities have a special power that allows them to trap Wario inside a dome-shaped barrier and force him to fight (as if that were necessary).

Because they're immobile, Crystal Entities don't do much fighting themselves. Instead, they summon smaller versions called Crystal Creatures and let them do most of the dirty work. Crystal Creatures are not to be taken lightly, but they aren't all that much of a threat to Wario. In fact, Wario finds a good use for them—he throws them at the Crystal Entity to defeat it.

WARIOWORLD™

PRIMA'S OFFICIAL STRATEGY GUIDE

Area-Specific Enemies

Some enemies appear only in their natural habitats. These enemies are usually much more dangerous than the run-of-the-mill variety listed above, so pay close attention.

Spooktastic World: Horror Manor

Door Spirit

These evil spirits guard several doors in the Horror Manor. They attack by firing bolts of electricity at Wario—quite a shocking experience! Wario likes to punch these things until he destroys them, but make him dodge their attacks as well.

Silver Door Spirit

The Silver Door Spirits are similar to their brass-colored cousins, but they're a bit tougher and have a special attack. When a Silver Door Spirit takes heavy damage, it flashes and looses a fat ray of pure electricity. When you see the Silver Door Spirit begin to flash, run clear of the powerful electric ray.

Swordfish

Swordfish are found only in watery areas of the Horror Manor. They like to swim underneath Wario and then surface, sticking Wario's plump purple rump with the blades on their backs. Punch these weak monsters until they're stunned, then do something nasty to them.

Spooktastic World: Wonky Circus

Cage Beast

Cage Beasts look like easy targets at a glance—they're trapped in a cage, after all. But when Wario gets close, they sprout arms and legs and begin to chase him around, swiping with their sharp claws. It takes quite a few punches to stun a Cage Beast, and a powerful move such as a Piledriver to defeat them.

Cobra

Cobras are easily defeated, immobile monsters. Punch a Cobra until you see it flash, then back away. After the Cobra strikes, move in again and keep punching.

Elephant

Leave Elephants alone. They use a powerful charging attack to trample Wario, and they're invulnerable while charging. If you must battle an Elephant, attack it from behind and defeat it with a powerful attack once it's stunned.

Thrillsville: Shivering Mountains

Freeze Cannon

Freeze cannons are among the few monsters that cannot be defeated. They shoot out long bursts of frost that freeze Wario in a block of ice. Wiggle ◎ from side to side if a Freeze Cannon freezes you. Although Wario can't defeat these enemies, he can temporarily put them out of action with a Ground Pound.

Fattington

Fattingtons have the coolest name of all enemies in the game, and also are among the most annoying. Their huge bellies bounce Wario backward, often dropping him into the Unithorn's Lair. Wario's punches are completely ineffective against Fattingtons. Throw an object or another enemy into them to stun them. Once a Fattington is stunned, Wario can pick it up (just barely!) and defeat it with a powerful attack.

Icicle Mite

Icicle Mites aren't really enemies, because they're incapable of attacking Wario. Instead, these odd creatures are useful: Wario can stick them into the ground with a Piledriver and then use them as platforms.

Thrillsville: Beanstalk Way

Monstrous Magnet

Monstrous Magnets are dangerous but useful monsters found only in the Beanstalk Way area. Although they fly, Wario can jump up and punch them or perform a Corkscrew Conk to stun them. Once a Monstrous Magnet is stunned, Wario can pick it up and throw it at a metal plate, to which it sticks. Wario may then use the Monstrous Magnet as a platform to reach higher ledges.

Ram

Rams are weak defensively but are offensive forces to be reckoned with. They attack by jumping into the air and slamming down on Wario, horns first. Punch a Ram to stun it and then defeat it with a powerful attack.

Wind Winder

Wind Winders are troublesome but harmless enemies that hover in the air. They use their propeller-like bases to blow gales of wind at Wario, pushing him away. A single jumping punch or Corkscrew Conk defeats a Wind Winder, which is incapable of directly harming Wario.

Sparkle Land: Mirror Mansion

Magician

Magicians are truly difficult enemies to overcome, especially when they attack in groups. They start out all tied up and highly vulnerable to punches. But instead of being defeated by a powerful attack, Magicians become more powerful, shedding their bonds and flying through the air. For the most part, leave these bothersome enemies alone.

Ninja Crow

Ninja Crows are fairly easy to handle one at a time. Unfortunately, they often attack in groups. Ninja Crows require only a few punches to stun, but their quick, powerful attacks are hard to predict and evade. Like Magicians, Ninja Crows are best left alone.

Witch

Witches are crafty, magical enemies that can only be seen in mirrors. They are otherwise completely invisible. Fortunately, Witches are only found in the Mirror Mansion area, and then only in places where there are plenty of mirrors about. They attack with magical projectiles, but you can easily beat them into a stunned state once you've nailed down their location.

Sparkle Land: Pecan Sands

Big Scorper

Big Scorpers are cowardly but nonetheless very dangerous enemies. They hide in the sand, with only their eyes and huge, red tail visible. Big Scorpers seem invincible at first, but you can stun them by executing three Ground Pounds onto their eyes. Use a powerful attack to finish off a Big Scorper.

Flying Spade

Flying Spades are similar to the Monstrous Magnets found in Beanstalk Way. As their name implies, they fly through the air and look like a shovel. Like the Monstrous Magnets, Flying Spades can be stunned and used as platforms to reach higher ledges. Jump and punch a Flying Spade twice to stun it, then throw it at a dark section of wall to make it stick.

Laser Jigglefish

The Laser Jigglefish is completely invulnerable until it attacks. It fires a powerful laser, shooting the ground below it and slowly turning over until it's firing straight up into the air. Once the laser cuts off, the Laser Jigglefish's weak spot—its soft underside—is exposed. Jump up and execute a Ground Pound onto the Laser Jigglefish's pink underbelly to stun it, then finish it off with a devastating attack.

Walkthrough of Wario World

Wario World is a linear game with four exciting stages to explore: Excitement Central, Spooktastic World, Thrillsville, and Sparkle Land. Each stage is divided into two areas and features an intense boss show-down at the end.

You must clear the first area of a stage before you can play through the second. After completing the stage's second area, you face the big, bad stage boss. When you defeat the boss, the next stage becomes available for explo-ration. Defeat all four stage bosses to unlock the final showdown against the evil black jewel.

How to Use This Walkthrough

What follows is a step-by-step walkthrough for each area of Wario World. Follow along with the maps, moving from the start of an area toward the goal. The num-bered step-by-step icons that appear on the maps ( ) are there to help guide you through each area in the proper order, so you don't miss anything.

When you encounter such an icon, check the walkthrough text to read up on anything of interest nearby.

Trapdoor Icons

When you come across a trapdoor, check the map for the area you're in to find the trapdoor's icon ( ). Trapdoor icons work just like the step-by-step kind—they're numbered so you can find each one in the trapdoor section of the walkthrough text. Refer to the map to find the trapdoor's number, then read how to clear each one.

Button and Treasure Chest Icons

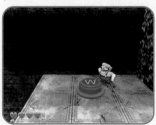

Each area in Wario World features eight colored Buttons ( ) and eight platforms of matching color. When Wario activates a Button by punching or attacking it, a Treasure Chest ( ) appears on the Button's matching platform. Until a platform's Button is activated, its Treasure Chest remains invisible.

Since there are eight colored Buttons in every area, you find eight colored Button icons on every area's map. To quickly locate a newly activated Button's Treasure Chest, check the map to find the Treasure Chest icon of the same color. Can't find a certain Button? Check the map for Button icons.

Other Icons

In addition to step-by-step and trapdoor icons, you see a few other icons on each area's map. Refer to the icon legend below for a description of every icon found on the maps.

Map Icon Legend

Icon	Description
START	Area's starting point
GOAL	Area's Goal Trapdoor
1	Step-by-step walkthrough
1	Wooden Trapdoor
1	Steel Trapdoor
W	Button (colored)
	Treasure Chest (colored)
	Garlic Dispenser
	Gold Statue Part
S	Spriteling
	Wooden Chest

Excitement Central: Greenhorn Forest

Excitement Central is the first stage of *Wario World*, and Greenhorn Forest is its first area. Here, Wario begins his quest to pound on the evil black jewel's monsters and reclaim every last one of his many lost treasures. As in every area in *Wario World*, Greenhorn Forest offers eight treasures to find, eight Gold Statue parts to collect, eight Red Diamonds to locate, and five Spritelings to rescue.

NOTE
You must have at least three Red Diamonds to enter the Greenhorn Forest's Goal Trapdoor.

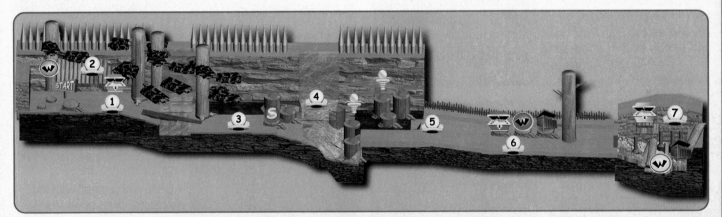

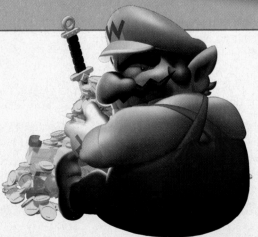

Legend

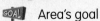 Area's goal

 Button (various colors)

Garlic Dispenser

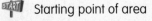 Walkthrough icon
(numbered)

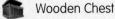 Gold Statue Part

Spriteling

Starting point of area

Steel Trapdoor (numbered)

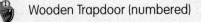 Treasure Chest (various colors)

Wooden Chest

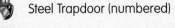 Wooden Trapdoor (numbered)

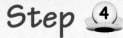 **WARIOWORLD**

Step

From the starting point, head down the trail to the right and look for a tall tree near a waterfall. The tree serves as a ladder. Climb all the way up and jump to the wooden platform to the left.

Step 2

Monsters! Don't worry—these are Magons, and they're a cinch to defeat. Show 'em what you can do, and don't be afraid to use the nearby Columns as weapons.

Hey, there's a pink Button up here, too! Run up to the Button and give it a punch to activate it.

The pink Button's Treasure Chest isn't very far away. It's sitting on the opposite corner of the wooden platform. Punch it open to claim Wario's first missing treasure, the Diamond!

Step 3

Wario notices a small box on a nearby stump and decides to check it out. It's a trapped Spriteling. The Spriteling teaches Wario the basics of jumping and fighting.

TIP

Rescue every trapped Spriteling, because they offer valuable hints as rewards. You also need their help in the final fight against the evil black jewel, so don't miss any.

Step

Hop across the tree stumps near the large waterfall to proceed. Over the last stump floats a Gold Statue part. Jump up and grab it, then continue.

NOTE

Collecting all eight Gold Statue parts from an area permanently extends Wario's Heart Meter by half a heart. Find them all.

Step

More Magon monsters await farther down the trail. This is a great spot to practice Wario's moves.

Once you've dealt with the monsters, climb up the ladder on the side of the nearby tree stump.

Hop across the stumps and collect the floating Gold Statue part. Only six more to find!

Step 6

There's a lot to see and do around here. Start off by smacking around the nearby monsters. Don't be afraid to pull off crazy moves.

A Wooden Chest sits nearby, on the stump to the right of the red Button. Punch the Wooden Chest open and claim your prize.

With the monsters out of the way, punch the red Button to make its Treasure Chest appear on the stump to the left. Open the Treasure Chest to collect the Ruby.

NOTE

Wooden Chests usually contain either gold coins or Garlic, but may have other items as well.

Step 7

Instead of jumping to the pole ahead, stay on the ground and go to the lower area first. Attack the yellow Button to activate it, then punch open the Wooden Chest for a random treat.

After you activate the yellow Button, head back up the hill to the left. Line up Wario with the foot imprint on the ground, then jump over and grab the pole to cross the gap.

Climb all the way up the pole closest to the wall and jump off it to reach the yellow Button's Treasure Chest, which contains the Opal. You've found three treasures!

Line up Wario with the foot imprint on the ground and jump from pole to pole to cross to the other side of the wide gap.

Step 8

Wario encounters his first Wooden Trapdoor here. Perform a Ground Pound to enter the trapdoor's sub-level.

Trapdoor 1

This first trapdoor is a breeze. Climb onto the stack of green blocks, and jump quickly across the Drop Blocks to reach the Red Diamond and Gold Statue part on the floating platform.

TIP

Remember, you can change the camera angle to get a better view of your surroundings. The camera is highly adjustable in trapdoor sub-levels, so take full advantage.

There's another Spriteling around here. Punch its confining box to rescue it. The Spriteling gives information on trapdoors and Red Diamonds.

Wario encounters his first Garlic Dispenser here. If you attack a Garlic Dispenser, it shoots out a clove of health-restoring Garlic and deducts coins from your purse, just like a vending machine. The cost of each clove of Garlic is shown in the number floating above the Garlic Dispenser, and the price goes up each time you buy a clove.

Step 9

Down the lower pathway, you encounter a stack of Rock Blocks. Punch the lowest Rock Block's weak side (the "X" design) to smash it and proceed down the path.

Hey, those Rock Blocks were hiding a Wooden Trapdoor! Ground Pound into the trapdoor's sub-level.

Trapdoor 2

The second Wooden Trapdoor Wario encounters is no more difficult than the first. Start by jumping onto the lowest floating block and make your way up the rest, collecting the Gold Statue part and Red Diamond.

After returning from the second Wooden Trapdoor, continue to follow the lower pathway to the right. You see a Bunny Spring at the end of the pathway. Ground Pound onto it to jump up the high ledge ahead. A dark-green Treasure Chest platform sits nearby, but you still have to find and activate the dark-green Button.

Step 10

Punch the small box on the nearby stump to rescue another Spriteling. It teaches you about using ⓑ to perform a Dash Attack, and how to perform a Power Throw.

After you rescue the Spriteling, a huge Clubosaur monster drops from the sky to fight Wario. This is a chance to put Wario's powerful moves to the test. Attack the Clubosaur from behind until you stun it, then hit it with a Power Throw, Piledriver, or Wild Swing-Ding.

Attack the nearby Wooden Chest for some coins or Garlic.

There's a Wooden Trapdoor in the vicinity as well. Ground Pound onto the top of the Wooden Trapdoor to enter and explore its sub-level.

Trapdoor 3

The third Wooden Trapdoor is trickier than the first two. Start by punching the middle stack of Rock Blocks three times to make it three blocks shorter. Then smash four Rock Blocks from one of the side stacks and one Rock Block from the other. This creates a set of steps, allowing you to reach the high floating platform and its Red Diamond.

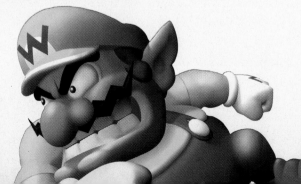

Step 11

Perform a Ground Pound on top of the Bunny Spring and bounce up to the higher ledge at left.

Two new enemies guard the Wooden Trapdoor here. These Cractyls can fly, so you usually need to jump and punch them. If they grab you, quickly move ◎ from side to side until you drop. Defeat the two Cractyls, then Ground Pound into the Wooden Trapdoor.

Trapdoor 4

Start by punching the first two Rock Blocks ahead, then jump onto them and up to the top of the stack of blocks. Grab the Gold Statue part from the top of the stack, then perform a Ground Pound on the center Rock Block, the one closest to the green-colored block.

Change the camera view to the top-down perspective and you see the Red Diamond surrounded by the stack of blocks. Jump back to the ground where you started, and punch away at the Rock Blocks ahead until you can reach the Red Diamond.

A nearby tree has been made into a ladder. Take note of the light-green Treasure Chest platform to the left, then climb the tree.

Step  12

At the top of the ladder, jump to the wooden platform at left. A group of monsters waits for you, but a few Columns in the vicinity help.

Farther left across the wooden platforms, the light-green Button sticks out from a tree trunk. Jump and punch the Button to activate it, then head back to the light-green Treasure Chest platform near the base of the ladder to claim your prize—the Amethyst!

Step 13

Climb back up to the top of the ladder, but this time jump to the wooden platforms on the right side. Continue along until you see a Gold Statue part. Grab the part and continue to cross the wooden platforms.

The farthest wooden platform to the right features a small gang of monsters and the dark-green Button. Defeat the monsters (the Piledriver works wonders), then punch the Button to activate it. Return to the dark-green Treasure Chest platform near the Bunny Spring to get the Amber.

Step

Another Gold Statue part floats above the rock in the middle of the shallow pool. Grab the part and then defeat the surrounding monsters.

The fifth Wooden Trapdoor sits on a second rock on the right side of the shallow pool. Execute a Ground Pound to enter the trapdoor's sub-level.

Trapdoor 5

The fifth trapdoor is a thinker. You must use the Glue Globe to reach the Red Diamond on a high floating platform, but a dangerous spiked ball is in your way.

If you look closely, you can see two open sections in the ring around the spiked ball. To avoid the spiked ball, carefully position Wario on the Glue Globe so that he passes through one of the ring's open areas as the Glue Globe makes its journey up to the floating platform.

Don't miss the Wooden Chest sitting against the wall near the shallow pool.

Near the shallow pool is another ladder-like tree. Once you've cleared the pool of goodies, climb to the top of the tree and jump onto the wooden platform at right.

Two Clubosaurs wait for you on the high wooden platform, but the Sculptures help even the odds. Once you've dealt with the monsters, jump and punch the light-blue Button sticking out from a nearby tree trunk.

Ground Pound the Bunny Spring to sail over the high wall of fallen logs and escape the shallow pool.

Step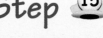

The light-blue Button's Treasure Chest is on the other side of the fallen logs. Smack it open to get the Sapphire.

Punch open the small wooden box sitting on a nearby stump to release another Spriteling. This grateful Spriteling warns about the dangers of falling off cliffs and into deep chasms.

The sixth Wooden Trapdoor is hiding behind a fallen log. Execute a Ground Pound to enter the Wooden Trapdoor's sub-level.

Trapdoor 6

This is probably the easiest trapdoor sub-level in the game. Make the blocks become steps by activating the large, red lever (punch it), then jump up the steps and grab the Red Diamond.

Take note of the purple Treasure Chest platform sitting on the ground near the two log bridges. You still need to find and activate the purple Button, but at least you know where to find its Treasure Chest.

Cross either log bridge to continue, but be forewarned: Whichever bridge you cross breaks, causing you to fall into the dreadful Unithorn's Lair! Escape the Unithorn's Lair by smashing open wooden boxes until you locate the Escape Spring. Once out of the Unithorn's Lair, cross the other log bridge to continue (it won't break).

Step

The fifth and final Spriteling for this area is sitting on a stump on the other side of the log bridge. It teaches you about Goal Trapdoors and ByeBye Balloons. A Garlic Dispenser is here if you need it.

There's the goal! Wario automatically begins to use Red Diamonds to remove the stone statue that guards the Goal Trapdoor. Don't enter the trapdoor just yet, though. Continue past the goal to the right.

A ByeBye Balloon floats near the Goal Trapdoor. ByeBye Balloons instantly take Wario back to the beginning of an area. If you want to return to the start of the Greenhorn Forest and collect any items you missed, jump and grab the ByeBye Balloon's Glue Globe.

Step

Smash through the Rock Blocks past the goal to find the dark-blue Button and a Wooden Trapdoor. Activate the Button, then Ground Pound into the trapdoor.

Trapdoor 7

This trapdoor features two levers and two floating platforms. Punching the lever to the right causes the lower, L-shaped platform to rotate; punching the lever to the left makes it move about. The object is to rotate and move the L-shaped platform to reach the higher platform and thus the Red Diamond.

Punch the lever to the right three times, and then punch the lever to the left twice. This puts the L-shaped platform in the perfect position for you to climb up and grab the Red Diamond.

After returning from the seventh trapdoor, continue down the path to the right. Smash open the nearby Wooden Chest for a random treat, then climb up the ladder carved into a tree.

Jump off the ladder to land on a log. Move left across the log until you see a purple Button below you. Jump out and Ground Pound the Button to activate it, then climb back up the ladder and continue across the log to the left.

Step 18

A group of monsters guards the eighth and final Wooden Trapdoor. Use the Columns to defeat the enemies, then Ground Pound into the trapdoor's sub-level.

Trapdoor 8

The eighth and final Wooden Trapdoor features a floating platform surrounded by spiked balls. Stand just below the floating platform and wait for a spiked ball to pass by overhead. Jump up and grab onto the platform, then quickly jump up to get the last Gold Statue part and Red Diamond.

Once you've returned from the Wooden Trapdoor, continue to the left. You have more monsters to deal with, one of which is a large Ankiron. Take out the other monsters first, then rapidly punch the Ankiron's head until it's stunned. Finish off the Ankiron with a powerful move.

The Ankiron was defending the dark-blue Button's Treasure Chest. Punch the Treasure Chest to obtain the Topaz.

You activated the purple Button earlier, so return to the purple Treasure Chest platform, which is sitting near the log bridge. Open the Treasure Chest to collect the Emerald. You've found all eight of Wario's missing treasures from Greenhorn Forest.

Now that you've rescued the five trapped Spritelings and found all of Wario's lost treasures, Gold Statue parts, and Red Diamonds, it's time to face the boss of the Greenhorn Forest. Return to the Goal Trapdoor and Ground Pound inside.

TIP

Use a Garlic Dispenser before entering the Goal Trapdoor if Wario's Heart Meter isn't full. A Garlic Dispenser stands a short distance from the goal in every area.

Area Boss: Greenfist

Greenfist is the first boss you face in *Wario World*, and he's a pushover. It only takes three powerful attacks to finish him off—the Piledriver works quite nicely. The skulls in the lower-right corner of the screen represent Greenfist's health.

As soon as the fight begins, run up to Greenfist and begin punching him as fast as you can. After a few hits, Greenfist becomes enraged and quickly begins to power up. Run away as soon as you see him flash.

After flashing, Greenfist begins to charge around the arena in a fury, chasing Wario and swinging wildly. Greenfist is invulnerable in this state, so stay away from him until his fury dies down. As the battle wears on, this attack becomes faster and more difficult to avoid.

Run up and continue to punch Greenfist after his fury attack has ended. After a couple of hits, Greenfist falls to the ground, stunned. Now's your chance. Pick him up and execute a powerful Piledriver.

Continue the rest of the fight against Greenfist in the same fashion. Punch him whenever he's not on a powered-up rampage, and hit him with a Piledriver when he's stunned. After just three Piledrivers, Greenfist is toast.

Excitement Central: Greenhorn Ruins

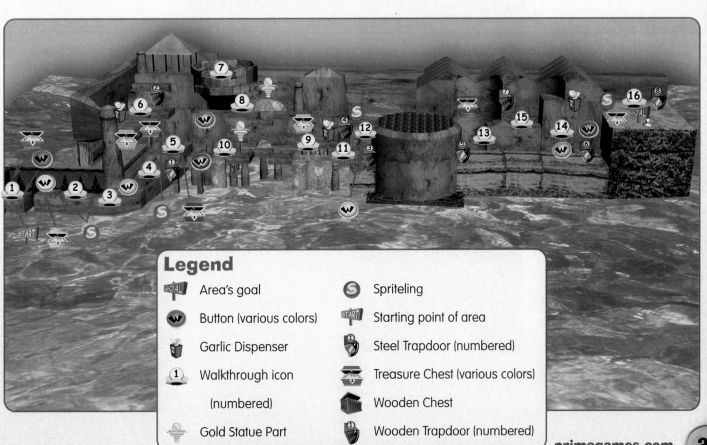

Legend

GOAL	Area's goal	**S**	Spriteling
W	Button (various colors)	**START**	Starting point of area
	Garlic Dispenser		Steel Trapdoor (numbered)
1	Walkthrough icon (numbered)		Treasure Chest (various colors)
	Gold Statue Part		Wooden Chest
			Wooden Trapdoor (numbered)

The second area of the Excitement Central stage is the Greenhorn Ruins. This area is a bit more difficult for Wario, so keep your wits about you. As with every area in *Wario World*, Greenhorn Ruins has eight treasures to find, eight Gold Statue parts to collect, eight Red Diamonds to locate, and five Spritelings to rescue.

NOTE

You must have at least three Red Diamonds to enter the Goal Trapdoor at the end of Greenhorn Ruins.

Step 1

Start by jumping onto the Rock Block near the area's starting point. From there, jump up to the red Button and activate it.

After you activate the red Button, jump back down and punch the weak side of the Rock Block you just used as a step. Underneath the Rock Block is the red Button's Treasure Chest. Collect the Porcelain Urn before you move on.

Attack the stack of Rock Blocks to the right of the starting point to reveal a ladder and a yellow Treasure Chest platform.

Destroy the remaining Rock Blocks to reveal the yellow Button. Activate the yellow Button, then open its Treasure Chest to obtain the Fine China. That's two treasures already! Climb the ladder to proceed.

Step 2

Wario sees the first trapped Spriteling on a circular pedestal. Free the Spriteling, who teaches you how to fight large groups of enemies by using the Piledriver and Wild Swing-Ding attacks.

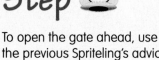

Farther down the path, put the Spriteling's advice to good use. Grab a Column or an enemy and use it to take out the surrounding monsters.

Another Spriteling is sitting on a second circular pedestal up the steps. Rescue the Spriteling for a hint on using the Piledriver and Wild Swing-Ding to turn gears, break iron doors, and deal with tricky traps. Smash open the nearby Wooden Chest for a random prize, then proceed to the right down the path.

Step 3

To open the gate ahead, use the previous Spriteling's advice. Stun one of the nearby Magons and use it to execute a Wild Swing-Ding. Swing the Magon into the yellow Swirly Spinner sticking out from the wall near the gate. The gate won't open unless you're spinning in the proper direction (in this case, clockwise).

Quickly run through the gate when it retracts. Jump and punch the light-green Button before heading up the steps.

Step 4

This next section of the Greenhorn Ruins is a perfect place to practice Wario's moves and fatten your coin purse at the same time. Two vase-like monster generators continually pump out those cowardly Magons. Spend some time brushing up on your fighting skills. They come in handy later.

A trio of Clubosaurs drops from the sky as you move ahead. Remember to attack them from behind, because they block all frontal advances.

The trapdoor ahead is the first of its kind: a Steel Trapdoor. They're sturdier than the wooden sort, and the only way to enter a Steel Trapdoor is to execute a Piledriver onto it. Use one of the Clubosaurs as your key into this first trapdoor.

Trapdoor 1

A Steel Trapdoor's sub-level is different from a Wooden Trapdoor's. Inside a Steel Trapdoor, you must show platform-navigating skill and make your way past an obstacle rather than solve a tricky puzzle. This first Steel Trapdoor doesn't present much of a challenge. It's the very first one, after all.

Walk along the path to reach the lever ahead. If you really want those floating gold coins, you can grab them and land safely by performing a Corkscrew Conk.

Punch the lever to activate the Glue Globe, which functions as a lift. Ride up to the higher platform, where a Gold Statue part awaits.

To reach the Red Diamond, move carefully across the floating blocks. Watch them for a few seconds to learn the pattern in which they move, then proceed across and grab the Red Diamond.

Step 5

From the Steel Trapdoor, head up the steps. You see the third Spriteling's box sitting on another circular pedestal. The Spriteling tells you how to use Glue Globes to navigate tricky environments.

There's the dark-blue Treasure Chest platform, but where could its Button be? Remember where you saw the dark-blue Treasure Chest platform for future reference.

A line of Glue Globes extends upward to a higher ledge. Line up with the foot imprint on the ground, and then jump from Glue Globe to Glue Globe as you make your way upward.

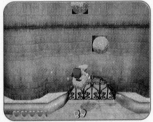

Step 6

Head left after making your way up the Glue Globes. Several Magons and Cractyls are waiting to fight, so punish them accordingly. A Garlic Dispenser stands nearby if you feel the need to heal up. Ground Pound into the nearby Wooden Trapdoor once the coast is clear.

Trapdoor 2

The second trapdoor's sub-level features two rings of gold coins circling a central pedestal. The Red Diamond sits atop the pedestal, protected by a ring of spiked balls that expand and contract in rhythm.

Timing is key for this sub-level. The circle of spiked balls is your only obstacle, so heed the movement as you make your way toward the Red Diamond.

After you return from the Wooden Trapdoor, head toward the camera, smacking Magons out of your way. The dark-green Treasure Chest platform is here, but you need to activate the dark-green Button before it's of any use.

Jump from the arrow to the next platform ahead. The light-green Button's Treasure Chest is sitting here, all alone. Open it for the Ceramic Vase, your third treasure from the Greenhorn Ruins.

After you grab the Ceramic Vase, you've nowhere to go except back the way you came. Return to the line of Glue Globes and make your way up the rest of them to an even higher ledge above.

Step ⑦

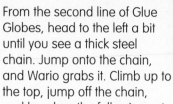

From the second line of Glue Globes, head to the left a bit until you see a thick steel chain. Jump onto the chain, and Wario grabs it. Climb up to the top, jump off the chain, and head up the following set of steps.

When you come to a large, circular spot, a giant Crystal Entity rises from the ground and a dome-shaped barrier appears, trapping you inside. You encounter several of these monsters as you progress through the game.

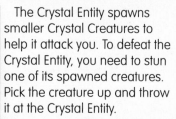

The Crystal Entity spawns smaller Crystal Creatures to help it attack you. To defeat the Crystal Entity, you need to stun one of its spawned creatures. Pick the creature up and throw it at the Crystal Entity.

The Crystal Entity reels after three direct hits, stunned. Now's your chance. Pick it up and execute a crystal-shattering Piledriver. This defeats the Crystal Entity, drops the barrier, and allows you to proceed.

TIP

Crystal Entities periodically attack with a deadly laser, so be on guard. It's easier to stun the flying Crystal Creatures—the other ones block all frontal attacks.

After you deal with the Crystal Entity, line up with the foot imprint and jump onto the nearby steel chain. Climb down, crossing over to a second chain as you go.

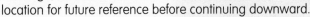

Step (8)

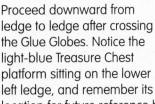

The pair of steel chains takes you down to a monster-filled section of the Greenhorn Ruins. Defeat the monsters, then activate the dark-green Button.

To quickly backtrack to the dark-green Treasure Chest platform, jump and punch Old Red-Mug until it falls over. Old Red-Mug's wide frame bridges a gap, allowing you to reach the dark-green Button's Treasure Chest in no time. Punch the Treasure Chest to open it and collect the Teapot.

With the Teapot added to your collection, backtrack across Old Red-Mug and continue to the right. A row of Glue Globes sticks out from the wall, allowing you to cross over the pit below.

It's almost impossible to miss the Gold Statue part that's hovering over the middle Glue Globe. Continue across the Glue Globes until you reach the other side.

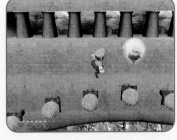

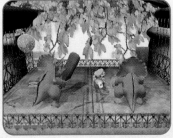

If you fall while crossing the row of Glue Globes, two Clubosaurs drop in to teach you a lesson. Use the Glue Globe to the left to climb out of the pit and try again.

Step (9)

Proceed downward from ledge to ledge after crossing the Glue Globes. Notice the light-blue Treasure Chest platform sitting on the lower left ledge, and remember its location for future reference before continuing downward.

The next ledge features a Garlic Dispenser. Use it if you need to before proceeding downward.

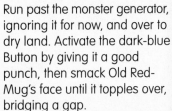

Stun your enemy of choice when you reach the watery, bottom ledge, and use it to open the gate to the left. Execute a clockwise Wild Swing-Ding on the nearby Swirly Spinner to force the gate open, then proceed to the left.

Step (10)

Run past the monster generator, ignoring it for now, and over to dry land. Activate the dark-blue Button by giving it a good punch, then smack Old Red-Mug's face until it topples over, bridging a gap.

Conveniently, the dark-blue Button's Treasure Chest is just on the other side of Old Red-Mug. Open the Treasure Chest for the Precious Pot. Only three more treasures to go.

Cross back over Old Red-Mug and look for a foot imprint on the ground just before the water. Jump from the imprint and grab the first Glue Globe sitting on top of a pillar.

A Gold Statue part is hovering over the last pillar. Exploration pays off! Add the Gold Statue part to your collection, then jump down and head over to the nearby monster generator.

Stun and pick up a Magon from the monster generator, then head right until you reach the gate you passed through earlier. Perform a counter-clockwise Wild Swing-Ding on the Swirly Spinner to open the gate, then toss the Magon aside and pass through.

TIP

Watch out for the narrow ledge near the Swirly Spinner as you open the gate. You can easily fall into the Unithorn's Lair if you're not careful.

Step 11

Continue along to the right until you encounter a large Ankiron. Remember to punch its head quickly—if you're too slow, it hides under its protective shell.

That Ankiron was guarding the light-blue Button. Punch the Button to activate it, but don't backtrack to its Treasure Chest just yet. Smash the Rock Blocks to the right instead.

The third trapdoor, which happens to be a Wooden Trapdoor, is hiding behind the wall of Rock Blocks. Ground Pound through the trapdoor and enter its sub-level.

Trapdoor 3

This is a simple puzzle to solve. A tall stack of floating blocks extends up, circled by spiked balls at various places. Start by jumping onto the lowest block, then jump to the next level of blocks as you begin to make your way up the stack.

Remember that you can alter the camera angle at any time to provide a better view as you navigate the stack. At the top of the blocks sits the Red Diamond.

When you return from the Wooden Trapdoor, get the light-blue Button's Treasure Chest. Head to the left until you reach the gate and Swirly Spinner. Perform a Corkscrew Conk to reach the elevated ledge, then use the Glue Globe to reach the ledge where the Treasure Chest is located. Open the chest and collect your sixth treasure from the Greenhorn Ruins, the Vase.

Return to the lower, watery area near the light-blue Button. A line of Glue Globes extends upward to a higher ledge. Jump from one Glue Globe to the next to reach the ledge above.

Step

Another Spriteling sits on top of a circular pedestal on the high ledge. When you free it, the Spriteling tells you about Battle Rings. Ground Pound into the Wooden Trapdoor before you move on to the Battle Ring.

NOTE

Battle Rings are found in many areas of *Wario World*. When you enter one, a large, dome-shaped barrier traps you inside for one minute, and large groups of monsters attack you in waves.

Trapdoor 4

This is an easy sub-level to clear. Climb the steps to reach the Arrow Block, then punch it. The Arrow Block zooms over to the far stack of blocks, where it acts as a step to help you reach the Gold Statue part and Red Diamond.

After you return from the Wooden Trapdoor, continue along to the right. You enter a large, circular area: a Battle Ring. Just as the Spriteling said, waves of monsters blink into existence until the one-minute timer expires. A barrier prevents your escape until time's up.

Almost every Battle Ring supplies you with several Columns to use as you see fit, which is a great help. Your best attack in any Battle Ring is the Wild Swing-Ding, which clears out hordes of enemies quickly and easily.

When the timer goes off, the battle is over. You're rewarded with a Wooden Chest for surviving each Battle Ring, which always contains gold coins. The more enemies you defeat, the more gold you get.

Proceed to the right after the Battle Ring, and you come to a foot imprint on the ground. Line up with the imprint and jump onto the steel chain ahead. Before you climb down the chain, notice the purple Treasure Chest platform on the ledge above.

Step

Below the steel chain you encounter a monster generator and a Steel Trapdoor. Stun a Magon from the monster generator and use it to perform a Piledriver onto the Steel Trapdoor.

Trapdoor 5

This Steel Trapdoor's sub-level is a simple obstacle course made up of several large gears. The gears rotate slowly, so watch your step as you jump across each one.

The smaller, flat gear sports a line of spiked balls that spin around. Be careful as you collect the gold coins from this gear, and don't worry if you have to leave some behind. Continue along until you reach the Gold Statue part and Red Diamond on the other side.

WARIOWORLD™

PRIMA'S OFFICIAL STRATEGY GUIDE

After you've collected the Gold Statue part and Red Diamond from the fifth trapdoor, run past the monster generator and punch Old Red-Mug's face until it falls over. Continue to the right past Old Red-Mug.

Step

Run past the monster generator and Swirly Spinner after Old Red-Mug, ignoring them for the moment. Smash a few of the Rock Blocks ahead, but don't smash all of them.

Use the Rock Blocks you didn't break as a step to jump onto the ledge above. Activate the purple Button on the ledge. The purple Button's Treasure Chest is coming up, but you have a few other things to do first.

Return to the monster generator you just passed by, stun a Magon when one pops out, and carry it over to the Rock Blocks. Use the Magon to enter the Steel Trapdoor on the other side of the Rock Blocks.

Trapdoor 6

This is another easy obstacle course to test your basic movement skills. Start by jumping out onto the blocks ahead, which are arranged to serve as a path. As you proceed, beware of the moving blocks and spiked balls that try to knock you off the pathway.

You're halfway to the Red Diamond once you reach the Gold Statue part. Try adjusting the camera angle for a better view as you cross the next line of moving blocks, and watch their movements carefully.

Pick the camera angle that gives you the best possible view of what's around you and where to jump next. Don't stand on any of the moving blocks too long or you're pushed off. Jump quickly from one block to the next, timing your jumps with care.

After clearing the sixth trapdoor, smash all the nearby Rock Blocks. They were covering the pink Button, which sticks out from the wall. Activate the pink Button, then return to the monster generator and Swirly Spinner near Old Red-Mug.

Stun and pick up a Magon when the monster generator spits one out, then execute a counterclockwise Wild Swing-Ding on the Swirly Spinner. The gate on the wall retracts, revealing a ladder to a higher ledge.

Quickly jump onto and climb up the ladder before the gate closes again. Head to the left once you reach the top of the ladder.

32

Step

After climbing the ladder, use the nearby Glue Globe to reach a small, elevated platform where an Ankiron stands guard. Relentlessly punch the Ankiron until it's stunned, then toss it aside.

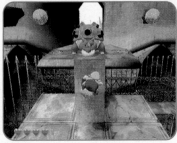

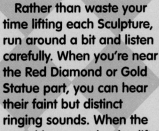

The Ankiron was guarding the seventh trapdoor. Walk into the small alcove and Ground Pound the Wooden Trapdoor to enter its sub-level.

Trapdoor 7

The seventh trapdoor is simple, but can be time consuming. It's a small room filled with Sculptures, two of which hide the Red Diamond and a Gold Statue part. The other Sculptures aren't hiding anything of interest.

Rather than waste your time lifting each Sculpture, run around a bit and listen carefully. When you're near the Red Diamond or Gold Statue part, you can hear their faint but distinct ringing sounds. When the sound becomes louder, lift the nearby Sculptures to find the goods.

Once you return from the seventh trapdoor, jump over to the Glue Globe to the left. From there, jump to the next platform ahead, where the purple Button's Treasure Chest is found. Punch the Treasure Chest to open it and claim the Lucky Figurine.

With the Lucky Figurine added to your treasures, return to the elevated platform where you recently fought an Ankiron. This time, jump and latch onto the Glue Globe to the right of the platform. Cross the row of Glue Globes, jumping from one to the next as you go.

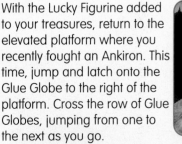

NOTE

If you fall while crossing the row of Glue Globes, you land near the Swirly Spinner. Activate the Swirly Spinner to retract the gate and then climb back up to try again.

Step

You encounter a Garlic Dispenser after crossing the Glue Globes. Two Clubosaurs drop from the sky to give you a hard time. Defeat the monsters and use the Garlic Dispenser to replenish Wario's Heart Meter.

The fifth and final trapped Spriteling is sitting on a circular pedestal just past the Garlic Dispenser. Several Cractyls guard the Spriteling, so be careful. The Spriteling tells you that the coming stages have many trapped Spritelings, and you'll be rewarded if you rescue them all.

The pink Button's Treasure Chest sits near the fifth Spriteling. Open the Treasure Chest to obtain the NES. That's the eighth and final treasure from the Greenhorn Ruins.

The goal and ByeBye Balloon are just beyond the final Spriteling. You need three Red Diamonds to remove the stone statue guarding the Goal Trapdoor. Before entering the Goal Trapdoor, however, stun a Cractyl and use it to enter the nearby Steel Trapdoor.

Trapdoor 8

Thankfully, the eighth trapdoor is a breeze. It consists of a "sea" of blocks that rise and fall in a simple pattern. There's no danger of being knocked off the undulating blocks, so cut straight across and grab the last Red Diamond and Gold Statue part.

Now that you've rescued the five trapped Spritelings and found all eight treasures, Red Diamonds, and Gold Statue parts, you're ready to face the boss of the Greenhorn Ruins. Use the nearby Garlic Dispenser if Wario's Heart Meter isn't full, then Ground Pound into the Goal Trapdoor.

Area Boss: Sandworm

Sandworm is the boss of the Greenhorn Ruins. The fight takes place in a bowl-shaped sand trap, which pulls you in toward the center of the arena. Be wary of this sand trap, as Sandworm uses it to its advantage throughout the fight.

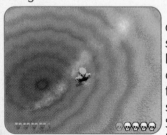

When Sandworm moves, it ducks below the surface of the sandy arena and zips to a new location. Sandworm tries to confuse you by traveling below the sand in this fashion. You can see a trail of dust whenever Sandworm moves about, however, which indicates where it'll pop up to attack next.

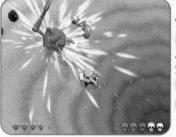

Charge up to Sandworm when it surfaces to attack and punch its head repeatedly. After several blows, Sandworm gets angry and begins to flash just like the previous area boss, Greenfist.

After powering up, Sandworm raises its frightening, scythe-like claws and begins to chase after you, attacking wildly. Sandworm is invulnerable during this attack, so run away as fast as you can. As with Greenfist, this furious attack becomes faster and more deadly as the battle wears on.

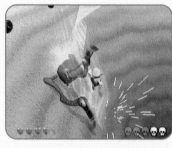

During Sandworm's other type of special attack, it zips to the center of the arena and begins spinning, which causes the sand trap to pull you in much faster. Sandworm then spits out several spiked balls, hoping to hit you with one. To avoid taking heavy damage, run and jump away from Sandworm during this nasty attack.

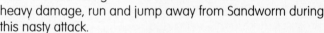

Sandworm never becomes stunned. Instead, it gradually takes damage as you hammer away with Wario's powerful punches. When all five of its health skulls have faded, this boss fight is over.

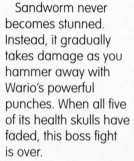

Excitement Central: Dinomighty's Showdown

The stage boss of Excitement Central is a huge, green dinosaur named Dinomighty. This is a fairly easy boss fight, as Dinomighty isn't the sharpest tool in the shed. Defeat Dinomighty to acquire the first Giant Treasure Chest Key and unlock the next stage.

Dinomighty's Attacks

Dinomighty often leaps into the air and comes crashing down in an attempt to flatten you. Even if Dinomighty misses, the force of her landing sends out a large shock wave capable of damaging you. Stay clear of Dinomighty when she leaps, and be ready to jump and avoid the resulting shock wave. As the battle wears on, Dinomighty jumps several times, sending out multiple shock waves in quick succession.

After being hit with a Piledriver, Dinomighty always jumps back up and crashes down in a rage. Be prepared for this and jump to dodge the shock wave that follows, or you take damage.

Occasionally, Dinomighty stomps the ground with her feet, hoping to flatten you underneath them. This attack doesn't create a shock wave, but Dinomighty uses it whenever you get too close.

If Dinomighty sees you, her eyes begin to glow red. Pay heed to this strong warning and run away. Start running to one side as soon as you see Dinomighty's eyes turn red—she soon lashes out with her long, powerful tongue.

Fighting Dinomighty

Since Dinomighty is so huge and Wario small, use stealth to your advantage. Run around and get behind Dinomighty to avoid detection. Dinomighty becomes confused, looking around to find you. While her back is turned, examine Dinomighty's tail.

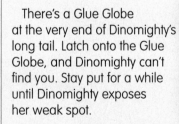

There's a Glue Globe at the very end of Dinomighty's long tail. Latch onto the Glue Globe, and Dinomighty can't find you. Stay put for a while until Dinomighty exposes her weak spot.

Eventually, Dinomighty catches on to your trick. She lifts her tail way up high and turns her head to see you hiding at the end of her lengthy extremity.

When Dinomighty looks at you, that's your chance to attack. Jump off her tail and perform a Ground Pound directly onto Dinomighty's giant head.

After you hit her head with a Ground Pound, Dinomighty becomes stunned and spews out a bunch of gold coins. Use Hyper Suction to quickly collect the loot, then run up to the stunned green giant and pick her up.

Once you've picked up Dinomighty, you can damage her. Execute a Piledriver to smash her head into the ground. You can also Power Throw Dinomighty into the lava that surrounds the arena.

After you hit her with five Piledrivers or Power Throws, Dinomighty is defeated. The first Giant Treasure Chest Key is yours.

Spooktastic World: Horror Manor

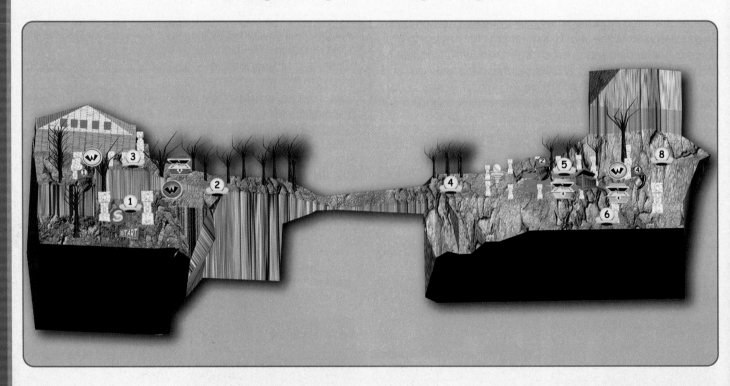

Legend

GOAL	Area's goal	S	Spriteling
W	Button (various colors)	START	Starting point of area
	Garlic Dispenser		Steel Trapdoor (numbered)
1	Walkthrough icon (numbered)		Treasure Chest (various colors)
	Gold Statue Part		Wooden Chest
			Wooden Trapdoor (numbered)

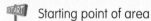

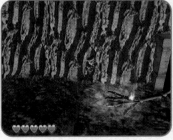

The first area of the Spooktastic World stage is Horror Manor. Horror Manor is a dark, foreboding place of pure evil, inhabited by zombies, ghosts, and spirits of every sort. This area has stronger enemies and trickier puzzles than its predecessor, upping the overall challenge. As with every area in *Wario World*, Horror Manor has eight treasures to find, eight Gold Statue parts to collect, eight Red Diamonds to locate, and five Spritelings to rescue.

NOTE

You must have at least four Red Diamonds to enter Horror Manor's Goal Trapdoor.

Step 1

You come across the first trapped Spriteling up the trail a short way from the area's starting point. When freed, the Spriteling gives you advice on how to defeat the Big Bone-Fist enemies in this area.

Several new monsters pop up from the ground as you continue past the first Spriteling. They look frightening, but these Zombie Magons are very similar to the weakling Magons you fought in previous areas. Zombie Magons are a bit more aggressive, but still not much of a threat.

This enemy is called a Big Bone-Fist. Later areas feature similar enemies, which block your path until they are defeated. Follow the Spriteling's advice and wait until the Big Bone-Fist performs its slam attack before you try to damage it.

When the Big Bone-Fist slams the ground trying to flatten you, jump up and execute a Ground Pound onto the blue, glowing jewel that lights up. Hit the Big Bone-Fist's blue jewel three times to defeat it and proceed.

Step 2

Past the Big Bone-Fist, several Zombie Magons guard the red Button. Defeat the monsters and activate the red Button.

The following hill is filled with Zombie Magons. Keep moving to avoid their speedy claws as you pummel them.

Head to the left after you've cleared the hill of monsters. The red Button's Treasure Chest is hidden in a small grove of dead trees. Open the Treasure Chest to collect the Candlestick.

Past the Treasure Chest is a small glowing circle on the ground. A Glue Globe Ghost rises up from the circle every few seconds. Latch onto the Glue Globe Ghost and ride it up to the high ledge to the left.

Step 3

Run along the outside fence of the brick building after you jump off the Glue Globe Ghost.

The yellow Button is on the ground where the fence turns a corner. Activate the yellow Button and continue to follow the fence.

The first trapdoor is a little past the yellow Button. It's a Wooden Trapdoor, so Ground Pound inside.

Trapdoor 1

This first trapdoor eases you in to the Horror Manor area. A large group of blocks floats in the center of a small room. Circle the blocks until you find a lower opening, then jump and climb inside.

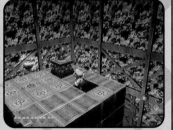

Go all the way inside the first alcove in the blocks, then turn left and jump up to continue along a short path. You can't really see what you're doing, so you have to "feel" your way around. Turn right at the next junction and follow a short path to its end. Jump up through the hole to reach the top of the blocks to find a Gold Statue part and a Red Diamond.

After returning from the first trapdoor, jump off the cliff and follow the trail back to the small hill where you fought all those Zombie Magons. This time, go right.

Step 4

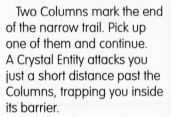

As you move along, the trail narrows and groups of smaller, weaker Zombie Magons pop up from the ground to attack. Punch or perform a Dash Attack to quickly get rid of the little pests.

Two Columns mark the end of the narrow trail. Pick up one of them and continue. A Crystal Entity attacks you just a short distance past the Columns, trapping you inside its barrier.

Use the Column you grabbed to execute a Wild Swing-Ding to make short work of the Crystal Entity. Finish it off with a Piledriver after it's stunned. Go right.

Step 5

A strange new object lies on the ground just past the Crystal Entity. This is called a Swirly Slab. If you perform a Wild Swing-Ding while standing on the Swirly Slab, it slowly winds upward, like an elevator.

Stun and grab a nearby Zombie Magon and use it to activate the Swirly Slab. Execute a Wild Swing-Ding while standing on the Swirly Slab, and it lifts you into the air. Jump off and grab the Gold Statue part hovering over a pillar close by.

The yellow Button's Treasure Chest is in the small graveyard. Open the chest to collect the Silver Candlestick. Open a nearby Wooden Chest for a random treat.

The second trapdoor also is in the small graveyard. Enter the Wooden Trapdoor to collect the goodies from its sub-level.

Trapdoor 2

This second trapdoor is fairly tricky, demanding quick reflexes and expert timing. Activate the lever, then quickly jump onto the platform as it begins to rise.

The first floating platform also has a lever. Punch the lever and immediately jump onto the next platform before it rises out of reach.

A Spriteling is trapped inside a small box near the Red Diamond. Rescue the Spriteling, who gives you a hint about using Swirly Slabs. Grab the Red Diamond and use the Escape Spring to return to the surface.

Once you return from the second trapdoor, exit the small graveyard and continue to the right. After a short distance, you see a light green Button on the ground near a wall. Activate the button and then continue to the right down the lower trail.

Step 6

Another Big Bone-Fist blocks the lower trail. Wait for it to use its slam attack, then jump up and Ground Pound its blue, glowing jewel. Continue along the trail to the right after defeating the Big Bone-Fist.

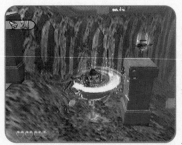

Several Bone Cractyls appear after the Big Bone-Fist. These are similar to the Cractyls you faced in previous areas. Jump and punch one to stun it, then grab it and perform a Wild Swing-Ding on the nearby Swirly Slab. Jump from the Swirly Slab to claim the Gold Statue part floating over a pillar close by.

Step 7

The trail becomes watery as you continue along, providing habitat for a new enemy. These bizarre monsters are called Swordfish because of the large blades that jut from their bodies. Keep moving, or they surface beneath your feet and attack with their large blades.

A Steel Trapdoor is a short distance ahead. Punch one of the nearby Swordfish to stun it, then use it to enter the third trapdoor.

Trapdoor 3

The third trapdoor can be trying. A large circle of blocks rotates counter-clockwise around a central platform, which holds a Wooden Chest. The Red Diamond sits on the far platform.

Jump onto one of the blocks as it passes, and proceed clockwise around the circle of blocks. If you follow the blocks counter-clockwise, you have to deal with the dangerous rings of spiked balls.

Be careful as you jump to each block, because some are smaller than others. If you fall, you have to start all over again.

At the opposite side of the sub-level is a moving platform. Use the platform to reach the Wooden Chest on the central platform.

Open the Wooden Chest, then use the moving platform to reach the Red Diamond. Time your jump to use one of the circling blocks as a step.

Now that you've returned from the third trapdoor, run up the circular building's steps to the right. The first Garlic Dispenser is at the top of the steps, ready to vend Wario some Garlic.

Use the ladder on the first tier of the circular building to reach the second tier above.

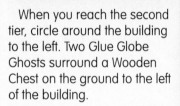

When you reach the second tier, circle around the building to the left. Two Glue Globe Ghosts surround a Wooden Chest on the ground to the left of the building.

Step

Use the Glue Globe Ghost farthest from the circular building first. When the Glue Globe Ghost travels all the way up, jump from it to sail over the wall to the left.

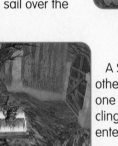

A Steel Trapdoor is on the other side of the wall. Stun one of the Bone Cractyls circling close by and use it to enter the fourth trapdoor.

Trapdoor 4

The fourth trapdoor's sub-level is very basic, but still presents a challenge. A line of blocks moves in a pattern ahead of the starting point. You must cross it to reach the Gold Statue part beyond.

As soon as the blocks move and stretch out in a straight line, jump onto them. Perform a Dash Attack to quickly charge to the other side of the blocks.

Even using the Dash Attack, you won't reach the other side of the blocks before they switch into a step-like arrangement. Quickly jump to the top block before they shift again into a vertical line.

You needed the Dash Attack because the blocks must still be in the step-like arrangement for you to jump to the next platform ahead. Jump from the top block to reach the platform and collect the Gold Statue part.

Traverse a similar line of blocks to reach the Red Diamond. These blocks switch their arrangement much faster than the others, making getting to the Red Diamond a difficult task.

The Dash Attack is counterproductive when moving along the second line of blocks unless you execute a Corkscrew Conk as they change into the step-like arrangement. Scamper up

to the top block before the blocks switch to the vertical line arrangement, then jump to the single stationary block ahead.

You're home free when you land on the stationary block. Jump to the platform ahead and nab the Red Diamond. Whew!

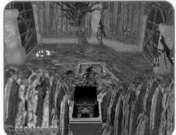

After you return from the fourth trapdoor, you see the light green Button's Treasure Chest on the ground in front of you. The chest contains the Forest Painting.

Jump to the lower trail after you grab the Forest Painting and return to the second tier of the circular building. Use the Glue Globe Ghost nearest the building to reach the third tier.

Round the third tier of the circular building, hopping over the spiked balls and punching the small Zombie Magons out of your way. Use the Glue Globe Ghost on the other side of the walkway to reach the building's rooftop.

Another Crystal Entity drops in to cause trouble atop the circular building. Defeat the Crystal Entity and activate the light-blue Button.

Step 9

Jump down from the circular building's rooftop and follow the trail as it rises to the right. Dodge or fight the monsters as you head for the large building in front of you: Horror Manor.

A nasty Door Spirit enemy guards the front door to Horror Manor. These monsters fire bolts of electricity that shock you if you don't avoid them.

Punch the Door Spirit repeatedly until it disappears, moving to one side when it begins to fire an electric bolt. When the Door Spirit is out of your way, enter Horror Manor.

Step 10

Horror Manor's main foyer is chock-full of undead enemies. Use the nearby Glue Globe Ghost to reach the upper balcony.

Another evil Door Spirit guards a doorway on the upper balcony. Pound the Door Spirit into submission and proceed through the doorway.

The doorway leads to a high outdoor balcony. Jump the gaps in the balcony as you run along it, making your way toward a trapped Spriteling. This thankful Spriteling teaches you about using Wario's Hyper Suction to quickly gobble up coins.

Return to Horror Manor and proceed along the upper balcony. The light-blue Button's Treasure Chest is close by, but walls of electricity guard it. Wait for the electric walls to drop, then quickly jump to the Treasure Chest and open it to collect the Crystal Ball!

The dark-green Button is on a balcony platform between two thick steel chains. Jump onto one of the chains, and then to the dark-green Button. Punch the Button to activate it, then use the other chain to reach the opposite end of the balcony.

What? Another Door Spirit guards a doorway on this side of the balcony, too! Hammer at the Door Spirit as you did the previous two. When you've dealt with it, enter the doorway.

Step 11

A trapped Spriteling waits to be rescued on the other side of the doorway. The Spriteling teaches you the advantages of using Autospin while performing a Wild Swing-Ding.

A Skeletal Ankiron is blocking the hallway past the Spriteling. Punch the Skeletal Ankiron's bony head as fast as you can to stun it, then defeat it with a Piledriver and move on.

A Silver Door Spirit guards the doorway past the Skeletal Ankiron. These are more powerful versions of regular Door Spirits. They can fire a powerful ray of electricity in addition to electric bolts. Punch the Silver Door Spirit until you see it flash, then step to one side to avoid its deadly electric ray.

Step 12

A Wooden Trapdoor is on the other side of the doorway that the Silver Door Spirit was guarding. Enter the trapdoor and collect the Red Diamond from its sub-level.

Trapdoor 5

The fifth trapdoor's sub-level is easy to solve, but can be hazardous to Wario's Heart Meter. The Red Diamond sits on a short pedestal in the center of the room, surrounded by two sets of electric currents.

The top-down camera view is invaluable in this situation. Use it to help you make careful, precise jumps toward the Red Diamond. If you're determined to open the Wooden Chest near the Red Diamond, punch it from the side or Ground Pound directly onto it to avoid a shock from the neighboring electric currents.

Proceed down the stairs that follow the Wooden Trapdoor. Activate the dark-blue Button on your way down, and open the Wooden Chest at the bottom of the stairs.

Oh, no! Another Silver Door Spirit! Defeat this monster with the same techniques you used to best the previous one, dodging its powerful electric ray when you see it flash. Enter the doorway beyond.

Step 13

The next room has a huge hole in the floor, with an arrow painted on the ground pointing toward it. Before you drop down the hole, check the ramp to the left.

Aha! A Gold Statue part hovers at the end of the left ramp! Collect the Gold Statue part, then drop into the hole in the center of the room to reach the basement of Horror Manor.

Step 14

You land smack in the middle of a Battle Ring! The Columns close by help you survive the one-minute battle. Proceed to the right once the smoke clears.

You eventually come to a section of the basement with a watery floor, a perfect habitat for those freaky Swordfish! Fortunately, a health-restoring Garlic Dispenser stands in an alcove nearby.

Stun a Swordfish and pick it up. Jump onto the nearby Swirly Slab and perform a Wild Swing-Ding using the Swordfish. Jump off the Swirly Slab to reach an elevated steel walkway to the right.

The dark-green Button's Treasure Chest is at the end of the steel walkway, guarded by a wall of electricity. Wait for the electric currents to shut off, then quickly run up to the Treasure Chest. Open the chest and nab the Castle Painting!

After you collect the Castle Painting, use the nearby Glue Globe Ghost to reach another steel walkway above.

On the higher steel walkway, run to the left.

CAUTION

Watch out for the huge spike traps that drop from the ceiling to crush you.

Wait for the second spike trap to retract, then leap from the end of the steel walkway to reach a distant ledge to the left where a Wooden Trapdoor is located. If you have trouble reaching the trapdoor, try executing a Corkscrew Conk. Enter the sixth trapdoor with a Ground Pound.

Trapdoor 6

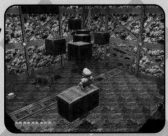

The puzzle on the sixth trapdoor's sub-level is easily solved. Jump onto the lowest pair of floating blocks, then watch the rest of the floating blocks for a few seconds. The blocks spin periodically in a set pattern. Be quick as you jump across them.

When you're comfortable with their pattern of rotation, jump to the closest of the floating blocks. Quickly jump across the rest, heading for the higher floating blocks on the other side. Collect the Gold Statue part and Red Diamond from the higher blocks and return to the surface.

After returning from the sixth trapdoor, drop from the ledge and head back to the Swirly Slab. Use the Swirly Slab to reach the higher walkway, and use the Glue Globe Ghost to get to the next walkway above. Proceed to the right once you land on the upper walkway.

Step

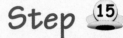

Use the ladder or jump down to the lower, watery chamber below, where a Steel Trapdoor is located. Stun a Sword-fish and use it to execute a Piledriver to enter the seventh trapdoor.

Trapdoor 7

The seventh trapdoor's sub-level can be time-consuming, but it isn't all that difficult. A group of large, floating blocks rotate counterclockwise but they switch back and forth to clockwise after a short period. The blocks are located between the starting platform and the Red Diamond's platform. Jump onto the first large block as it moves past the starting platform.

The idea is to cross the collection of floating blocks and reach the Red Diamond's platform. If you make careful jumps and plan your next move wisely, you can avoid the slippery, dangerous ice blocks altogether. Jump from one block to the next until you reach the Gold Statue part and Red Diamond.

Run onto the steel mesh ramp after you return from the seventh trapdoor. A large machine cog near the ramp slowly spins clockwise. Jump onto one of the Glue Globes that stick out from the cog and ride upward.

Once the cog takes you all the way up, jump off the Glue Globe and onto the top of the cog. From there, jump over and latch onto the Glue Globe to the right, then jump and land on the high steel walkway ahead.

Step 16

This elevated steel walkway features two sets of dangerous electric walls. To proceed unscathed, jump past each one as soon as the electric currents shut off.

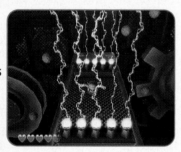

Turn left at the walkway's T-intersection. The dark-blue Button's Treasure Chest is nearby, waiting to be opened. Collect the Knight's Helmet from the chest, then run to the right down the walkway.

At the other end of the walkway sits a Wooden Chest. Open the chest for a random treat, then backtrack to the electrified walls on this walkway. As you did before, jump past the walls when their electric currents shut off.

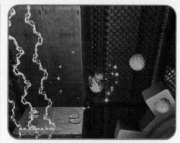

Past the electrified walls, this walkway has two footprints. Line up with the print on the right, and jump across the two Glue Globes ahead.

Jump from the second Glue Globe and land on top of the large machine cog below. Jump from the cog and grab onto the nearby steel chain. Climb the chain and then jump over to the platform to the right, where the purple Button is located.

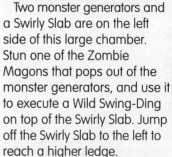

Jump down to the large chamber below after activating the purple Button. The pink Button is on the ground in the far right corner. Activate it, then head over to the left.

Two monster generators and a Swirly Slab are on the left side of this large chamber. Stun one of the Zombie Magons that pops out of the monster generators, and use it to execute a Wild Swing-Ding on top of the Swirly Slab. Jump off the Swirly Slab to the left to reach a higher ledge.

This ledge features a Skeletal Ankiron and a Steel Trapdoor. Ferociously punch the Ankiron until you stun it, then pick it up and use it to enter the eighth and final trapdoor.

Trapdoor 8

If you were hoping that the last trapdoor in the Horror Manor area would be straightforward, you're in luck! Your only task is to traverse the crooked line of floating blocks to reach the Red Diamond's platform.

Some of the floating blocks are extremely small, which makes crossing them an edge-of-your-seat experience. Use the camera angle shown in the screenshot above for the best view as you cross the blocks. The final Red Diamond and Gold Statue part are waiting on the far platform.

Now that you've returned from the final trapdoor, go after the purple Button's Treasure Chest. Jump left off the trapdoor's ledge and land in the watery chamber below. Ride on one of the nearby cog's Glue Globes, then jump to the Glue Globe that's floating above and to the left.

Jump left off the floating Glue Globe and land on the high steel walkway. Proceed down the walkway, jumping past the electrified walls when their nodes shut off.

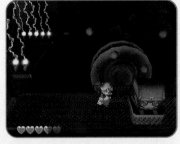

The purple Button's Treasure Chest is at the end of the steel walkway. Open it and collect the Gladiator's Helmet, then backtrack to the purple Button's small, elevated platform.

Jump to the chain to the right from the purple Button's small platform, then drop down to the top of the large machine cog below.

From there, jump over to the first Glue Globe to the right. Jump from that Glue Globe to the next one, then jump and land on the ledge ahead.

Step 17

Watch out for the pair of huge spike traps that fall from the ceiling on this ledge. A trapped Spriteling sits between the two spike traps. The Spriteling gives you a hint about defeating the boss of the Horror Manor area.

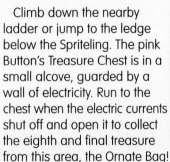

Climb down the nearby ladder or jump to the ledge below the Spriteling. The pink Button's Treasure Chest is in a small alcove, guarded by a wall of electricity. Run to the chest when the electric currents shut off and open it to collect the eighth and final treasure from this area, the Ornate Bag!

The goal also is on this ledge. Feed the stone statue guarding the Goal Trapdoor four Red Diamonds to remove it. If Wario's Heart Meter is low, don't enter the Goal Trapdoor just yet. Instead, jump up the line of Glue Globes on the wall to the right of the goal.

Jump left from the highest Glue Globe on the wall and grab onto the thick steel chain hanging there. Jump from chain to chain until you come to a small segment of steel walkway.

A Garlic Dispenser is on this walkway. Gobble some Garlic to replenish Wario's Heart Meter and return to the goal. When you're ready, Ground Pound onto the Goal Trapdoor and prepare to battle the boss of the Horror Manor area.

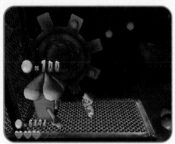

Area Boss: Brawl Doll

Brawl Doll is the evil boss of the Horror Manor area and he has a few tricks up his sleeve, so be wary! All in all, this is a fairly easy boss fight as long as you use the surrounding environment to your advantage. Defeat Brawl Doll to unlock the next area of Spooktastic World.

As soon as the fight begins, run over to a nearby Column, pick it up, and execute a Wild Swing-Ding.

Brawl Doll stays airborne throughout most of the fight, but he has to come into close quarters at some point if he wants to attack you. As long as you keep swinging Columns around, Brawl Doll gets smacked every time he drops in to attack.

It only takes one Wild Swing-Ding blow to stun Brawl Doll. Press Ⓑ to throw the Column after you hit Brawl Doll, then pick him up while he's vulnerable.

While carrying Brawl Doll, jump up and execute a devastating Piledriver! This powerful attack takes away one of Brawl Doll's five health skulls.

After you successfully damage Brawl Doll, he flies to the far end of the arena and fires out multiple energy projectiles. This attack takes Brawl Doll a few seconds to set up. Grab another Column while he flies off.

At first, the energy projectiles are easy to avoid. As the fight wears on and Brawl Doll takes more damage, this attack becomes much more powerful and difficult to avoid. Wario drops the Column he's carrying if he's hit by a projectile, forcing you to grab another.

Continue to use Columns and perform Wild Swing-Ding attacks until Brawl Doll is defeated. Don't worry about running out of Columns. They reappear if you use them all up. Brawl Doll finally succumbs after five painful Piledrivers.

Spooktastic World: Wonky Circus

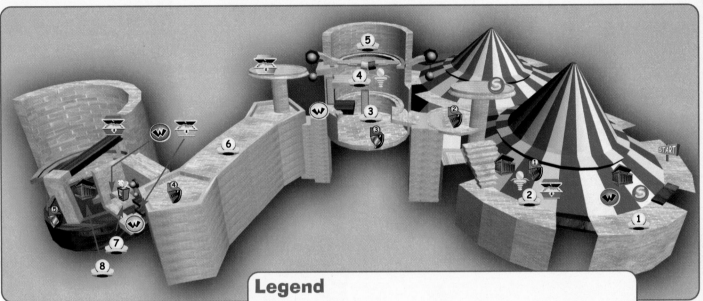

Legend

GOAL	Area's goal	**S**	Spriteling
W	Button (various colors)	**START**	Starting point of area
	Garlic Dispenser	**1**	Steel Trapdoor (numbered)
1	Walkthrough icon (numbered)		Treasure Chest (various colors)
	Gold Statue Part		Wooden Chest
		1	Wooden Trapdoor (numbered)

The second area of the Spooktastic World stage is the Wonky Circus. All sorts of new enemies and obstacles fill this zany, circus-themed area to further test your fighting skills. As with every area in *Wario World*, Wonky Circus has eight treasures to find, eight Gold Statue parts to collect, eight Red Diamonds to locate, and five Spritelings to rescue.

NOTE
You must have at least four Red Diamonds to enter the Wonky Circus Goal Trapdoor.

Step

As soon as you enter the Wonky Circus area, you're surrounded by a group of new enemies: Clowns! These monsters are similar to Magons, so they aren't much of a threat by themselves.

Watch out for the huge cannonballs that fire from the circus tent as you cross the narrow wooden bridge ahead. Their painted-on clown faces might be smiling, but you won't be if you're knocked into the Unithorn's Lair.

More Clowns gather past the wooden bridge. Pick up a Column and perform a Wild Swing-Ding attack to defeat them quickly.

Jump onto the small wooden platform sticking out from the circus tent when the Clowns are out of the way. From there, jump to the right to rescue a trapped Spriteling sitting on another platform. The Spriteling gives you advice on defeating the upcoming Electric Clown Fence.

After freeing the Spriteling, jump into the small recess in the tent and open the Wooden Chest sitting there. Next, jump over to the red Button and activate it before moving on to the left.

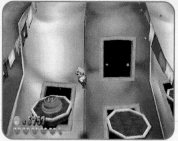

Wait for the huge cannon-balls to shoot past before crossing this second wooden bridge.

More Clowns patrol on the other side of the second wooden bridge. Stun one and use it to execute a Wild Swing-Ding to take out the rest. Once the Clowns are gone, jump onto another small wooden platform sticking out from the circus tent.

Jump to the right from the central wooden platform and land near the red Button's Treasure Chest. Smash the chest to collect your first treasure—the Bugle.

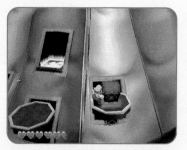

The first Gold Statue part hovers over the small wooden platform to the left. Nab the Gold Statue part, then jump over to the nearby Wooden Trapdoor and enter its sub-level.

Trapdoor 1

This first trapdoor isn't much of a challenge, but you may walk out of it with a low Heart Meter if you're not careful. Clusters of spiked balls circle both ladders that lead up to the higher balcony of the small room. Watch carefully to spot gaps between some of the spiked balls.

Time your movements carefully as you attempt to grab onto the ladder. Wario has just enough space to fit between the gaps in the spiked balls—there isn't much margin for error. Climb the ladder to avoid being hit by the spiked balls above and below you, then walk along the balcony and collect the Gold Statue part and Red Diamond.

Continue onward to the left when you return from the first trapdoor. Cross the next wooden bridge ahead, then jump up and open the Wooden Chest sitting atop the small platform on the other side.

Step 2

An Electric Clown Fence blocks your progress past the third wooden bridge. Clowns periodically drop in to attack. Stun one and pick it up. Charge up a Power Throw by holding down Ⓑ, then hurl the stunned Clown at the fence's moving target. One well-aimed, fully charged Power Throw downs the Electric Clown Fence, allowing you to proceed up the steps ahead.

A trio of fat Pigeon enemies guards a Wooden Trapdoor up the steps. These monsters are very similar to Cractyls. They try to snatch you with their claws and carry you away. If a Pigeon grabs you, shake Ⓒ from side to side. After you defeat them, enter the second trapdoor.

Trapdoor 2

The second trapdoor's sub-level features several Glue Globes that extend upward in the middle of the room. Spiked balls block the ladders that lead to the room's upper balcony, so you need to use the Glue Globes.

Jump from one Glue Globe to the next as you work your way up to the balcony. Once there, open the Wooden Chest and collect the Red Diamond.

After exiting the second trapdoor, run up the ramp to the left. Ignore the odd-looking trapeze for the moment and follow the wooden walkway along the outside wall.

Step 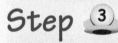 3

The narrow walkway abruptly ends with a ladder that leads downward. Climb down the ladder or simply jump off the walkway to proceed.

A Crystal Entity attacks you once you reach the lower circular area. Use the smaller Crystal Creatures it spawns as weapons to defeat it, as you did earlier with Crystal Entities.

The Crystal Entity's confining barrier disappears after its defeat, allowing you to access a nearby Steel Trapdoor. Several Clowns drop in to attack. Use one of them to perform a Piledriver and enter the third trapdoor.

Trapdoor 3

This unusual sub-level consists of an enormous ring of wide, rectangular blocks that circle a small central platform. The massive ring of blocks slowly rotates vertically around the central platform.

Start by jumping onto the first rectangular block. Run across the block and jump to the next one ahead. Continue jumping from one block to the next until you land on the far rectangular block, directly opposite the starting platform.

Stand on this block as the ring makes its slow trip into a vertical formation. Keep adjusting the camera angle so you can see the central platform and the line of gold coins that extends upward from it.

As the ring of blocks continues to rotate vertically, run onto the side of the block you're standing on to avoid falling off. As the ring of blocks completes its rotation, you see a single gold coin floating in the air, marking the position of the central platform below.

Shift the camera angle to the top-down perspective so you can see directly below you. Use the single gold coin as your guide and make a leap of faith off the rectangular block. As you fall, follow the long line of gold coins to ensure you land on the central platform below. Collect the Red Diamond and Gold Statue part from the central platform.

Now that you've cleared the third trapdoor, climb up the ladder to return to the wooden walkway above. Backtrack around the walkway and approach the odd-looking trapeze you passed earlier.

Circle around the trapeze, positioning Wario as shown in the screenshot at left. Dash Attack the trapeze from this position. You're flung to the left across the gap.

Walking into the trapeze lands you on a distant platform on the other side of the gap. Nothing here is of interest, so climb the nearby ladder to reach a higher platform.

Spookastic World: Wonky Circus

Step 4

After climbing the ladder, turn left to find the yellow Button. This is a dead end, so activate the yellow Button and go back toward the ladder.

On the right side of the ladder is another trapeze. Walk into the trapeze to sail over the gap to the right. As you soar through the air, you automatically collect a Gold Statue part hovering over the gap.

Continue to the right until you see a small wooden pedestal with a foot imprint on top. Jump onto the pedestal and wait for a Glue Globe attached to a pole to swing by. Jump up and grab the Glue Globe when it pauses briefly over the foot imprint.

The Glue Globe Pole goes around and around, pausing at four spots. You encounter many more Glue Globe Poles in this area. Ride on the Glue Globe until it pauses for a moment in the three o'clock position, then jump over to the platform on the right.

Watch out for the huge, clown-faced cannonballs that try to knock you off this small platform. A trapped Spriteling sits on the right side of the platform. Rescue the Spriteling, who tells you about using © to peek around and see what's coming up next.

TIP

The Spriteling's tip is a good one. Use © to get a better view of your surroundings. This trick is especially useful in the Wonky Circus.

After rescuing the Spriteling from the small platform, hop back onto the Glue Globe Pole and ride around until it pauses at the nine o'clock position. Jump to the platform to the left, which looks like a giant hand.

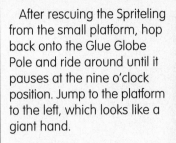

Step 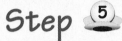 5

Proceed to the left across the giant hand, stopping when you reach the wooden part of this odd platform. While you stand on the wooden section, five bowling pins appear on a ledge along the far outside wall, and a cannonball appears next to you.

Pick up the cannonball and turn to face the flamingo-like bowling pins. Hold down ⑧ to charge up a Power Throw. A spotlight shines against the far wall, indicating the spot where the cannonball will land when you throw it.

The pins quiver when you're perfectly lined up to hit them with the cannonball, so it's easy to set up each Power Throw. A Wooden Chest appears as your reward for knocking down all five pins.

Once you're finished smacking the bowling pins around, proceed to the left across another giant hand. Line up with the foot imprint on the hand's fingertip and jump onto the Glue Globe Pole as it pauses next to you.

Ride the Glue Globe Pole up to the twelve o'clock position, then jump to the platform on the left. Watch out for the huge cannonballs as you cross the short platform to reach the yellow Button's Treasure Chest. Open the chest and claim the Tambourine.

After collecting the Tambourine, head back across the small platform and hop back onto the Glue Globe Pole. Ride on the Glue Globe Pole until it pauses at the nine o'clock position, then jump off and land on the small iron ramp to the left.

Step 6

Jump down from the small iron ramp and start running down the walkway, toward the camera. As you run, three giant Elephants drop from the sky behind you and charge! Run to the end of the walkway, where you see a Wooden Trapdoor. Enter the trapdoor quickly to avoid being crushed by the charging Elephants.

Trapdoor 4

The fourth trapdoor's sub-level is fairly straightforward. All the good stuff is on top of the small room's upper balcony, but spiked balls guard the two ladders in the room. The spiked balls move back and fourth, so carefully avoid the spiked ball as you climb one of the ladders.

Now that you've reached the balcony, run along it and collect the Gold Statue part. Turn to face the Red Diamond, which sits on a block floating over the center of the room.

The two blocks that float on either side of the Red Diamond are called Marshmallow Blocks. These blocks vanish a second after you step on them. Jump from the balcony and land on a Marshmallow Block, then jump immediately to the Red Diamond before the block disappears.

With the Gold Statue part and Red Diamond collected from the fourth trapdoor, proceed left. Line up with the foot imprint on the ground and jump onto the Glue Globe Pole when it passes. Try shifting the camera by pressing ◄◎ before you jump for a better view of the Glue Globe Pole.

Step 7

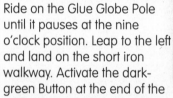

Ride on the Glue Globe Pole until it pauses at the nine o'clock position. Leap to the left and land on the short iron walkway. Activate the dark-green Button at the end of the walkway, then return to the Glue Globe Pole.

Jump onto the Glue Globe Pole and ride on it until it pauses at the six o'clock position. Leap to the left and grab the thick rope there. Shimmy down the rope.

The rope leads to a small iron platform where a Garlic Dispenser stands, ready to be of service. Use the Garlic Dispenser to replenish Wario's Health Meter, then climb down the nearby ladder.

Turn right after climbing down the ladder and carefully cross the narrow walkway. Two sets of giant, clown-faced cannonballs fire at you, trying to knock you into the Unithorn's Lair. Avoid the cannonballs and activate the light-green Button on the lower iron platform nearby.

After activating the light-green Button, backtrack to the Garlic Dispenser. Climb up the rope and jump onto the Glue Globe Pole as it passes by. Ride on the Glue Globe Pole until it pauses at the six o'clock position, then jump to the small platform at right. Open the light-green Button's Treasure Chest to collect the Triangle.

That's all there is to do around here, so jump back onto the Glue Globe Pole and ride until it pauses at the six o'clock position. Jump over to the Garlic Dispenser's platform, then drop to the stone walkway below and enter the tall doorway at left.

Step

A wooden walkway runs along the outside wall past the tall doorway. The walkway is patrolled by several Gatorbabies, which are strong, club-wielding monsters similar to Clubosaurs. The wooden walkway holds nothing of interest, so jump over the railing to the large, circular area below.

Several large cages sit in a semicircle on the floor below the wooden walkway. These aren't merely cages, however: They're Cage Beasts. These horrible monsters sprout arms and legs and chase you around, swiping at you with their large claws. It takes several punches to stun them.

A Wooden Chest sits in the middle of the floor below the wooden walkway. Punch the chest to open it and receive a random goodie.

A Steel Trapdoor is located down here as well. Stun a Cage Beast (or grab a Gatorbaby from the wooden walkway) and use it to enter the fifth trapdoor's sub-level.

Trapdoor 5

The fifth trapdoor's sub-level is made up of three floating platforms in a row. Two pairs of Glue Globes are on either side of the central platform. The Glue Globes chase each other in a circular pattern.

Select a camera angle that gives you the best possible view and watch the Glue Globes circle for a few seconds. Once you've got the timing down, jump onto one of the Glue Globes as it passes. Jump off the Glue Globe and land on the central platform.

The second pair of Glue Globes circles much faster. Fortunately, their increased speed makes them easier to grab onto. Jump from the Glue Globes to reach the Wooden Chest and Red Diamond on the final platform.

After you clear the fifth trapdoor, notice the nearby Rock Block embedded into the floor and the wooden ladder above it. Do not break the Rock Block. Instead, jump onto and climb the wooden ladder.

The ladder leads up to a high, narrow wooden plank. Two new enemies, called Cobras, block your path across the narrow plank. Punch the Cobras repeatedly until you see them flash.

A Cobra is about to strike when it flashes, so dodge to one side or take a couple of steps backward.

Keep beating on the first Cobra with punches, dodging its strikes. Power Throw the first Cobra into the next one ahead to quickly clear the plank of enemies.

The dark-green Button's Treasure Chest sits on the other side of the high wooden plank. Open the chest to acquire the Clarinet.

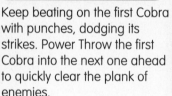

After adding the Clarinet to your collection of treasures, backtrack across the plank and climb back down the wooden ladder. Perform a Ground Pound onto the Rock Block below the ladder to proceed.

Step

After Ground Pounding the Rock Block, you fall a long way before landing in a large stone courtyard. A Crystal Entity attacks as soon as you land, trapping you inside its barrier. Defeat the Crystal Entity and proceed to the right.

A foot imprint on the ground helps you line up with the Glue Globe Pole ahead. If you're low on health, ride on the Glue Globe Pole until it pauses at the twelve o'clock position and head over to the Garlic Dispenser on the small walkway there. Otherwise, use the Glue Globe Pole to continue onward to the right.

You encounter another Glue Globe Pole a short distance ahead. This one is dangerous, because it passes between two fire traps. Watch the fire traps carefully and use the Glue Globe Pole to cross the gap just after the fire traps have shut off.

Step

Two Gatorbabies greet you on the small stone walkway past the fire traps. Stun a Gatorbaby and use it to enter the Steel Trapdoor on the ground.

Trapdoor 6

The sixth trapdoor's sub-level consists of two floating platforms—the starting platform and the far one where the Red Diamond is located. Use a Glue Globe Pole to reach the far platform and claim the Red Diamond.

This Glue Globe Pole is different from others you've seen so far. Instead of traveling in circles, the pole slowly retracts until the Glue Globe touches the starting platform. After it has fully retracted, the pole extends again.

To reach the far platform, jump from the Glue Globe Pole as soon as it begins to extend. The Glue Globe Pole shoots out so quickly that it sends Wario flying through the air when you time your jump correctly. Watch the Glue Globe Pole carefully to get its timing down before you use it to reach the far platform and claim the Red Diamond.

The far platform also has a trapped Spriteling, who, when freed, teaches you how to perform a Dash Attack.

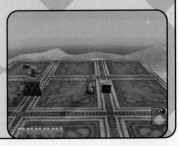

After returning from the sixth trapdoor, look for a foot imprint on the ground nearby. Use the foot imprint to help you jump onto the Glue Globe Pole that swings by overhead.

Ride on the Glue Globe Pole until it pauses at the twelve o'clock position. Next, jump onto the tiny bit of iron walkway to the left, where the light-blue Button is located. Be careful of the fire trap as you jump to reach the light-blue Button.

Drop off the left side of the tiny iron walkway after activating the light-blue Button and land on the slightly larger walkway below. Use the nearby foot imprint to line up with the Glue Globe Pole to the left, then jump onto the Glue Globe and use it to reach the platform ahead.

Step

Ignore the large, odd-looking object on this wide platform for the moment and run across to the far left side. Line up with the foot imprint on the ground there and jump onto the nearby Glue Globe Pole. Ride on the Glue Globe Pole until it pauses at the nine o'clock position, then jump to the left and land on another ledge.

Once you land on the ledge, move to the left and climb down the short ladder to reach a tiny platform. Use the Glue Globe Pole to cross the wide gap and land on the small platform to the left.

Climb up the next short ladder to reach a small platform with the light-blue Button's Treasure Chest. Open the Treasure Chest to obtain the Trombone. With the Trombone in hand, backtrack to the wide platform where you noticed the large, odd-looking object a moment ago.

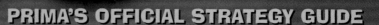

Ignore the large, odd-looking object once again (you use it soon) and grab onto the Glue Globe Pole found on the left side of the wide platform—the same one you recently used to reach the light-blue Button's Treasure Chest. This time, ride the Glue Globe Pole until it pauses at the twelve o'clock position, then jump over to a tiny bit of iron walkway where a trapped Spriteling is located. The Spriteling teaches you the advantages of using Garlic Dispensers.

Now check out that odd-looking object, which is called a Corkscrew Lift. Activate the Corkscrew Lift by punching the ⑧ logo on its side. The circular platform at the bottom of the Corkscrew Lift spins upward, rising like an elevator.

Climb the little ladder nearby and jump from the small iron platform onto the now-raised Corkscrew Lift. Jump from the Corkscrew Lift to reach the ledge to the right.

Step ⑫

Use the second Corkscrew Lift (or simply run up the nearby ramp) to reach a higher portion of this ledge, where a third Corkscrew Lift and Wooden Chest are located. Open the Wooden Chest, then use the third Corkscrew Lift to reach the wooden platform above.

The wide, circular wooden platform is a perfect spot for a Battle Ring. Use the surrounding Columns to help you defeat the waves of monsters until the one-minute timer expires. Once the battle is over, continue to the right.

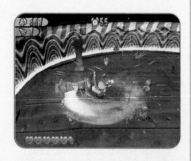

The wooden platform ends at a narrow stone walkway. Run over to the foot imprint on the ground, and from there jump onto the nearby Glue Globe Pole when it pauses at the six o'clock position.

Step ⑬

Ride on the Glue Globe Pole until it pauses at the twelve o'clock position, then jump off, landing on the small ledge to the left. Activate the dark-blue Button you find on the ledge, then jump back onto the Glue Globe Pole.

NOTE

If you happen to fall while navigating the next few Glue Globe Poles, you land on a wide section of ground patrolled by two large Elephant monsters. Use the nearby rope to climb back up to safety and try again.

Jump off the Glue Globe Pole when it pauses at the three o'clock position and land on a tiny ledge to the right. Make sure you're lined up with the foot imprint on the tiny ledge, then jump onto the Glue Globe Pole to the right.

Ride on the Glue Globe Pole until it pauses at the twelve o'clock position, then jump onto the high ledge to the right. Cross the ledge and collect the Gold Statue part that's hovering near the wall, being careful to avoid the huge, clown-faced cannonballs.

With the Gold Statue part acquired, return to the Glue Globe Pole. This time, ride around until it pauses at the six o'clock position. Jump over to the lower ledge at right and continue onward.

Use the next Glue Globe Pole to reach a small wooden walkway where the dark-blue Button's Treasure Chest is located. Open the Treasure Chest to find the Sax, then continue along the wooden walkway.

At the end of the short wooden walkway you see a foot imprint. Wait for a Glue Globe Pole to swing by, then latch onto it and ride around until it pauses at the six o'clock position.

Step 14

Jump off the Glue Globe and land on the lower walkway below to find the purple Button. Activate it and follow the narrow walkway around to the left, avoiding the clown-faced cannonballs and defeating the Cobra as you go.

An Electric Clown Fence blocks your progress past the Cobra. Stun a Clown that drops in to attack and use it to execute a Power Throw. Hit both of the Electric Clown Fence's moving targets to down the fence, then run up the ramp ahead.

A Wooden Chest sits in a corner just up the ramp, with a thick rope hanging next to it. Open the Wooden Chest and then climb up the rope. Backtrack across the many Glue Globe Poles and return to the wooden walkway.

Step 15

Use the Glue Globe Pole at the other end of the wooden walkway to reach the purple Button's Treasure Chest, which is sitting on the walkway below. Jump off the Glue Globe Pole when it pauses at the three o'clock position to land near the Treasure Chest. Open the chest and collect the Drum.

With the Drum added to your collection of treasures, follow the walkway along to the right. A couple of Cobras guard the walkway. Stun one and pick it up. Power Throw the stunned Cobra into the pink Button sticking out of the far wall to activate it, then continue to the right.

Past the pink Button is another Electric Clown Fence. Power Throw the nearby Clowns into the fence's moving targets as you did the others. Continue along the stone walkway, heading up the ramp and crossing the curved bridge to the right.

Step 16

As you cross the curved bridge, defeat the monsters you encounter, including a Circus Ankiron. A Garlic Dispenser and Wooden Trapdoor are on the far right side of the bridge. Fill up Wario's Health Meter and then enter the seventh trapdoor.

Trapdoor 7

Fortunately, the seventh trapdoor's sub-level is a piece of cake. Use the Glue Globe Pole (or climb up the ladder) to reach the small room's upper balcony.

Rescue the trapped Spriteling on the upper balcony. The Spriteling gives you a valuable hint on defeating the boss of the Wonky Circus area. After rescuing the Spriteling, look over at the Red Diamond on the opposite side of the balcony.

Two long rows of spiked balls make it impossible to reach the Red Diamond unharmed unless you use the floating, rotating blocks. Jump onto one of the blocks and ride it over to the Red Diamond. If you have difficulty crossing the rotating blocks, you can reach the Red Diamond by jumping through the spiked balls and taking a bit of damage.

After returning from the seventh trapdoor's sub-level, head back across the curved bridge. You find a foot imprint on the ground about halfway across the bridge, near the Circus Ankiron. Jump onto the Glue Globe Pole as it pauses in the six o'clock position, and ride it to the nine o'clock position. Jump to the next Glue Globe to the left. Watch out for the fire trap.

The Glue Globe Pole takes you right next to a Gold Statue part. Leap from the Glue Globe and nab the Gold Statue part as you fall.

Return to the foot imprint on the curved bridge and jump onto the Glue Globe Pole when it pauses overhead. Ride on the Glue Globe Pole until it pauses at the three o'clock position, then jump up to the next Glue Globe Pole above.

Step 17

Ride the Glue Globe Pole up to the twelve o'clock position, then jump onto the wooden platform above you. The pink Button's Treasure Chest sits off to the side. Open the chest to claim the eighth and final treasure from this area, the Nintendo 64.

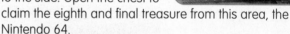

Jump onto the higher part of the wooden platform, where the eighth and final trapdoor is found. Use one of the nearby Clowns to enter the Steel Trapdoor's sub-level.

Trapdoor 8

The Wonky Circus area's final trapdoor isn't too much of a pain, but it can be tricky at first. A long line of floating blocks presents an obstacle course that you must overcome to reach the Red Diamond and Gold Statue part on the opposite side. Start off by quickly jumping across the Marshmallow Blocks ahead.

A rotating circle of spiked balls guards the next line of stable blocks. Time your jump carefully to pass over the spiked balls and continue unscathed.

Past the sole Marshmallow Block is another line of stable blocks guarded by rotating spiked balls. Again, time your movements carefully and run past the spiked balls.

The final obstacle is a trio of Marshmallow Blocks. Hop from one Marshmallow Block to the next, then jump over to the small moving platform. Ride the moving platform over to the final Red Diamond and Gold Statue part.

Now that you've cleared the final trapdoor, jump off the elevated wooden platform to land on the lower section to the left. Run up to the Goal Trapdoor and feed the stone statue four Red Diamonds to get rid of it. Once the statue is gone, enter the Goal Trapdoor to face the boss of the Wonky Circus area.

NOTE

If you need to replenish Wario's Heart Meter, use the Garlic Dispenser standing at the far right side of the curved bridge.

Area Boss: Clown-a-Round

Clown-a-Round is the boss of the Wonky Circus area. He has several heads and uses them as weapons against Wario. The arena consists of two circular platforms with a tightrope stretching between them, which Clown-a-Round uses to move between the two platforms.

Clown-a-Round follows a specific pattern throughout the entire fight. First, he uses a huge ball to cross the tightrope and reach the opposite platform. Jump and grab one of the Glue Globes on the side of the large ball and follow Clown-a-Round as he rolls across the tightrope.

As soon as Clown-a-Round crosses the tightrope, he jumps off his ball and hurls it to the opposite platform. The ball is volatile and causes a massive explosion when it lands in the center of the opposite platform. Don't be there when it lands.

After throwing his ball, Clown-a-Round reveals his weak spot—his head. Clown-a-Round's *real* head isn't on top of his shoulders, however, it's on his fat belly! Clown-a-Round pulls off his fake head and throws it at Wario. As the battle wears on, Clown-a-Round sprouts several fake heads and throws them all at once.

As soon as Clown-a-Round throws his ball, his real head emerges from his round belly. Punch Clown-a-Round in his face (belly?) repeatedly, until he's stunned. Pick up Clown-a-Round when he's dazed and slam him into the ground with a powerful Piledriver.

As the battle wears on, you find fewer Glue Globes to stick to on Clown-a-Round's giant ball. This makes it difficult to follow him as he crosses the tightrope toward the opposite platform. If you aren't able to follow Clown-a-Round, move to one of your platform's tiny side alcoves to avoid his incoming giant ball and its devastating explosion.

Continue to punch Clown-a-Round's belly (face?) to stun him, and then give him a painful Piledriver. The fight ends when you succeed in knocking out all five of Clown-a-Round's health skulls.

Spooktastic World: Dual Dragon's Showdown

The boss of the Spooktastic World stage is a huge, two-headed dragon known as the Dual Dragon. The boss show-down against this enormous creature is the toughest yet. Keep your wits about you and make use of everything you've learned so far, and you should defeat the Dual Dragon without too much trouble. Pound the Dual Dragon into submission to get the second Giant Treasure Chest Key and unlock the next stage.

Dual Dragon's Attacks

The Dual Dragon has only three attacks, but that's more than enough. In its first and most common attack, one of the Dual Dragon's heads opens wide and exhales a massive burst of fire.

At first evade the fire by moving to one side or the other. As the battle wears on, the fire also rains balls of flame on you as it shoots by. It's almost impossible to avoid being scorched. While one of the Dual Dragon's heads is executing the fire-breathing attack, the other must dodge the long line of sizzling flame.

The Dual Dragon's heads work as a team in its second attack. One opens its mouth and spits out several Glue Globes; the other sucks them up. If you're unlucky enough to get stuck to a Glue Globe, you're sucked into the other head's mouth, chewed up, and then spit back out. The Dual Dragon spits out more Glue Globes as the fight heats up.

Finally, the Dual Dragon also uses its two spiked tails to smack you around. If you stand too close to one of the tails, it slams down and flattens you. Stay in the center of the small arena to avoid being crushed by the Dual Dragon's powerful tails.

Fighting the Dual Dragon

There's only one way to damage the Dual Dragon: Trick it into attacking itself. Run up to and punch one of the Dual Dragon's heads. After several punches, you stun the head, which droops to the ground.

Spooktastic World: Dual Dragon's Showdown

While one Dual Dragon head is out cold, the other may foolishly attempt its fire-breathing attack. When this happens, the Dual Dragon's stunned head can't dodge the incoming fire. The Dual Dragon loses one health skull each time it accidentally burns itself. That's the only way to damage the Dual Dragon.

It's important not to stand next to either of the Dual Dragon's spiked tails, lest these powerful tails come crashing down on you.

The Glue Globe attack may seem effective at first, but it's easily avoided if you're ready for it. Jump whenever you become attached to a Glue Globe. If a bunch of Glue Globes are nearby, jump rapidly. As long as you keep jumping off the Glue Globes, you needn't worry about being sucked in.

When you trick the Dual Dragon into burning itself five times, you defeat it. Well done! You have the second Giant Treasure Chest Key.

Thrillsville: Shivering Mountains

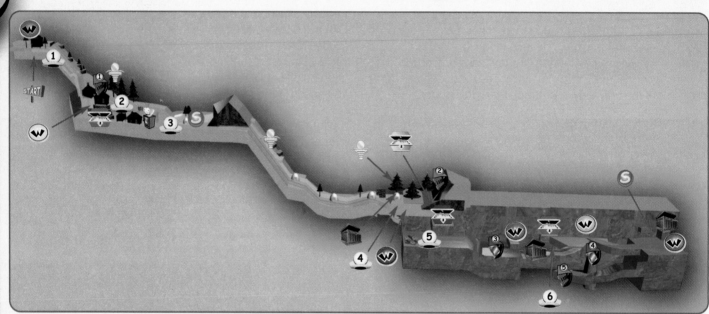

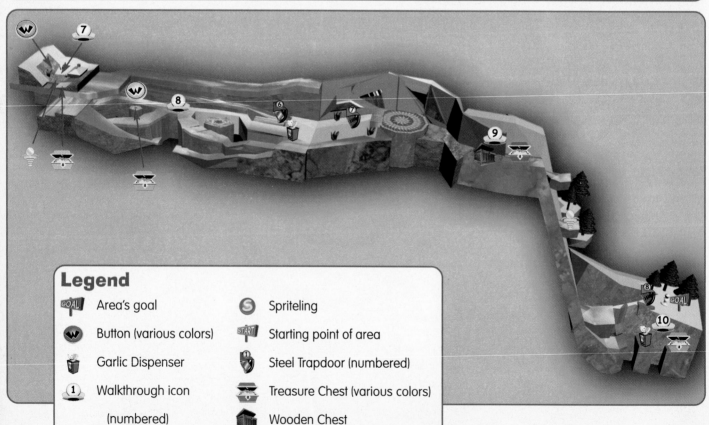

Legend

GOAL Area's goal

W Button (various colors)

Garlic Dispenser

1 Walkthrough icon
(numbered)

Gold Statue Part

S Spriteling

START Starting point of area

1 Steel Trapdoor (numbered)

Treasure Chest (various colors)

Wooden Chest

1 Wooden Trapdoor (numbered)

Thrillsville: Shivering Mountains

The first area of the Thrillsville stage is Shivering Mountains. This frozen, snow-covered area features many new enemies, and the harsh weather conditions make traversing the Shivering Mountains a difficult task. As with every area in *Wario World*, Shivering Mountains has eight treasures to find, eight Gold Statue parts to collect, eight Red Diamonds to locate, and five Spritelings to rescue.

NOTE

You must have at least five Red Diamonds to enter the Shivering Mountains Goal Trapdoor.

Step 1

Near the starting point of the Shivering Mountains area is a Bunny Spring. Ground Pound onto the Bunny Spring to reach the roof of the small house and activate the red Button there.

TIP

You can get stuck in the snow-covered ground if you Ground Pound onto it in Shivering Mountains. If it happens, press Ⓐ to climb back out.

Ahead is a huge, ice-covered hill. Make sure you're on the far side, away from the camera, when you slide down the hill, as pictured above. Wario automatically slides straight down the hill. You don't need to control him once he starts sliding.

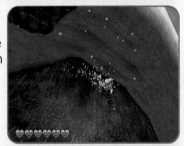

Slide off this jump (shown above) to land on the snow-covered rooftop ahead. There's no other way to reach the rooftop, so hit the jump.

Step 2

When you land on the rooftop after the long, icy hill, line up with the foot imprint there and jump to the Glue Globe on the right. From there, jump over to the Wooden Trapdoor and enter its sub-level.

Trapdoor 1

This first trapdoor's sub-level is simple. A tall stack of Rock Blocks extends upward beyond your view. Several spiked balls circle the Rock Blocks, which are your only obstacles.

Punch the weak side of each Rock Block to destroy it, being careful to avoid the spiked balls as they circle the blocks. The stack gets shorter with every Rock Block you destroy. Destroy them all to claim the Red Diamond, which sits atop the Rock Block stack.

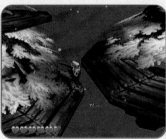

After you return from the first trapdoor, jump onto the hill behind the house. Run up the hill, then turn and jump onto the lowest wooden platform.

The Freeze Cannons shoot out long bursts of icy-cold frost. Wario freezes when the ice hits him. Shake ⊙ from side to side to break the ice. You can stun a Freeze Cannon by Ground Pounding it, but you can't destroy it.

Jump to the next wooden platform directly above you. It's the only one you can jump to.

Head to the right across the wooden platform, avoiding the Freeze Cannon, and use the Glue Globe on the other side to reach the next wooden platform above.

Run to the opposite side of this wooden platform and jump across the line of Glue Globes to reach the next wooden platform to the left.

Continue to the left across another line of Glue Globes, landing on yet another wooden platform. Use the Glue Globe on the left side of this platform to reach the next one above, where a Gold Statue part awaits.

Backtrack to the rooftop you landed on after sliding down the long, icy hill. Drop off the left side of the roof to land next to the yellow Button.

The red Button's Treasure Chest sits on a small ice block at the foot of the long, icy hill. Open the Treasure Chest to collect the Nice Glass.

Run to the right after opening the red Button's Treasure Chest. Jump onto the snowy patches to avoid slipping on the icy slope and falling into the Unithorn's Lair. Watch out for the Snow Bomber monsters flying about, and the nearby electric currents.

Jump up the slope as soon as the electric currents shut off, using the snow to keep your footing. When you reach the level area above, follow the path to the right.

A Garlic Dispenser stands nearby if you're in need of Garlic. Continue to the right after eating your fill.

Step ③

The trail leads to a snowy hill where several small igloos are located. Watch out for the crazy Sled Creatures that zip down the hill.

A Spriteling is trapped atop an igloo at the top of the hill. After being rescued, the Spriteling tells you the weak spot of an upcoming enemy, the Angler Mangler, and hints at how to defeat it.

Continue across the snowy hill, dodging the Sled Creatures, until you come to a giant fish head—the Angler Mangler. A wall of ice appears behind you, trapping you in. You must defeat this enemy to pass it.

The Angler Mangler uses ice-based attacks that freeze you in place. It relies on its helper, the Barrel Buster, to attack you while you're frozen. Dodge the freezing-cold ice blocks that the Angler Mangler spits out at you, and punch the Barrel Buster until it's stunned.

Pick up the stunned Barrel Buster and stand directly underneath the Angler Mangler's weak spot—the giant, glowing extremity that hangs above its head. Execute a Piledriver, and the Barrel Buster's head shoots straight up into the Angler Mangler's glowing weak spot.

Dodge the Angler Mangler's icy attacks and continue to attack it by Piledriving Barrel Busters. When you score three direct hits on its weak spot, the Angler Mangler is defeated.

There's another steep, ice-covered hill past the Angler Mangler. Slide down the far side of the hill away from the camera, as shown in the screenshot above, just as you did on the previous hill.

A Gold Statue part hovers over the first jump on the far side of the hill. Grab it as you slide off the jump, and continue sliding straight down the hill.

NOTE

Don't worry if you miss the Gold Statue part on the icy hill. You can use the ByeBye Balloon at the goal to return to the start of this area and try again.

Step ④

After sliding down the center of the icy hill, you land in a snowy area that is otherwise inaccessible. A Crystal Entity attacks immediately. Defeat the monster and continue to the right.

A Polar Bear also is nearby. This enemy is similar to a Clubosaur or Gatorbaby, so you already know how to deal with the likes of it.

The dark-blue Button sits atop an igloo to the right. Activate the dark-blue Button, then head back over to the left.

Use the nearby Bunny Spring to reach the top of the high ledge. Open the Wooden Chest that sits atop the ledge, then jump onto the wooden platform to the right.

Cross the wooden platform and jump to the next one ahead. Dodge the Freeze Cannon on the second wooden platform and jump onto the snowy ledge to the far right.

The yellow Button's Treasure Chest sits under a tall tree on the snowy ledge. Open the Treasure Chest to receive the Ancient Chalice.

A pair of Ice Ankirons waits on this snowy ledge as well. There's no reason to fight them, except that it's fun! The Sculptures close by might be of use if you tackle these tough monsters.

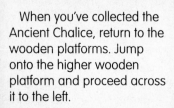

When you've collected the Ancient Chalice, return to the wooden platforms. Jump onto the higher wooden platform and proceed across it to the left.

Jump over to the next wooden platform ahead and run across it to the left, dodging the Freeze Cannon. Use the Glue Globe on the far left side of this wooden platform to reach the next one above.

Run to the right across this high wooden platform and jump onto the nearby Glue Globe. Don't cross the row of Glue Globes ahead. Instead, jump to the highest wooden platform directly above you.

Nab the Gold Statue part from the left side of the tallest (and smallest) wooden platform. Return to the row of Glue Globes after collecting the Gold Statue part and proceed across them to the right.

Continue crossing Glue Globes and wooden platforms, constantly heading right. You eventually reach a high, snowy cliff and the second trapdoor. Dodge or defeat the pair of Snow Bombers and enter the Wooden Trapdoor.

Trapdoor 2

You couldn't ask for a more straightforward trapdoor sub-level than this. A line of floating blocks extends upward and out of sight. Jump and grab the lowest floating block, but don't pull yourself up onto it.

Instead, continue jumping and grabbing onto the side of each block, moving quickly past the Marshmallow Block. The Red Diamond and a trapped Spriteling are on the high floating platform. When rescued, the Spriteling hints at using Icicle Mites to reach high places.

Jump down off the high cliff and head back toward the dark-blue Button you activated a while ago. A single Rock Block is embedded in the ground near the dark-blue Button. Perform a Ground Pound onto the Rock Block to smash it and land in an underground cavern.

Step

If you had slid down the sides of the previous icy hill, you would have ended up in this icy cavern. You enter a Battle Ring as soon as you land here. Proceed to the right after time expires.

Several new enemies—Icicle Mites—jump from the ground as you run down the icy pathway past the Battle Ring. They can't attack you, but they do serve an important purpose. Ignore the first two groups of Icicle Mites that pop up and run to the end of the pathway.

Two more Icicle Mites jump from the ground near the high wall at the end of the pathway. Punch one of them until it's stunned, then pick it up and perform a Piledriver with it near the high wall. The Icicle Mite's pointy top sticks into the ground, allowing you to use its flat, circular underside as a step. Jump onto the Icicle Mite, and then onto the ledge above the wall.

The ledge hosts a monster generator and Steel Trapdoor. Wait for a red Snowman to pop out of the monster generator, then use it in a Piledriver to enter the third trapdoor.

Trapdoor 3

This sub-level seems complicated at first glance, but it's simple. Five levers on the starting platform control the five floating blocks that stretch between you and the Red Diamond's platform. Manipulate the levers to arrange the floating blocks more or less in a straight line, then cross over them to acquire the Red Diamond.

Defeat or run past the Ice Ankiron and approach the dark-blue Button's Treasure Chest on the far left side of the ledge. Open the Treasure Chest to claim the Nice Saucer.

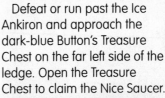

Jump up onto the higher ledge near the monster generator after you return from the Steel Trapdoor. Turn left and jump across the gap ahead to the next ledge.

Backtrack to the right and jump over the gap to the next platform ahead. Line up with the foot imprint found on this platform and jump to the icy pole to the right. Jump to the next pole, and finally down onto another ledge.

Step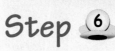

The purple Button sits on the far right corner of the icy ledge past the pair of poles. Two Ice Ankirons guard the purple Button, but you can activate it and drop to the pathway below without having to fight them if you wish.

A Wooden Chest stands in a corner on the lower pathway. Open it for a random treat.

The lower pathway has more Icicle Mites. Use them to climb back up to the Steel Trapdoor and monster generator's ledge if you need to. Otherwise, continue along to the right.

The pathway begins to narrow as you head to the right, and you soon encounter a large block of ice that prevents you from proceeding. Perform a Dash Attack to smash the ice block and clear the path ahead. Beat up or just ignore the harmless Turtle that was carrying the ice block on its back.

Watch out for the electric currents that stretch across the pathway as it narrows. Jump over them and continue to the right.

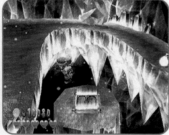

Another ice block carried by a Turtle blocks your progress at the bend in the path. Dash Attack the ice block to get it out of your way, then stun the hapless Turtle. Pick it up and jump over to the small, circular platform to the right, where a Steel Trapdoor is located. Use the Turtle to enter the fourth trapdoor.

Trapdoor 4

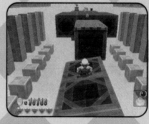

This is another straightforward sub-level to breeze through. A trio of large, slowly rotating blocks spans the gap between the starting platform and the platform with the Red Diamond. Simply jump from one block to the next, collecting gold coins if you choose, until you reach the Red Diamond's platform.

A trapped Spriteling sits near the Red Diamond. Free the Spriteling, who warns you about the danger the Fattingtons on the narrow walkways present.

After returning from the fourth trapdoor, drop down onto the Glue Globe below the small, circular platform. Jump off the Glue Globe and land on the narrow walkway below.

Run left once you land on the narrow walkway, and Dash Attack the large ice block you encounter. Jump onto the Glue Globe ahead to cross the narrow gap safely.

The fifth trapdoor is at the end of this narrow walkway. Enter the Wooden Trapdoor's sub-level to get the goodies there.

Trapdoor 5

Another simple sub-level! Punch the lever to activate it, and the five Rock Blocks on the floor flash in sequence. Punch each Rock Block in the same order they flashed to reveal the Red Diamond and a Gold Statue part. You have to exit and re-enter the trapdoor if you make a mistake, so watch the blocks carefully.

Run to the right after returning from the fifth trapdoor, following the walkway to the right until you come to a monster generator and the dark-green Button. Stun one of the red Snowmen when it pops out of the generator and pick it up, then jump and throw the Snowman at the dark-green Button on the wall to activate it.

Turn left and head up the higher pathway after activating the dark-green Button, ignoring the Icicle Mites that pop up from the ground nearby. Dash Attack the ice blocks that get in your way and jump over the electric currents as you follow the upper pathway to the left.

Stop when you see the light-green Button high up on a far wall. Dash Attack the nearby ice block, then stun the Turtle that was underneath it. Pick up the Turtle and stand on the small, circular chunk of ice near the light-green Button. Charge up a Power Throw, then jump and hurl the Turtle into the light-green Button to activate it.

When the light-green Button is activated, continue along the pathway to the left. Smash the ice block out of your way to reach the dark-green Button's Treasure Chest beyond. Open the Treasure Chest and collect the Ornate Decanter.

Backtrack to the right along the upper pathway, past the light-green Button, until you reach the pair of Icicle Mites you ran past earlier. Stun one, and execute a Piledriver in the corner made by the far wall and tall cliff. Use the embedded Icicle Mite to jump up and onto the ledge.

A trapped Spriteling sits atop the high ledge. The Spriteling says that it's difficult to climb the mountain ahead, but also hints that you find something valuable at the top.

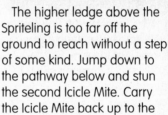

The higher ledge above the Spriteling is too far off the ground to reach without a step of some kind. Jump down to the pathway below and stun the second Icicle Mite. Carry the Icicle Mite back up to the ledge you just came from, again using the Icicle Mite you previously embedded into the walkway as a step.

Plant the Icicle Mite you're carrying into the ground of the ledge with a Piledriver, and use it as a step to reach the higher ledge above.

Step 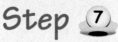 7

The ledge above the Spriteling features a Bunny Spring and Wooden Chest. Ignore the Bunny Spring for the moment and open the Wooden Chest. Proceed down the narrow path to the right after opening the chest.

Jump onto the Glue Globe that hangs over the small gap in the narrow pathway. Jump off the Glue Globe, aiming for the light-blue Button directly below. Punch or execute a Ground Pound to activate the light-blue Button as you drop past it.

Return to the Icicle Mites and use them both as steps to reach the high ledge where you saw the Bunny Spring. Bounce off the Bunny Spring and grab the nearby ladder, then climb up.

A Polar Bear patrols the icy grounds at the top of the ladder. Beat on the Polar Bear until you stun it, then jump and throw it at the pink Button sticking out from the side of the snowy cliff.

A pair of Snow Bombers guards a Gold Statue part hovering over the small bridge close by. Run across the bridge and collect the Gold Statue part.

The light-blue Button's Treasure Chest is sitting on the ground on the other side of the short bridge. Open the chest to collect the Glass Decanter. After you add it to your treasure collection, climb down the ladder and return to the pathway below.

Step 8

Run to the right across the higher pathway, heading toward the light-blue Button. You encounter a new enemy along the way—a Fattington.

Carefully dodge the Fattington and jump to the small circular platform just below the high walkway to reach the light-green Button's Treasure Chest. Open the Treasure Chest to acquire the Nice Cup.

Jump back onto the higher walkway and proceed along to the right, avoiding the jelly-like Fattingtons as you go. The higher walkway eventually leads to the sixth trapdoor, which is guarded by an Ice Ankiron. Stun the Ice Ankiron with rapid punches, then use it to enter the Steel Trapdoor.

Trapdoor 6

You just can't argue with another straightforward sub-level. Cross the long stretch of moving blocks to reach the Red Diamond and Gold Statue part on the far platform.

After returning from the sixth trapdoor's sub-level, run off the ledge to the right and drop down to the snowy path below. A Garlic Dispenser stands near the base of the ledge. Use it to regain some health.

Jump onto the small, lower ledge near the Garlic Dispenser where a Sculpture sits. Pick up the Sculpture and run up the hill to the right, staying on the snowy trail to avoid slipping on ice.

Several Fattingtons drop in to cause you trouble as you run up the steep, snowy hill. Throw the Sculpture at the first Fattington to stun it, then pick up the Fattington and throw it at the next one that drops in. Continue in this fashion until you come to the top of the hill.

The seventh trapdoor is on a small ice platform near the top of the steep hill. Jump to the first ice platform, then jump over to the Wooden Trapdoor and enter its sub-level.

Trapdoor 7

This trapdoor's sub-level consists of several rings of spiked balls and Glue Globes leading upward to a high floating platform where the Red Diamond and a Gold Statue part are located. Jump onto each Glue Globe as you ascend the rings, timing your jumps carefully to avoid the dangerous spiked balls.

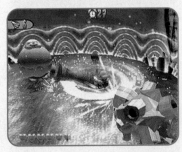

Proceed to the right when you return from the seventh trapdoor. The large circular platform ahead is home to a Battle Ring. Continue to the right after you finish smacking monsters around.

You encounter another Angler Mangler a short distance past the Battle Ring. Defeat the Angler Mangler as you did the previous one: Stun the Barrel Busters and use them to execute Piledrivers beneath the Angler Mangler's bulbous, glowing weak spot. Continue to the right after you defeat the Angler Mangler.

Step

Several Sled Creatures zoom down the snowy hill beyond the second Angler Mangler. Take a moment to open the Wooden Chest on a small ice platform before continuing to the right, avoiding the Sled Creatures as you go.

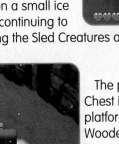

The purple Button's Treasure Chest is sitting on a small ice platform to the right of the Wooden Chest. Open the Treasure Chest to receive the Glass Bowl.

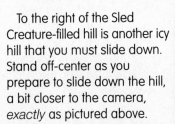

To the right of the Sled Creature-filled hill is another icy hill that you must slide down. Stand off-center as you prepare to slide down the hill, a bit closer to the camera, *exactly* as pictured above.

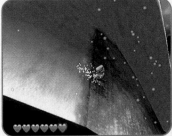

If you slid from the correct starting position at the top of the hill, you collect a Gold Statue part on your way down. Keep sliding downward until you reach the landing at the bottom.

NOTE

Don't worry if you miss the Gold Statue part on your first attempt. After you defeat the boss of the Shivering Mountains area, the ByeBye Balloon appears at the starting point. Use it to quickly return to this steep hill and try again.

Step 10

A Garlic Dispenser stands at the bottom of the icy hill. Fill up on Garlic before you jump across the gap to the right.

The ByeBye Balloon and the pink Button's Treasure Chest are found on the ledge across the gap. Open the Treasure Chest to collect the Jade Box.

NOTE

If you missed either (or both) of the two Gold Statue parts while you were sliding down the steep, icy hills in this area, use the ByeBye Balloon to return to the starting point and try for them again.

After you nab the Jade Box, jump up the short line of Glue Globes on the far wall to reach a higher ledge above. The area's goal is on the snowy ledge.

The stone statue that guards the Goal Trapdoor requires five Red Diamonds to remove. Before you enter the Goal Trapdoor, stun one of the monsters that pops out of the nearby monster generator and use it to enter the Steel Trapdoor close by.

Trapdoor 8

The eighth trapdoor has a dangerous but simplistic sub-level. Several rings of spiked balls circle and rotate around the central floating platform, where the Red Diamond and a trapped Spriteling are located. Watch the spiked balls' movements for a few seconds before you carefully jump across to the central platform.

Rescue the trapped Spriteling once you reach the narrow, central platform. The Spriteling gives you a clue as to how to beat the area's boss.

Enter the Goal Trapdoor after clearing the nearby Steel Trapdoor to face the Shivering Mountains area's boss. If you were injured in the trapdoor's sub-level, drop down to the ledge below and use the handy Garlic Dispenser to heal up.

Area Boss: Winter Windster

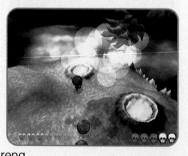

The boss of the Shivering Mountains area is the Winter Windster. The Winter Windster flies high above the circular arena, attacking from the sky with various projectiles. The fight against the Winter Windster seems difficult at first, but it becomes easier once you learn ways to ground him.

The Winter Windster drops several cannonballs as he flies about, circling the arena. He hopes to flatten you with one of them, but the cannonballs serve a much more important purpose. Pick up a cannonball and toss it into one of the small, lava-filled craters on the ground of the arena.

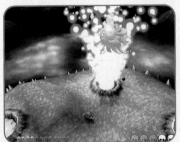

The cannonball reacts with the lava, causing a huge volcanic eruption. If the Winter Windster flies over a lava-filled crater when it goes off, the erupting lava hits him and knocks him to the ground, stunned.

Pick up the Winter Windster when he's stunned and pull off a punishing Piledriver, slamming his huge melon into the earth. The Winter Windster loses one health skull for each Piledriver he receives. This is the most basic way to ground and damage the Winter Windster...but there's an easier way.

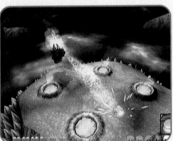

The Winter Windster executes one of his prominent attacks—ice breath—from the sky. Use this attack to trick the Winter Windster into dropping to the ground. Stand as far away as possible when you see the Winter Windster begin to use his ice breath attack, but allow the attack to freeze you in place.

The Winter Windster drops to the ground and starts charging at you as soon as you're frozen. Rapidly move ◎ from side to side until you break free, then run toward the incoming Winter Windster. Punch the Winter Windster before it has a chance to attack, stunning it with a few solid blows. You know what to do now!

In addition to his run-of-the-mill attacks, the Winter Windster has a unique attack that you should avoid. A few times during the fight, the Winter Windster's eyes begin to glow bright red. When you see the Winter Windster's eyes begin to glow red, turn around quickly so that Wario isn't looking at him.

If you look into the Winter Windster's eyes, he suddenly flashes and splits into several thick gusts of condensed air The gusts of air fly into Wario's mouth, making him expand and float off like a balloon. Quickly move ◎ from side to side to break free of the Winter Windster's special attack, or you float over the edge of the arena.

Continue to use the cannon-balls and lava-filled craters or the sneaky ice breath technique to ground the Winter Windster, then attack him with a Piledriver while he's stunned. Five solid Piledrivers defeat the Winter Windster.

Thrillsville: Beanstalk Way

Legend

GOAL	Area's goal	S	Spriteling
W	Button (various colors)	START	Starting point of area
	Garlic Dispenser	1 (steel)	Steel Trapdoor (numbered)
1	Walkthrough icon (numbered)		Treasure Chest (various colors)
	Gold Statue Part		Wooden Chest
		1 (wooden)	Wooden Trapdoor (numbered)

The second area of the Thrillsville stage is Beanstalk Way. This lush area is full of giant flowers that serve as platforms, and several new enemies. As with every area in *Wario World*, Beanstalk Way has eight treasures to find, eight Gold Statue parts to collect, eight Red Diamonds to locate, and five Spritelings to rescue.

NOTE

You must have at least five Red Diamonds to enter Beanstalk Way's Goal Trapdoor.

Step 1

The yellow Button's Treasure Chest platform is on a short stump just to the right of the starting point, close to a shallow stream. You won't come across the yellow Button for quite some time, so remember where its Treasure Chest platform is for future reference.

An odd-looking brown pod sits on top of another short stump on the other side of the stream. Climb onto the pod and hit it with a Ground Pound. The pod opens into a flower with a swirly design on it—a Swirly Slab.

Stun one of the large, brown Wolves that pops out of the nearby monster generator and carry it onto the Swirly Slab. Perform a Wild Swing-Ding to raise the Swirly Slab and collect the Gold Statue part that hovers high above.

Ground Pound the other nearby pod, which is on the ground close to the tall beanstalk, to reveal a second Swirly Slab. Wild Swing-Ding another large Wolf while standing on the Swirly Slab to raise it, then jump to the ladder that runs up the tall beanstalk and climb up.

Step 2

Jump over the first set of large leaves on either side of the beanstalk's ladder, landing on the wide part of the lower leaf on the left side. Jump across the leaf to reach a small clearing farther left.

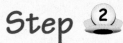

CAUTION

Many large leaves in this area serve as platforms. Be careful not to walk onto the narrow part of a leaf, lest you slip and fall off.

The first trapped Spriteling sits atop a short stump in the clearing beyond the two leaf platforms. The Spriteling briefs you on defeating the upcoming Tree Freak monsters.

The light-green Button sticks out from the side of the cliff to the far left. Jump and punch the light-green Button to activate it, then turn around and head to the right, back across the small clearing.

Ground Pound the pod on the ground at the far right side of the small clearing to reveal a Swirly Slab. Stun one of the nearby Hawks and use it to raise the Swirly Slab by executing a Wild Swing-Ding. Jump off the Swirly Slab and land on the leaf platform to the right,

then cross the next leaf and return to the tall beanstalk's ladder. Continue climbing the ladder, ignoring the leaf platform to the right for the moment.

Step 3

You see another large leaf to the left farther up the beanstalk's ladder. Jump onto the wide part of the leaf, then jump to the Glue Globe to the left. Jump off the Glue Globe to reach another small clearing.

A pair of new enemies guards the red Button on this small clearing. These big, blue monsters are Stingrays, which can't be harmed by conventional attacks. Pick up one of the nearby Sculptures and use it as a weapon against the Stingrays to defeat them, then activate the red Button.

Use the Glue Globe and leaf platform to return to the tall beanstalk's ladder after you activate the red Button. Climb down the ladder and jump to the first leaf platform to the right. Cross the row of leaf platforms and Glue Globes to reach a small clearing farther right.

Step 4

The first trapdoor is on top of a short stump in the small clearing to the right. Ground Pound the Wooden Trapdoor to enter its sub-level.

Trapdoor 1

The first trapdoor's sub-level is a thinker, but it's not too complicated. A tall collection of Rock Blocks stretches up beyond your view. You must break some of the Rock Blocks to climb up the stack and reach the Red Diamond at the top.

Begin by smashing away five Rock Blocks from one of the stacks, lowering it enough that you can jump on top of it. Next, break two Rock Blocks from a neighboring stack. Jump from the lower stack to the higher one, then finally up to the Red Diamond.

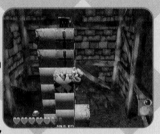

A trapped Spriteling sits near the Red Diamond at the top of the stack. When rescued, the Spriteling tells you how to cross the upcoming Tulipatooie's Glue Globes.

The red Button's Treasure Chest sits atop another small stump near the first trapdoor. Open the Treasure Chest to get the Nice Goblet.

A Wooden Chest sit in this small clearing, in the middle of a small stream. Open the Wooden Chest for a random surprise.

Return to the tall beanstalk's ladder by using the Glue Globes and leaf platforms near the Wooden Trapdoor. Climb all the way up the beanstalk, then jump off its ladder and land in the tiny hut above. Exit the hut to the right to reach another small, grassy clearing.

Step ⑤

Two Stingrays and a pair of Hawks ambush you on the small, grassy clearing. Use the nearby Sculptures to defeat the enemies, then continue to the right.

A Tree Freak blocks your progress past the small, grassy clearing. You must destroy the Tree Freak to continue to the right. Run up to the Tree Freak and punch it to make its fruit drop to the ground.

You must pick up a fruit and throw it at the Tree Freak, but the Tree Freak's fruits are covered with thorns on one side. Perform a Ground Pound on the grass to shake the earth, and the fruits flip over.

Approach a fruit from its non-thorny side and pick it up. Throw the fruit directly at the green pod that sticks out from the Tree Freak's thick trunk.

Striking the Tree Freak's pod with one of its thorny fruits causes the pod to open, revealing the Tree Freak's flowery weak spot. Quickly collect another fruit and throw it into the Tree Freak's exposed flower to destroy the Tree Freak, then continue along to the right.

Step 6

You encounter a Tulipatooie down the grassy trail a short distance past the Tree Freak. Don't jump to the Tulipatooie's Glue Globe just yet. Drop to the watery area below instead.

Inside the shallow cave near the Tulipatooie is a Wooden Chest. Smash the Wooden Chest to receive a random treat.

Run out of the cave after opening the Wooden Chest and head to the right. Ignore the monster generator and Swirly Slab pod on the ground for the moment and continue to the right to find the second trapdoor. Defeat the nearby Grizzlies (or ignore them) and enter the Wooden Trapdoor's sub-level.

Trapdoor 2

Jump onto the Glue Globe as it slowly passes by. The Glue Globe travels through two rings with spiked balls in their centers.

To avoid being hit by the spiked balls, position Wario on the Glue Globe so he passes through the open slots on the rings. Ride the Glue Globe up to the high floating platform, where you find a Gold Statue part and Red Diamond.

Run into the shallow cave behind the second trapdoor after you return from its sublevel. Jump and punch the yellow Button on the wall of the cave to activate it, then exit the cave and head over to the nearby Swirly Slab pod and monster generator.

Ground Pound the pod on the ground to reveal a flowery Swirly Slab, then stun a Wolf and use it to help you raise the Swirly Slab. Jump to the wooden ladder from the Swirly Slab and climb to the grassy ledge above.

Now backtrack to the yellow Button's Treasure Chest platform, which, you recall, you saw near the starting point of this area. Jump onto the Tulipatooie's Glue Globe to the left, then quickly jump off the Glue Globe and land on the grassy ledge to the left before the Tulipatooie sucks you in. Backtrack to the yellow Button's Treasure Chest and open it to collect the Violin.

Step 7

When you've acquired the Violin, make the long journey back to the Tulipatooie. Cross the Tulipatooie's Glue Globe and land on the grassy ledge to the right. Climb to the top of the nearby beanstalk's ladder.

The third trapdoor is on a small ledge to the left of the beanstalk. Jump from the top of the beanstalk and enter the Wooden Trapdoor.

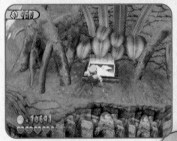

Trapdoor 3

The third trapdoor's sub-level is a quick one. The Red Diamond sits atop a high floating platform. A single block sits on the ground below the center of the platform, and a lever is just to the left of the block. Wooden Chests periodically drop in from above. They all contain bombs.

The idea is to use one of the Wooden Chest's bombs to activate the lever while standing on the single block. Stand on the block and toss a bomb at the lever. When the lever is activated, the block rises toward the floating platform like an elevator. Collect the Red Diamond and Gold Statue part from the floating platform.

After returning from the third trapdoor, climb back down the beanstalk's ladder to reach the ledge below. Line up with the foot imprint on the right side of the ledge, and watch the second Tulipatooie as it spits out and sucks in its Glue Globe. To cross the gap safely, time yourself and jump when the Tulipatooie begins to spit out its Glue Globe. Otherwise, you get sucked in.

Step 8

A Garlic Dispenser stands on the edge of the grassy ledge, to the right of the second Tulipatooie. Make good use of this Garlic Dispenser before continuing up the grassy trail ahead.

A huge cluster of monsters—Wolves, Hawks, Grizzlies, and a Rhino Ankiron—wait to fight at the top of the grassy trail. Use powerful moves to clear out most of the enemies, but save one so you can enter the nearby Steel Trapdoor.

Trapdoor 4

The fourth trapdoor's sub-level starts you off on a high floating platform. The Red Diamond's platform is far, far below. To reach it, you must plummet from the starting platform. Use the single gold coin as your guide to land safely on the platform below and collect the Red Diamond.

A tiny, *tiny* platform is far below the Red Diamond's platform. Jump and fall down to the minute platform, following the long line of gold coins. As you fall, you also collect a Gold Statue part.

Proceed to the right after returning from the fourth trapdoor. A single Rock Block is embedded in the ground nearby. Ground Pound through the Rock Block and you drop to a lower platform. As you fall, you automatically collect the Gold Statue part that hovers directly below the Rock Block.

Step 9

After smashing through the Rock Block, you land in the middle of a circular Battle Ring. Beat the stuffing out of waves of monsters until the timer expires, then continue onward to the right.

The light-green Button's Treasure Chest is on the ground just to the right of the Battle Ring. Open the Treasure Chest to acquire the Earring. Then continue following the grassy trail down and to the right, using the short wooden bridge to cross the wide stream.

Step 10

You encounter two pairs of new enemies on the far side of the stream. The first are called Wind Winders—cute little guys that fly about, pushing you backward with strong gusts of wind. Defeat these enemies easily with a single jumping punch.

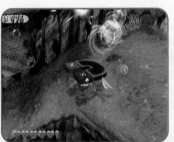

The other new enemies are more dangerous, but also more useful. The large Monstrous Magnets fly over-head, firing bolts of electricity at you. Jump and punch one of the Monstrous Magnets until it falls to the ground, then pick it up.

Carry the stunned Monstrous Magnet back a little way to a large metal plate nailed to the side of the nearby cliff. Throw the Monstrous Magnet at the plate and it sticks, creating a platform. Jump onto the Monstrous Magnet, then up to the grassy ledge above.

The purple Button sits on the ground at the far left side of the grassy ledge. Activate it, then jump down from the ledge and head to the right until you encounter more Monstrous Magnets.

Stun a Monstrous Magnet, and this time throw it to the metal plates across the gap to the right. Use the Monstrous Magnet as a platform to reach the higher ledge to the right.

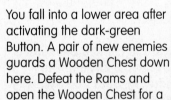

More Monstrous Magnets appear on this higher ledge, and more metal plates appear on the other side of the gap to the right. Don't worry about using the Monstrous Magnets just yet. Jump into the gap and, as you fall, either punch or Ground Pound the dark-green Button sticking out of the nearby wall to activate it.

Step 11

You fall into a lower area after activating the dark-green Button. A pair of new enemies guards a Wooden Chest down here. Defeat the Rams and open the Wooden Chest for a random treat, then Ground Pound the Rock Block embedded in the earth nearby.

You land in an even lower area below the Rock Block. The light-blue Button sticks out of the wall to the left. Stun one of the Wolves that pops out of the nearby monster generator and pick it up. Jump and throw the stunned Wolf into the light-blue Button to activate it.

On the right side of the monster generator is a Steel Trapdoor. Stun another Wolf and use it to enter the fifth trapdoor.

The dark-green Button's Treasure Chest sits on a small, grassy ledge at the top of the vine. Jump off the vine. Land near the Treasure Chest, collecting the Gold Statue part hovering in the air as you jump across. Open the Treasure Chest to receive the Jeweled Sword.

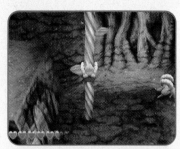

Trapdoor 5

This sub-level features an enormous, odd-shaped floating block that slowly rotates in place. The odd-shaped block stands between you and the platform with the Red Diamond.

With the Jeweled Sword added to your collection of treasures, jump off the Treasure Chest's ledge to the left. Run past the pair of Rams (or stop and beat 'em up) and come to another thick vine. Climb the vine and jump to the grassy ledge to the left.

Pick up a lonely Sculpture sitting on the grass and continue to the left. Use the Sculpture to enter the Steel Trapdoor in the middle of the wide stream.

Jump onto the block and make your way around it, heading for the Red Diamond's platform on the opposite side. The block rotates slowly, so don't worry about taking a fall. Jump to the Red Diamond's platform once you've reach a satisfactory location.

Trapdoor 6

You've been to a sub-level similar to this one before. Three levers on the starting platform control three floating platforms that span the long gap between you and the Red Diamond.

Next to the Red Diamond is a trapped Spriteling. The Spriteling, once freed, hints that treasures are to be found at the cliff bases in this area.

Activate each lever to manipulate the floating platforms. Set the platforms moving so you can ride on them and jump from one to the next.

Continue onward to the right after returning from the fifth trapdoor. Ground Pound the nearby pod and use a Wolf to raise the Swirly Slab. Jump and grab onto the vine above the Swirly Slab and climb to the top.

The Red Diamond's platform also harbors a trapped Spriteling. Rescue it and it hints at the usefulness of the Monstrous Magnets.

Thrillsville: Beanstalk Way

After returning from the sixth trapdoor, follow the Spriteling's advice and return to the Monstrous Magnets. Use the Monstrous Magnets as platforms and proceed to the right.

Step 12

Past the Monstrous Magnets are a Swirly Slab pod and a monster generator. If you need to, use the Swirly Slab to return to previous parts of this area. Otherwise, continue to the right.

The grassy hill turns to dirt as you continue right. Move to the top of the hill and you see several small caves. Crazed Rams charge out of the caves, one after the other, making this a dangerous hill to cross. You're sent flying if a charging Ram hits you, so take pains to avoid them.

You stand a good chance of being hit by a charging Ram even if you cross the hill very carefully. When a Ram plows into you, you fly over the edge of a steep cliff. You'll soon end up in the Unithorn's Lair. As you fall, however, you also catch a glimpse at ledges, Glue Globes, and a Wooden Chest. This must be the treasure-laden cliff base that the Spriteling was talking about.

Use the line of Glue Globes on the left side of the hill to safely reach the ledges at the base of the cliff. Time your jump over to the first Glue Globe carefully to avoid being hit by the suicidal Rams.

The first ledge on the left side of the cliff's base has a Wooden Chest. Open it for a random prize.

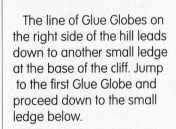

The dark-blue Treasure Chest platform is located on another small ledge on the hill, just to the right of the light-blue Button's Treasure Chest. You still need to find and activate the dark-blue Button, but remember the location of its Treasure Chest platform for future reference.

The line of Glue Globes on the right side of the hill leads down to another small ledge at the base of the cliff. Jump to the first Glue Globe and proceed down to the small ledge below.

Cross the short bridge on the left side of the ledge and collect the Gold Statue part on the other side, then climb back up the line of Glue Globes.

The pink Button sits on the ledge below the Wooden Chest. Activate the pink Button, then use the line of Glue Globes to climb back up to the top of the hill.

Run along to the right once you reach the top of the hill, carefully avoiding the Rams. The light-blue Button's Treasure Chest is found on a small ledge between two lines of charging Rams. Open the Treasure Chest and collect the Gold Tiara.

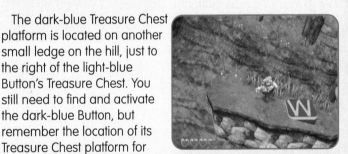

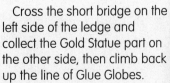

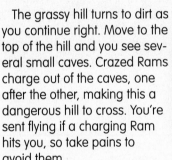

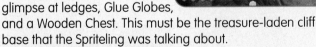

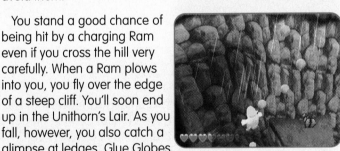

Continue along to the right past the hill and charging Rams. A Garlic Dispenser stands to the right of the hill, ready to dish out health-replenishing Garlic.

Another Tree Freak blocks your progress to the right. Defeat this Tree Freak in the same manner you did the previous one, using its fruit to attack its weak spot. Continue onward to the right after you defeat the Tree Freak.

Step 13

Drop off the cliff beyond the Tree Freak to a small ledge. Use the Monstrous Magnets that fly in to attack as platforms to reach the line of Glue Globes extending upward.

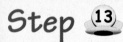

Step 14

The Glue Globes lead to a large, circular platform—a Battle Ring. Use Wario's Wild Swing-Ding attack to clear out the waves of monsters.

A Crystal Entity attacks as soon as you land on the huge flower. Defeat the Crystal Entity, then walk back over to the Glue Globes you used to reach the massive yellow flower.

Head right across the circular platform after the Battle Ring's timer expires. Line up with the foot imprint you see on the ground and jump onto the Glue Globe below. Jump to the next Glue Globe and then onto the huge flower platform.

You can see the dark-blue Button on the side of the wall below the Glue Globes. Line up as best you can and make a jump to the dark-blue Button. Ground Pound the dark-blue Button as you fall toward it to activate it. Wario grabs onto the dark-blue Button after Ground Pounding it.

Step 15

Jump to the left to reach a lower clearing and the purple Button's Treasure Chest. Open the chest to collect the King's Crown.

The seventh trapdoor is just to the right of the purple Button's Treasure Chest. Use one of the nearby Rams to enter the Steel Trapdoor's sub-level.

Trapdoor 7

This unique sub-level features a long line of floating blocks that stretch between your starting position and the Red Diamond's far platform. Many of the blocks quickly move up and down.

The idea is to stand on each moving block and jump off it just as it begins to move upward. You can jump very high by timing your jump correctly. Watch the blocks carefully as they move up and down, and use the side camera angle for a better view. Jump from block to block until you reach the far platform and the Red Diamond.

Thrillsville: Beanstalk Way

A trapped Spriteling sits near the Red Diamond. Rescue the Spriteling, who gives you advice on fighting the boss of the Beanstalk Way area.

Move along to the right after returning from the seventh trapdoor. Ground Pound the pod on the far right side of the clearing to reveal a Swirly Slab. Use a nearby Ram to raise the Swirly Slab, then jump onto the small, white flower to the left.

The next flower platform to the left has a Wooden Chest atop it. Open the Wooden Chest, then continue moving left across the flower platforms.

Make your way back to the dark-blue Button's Treasure Chest platform, which you saw on the big hill with all those crazy, charging Rams. Open the dark-blue Button's Treasure Chest to obtain the Nice Scepter.

Backtrack to the right, all the way back to the huge yellow flower. Drop to the clearing below the yellow flower and use the Swirly Slab on the far right side of the clearing again. Jump from the raised Swirly Slab, this time landing on the grassy ledge to the right. Alternatively, you can perform a Corkscrew Conk from the small, white flower platform to reach the grassy ledge.

Step

Another Tree Freak blocks the grassy pathway ahead. This is a strong Tree Freak, which takes three hits to defeat. Proceed up the pathway after dealing with the Tree Freak.

Ignore the monster generator and continue to follow the path as it turns, moving around the fence and toward the camera. The pink Button's Treasure Chest sits on the ground past a Sculpture, near the eighth trapdoor. Open the Treasure Chest to collect the final treasure from Beanstalk Way, the Game Boy Advance.

Run over to the nearby Wooden Trapdoor. Ground Pound the trapdoor to reach the eighth and final sub-level.

Trapdoor 8

The eighth trapdoor features a simple but dangerous sub-level. The Gold Statue part and Red Diamond are in the middle of the small room. The Red Diamond floats on a block just above the Gold Statue part. A large shadow from the Rock Blocks above surrounds the two goodies.

The Rock Blocks drop from the ceiling, pounding anything that tries to get close to the goods. If you're caught beneath a falling Rock Block, you're flattened. Carefully navigate the Rock Blocks, jumping over them after they've fallen, to avoid getting crushed as you collect the final Gold Statue part and Red Diamond.

Run back to the monster generator you passed a moment ago. Line up with the foot imprint on the ground near the monster generator and jump to the Glue Globe to the left. Jump from one Glue Globe to the next, making your way across.

Jump from the leaf platform at the end of the Glue Globes and grab the ladder that runs up the tall beanstalk to the left. Climb the ladder, taking care to avoid the two spiked balls that circle the beanstalk.

Step 17

Run across the short wooden bridge to the right of the tiny hut at the top of the beanstalk. A Garlic Dispenser stands at the edge of the grassy ledge on the other side of the short bridge. Make use of the Garlic Dispenser before continuing to the right.

A large group of various monsters gets in your way as you cross the grassy clearing. Dish out some pain, then continue along to the right.

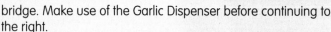

The goal lies beyond the group of monsters, on the far right side of the grassy clearing. Feed the Goal Trapdoor's guardian statue five Red Diamonds to remove it, then enter the Goal Trapdoor to face Beanstalk Way's boss.

TIP

If you need to refill Wario's Heart Meter, cross the grassy clearing and use the nearby Garlic Dispenser.

Area Boss: Spideraticus

Spideraticus is the boss of the Beanstalk Way area. This giant spider's sticky web makes up most of the circular arena. Be quick and avoid getting stuck on his spider webs, and you easily defeat Spideraticus.

Begin running around the non-webbed outside of the arena as soon as the fight begins. Spideraticus stays in the center of his web throughout the fight. Jump over the shock wave that Spideraticus sends out when he jumps into the air and comes crashing down on his web.

Keep running along the outside of the arena until Spideraticus spits out five Glue Globes. Jump onto one of the Glue Globes before Spideraticus sucks them back in.

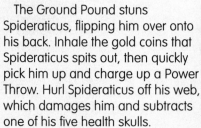

Spideraticus sucks in his Glue Globes one at a time. As you're pulled in close to Spideraticus, jump off the Glue Globe and execute a Ground Pound onto his head or midsection.

The Ground Pound stuns Spideraticus, flipping him over onto his back. Inhale the gold coins that Spideraticus spits out, then quickly pick him up and charge up a Power Throw. Hurl Spideraticus off his web, which damages him and subtracts one of his five health skulls.

While Spideraticus is bouncing around after being thrown, turn around and run off his sticky spider web to safety. You can't jump while standing on Spideraticus's web, which makes avoiding his shock wave attack impossible.

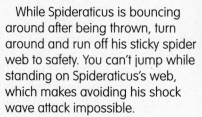

Continue fighting Spideraticus in the same manner, using his Glue Globes to get in close and attack. Spideraticus is defeated when all five of his health skulls have been knocked out.

Thrillsville: Red-Brief J's Showdown

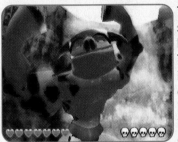

The boss of the Thrillsville stage is a giant, bipedal bull by the name of Red-Brief J. This nasty, briefs-wearing bull is a tough boss. His attacks are fierce, and even his arena is hostile, surrounded by boiling lava. Beat the odds and crush Red-Brief J to acquire the third Giant Treasure Chest Key and unlock the fourth and final stage.

Red-Brief J's Attacks

Red-Brief J has a wider variety of attacks than any boss you've faced to this point. Just walking around is a form of attack for Red-Brief J—he creates a plume of fire with every step.

Red-Brief J's most common attack makes sense when you consider that he's a big bull. He begins to power up and charges at Wario, moving at full speed. This charging attack is Red-Brief J's most dangerous, because it's difficult to avoid. As the fight wears on, Red-Brief J charges several times at once!

When Red-Brief J begins to flash, drawing in purple-colored energy, he's about to unleash another powerful attack. Red-

Brief J leaps into the air and crashes down onto the metal arena with such force that the arena dunks into the lava. Jump just before Red-Brief J lands to avoid being burned up.

In an attack similar to his charge attack, Red-Brief J jumps up and begins to spin, drawing in white-hot energy. He then darts out at Wario from above! Run around the arena to dodge this speedy, airborne attack.

As he gets angrier, Red-Brief J comes out with yet another attack. He points at Wario, begins to power up, and then fires a ball of fire from the end of his hoof. Again, keep moving around to dodge Red-Brief J's fireballs.

But wait, there's more! Red-Brief J's final attack type begins when he starts summoning red-colored energy. Red-Brief J starts to twirl like a ballerina and chases after Wario. Run away from Red-Brief J to avoid his mighty ballerina attack.

Fighting Red-Brief J

Unlike most other bosses, Red-Brief J is immune to Wario's powerful punches. Don't even bother punching or otherwise attacking Red-Brief J. He just gets angrier and lashes out. Keep your distance from Red-Brief J throughout the fight.

Five dunks in the lava, and Red-Brief J is toast. Excellent work! You've earned the third Giant Treasure Chest Key!

Red-Brief J's one weakness is in his charging attack. Dodge each charge until the attack ends. After he executes his final charge, Red-Brief J teeters on the edge of the arena, near the lava.

Run to the top of the octagonal arena and perform a Ground Pound. The force of your Ground Pound drops most of the arena into the lava, dunking the off-balance bull into its boiling heat. Red-Brief J loses one of his five health skulls each time you dunk him into the lava.

Red-Brief J adds another charge for every health skull he loses, making his charging attack very difficult to avoid toward the end of the fight. Keep your distance and move quickly, dodging the bull each time he charges.

Sparkle Land: Mirror Mansion

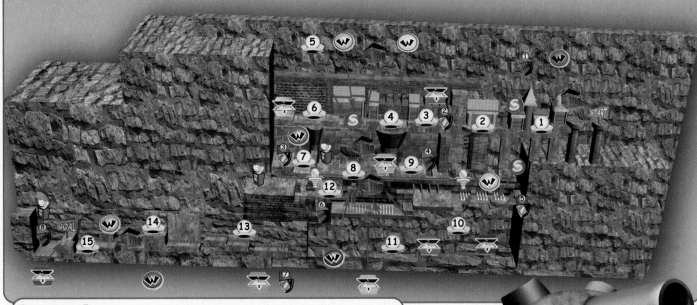

Legend

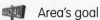 Area's goal	**S** Spriteling
W Button (various colors)	**START** Starting point of area
Garlic Dispenser	Steel Trapdoor (numbered)
(1) Walkthrough icon (numbered)	Treasure Chest (various colors)
Gold Statue Part	Wooden Chest
	Wooden Trapdoor (numbered)

Mirror Mansion is the first area of the Sparkle Land stage. This area is made confusing by its many mirrors, which you must use to see the hidden items, objects, and platforms reflected in them. As with every area in **Wario World**, Mirror Mansion has eight treasures to find, eight Gold Statue parts to collect, eight Red Diamonds to locate, and five Spritelings to rescue.

NOTE
You must have at least six Red Diamonds to enter the Mirror Mansion's Goal Trapdoor.

Step (1)

Run to the left from the starting point. You encounter a Stuffed Ankiron on your way. Punch it rapidly to stun it, give it a Piledriver, then continue left.

Farther to the left, a Rock Block drops from above. Jump onto the Rock Block when it drops and ride it up to a Wooden Chest on a ledge above. Open the Wooden Chest, then continue to the left.

The red Button and first trap-door are farther to the left. Activate the red Button, then enter the Wooden Trapdoor.

Trapdoor 1

This trapdoor's sub-level is similar to one you've seen before. Activating the lever causes 10 Rock Blocks on the ground to flash in sequence. Break the Rock Blocks in the order in which they flashed to reveal the Red Diamond and a Gold Statue part. Write down the sequence if you have trouble remembering it. You must exit and re-enter the trapdoor if you make a mistake.

Backtrack to the right after returning from the first trap-door's sub-level. Run past the moving Rock Block you used as an elevator to reach the Wooden Chest, and run along the lower pathway to proceed. To avoid being crushed, wait for the Rock Block to fall and run underneath it as it begins to rise again or just break it while on top of it.

You encounter two more falling Rock Blocks as you proceed across the lower pathway. Smash the Rock Blocks when they fall in front of you and continue moving left.

Use the fourth falling Rock Block as an elevator to reach the trapped Spriteling on the ledge above. Run under the Rock Block as it rises, then jump onto it after it falls. The Spriteling informs you that in certain places in the Mirror Mansion, you must use your reflection in the mirrors to see what you're doing.

Step ②

Jump down from the ledge and run up the steps to the left. Past another Stuffed Ankiron, you come to a gate with a Swirly Spinner. Use one of the monsters that pop out from the nearby monster generator and activate the Swirly Spinner with a counterclockwise Wild Swing-Ding. Run through the gate before it closes and continue onward to the left.

Step ③

You come to Mirror Mansion's first mirrored section up the steps to the left. Follow the Spriteling's advice and use © to get a better view of your reflection in the mirrors against the far wall. Stun one of the Ninja Crows that come out of the walls and use it to enter the Steel Trapdoor nearby.

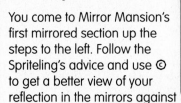

NOTE
What you see in mirrors are only reflections. If you see an object of interest reflected in a mirror, don't move toward the reflection itself! Move toward the source of the reflection.

Trapdoor 2

The second trapdoor's sub-level is not for the faint of heart! Several large rings of blocks fill the long gap between the starting platform and the Red Diamond, creating a sort of tunnel. The rings spin one way for a time, then slow down and spin in the opposite direction. You must jump from one ring to the next as you make your way over to the Red Diamond and Gold Statue part.

Wait for the ring of blocks you're standing on to slow down before jumping to the one ahead. Use © to get a better view of the small gaps between the rings. The last few rings of blocks spin at high speed, so time your jumps carefully!

Sparkle Land: Mirror Mansion

Head to the left after returning from the second trapdoor. The reflection of the red Button's Treasure Chest can be seen in the mirrors, up a short flight of stairs. Jump up the stairs and open the Treasure Chest for the Big Mirror!

Notice a ladder's reflection in the mirrors of the far wall just to the left of the red Button's Treasure Chest. Because the ladder you see is only a reflection, move toward the camera, away from the far wall (push ↓), to grab the ladder and climb up.

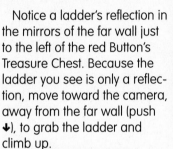

Step 4

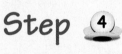

You come to another area with mirrors on the far wall to the left of the ladder. Watch out for the large, pink wheels that roll by as you move to the left. Look for the yellow Button's reflection in the mirrors of the far wall.

You're seeing the yellow Button's reflection in the far wall's mirror. The yellow Button itself sticks out from the side of the wall opposite its reflection. Activate the yellow Button and continue left.

A Glue Globe is reflected in the far wall's mirrors, farther to the left. Move toward the camera, away from the Glue Globe's reflection, and jump onto the Glue Globe. Jump to the left to reach a higher ledge above.

Step 5

An odd-looking lion and a Wooden Chest are farther to the left. Open the Wooden Chest for a random treat, then approach the funny-looking lion.

No wonder the lion looked so weird—it's not real! It's a wooden cutout made to look like a lion. Strangely, there's a Glue Globe on the end of the lion's tail.

Punching the lion activates it, and it slowly scampers across the spikes ahead. Jump onto the lion's Glue Globe to safely ride over the dangerous spikes.

The light-green Button is on a small ledge about halfway across the spikes. Jump off the lion and land near the light-green Button. Punch the Button to activate it, then jump over the spikes and land on the small platform across from the light-green Button.

A trapped Spriteling sits on the small platform across from the light-green Button. The Spriteling hints at how to defeat the upcoming Terrible Portrait monster. After rescuing the Spriteling, wait for the lion to make its return trip, then ride the lion back to where you first encountered it.

Activate the lion again when it stops, then jump back onto its Glue Globe and ride across the spikes. Stay on the lion until it reaches the opposite end of the spiked floor, then jump onto the monster-laden ledge above.

Step 6

To the left of the spiked floor, a Terrible Portrait ambushes you. These large, creepy monsters trap you and force you to battle them to the finish.

The Terrible Portrait mainly uses its long arms to attack you. The hands summon various elements, such as fire and ice, to attack you. Dodge the hand's attacks until the Terrible Portrait spawns a Barrel Buster to help it attack you.

Stun the Barrel Buster and run under one of the Terrible Portraits hands (preferably one that isn't about to attack). Execute a Piledriver to make the Barrel Buster's head shoot upward and strike the Terrible Portrait's hand.

Hit the Terrible Portrait twice with the Barrel Buster to defeat it. The Terrible Portrait explodes, allowing you to continue onward to the left.

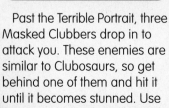

Past the Terrible Portrait, three Masked Clubbers drop in to attack you. These enemies are similar to Clubosaurs, so get behind one of them and hit it until it becomes stunned. Use the stunned Masked Clubber to take out the other two with a Wild Swing-Ding or Piledriver.

After defeating the three Masked Clubbers, climb up the steel mesh on the far wall. Watch out for the spiked balls as you cross the steel mesh, and drop to the small ledge below, which holds the yellow Button's Treasure Chest.

Open the Treasure Chest to get the Antique Clock. Add it to your treasures, then drop down the nearby hole in the ledge to proceed.

Step  7

After you fall through the hole, you land near the third trapdoor. A new type of enemy guards the Steel Trapdoor. Punch the Magician until he's stunned, then use him to enter the Steel Trapdoor.

Trapdoor 3

The third trapdoor's sub-level features an assortment of floating blocks. You must navigate the floating blocks to reach the Red Diamond. Start by jumping across the line of floating blocks ahead.

Follow the blocks until you come to a junction. It doesn't matter which way you go, so pick a direction and continue across the blocks.

You come to a line of floating blocks that extend upward and out of sight. Jump to the lowest block and grab its edge. Continue jumping and grabbing the edge of each block above, making your way to the top block.

You end up on a block floating above the Red Diamond's platform. Drop onto the platform and claim the Red Diamond.

A series of moving blocks stretches past the Red Diamond's platform. Jump to the first block and make your way across.

A Gold Statue part hovers atop the final platform. Jump off the last moving block and collect the Gold Statue part, then use the nearby Escape Spring to return to the Mirror Mansion.

Proceed to the right after returning from the third trap-door. You come to a mirrored floor patrolled by several Magicians. The dark-green Button is reflected in the floor. Use the steel mesh on the far wall to climb above the dark-green Button, then execute a Ground Pound to activate it.

Continue across the steel mesh to the right, using your reflection in the floor to see what you're doing. Avoid the spiked ball you encounter as you cross the mesh by watching its movements. Follow the steel mesh to the right until it ends.

Step 8

A Garlic Dispenser stands on the mirrored floor at the end of the steel mesh. Use the Garlic Dispenser to replenish Wario's Heart Meter, then continue to the right.

On the far right side of the mirrored floor sits the light-green Button's Treasure Chest. Open the Treasure Chest to get the Gold Mirror.

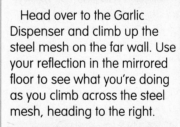

Head over to the Garlic Dispenser and climb up the steel mesh on the far wall. Use your reflection in the mirrored floor to see what you're doing as you climb across the steel mesh, heading to the right.

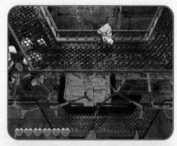

You eventually end up on a high steel walkway. A Wooden Chest sits in the corner of the walkway, visible only by its reflection on the floor below. Open the Wooden Chest, then continue across the walkway.

Watch out for the gap in the walkway. You have a hard time seeing it if you're not looking at the walkway's reflection in the floor below. Jump the gap and follow the steel walkway to its end.

Step 9

The walkway abruptly ends at a drop-off. Jump to the chamber below, which holds the fourth trapdoor. Execute a Ground Pound to enter the Wooden Trapdoor's sub-level.

Trapdoor 4

The fourth trapdoor's sub-level is simple, but still quite tricky. A staircase made of floating blocks leads up to a higher balcony where the Red Diamond is located. The blocks periodically flip, which makes crossing them difficult. **Watch the blocks carefully as you make precision jumps up to the Red Diamond.**

A Gold Statue part hovers on the opposite balcony. To get to it, you must perform a well-timed Corkscrew Conk.

Look for a nearby hole in the floor after you return from the fourth trapdoor's sub-level. Drop into the hole to proceed.

Step 10

Dropping through the hole lands you in the middle of a Battle Ring. Defeat waves of monsters until time runs out, then proceed to the right.

Hop across the grassy ledges of the spiked floor section to the right. Activate the light-blue Button from the second grassy ledge.

Punch the nearby wooden lion to get it moving and jump onto its Glue Globe. Jump off the lion halfway across the spiked floor and land on a small platform with a trapped Spriteling. After you rescue it, the Spriteling says that some monsters are invisible and can only be seen in mirrors.

Wait for the lion to make its return trip and hop onto it as it moves by. Activate the lion again and ride it to the other side of the spiked floor.

The platform across the spiked floor features the fifth trapdoor and the dark-blue Button's Treasure Chest platform. You need to find and activate the dark-blue Button, so use one of the nearby monsters to enter the Steel Trapdoor.

Trapdoor 5

The fifth trapdoor's sub-level features several rings of floating, spinning blocks. The rings of floating blocks are arranged in a large circle, which also spins in a clockwise pattern. Jump from one floating block to the next as you make your way to the Red Diamond on the far platform.

It would be simple to stand on a block and ride around on it until you reach the Red Diamond, but you'd have to repeatedly dodge the spiked balls to the right of the starting platform. It's easier to go against the grain and head counterclockwise as you jump from block to block. Watch for the Drop Blocks as you go. Avoid them if at all possible.

The central platform has a Gold Statue part hovering over it. Use the moving platform to reach the Gold Statue part, then turn around and head for the Red Diamond.

After returning from the fifth trapdoor's sub-level, climb the nearby ladder to reach a higher ledge. Defeat the monsters on the ledge, then climb onto the steel mesh on the wall close by.

The spiked ball you encounter as you climb across the steel mesh moves up and down along the vertical part of the mesh. Wait for the spiked ball to float above the mesh, then sneak in underneath it and hurry along.

A Gold Statue part floats at the far left end of the steel mesh. Grab the Gold Statue part and drop off the mesh, then start heading to the left across the Battle Ring.

Step 11

On the Battle Ring's left side is another spiked floor. Punch the wooden lion to activate it and ride the lion across the spikes.

The dark-blue Button is on the wall at the far left side of the spiked floor. Jump off the lion and activate the dark-blue Button, then quickly jump back onto the lion's Glue Globe and ride it back across the spiked floor.

The light-blue Button's Treasure Chest is sitting on a small ledge about halfway across the spiked floor. Jump to the Treasure Chest and open it for the Bronze Mirror. Quickly jump back onto the lion's Glue Globe as it continues to the right.

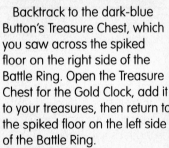

Backtrack to the dark-blue Button's Treasure Chest, which you saw across the spiked floor on the right side of the Battle Ring. Open the Treasure Chest for the Gold Clock, add it to your treasures, then return to the spiked floor on the left side of the Battle Ring.

Activate the lion on the left side of the Battle Ring and ride it across the spiked floor again. A line of Glue Globes leads upward to a higher platform about halfway across the spiked floor. Jump off the lion and onto the lowest Glue Globe, then follow the Glue Globes upward.

More Glue Globes are found at the high platform. Jump across the Glue Globes, heading right, until you come to a Wooden Chest.

Drop to the lower ledge on the right side of the Wooden Chest, where you find the dark-green Button's Treasure Chest. Open the Treasure Chest to acquire the Stained Glass.

Step 12

Head back across the Glue Globes to the left until you reach a large area with mirrors on the far walls. Look for a hole in the floor nearby and drop down.

The hole leads down to the sixth trapdoor. Use a Ground Pound to enter the Wooden Trapdoor's sub-level.

Trapdoor 6

This sub-level tests your ability to execute the Corkscrew Conk. You must first use the Corkscrew Conk to leap across to the far balcony, activating the central lever as you go. If you fall off the balcony, use the Glue Globe to climb back up.

After you activate the central lever, another one lowers to one side. Again, you must execute a Corkscrew Conk to activate the lever. A third lever then lowers on the other side. Activate the third lever with another Corkscrew Conk to reveal the Red Diamond and a trapped Spriteling.

When rescued, the Spriteling informs you that in areas ahead, there may appear to be no way to proceed. He suggests that you search for hints reflected in mirrors.

Climb up the ladder to return to the mirrored area after exiting the sixth trapdoor. Move to the left, where a Swirly Spinner sticks out of a nearby pillar. Check the mirrors on the far wall to see a pair of Glue Globes leading up the back of the pillar. Jump up the Glue Globes to reach a Gold Statue part hovering over the pillar.

This mirrored area has several Witches, but they're invisible. You can only see a Witch's reflection in the mirrors on the far wall.

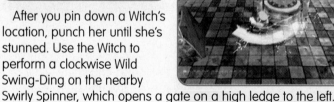

After you pin down a Witch's location, punch her until she's stunned. Use the Witch to perform a clockwise Wild Swing-Ding on the nearby Swirly Spinner, which opens a gate on a high ledge to the left.

The pillar to the left of the Swirly Spinner also has a Glue Globe on its backside, which is reflected in the far wall's mirror. Jump onto the Glue Globe and up to the pillar's top, then leap over to the high left ledge before the gate closes.

Past the gate to the left is a Garlic Dispenser. Use it, then drop into the nearby hole in the floor to proceed.

Step 13
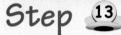

You find the Red Diamond on the third floating platform, but you're not finished yet. This platform has a Glue Globe Pole as well. Use it to reach the next floating platform ahead and collect the Gold Statue part you find there.

As you fall through the hole, you catch a glimpse in the tall mirror of an odd-looking flying contraption. The flying contraption can't be reached. It just follows you around and constantly fires enemies and bombs at you.

Jump the small gap to the right after you land. Here you find the pink Button's Treasure Chest platform and the seventh trapdoor. You still need to find and activate the pink Button, so use an enemy or the nearby Sculpture to enter the Steel Trapdoor.

You can't go any farther to the right, so turn around and start going left after returning from the seventh trapdoor. You soon encounter another Terrible Portrait. Defeat it by using the Barrel Busters as weapons against it, then continue onward to the left.

Trapdoor 7

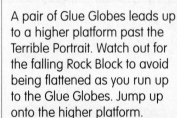

This crazy sub-level forces you to use Glue Globe Poles to leap across wide gaps to distant platforms. Jump onto the first Glue Globe Pole and watch it closely for a few seconds to get its timing down. Jump just as the Glue Globe Pole begins to shoot forward, landing on the distant platform ahead.

Step  14

A pair of Glue Globes leads up to a higher platform past the Terrible Portrait. Watch out for the falling Rock Block to avoid being flattened as you run up to the Glue Globes. Jump up onto the higher platform.

The second platform has another Glue Globe Pole. Follow the same procedure as before, using the Glue Globe Pole to soar over to the next distant platform.

Continue to the left until you come to the pink Button on the ground. Activate the pink Button, then retrace your steps back to the pink Button's Treasure Chest platform you noticed a short time ago. Open the pink Button's Treasure Chest to get the Crazy Glasses.

Return to the platform where you found the pink Button. Drop to the lower platform to the right of the pink Button (which is now gray), where you find a Wooden Chest and the purple Button. Open the chest and activate the purple Button, then proceed to the left.

Farther left, you can barely make out the reflection of a Glue Globe in the shattered mirror on the far wall. Jump onto the Glue Globe and up to the platform above.

Step

Nice work! You've reached the goal! You're not finished yet, however. Feed the stone statue six Red Diamonds to remove it from the Goal Trapdoor, then drop onto the lower platform to the left of the goal.

On the goal's lower left side is a Garlic Dispenser, the ByeBye Balloon, the eighth trapdoor and the purple Button's Treasure chest. Open the Treasure Chest to collect the final treasure from the Mirror Mansion, the Gold Pocket Watch. Next, fill up on Garlic from the nearby Garlic Dispenser before you Ground Pound into the Wooden Trapdoor.

Trapdoor 8

This last sub-level is straightforward. Use the Glue Globe to reach the upper balcony of the small room, where you spot a trapped Spriteling. The Spriteling gives you a hint about beating the area's boss.

You must execute a Corkscrew Conk to reach the Red Diamond on the opposite balcony. This is made difficult by the rings of spiked balls that rotate between the two balconies. Watch the spiked balls rotate before attempting to Corkscrew Conk through the central ring.

If the spiked balls in the sub-level hit you, use the Garlic Dispenser again after you return from the eighth trapdoor. When Wario's Heart Meter is full, use the Glue Globes you see in the broken mirror on the far wall to return to the goal. Enter the Goal Trapdoor and prepare to face the Mirror Mansion boss.

Area Boss: Mean Emcee

The boss of the Mirror Mansion area is called the Mean Emcee. This large, cowardly boss is easily hurt, but difficult to defeat.

Run up to the Mean Emcee and punch him as soon as the fight begins. The Mean Emcee becomes frightened after several punches and darts underneath one of three tall cups to the rear of the arena.

The three tall cups lower, hiding the Mean Emcee beneath one of them. The cups then begin to shift positions slowly. Keep track of the cup that the Mean Emcee is hiding under as the cups shift.

When the cups stop moving, run to the one you believe the Mean Emcee is hiding under. Punch the cup you've chosen, and the cup lifts into the air. If you chose the correct cup, you see a flash of red light—the Mean Emcee has vanished!

Don't worry. The cowardly Mean Emcee hasn't gone far. Jump up and punch the cup. The Mean Emcee falls from it, stunned that you found his hiding spot. Pick up the Mean Emcee and execute a Piledriver, which knocks out one of his five health skulls.

The Mean Emcee jumps up and twirls his magic baton. Stay clear of the Mean Emcee while he performs this powerful spinning attack.

When he stops twirling his baton, run over to the Mean Emcee and punch him *once*. The Mean Emcee begins to power up after you hit him the first time. If you continue to hit him, you won't be able to dodge his next attack!

The Mean Emcee begins to spin after powering up, zipping out at Wario. You should have plenty of time to dodge this fast spinning attack as long as you punched him only once and backed away after he began to power up.

The Mean Emcee is out of tricks after he finishes his spinning attack. Run up to him and punch repeatedly until he darts under another cup.

The cups shift faster and faster as the Mean Emcee takes damage. When the Mean Emcee has only one health skull remaining, the cups shift so fast it's nearly impossible to follow them! Several Ninja Crows pop out and attack you if you choose the wrong cup. Ignore the annoying Ninja Crows and focus on defeating the Mean Emcee.

Five Piledrivers defeat the Mean Emcee. Follow the steps outlined above as you battle the Mean Emcee, and the only hard part of this boss fight is choosing the correct cup!

Sparkle Land: Pecan Sands

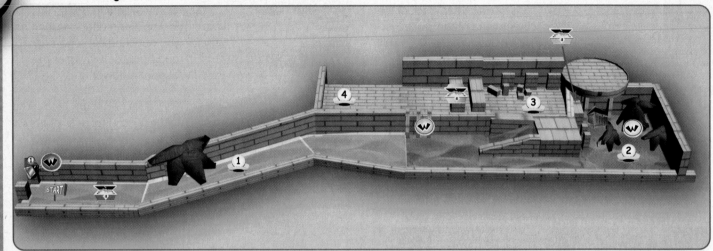

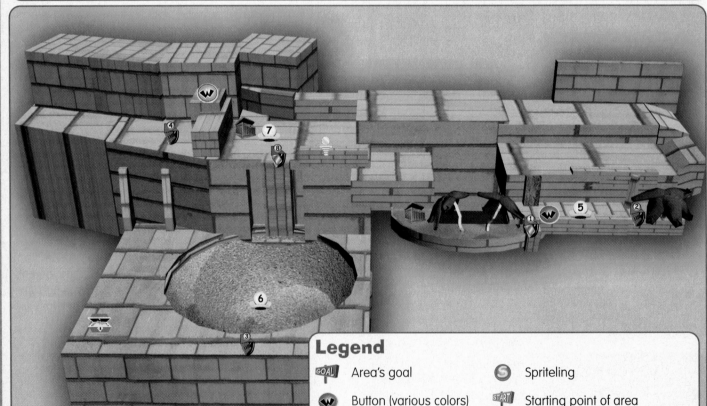

Legend

GOAL	Area's goal	**S**	Spriteling
W	Button (various colors)	**START**	Starting point of area
	Garlic Dispenser		Steel Trapdoor (numbered)
1	Walkthrough icon (numbered)		Treasure Chest (various colors)
	Gold Statue Part		Wooden Chest
			Wooden Trapdoor (numbered)

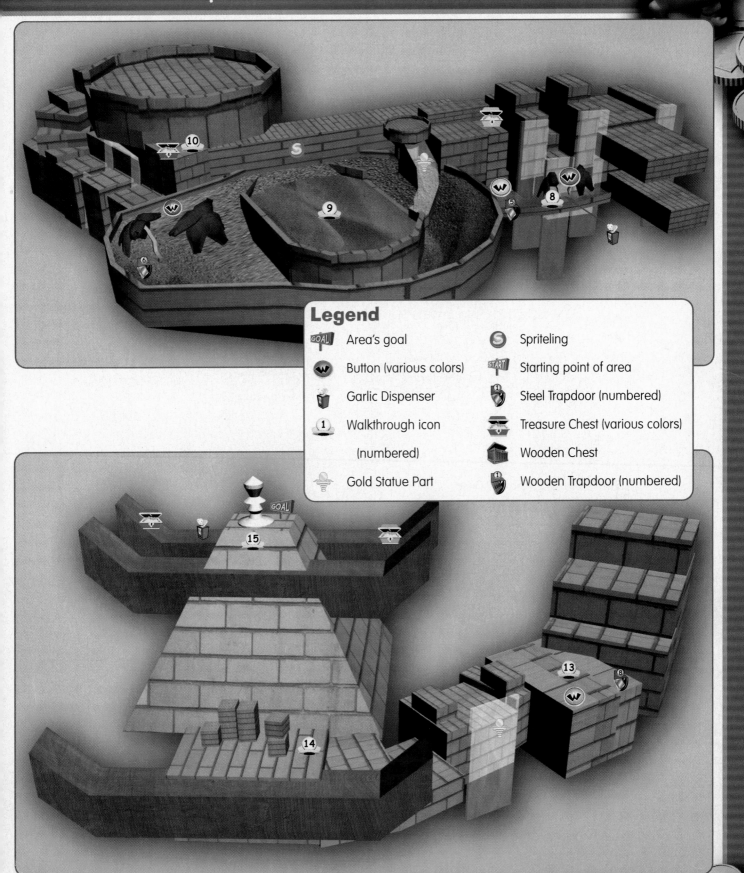

Legend

GOAL	Area's goal	S	Spriteling
W	Button (various colors)	START	Starting point of area
Garlic Dispenser		Steel Trapdoor (numbered)	
1	Walkthrough icon (numbered)		Treasure Chest (various colors)
	Gold Statue Part		Wooden Chest
			Wooden Trapdoor (numbered)

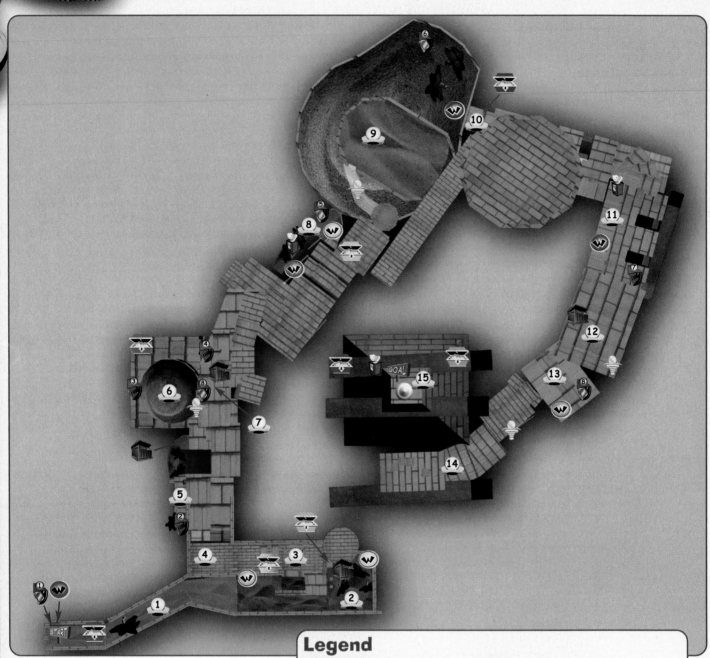

Legend

GOAL	Area's goal	⑤	Spriteling
Ⓦ	Button (various colors)	**START**	Starting point of area
	Garlic Dispenser		Steel Trapdoor (numbered)
①	Walkthrough icon (numbered)		Treasure Chest (various colors)
	Gold Statue Part		Wooden Chest
			Wooden Trapdoor (numbered)

The second area of the Sparkle Land stage is Pecan Sands. This relatively small, sandy area is dominated by a massive central temple. It's the game's final area, so expect it to put all your skills to the test! As with every area in *Wario World*, Pecan Sands has eight treasures to find, eight Gold Statue parts to collect, eight Red Diamonds to locate, and five Spritelings to rescue.

> ## NOTE
> You must have at least six Red Diamonds to enter the Pecan Sands Goal Trapdoor.

Step

From the starting point, run to your right; you soon come to the red Button's Treasure Chest platform. You still need to find and activate the red Button, but remember where its Treasure Chest platform is for future reference.

Continue right to encounter a monster generator. Two large Club Mummies, similar to Clubosaurs and the like, patrol nearby. Use Columns to defeat the monsters quickly, then continue to the right.

A long, wide ramp leads upward, past the monster generator. Ignore the ramp for the moment and proceed to the right across the sand.

Step ②

A Crystal Entity ambushes you on the sand near the ramp. Defeat it and continue around the bend to the right.

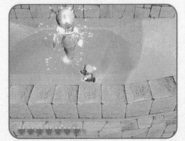

In a small alcove near a wall to the far right, open a Wooden Chest for a random goodie.

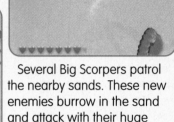

Several Big Scorpers patrol the nearby sands. These new enemies burrow in the sand and attack with their huge tails. Ground Pound their eyes, which barely peek out from the sand, to stun them. Finish them off with a powerful attack.

> ## CAUTION
> Wario becomes stuck if he Ground Pounds onto the sand, just as he became stuck in the deep snow of Shivering Mountains. Quickly press Ⓐ to climb out of the sand if you're stuck.

The yellow Button sits on the sand in the corner of the nearby wall. Activate the yellow Button and retrace your steps to the ramp you noticed a moment ago.

Step ③

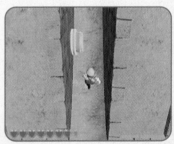

The light-green Button sticks out from a wall in a small alcove near the ramp. Jump up and punch the light-green Button to activate it, then proceed up the ramp to the right.

The ramp takes you close to the huge central temple. As you head up the ramp, a wind trap blows sandy gales at you from a small alcove. Jump over the gale as you run up the ramp to avoid being knocked backward.

Jump onto a small ledge to the right of the wind trap. The light-green Button's Treasure Chest is at the end of the ledge. Open the Treasure Chest and collect the Ancient Relief.

You encounter two more wind traps to the left of the first one. The yellow Button's Treasure Chest is near the farthest wind trap. When the wind trap stops, jump to the Treasure Chest and open it to get the Ancient Necklace.

Step 4

A Crystal Entity attacks to the left of the yellow Button's Treasure Chest. Defeat it and proceed down the ramp to the left.

On the ledge at the bottom of the ramp is a foot imprint. Ignore it for the moment and drop off the ledge, landing on the sandy area below.

Step 5

At the far left side of this long sandy strip is a Wooden Chest. Open it for a random treat, then run to the right across the sand.

The red Button sits on top of a short wall. Jump onto the wall and punch the red Button to activate it.

After activating the red Button, stun a Big Scorper and pick it up. Carry the Big Scorper onto the wall near the red Button, then jump over to the top of the pillar ahead. Jump to the top of the next pillar to the left, where the first trapdoor is located. Use the Big Scorper to enter the Steel Trapdoor's sub-level.

Trapdoor 1

This first trapdoor's sub-level is very straightforward. A large floating platform features several levers. Start by activating the levers on the far side of the large platform, working your way toward the centermost lever.

The large platform shifts each time you activate a lever, taking on a pyramid-like shape. Collect the gold coins that appear around every other tier of the pyramid as you activate the levers.

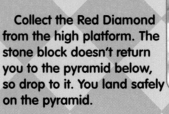

Stand on the center stone block and activate the lever closest to the block. This causes the stone block to rise, lifting you to a high-floating platform.

Collect the Red Diamond from the high platform. The stone block doesn't return you to the pyramid below, so drop to it. You land safely on the pyramid.

If you look through the hole at the top of the pyramid where the stone block used to be, you can just barely see a tiny platform far below the pyramid. Drop down through the hole and land on the tiny platform below, where a Spriteling is trapped. Rescue it, and the Spriteling tells you how to defeat the Big Scorpers.

After you return from the first trapdoor, jump back over to the red Button and back onto the sandy strip. The second trapdoor is on the far right side of this sandy strip. Perform a Ground Pound to enter the Wooden Trapdoor's sub-level.

Trapdoor 2

The second trapdoor's sub-level is a small room filled with Arrow Blocks. The object is to manipulate the Arrow Blocks to reach the goodies on the high balcony.

Begin punching the Arrow Blocks on the floor over to the side of the room where two adjacent Arrow Blocks float just off the ground.

When you've punched most of the Arrow Blocks to the far side of the room, a chain reaction begins that eventually shoots the two floating Arrow Blocks upward.

If the floating Arrow Blocks don't automatically fly upward, jump onto one of them and execute a Ground Pound when another Arrow Block is directly underneath it. The collision sends you flying!

Use the floating Arrow Blocks to reach the higher balcony. Jump over to the trapped Spriteling sitting on the balcony and rescue it. The Spriteling tells you how to defeat the upcoming Stone-Cold Statue enemies.

After freeing the Spriteling, use the floating Arrow Blocks to reach the high platform. Collect the Red Diamond from the high platform, then use the Escape Spring below to return to the surface.

After returning from the second trapdoor's sub-level, run to the left, back toward the red Button you activated a moment ago. Jump onto the short wall near the red Button, then drop to the starting point of the Pecan Sands area below.

The red Button's Treasure Chest is right where it should be—just to the right of the starting point. Open the Treasure Chest to receive the Ancient Ring. Proceed to the right, running up the ramp ahead and then crossing the wind traps to the left as you return to the small ledge where you noticed the foot imprint earlier.

Line up with the foot imprint. To the left is a cascade of sand and Glue Globes, falling from the side of the temple above. Jump across the Glue Globes as they pour down with the sand to reach a ledge on the opposite side.

Step 6

A Club Mummy and Mummy Ankiron patrol the platform on the other side of the sand cascade. Either defeat or ignore these enemies, then jump down to the sandy area below.

You land near a huge, bowl-shaped sand trap. The boss from the Greenhorn Ruins area, Sandworm, makes a stunning reappearance! Sandworm hasn't learned any new tricks; he's just gotten meaner. Defeat Sandworm the same way you did before, by punching him repeatedly and avoiding his predictable attacks.

The third trapdoor is on the outside wall near the giant sand trap. Execute a Ground Pound to enter the Wooden Trapdoor's sub-level.

Trapdoor 3

The third trapdoor's sub-level features more Arrow Block-manipulating antics. Start by climbing one of the small room's ladders to the upper balcony, where you find a Gold Statue part.

The Red Diamond sits atop a single block floating high above the center of the small room. There are several ways to manipulate the Arrow Blocks to reach the Red Diamond. To keep things simple, start by performing a Ground Pound onto one of the two Arrow Blocks that float just over the balcony's short lip.

Hop down from the Arrow Block and stand on the balcony's lip, directly below the other Arrow Block. Punch the Arrow Block that you just Ground Pounded to send it flying up against the wall.

Jump up and punch the other Arrow Block to send it over to the wall as well. The Arrow Block comes to a stop against the wall, floating just above the other one. Jump onto the higher Arrow Block and turn to look at the Red Diamond.

Now you're set up to reach the Red Diamond! Switch the camera view to the top-down perspective and execute a Ground Pound onto the higher Arrow Block. The Ground Pound slams the upper Arrow Block into the one directly beneath it. The reaction causes the upper Arrow Block to rise into the air.

Jump over to the Red Diamond as soon as you're high enough to make it. If you stay on the rising Arrow Block for more than a few seconds, you're transported back to the surface as if you'd used the Escape Spring!

Run past the large sand trap, heading to the left after you return from the third trapdoor. The dark-green Button's Treasure Chest platform sits on the sand near the outside wall. You still need to find and activate the dark-green Button, but remember its Treasure Chest platform location for future reference.

Near the dark-green Button's Treasure Chest platform is an odd-looking weathervane. Punch the weathervane to activate it, and a sudden squall whisks you into the air. Use the weathervane to reach the high landing nearby.

Step 7

The wind from the weathervane takes you to a platform patrolled by another Club Mummy/Mummy Ankiron duo. Defeat the two monsters and open the nearby Wooden Chest for a random goodie.

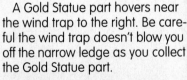

A Gold Statue part hovers near the wind trap to the right. Be careful the wind trap doesn't blow you off the narrow ledge as you collect the Gold Statue part.

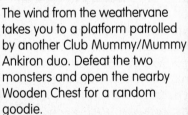

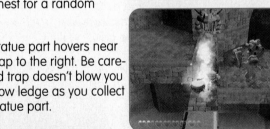

Line up with the foot imprint on the left side of the landing and jump up the Glue Globes that pour out from a small sand cascade ahead. Grab onto the edge of the ledge above, and pull yourself up onto the ledge. Enter the Wooden Trapdoor you find there.

Trapdoor 4

The fourth trapdoor's sub-level is mercifully straightforward. A trapped Spriteling sits on the ground nearby. The rescued Spriteling gives you information on how to handle the upcoming Laser Jigglefish monsters.

Use the pair of Arrow Blocks on the ground to reach the small room's upper balcony. Jump on top of the Arrow Blocks and perform a Ground Pound. Quickly jump off the rising Arrow Block and land on the balcony before you're crushed against the unyielding block above.

It's short work getting to the Red Diamond. Jump over one of the large spiked balls as it moves toward you. Before the spiked ball makes its return trip, quickly run over to the Red Diamond.

After returning from the fourth trapdoor's sub-level, jump across the cascading Glue Globes to the left. The dark-green Button sticks out from the side of the wall to the left. Jump from a Glue Globe and punch the dark-green Button to activate it. Head to the right, back across the cascading Glue Globes, and backtrack to the dark-green Button's Treasure Chest platform, which you noticed a short while ago. Open the chest to collect the Small Pyramid.

Use the nearby weathervane again to return to the cascading Glue Globes. Cross the Glue Globes to reach a higher platform to the left, where you encounter a Stone-Cold Statue. Pound on the Stone-Cold Statue's weak spots, the glowing green orbs, while avoiding its attacks.

Step 8

Don't climb up the ladder beyond the Stone-Cold Statue just yet. Instead, drop to the lower sandy area. Fill up on Garlic, using a Garlic Dispenser in a small recess in the temple's wall. Then head to the left.

The light-blue Button is on the far left side of the sandy area. Activate the light-blue Button and then run toward the camera and the outside wall.

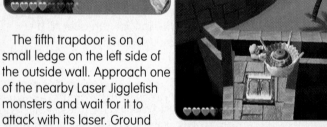

The fifth trapdoor is on a small ledge on the left side of the outside wall. Approach one of the nearby Laser Jigglefish monsters and wait for it to attack with its laser. Ground Pound the Laser Jigglefish while its underside is exposed to stun it, then use the Laser Jigglefish to enter the Steel Trapdoor.

Trapdoor 5

This trapdoor's sub-level features a long line of rotating platforms that stretch between the starting point and the far platform, which holds the Red Diamond. Each rotating platform spins in a slightly different pattern from the others, and they all feature a pair of spiked balls as well as a hole in their centers. This extremely trying obstacle course puts all of your jumping skills to the test.

Carefully jump from one revolving platform to the next. Crossing the platforms is not an easy task. Even experts can expect to fall several times. The secret to reaching the Red Diamond lies in timing your jumps carefully. Don't get flustered by the sudden rotation of the platforms. Watch them carefully and learn to predict their patterns of rotation.

The platform's spiked balls are very dangerous. Hitting one almost always causes you to fall. If they're moving toward you, you can jump the spiked balls and land safely behind them.

The final rotating platform not only spins faster than the rest, but it also slowly moves back and forth between the Red Diamond platform and the second-to-last rotating platform. Don't jump prematurely to the Red Diamond. Stay on this last revolving platform until you know you can make the jump, then collect your hard-earned Red Diamond and Gold Statue part.

After you return from the fifth trapdoor, use the weathervane on the far right side of the sandy area to reach a high platform above. Cross the cascading Glue Globes to the left once again to reach the platform where you battled the Stone-Cold Statue.

Climb up the nearby ladder to reach a higher platform. The light-blue Button's Treasure Chest sits in a corner to the right. Open the Treasure Chest to collect the Ancient Bracelet.

To the left of the light-blue Button's Treasure Chest is a huge, curvy slide. Collect the Gold Statue part as you bomb down the slide.

Step 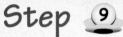 9

A Battle Ring waits at the bottom of the giant slide! Defeat the waves of monsters until time runs out, then exit the Battle Ring to the left.

The dark-blue Button sits on the sand in a small recess in the wall of the temple. Activate the dark-blue Button and continue to the left.

The sixth trapdoor is to the left of the dark-blue Button. Use a Big Scorper to enter the Steel Trapdoor.

Trapdoor 6

This straightforward but challenging sub-level consists of a long stretch of various floating blocks. You must navigate the blocks with skill to reach the Red Diamond on the far platform. Start by jumping to the first floating block, then jump over the spiked ball ahead and land on the block beyond.

The next block ahead is a Drop Block with a spiked ball atop it. Jump and grab the edge of the Drop Block. It begins to sink!

Hang on the edge of the Drop Block until it falls a short distance, then hop up onto it and make a quick jump to the next Drop Block ahead. Grab the edge of the second Drop Block, wait for it to fall a bit, then climb up and jump onto the platform ahead.

The Red Diamond is on the floating platform. Collect the Red Diamond, then jump onto the larger of the two spinning, moving blocks ahead. Ride the larger block over to a small platform.

Your next task is to run across a curvy line of Marshmallow Blocks. Pick a camera angle you like and start running across the Marshmallow Blocks, which rapidly disappear behind you.

The Marshmallow Blocks lead to the final platform and a Gold Statue part. Collect the Gold Statue part and then return to the surface, using the nearby Escape Spring.

After returning from the sixth trapdoor, return to the Battle Ring you conquered a short time ago. Jump on top of one of the two Columns near the Battle Ring, near the temple wall. Jump from the Column and land on one of two tiny ledges.

Jump from the tiny ledge to a slightly larger ledge above, where you find a trapped Spriteling. Rescue it, and the Spriteling gives you a hint to help you defeat the upcoming boss.

Drop from the Spriteling's ledge and head left a bit. Climb the ladder you come to.

Step 10

A Wooden Chest sits on the platform at the top of the ladder. Open the Wooden Chest, then proceed left.

Walk toward the camera a bit, toward the outside wall, to see a narrow walkway blocked by Sculptures. Lift the Sculptures and toss them aside as you continue moving toward the camera.

The dark-blue Button's Treasure Chest is at the very end of the narrow walkway. Open the Treasure Chest to claim the Anubis Statue, then backtrack along the narrow walkway and head left.

Jump up the pile of loose brick blocks near the steel mesh to reach a small ledge. To the left are several ledges. Continue jumping from one ledge to the next.

You come to the seventh trapdoor on the last ledge to the left. Ground Pound the Wooden Trapdoor and enter its sub-level.

Trapdoor 7

The seventh trapdoor is simple in design yet quite difficult to clear. A Gold Statue part and a Red Diamond are on the small room's upper balcony. A pair of ladders leads up to the balcony, but the ladders are blocked by spiked balls. You must activate the elevated lever to move the spiked balls.

The lever is too high to reach without executing a precision Corkscrew Conk—the most difficult Corkscrew Conk you ever have to perform. Start out on top of the short stack of blocks, facing the adjacent Marshmallow Block and the lever.

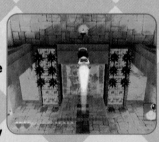

Start running toward the Marshmallow Block. The instant you step on the Marshmallow Block, execute a quick Dash Attack and press Ⓐ to perform a Corkscrew Conk. Do all of this before the Marshmallow Block disappears!

Hitting the lever is no easy task. If you Dash Attack before you touch the Marshmallow Block, your Dash Attack is interrupted by the minuscule gap between the top block and the Marshmallow Block. Just keep trying until you finally nail the Corkscrew Conk and the spiked balls shift off the ladders.

The spiked balls don't go away completely. They just move up and down, lifting off the ladders and then coming back down to block them again. Time your movements carefully as you climb up the ladder and onto the balcony. The Gold Statue part sits right on the balcony, waiting to be taken.

Watch out for the Rock Blocks that try to flatten you on the sides of the balcony. Jump onto one of them after it falls, then cross the rest of the blocks to reach the Red Diamond.

Jump back across the ledges after returning from the seventh trapdoor. Climb up the steel mesh to reach a higher platform.

Step 11

A Garlic Dispenser waits to heal your wounds on the platform above the steel mesh. Make good use of it.

A set of steps winds upward to the left of the purple Button. Before you head up the steps, walk around behind them and collect a Gold Statue part hidden in a small alcove.

The purple Button sticks out from the temple's wall on the sandy area to the left. Activate the purple Button with a jumping punch, then proceed to the left.

Step 12

Head up the short flight of winding steps after nabbing the Gold Statue part. Open the Wooden Chest at the top of the steps, then continue left.

Step 13

A Laser Jigglefish guards the next platform, down some steps to the left. Stun the Laser Jigglefish by executing a Ground Pound on its exposed underside, then carry it over to the eighth and final trapdoor. Use the Laser Jigglefish to enter the Steel Trapdoor's sub-level.

Trapdoor 8

This massive obstacle course is made up entirely of floating blocks, and it puts all your jumping skills to the ultimate test! Start out by running down the line of blocks ahead, following them around to the left.

You eventually end up at far left side of the floating block maze, as pictured above. Jump the nearby gap and continue onward.

Jump to the path of floating blocks at left, and cross the Drop Blocks as you continue onward. Jump quickly across the upcoming Marshmallow Blocks that follow the bend in the path.

Execute a Corkscrew Conk to leap over the next wide gap. If you miss, you have a good chance of landing on the lower blocks. Climb back up and try again!

The path of floating blocks eventually leads to a small platform that moves up and down like an elevator. Jump onto the moving platform as it lowers, then jump or execute a Corkscrew Conk from the moving platform to reach the blocks to the right.

Move past the moving platform, jumping up the stepped blocks ahead. When you come to the junction pictured here, jump up the stepped blocks to the right.

Navigate the gaps in the pathway as you make your way to the bottom of the tall, vertical arrangement of floating blocks. Make your way up the blocks in a zigzag fashion until you reach the top, then continue along the upper path.

The upper path of floating blocks leads to a Wooden Chest. Open the Wooden Chest for a random treat, then continue along the path.

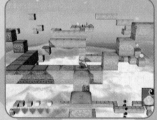

The moving block ahead takes you to a junction in the path. Head up the stepped blocks to the right.

The path abruptly ends at the top of the stepped blocks. Look below to see a small row of floating blocks and a block moving up and down next to them. Jump down to the lower blocks, then use the moving block to reach the path above.

Don't worry. You're almost done. Follow the path of blocks beyond the moving block, jumping the gaps as you go. The path eventually leads to a platform, where you find a trapped Spriteling. When rescued, the Spriteling informs you that there are 40 Spritelings to save in all.

If you look around carefully, you can see the Red Diamond on a platform far below the Spriteling. Drop to the Red Diamond and claim your hard-earned prize!

After you pop out of the eighth trapdoor, look for the pink Button atop the outside wall to the left of the Steel Trapdoor. Punch the pink Button to activate it, then continue onward to the left.

Line up with the foot imprint at the left edge of this ledge and jump to the closest Glue Globe as it falls down the sand cascade to the left. Jump across the cascading Glue Globes, collecting the Gold Statue part that hovers in the middle of the sand cascade.

Sparkle Land: Pecan Sands

Step 14

Proceed up the steps to the left of the cascading Glue Globes. A trio of Flying Spades drops in to attack you when you come to a dark section of the temple wall. These enemies are similar to the Monstrous Magnets you encountered in Beanstalk Way. Stun and throw them at the dark section of the temple's wall to create platforms, then use those platforms to reach the top of the temple.

Step 15

Now that you've reached the top of the temple, you're very near the goal. The only thing left in your way is a Stone-Cold Statue that blocks a ladder to the Goal Trapdoor. Defeat the Stone-Cold Statue by repeatedly punching its green, glowing weak spots.

As usual, a Garlic Dispenser stands near the goal. Stop for a second to fill up on Garlic before proceeding.

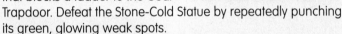
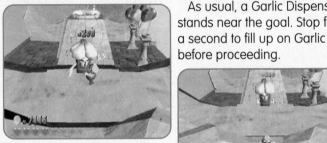

The purple Button's Treasure Chest is out on the ledge near the Garlic Dispenser. Open the Treasure Chest to collect the Monarch Mask!

On the exact opposite ledge from the purple Button's Treasure Chest you find the pink Button's Treasure Chest. Open the pink Button's Treasure Chest to receive the final treasure from this area, the Nintendo GameCube. Now that's one *sweet* treasure!

Only one thing left to do now! Climb up the ladder and stand next to the Goal Trapdoor. Feed the stone statue six Red Diamonds to get rid of it. When the stone statue is gone (and Wario's Heart Meter is full), Ground Pound the Goal Trapdoor to face the area boss.

Area Boss: Ironsider

The boss of Pecan Sands area is Ironsider. This powerful boss is made of solid, tempered iron! You can't damage the Ironsider with mere punches. You have to improvise.

As soon as the fight begins, run up to and punch one of the giant fists that drop from above. Keep punching the fist until it's stunned, then pick it up and throw it at the Ironsider. You don't need to use a Power Throw. A regular throw works just fine. Each successful throw knocks out one of the Ironsider's five health skulls.

The Ironsider moves by jumping to one of the nine solid squares on the ground of the arena. When he lands on a square, he sends out a powerful shock wave. Jump the Ironsider's shock waves to avoid taking damage.

The Ironsider begins to breathe wide-sweeping bursts of fire. There's only one sure way to avoid this powerful attack: Execute a Ground Pound to burrow into the sand. You're immune to the Ironsider's fire while stuck in the sand, but the large fists can still damage you in your vulnerable state.

Continue to stun the large fists and hurl them at the Ironsider while avoiding his powerful attacks. When you knock out all five of his health skulls, you've defeated the Ironsider.

Sparkle Land: Captain Skull's Showdown

The fight against Captain Skull, the Sparkle Land stage's boss, takes place on a broken pirate ship with a gaping hole in the middle. Captain Skull is the most difficult boss in *Wario World*, and defeating him requires skill and precision rather than all-out button mashing.

Captain Skull's Attacks

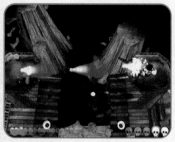

Captain Skull is a sea-terrorizing pirate to the root—he even has a giant cannon for an arm! He makes good use of this arm cannon, blasting energy projectiles and flaming cannonballs at you from long range.

Every once in a while, Captain Skull powers up a mega attack. He aims his arm cannon and summons energy, then unleashes an enormous, volatile cannonball. The attack is devastating if it hits, but it's usually easy to dodge once you learn the trick.

Captain Skull always aims and fires the huge cannonball where you're standing when he first begins to power up the attack. When Captain Skull's arm cannon begins to power up, run far away!

After losing a few health skulls, Captain Skull blocks every punch you throw at him by using his arm cannon as a shield. If you continue to punch Captain Skull while he's blocking, he becomes enraged and flashes! He then executes a fast spinning attack—his one and only close-range assault.

Fighting Captain Skull

Captain Skull is a pushover at first. All you have to do is get close to him and punch away until he's stunned. Pick him up and execute a painful Piledriver to knock out one of his five health skulls.

After he's lost three health skulls, Captain Skull becomes more difficult to stun because he blocks your punches with his arm cannon. You must find another way to stun the evil captain.

To stun Captain Skull after he begins to block your punches, Power Throw projectiles at him. This works best if you're both standing atop the two lookout towers on either side of the broken pirate ship. Use the glowing energy rings to bounce up to a lookout tower when Captain Skull is atop the opposite one. Use Wario's shadow as a guide to a safe landing on top of the lookout tower.

Sparkle Land: Captain Skull's Showdown

Stay on top of the opposite lookout tower as long as Captain Skull doesn't fire a giant cannonball at you. Eventually, Captain Skull fires a volley of flaming cannonballs over to your lookout tower. If you stand near the lookout tower's edge that's closest to Captain Skull on the opposite tower, the flaming cannonballs usually miss you.

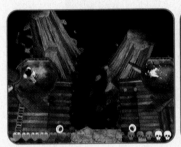

Pick up one of the cannonballs after it's cooled off and turn to face Captain Skull on the opposite tower. Quickly charge up a Power Throw, take aim, and fire! A well-aimed cannonball flies over to Captain Skull, smacking him upside the head.

Being hit with the cannonball stuns Captain Skull, but you have to move quickly to reach him. Jump down and land on the glowing energy rings, which propel you high into the air. Then, using Wario's shadow as a guide, hold down ← or → to sail over to the opposite deck's energy ring.

Land on the opposite energy ring to bounce up onto Captain Skull's lookout tower. Pick up the still-stunned captain and execute a powerful Piledriver. This is the fastest and easiest way to damage Captain Skull after he begins to block your punches. To reach the stunned boss before he wakes up, get comfortable at using the energy rings.

Continue to stun Captain Skull by Power Throwing his cannonballs back at him when he's standing atop one of the ship's lookout towers. Use the pair of energy rings to reach the stunned Captain Skull, then give him a punishing Piledriver! When you knock out all five of Captain Skull's health skulls, he's defeated! The fourth and final Giant Treasure Chest Key is yours.

Final Boss: Evil Black Jewel

After you defeat all four stage bosses and collect all four Giant Treasure Chest Keys, you can battle the evil black jewel. Run up to the Giant Treasure Chest in Treasure Square. A short cinema plays, showing the evil black jewel arising from the Giant Treasure Chest to do battle against Wario.

The Evil Black Jewel's Attacks

The evil black jewel has only three attacks. The most common is a laser that it emits from its single eye. The laser carves a line into the arena, which bursts into a wall of fire. Take the hit and jump through the wall of fire if you're in a rush, but it's safer to wait until the flames die down.

The evil black jewel tries to trap you between two walls of fire with its laser eye attack. Should you become trapped, the evil black jewel shoots out large fireballs that have limited homing capabilities. Dodge the fireballs until one of the walls of fire dies down, allowing you to escape.

When you're stuck between two walls of fire, the evil black jewel sometimes slams repeatedly onto the center of the arena, sending out multiple shock waves. Jump to avoid each incoming shock wave until you can escape.

Fighting the Evil Black Jewel

The evil black jewel hovers high above the center of the large, circular arena, completely out of reach. You must find a way to ground the evil black jewel so you can damage it.

As the fight begins, the evil black jewel releases five Spritelings trapped inside translucent crystals. The Spritelings become stuck in the floor around the outside of the circular arena.

Final Boss: Evil Black Jewel

Run around the outside of the arena, using the Dash Attack for extra bursts of speed. Punch each Spriteling's crystal as you run along. The crystals shatter, sending each Spriteling flying into the evil black jewel!

After you've smashed all five of the Spritelings' imprisoning crystals, the evil black jewel drops to the ground, stunned. Dash Attack over to the stunned evil black jewel, pick it up and execute a ground-shaking Piledriver!

The evil black jewel rises back into the air and releases five more crystallized Spritelings. Run around the arena, smashing each crystal, and give the evil black jewel a Piledriver when it's stunned. Use the Dash Attack for extra speed bursts.

The evil black jewel loses one of its eight health skulls every time you execute a Piledriver with it. You win the fight when all eight of the evil black jewel's health skulls have been knocked out.

The End

For rescuing all the Spritelings and helping them to defeat the evil black jewel, the Spritelings agree to rebuild Wario's castle and put everything back to the way it was.

If you rescued all 40 Spritelings from the game's eight areas, they perfectly rebuild Wario's castle for him. If you didn't rescue all 40 Spritelings, they can't quite restore Wario's castle to its full glory, but it's still better than nothing!

Wario's Checklist

So you think you've found everything in Wario World? Better be sure—Wario wants *all* his stuff back, posthaste! As you collect each treasure, find each Red Diamond and Gold Statue part, and rescue each trapped Spriteling, use the handy checklists in this section to track your progress. Just don't expect Wario to reward your hard work—that treasure is *his*!

Excitement Central: Greenhorn Forest

Wario's Treasures		Red Diamonds	
Treasure		Red Diamond	
Diamond	❏	1	❏
Ruby	❏	2	❏
Opal	❏	3	❏
Amethyst	❏	4	❏
Amber	❏	5	❏
Sapphire	❏	6	❏
Topaz	❏	7	❏
Emerald	❏	8	❏
Gold Statue Parts		Spritelings	
Gold Statue part		Spriteling	
1	❏	1	❏
2	❏	2	❏
3	❏	3	❏
4	❏	4	❏
5	❏	5	❏
6	❏		
7	❏		
8	❏		

Excitement Central: Greenhorn Ruins

Wario's Treasures		Red Diamonds	
Treasure		Red Diamond	
Porcelain Urn	❏	1	❏
Fine China	❏	2	❏
Ceramic Vase	❏	3	❏
Teapot	❏	4	❏
Precious Pot	❏	5	❏
Vase	❏	6	❏
Lucky Figurine	❏	7	❏
NES	❏	8	❏
Gold Statue Parts		Spritelings	
Gold Statue part		Spriteling	
1	❏	1	❏
2	❏	2	❏
3	❏	3	❏
4	❏	4	❏
5	❏	5	❏
6	❏		
7	❏		
8	❏		

Spooktastic World: Horror Manor

Wario's Treasures

Treasure	
Candlestick	☐
Silver Candlestick	☐
Forest Painting	☐
Crystal Ball	☐
Castle Painting	☐
Knight's Helmet	☐
Gladiator's Helmet	☐
Ornate Bag	☐

Red Diamonds

Red Diamond	
1	☐
2	☐
3	☐
4	☐
5	☐
6	☐
7	☐
8	☐

Gold Statue Parts

Gold Statue part	
1	☐
2	☐
3	☐
4	☐
5	☐
6	☐
7	☐
8	☐

Spritelings

Spriteling	
1	☐
2	☐
3	☐
4	☐
5	☐

Thrillsville: Shivering Mountains

Wario's Treasures

Treasure	
Nice Glass	☐
Ancient Chalice	☐
Nice Saucer	☐
Ornate Decanter	☐
Glass Decanter	☐
Nice Cup	☐
Glass Bowl	☐
Jade Box	☐

Red Diamonds

Red Diamond	
1	☐
2	☐
3	☐
4	☐
5	☐
6	☐
7	☐
8	☐

Gold Statue Parts

Gold Statue part	
1	☐
2	☐
3	☐
4	☐
5	☐
6	☐
7	☐
8	☐

Spritelings

Spriteling	
1	☐
2	☐
3	☐
4	☐
5	☐

Spooktastic World: Wonky Circus

Wario's Treasures

Treasure	
Bugle	☐
Tambourine	☐
Triangle	☐
Clarinet	☐
Trombone	☐
Sax	☐
Drum	☐
Nintendo 64	☐

Red Diamonds

Red Diamond	
1	☐
2	☐
3	☐
4	☐
5	☐
6	☐
7	☐
8	☐

Gold Statue Parts

Gold Statue part	
1	☐
2	☐
3	☐
4	☐
5	☐
6	☐
7	☐
8	☐

Spritelings

Spriteling	
1	☐
2	☐
3	☐
4	☐
5	☐

Thrillsville: Beanstalk Way

Wario's Treasures

Treasure	
Nice Goblet	☐
Violin	☐
Earring	☐
Jeweled Sword	☐
Gold Tiara	☐
King's Crown	☐
Nice Scepter	☐
Game Boy Advance	☐

Red Diamonds

Red Diamond	
1	☐
2	☐
3	☐
4	☐
5	☐
6	☐
7	☐
8	☐

Gold Statue Parts

Gold Statue part	
1	☐
2	☐
3	☐
4	☐
5	☐
6	☐
7	☐
8	☐

Spritelings

Spriteling	
1	☐
2	☐
3	☐
4	☐
5	☐

Sparkle Land: Mirror Mansion

Wario's Treasures

Treasure

Big Mirror	❑
Antique Clock	❑
Gold Mirror	❑
Bronze Mirror	❑
Gold Clock	❑
Stained Glass	❑
Crazy Glasses	❑
Gold Pocket Watch	❑

Gold Statue Parts

Gold Statue part

1	❑
2	❑
3	❑
4	❑
5	❑
6	❑
7	❑
8	❑

Red Diamonds

Red Diamond

1	❑
2	❑
3	❑
4	❑
5	❑
6	❑
7	❑
8	❑

Spritelings

Spriteling

1	❑
2	❑
3	❑
4	❑
5	❑

Sparkle Land: Pecan Sands

Wario's Treasures

Treasure

Ancient Relief	❑
Ancient Necklace	❑
Ancient Ring	❑
Small Pyramid	❑
Ancient Bracelet	❑
Anubis Statue	❑
Monarch Mask	❑
Nintendo GameCube	❑

Gold Statue Parts

Gold Statue part

1	❑
2	❑
3	❑
4	❑
5	❑
6	❑
7	❑
8	❑

Red Diamonds

Red Diamond

1	❑
2	❑
3	❑
4	❑
5	❑
6	❑
7	❑
8	❑

Spritelings

Spriteling

1	❑
2	❑
3	❑
4	❑
5	❑

Wario Ware™, Inc. Mega Microgame$ Trial Versions

After you connect the Game Boy Advance and turn on the power, have Wario punch one of the *Wario Ware, Inc. Mega Microgame$* trial version icons that appear near the Giant Treasure Chest in Treasure Square. A message informs you that the selected trial version is being downloaded onto your Game Boy Advance. When the download completes, press Ⓐ at the title screen and enjoy!

Collecting all eight treasures from an area in *Wario World* unlocks a *Wario Ware, Inc. Mega Microgame$* trial version. If you collect all the treasures from each area in the game, you unlock eight trial versions!

Connecting a Game Boy Advance

To play the exciting *Wario Ware, Inc. Mega Microgame$* trial versions, you need a Game Boy Advance and a Nintendo GameCube/Game Boy Advance Link Cable. Connect the Game Boy Advance to the GameCube by plugging the Link Cable into the second controller slot, then turn on the Game Boy Advance.

After you download a trial version, you can disconnect your Game Boy Advance and take it anywhere. The trial version remains on your Game Boy Advance until you turn off the power.

If the download fails, you receive an error message. Make sure the Nintendo GameCube/Game Boy Advance Link Cable is properly connected and try again. You cannot have a game inserted in the Game Boy Advance while downloading or playing a *Wario Ware, Inc. Mega Microgame$* trial version.

Trial Version Tips

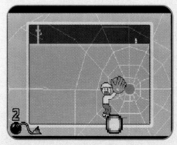

If you're stuck on a certain trial version or can't figure out what you're supposed to do, you've come to the right place. The following hints and tips help you become the best *Wario Ware, Inc. Mega Microgame$* trial version player you can be.

Wario Ware, Inc. Mega Microgame$ Basics

Wario Ware, Inc. Mega Microgame$ are simple yet challenging games that last only a few seconds. Anyone can play and enjoy them!

You get a one- or two-word explanation of what you need to do to pass each Microgame—"Jump!" or "Dodge!", for example.

A sub-screen appears before and after each Microgame. At the sub-screen, Wario grins when you successfully pass one Microgame, and then you're thrown into the next one. If you fail to complete a Microgame for any reason, including running out of time, Wario grimaces at the sub-screen, and one of the four indicators dims. When all four indicators are dimmed, the game is over.

The object is to see how far you can progress through each trial version. There's no end to the Microgame$, they just keep coming and steadily become more difficult to pass. The game speeds up at certain intervals and slows down at others, adding to the overall challenge.

Trial Version I

After properly connecting your Game Boy Advance, punch the left-most *Wario Ware, Inc. Mega Microgame$* trial version icon on the left side of the Giant Treasure Chest in Treasure Square. Download the first trial version, then press Ⓐ at the title screen to start the game.

Press Ⓐ to jump over the mobile that cruises toward you. The mobile sometimes pauses for a second, which can throw off your timing. Wait for it to get close, then jump.

 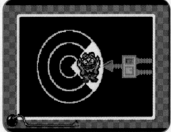

Press Ⓐ to stop Wario from spinning around in this dizzying Microgame. Line up the white pie slice with the red pointer to stop Wario. Watch out! The pie slice gets smaller as you play.

 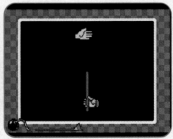

Patience is the key to beating this Microgame. Wait for the hand above to drop the pink stick, then press Ⓐ as the stick falls past the lower hand. The stick gets shorter as you play.

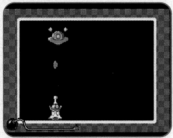

You need quick reflexes to pass this challenging Microgame. Move around and press Ⓐ to fire a bullet at the spaceship above. As you progress through the game, there are more spaceships to destroy. You fail if you miss one spaceship, so aim carefully!

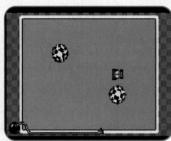

In this challenging Microgame, avoid the rolling, checkered balls that try to flatten you. Keep a careful eye on the balls and stay clear of them. In later levels, you must dodge more balls.

This Microgame tests your reflexes. Press Ⓐ to grab the cup as it zips past Wario. You get only one chance, so don't miss.

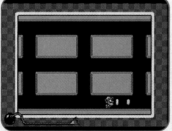

Here you must move Wario around and collect the nearby coins. More coins appear in later levels. Instantly determine the shortest route to collect them all within the time limit.

Trial Version 2

After properly connecting your Game Boy Advance, punch the *Wario Ware, Inc. Mega Microgame$* trial version icon that's second from the left on the left side of the Giant Treasure Chest in Treasure Square. Download the second trial version, then press Ⓐ at the title screen to start the game.

Press Ⓐ when the skier reaches the hill's dark-blue section to hit the jump and soar through the air. The dark-blue section narrows as you reach the higher levels, making it more difficult to time your jump.

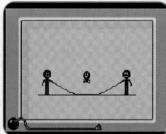

This Microgame has you jumping rope. Watch the rope carefully and press Ⓐ to jump when it lowers. In later levels, your character becomes heavier and can't jump very high, making the rope-jumping more challenging.

Focus your power to chop a log in this tricky Microgame. Closely watch the power bar on the screen's right side, and press Ⓐ when the bar fills up to the red section. The bar's red area is smaller in later levels.

The object of this Microgame is to steer around the large white ball and reach the goal before time expires. Watch out—the goal becomes smaller in the later levels.

Catch the ball before it smashes through the screen in this Microgame. Move your character around and position your glove to catch the ball as it curves toward the screen. Your glove gets smaller as you progress through the game.

 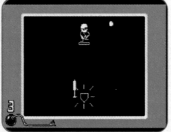

A pitcher hurls the heat toward home plate in this Microgame. Watch the pitch carefully to judge whether it's a fastball or a change-up, then press Ⓐ to smack a home run.

Move the trampoline from side to side to keep the little man bouncing through the air. The trampoline gets smaller in later levels.

Trial Version 3

 After properly connecting your Game Boy Advance, punch the *Wario Ware, Inc. Mega Microgame$* trial version icon that second from the right on the left side of the Giant Treasure Chest in Treasure Square. Download the third trial version, then press Ⓐ at the title screen to start the game.

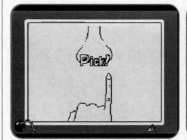 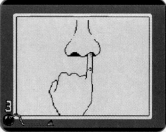

This gross Microgame actually has you picking your nose! Press Ⓐ when the finger is lined up with a nostril for a successful pick. As you progress through the game, you have to line up two fingers at once.

In this odd Microgame, pinch a little creature with tweezers. Press Ⓐ when the tiny creature jumps to pass this odd Microgame.

 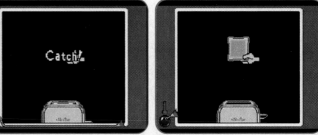

Catch the toast when it pops out of the toaster. It's easier to catch the toast when it begins to drop than to snag it on the way up. In later levels, the toast has numerous bite marks, making it harder to grab.

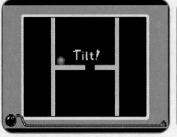 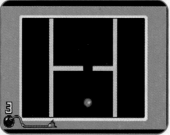

Tilt the machine to make the ball drop through the hole in this Microgame. Don't tilt too much or the ball rolls past the hole. At higher levels, you must tilt the ball through several holes.

 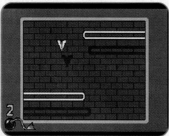

Steer the paper airplane in wide, zigzagging turns around the long barriers. The barriers get bigger and wider as you progress through the game, making them more difficult to avoid.

Ready, set, thread! That's right—thread the needle by moving the hand up or down to line up with the hole. The hand moves toward the needle slowly, so don't move it up or down too soon.

 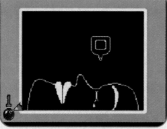

This person needs to wet his dry eyes. Press Ⓐ when the squirt bottle is over the person's eye to wet it with a drop. The bottle is positioned higher and moves faster in the later levels, making it tough to line up.

Trial Version 4

After properly connecting your Game Boy Advance, punch the right-most *Wario Ware, Inc. Mega Microgame$* trial version icon on the left side of the Giant Treasure Chest in Treasure Square. Download the fourth trial version, then press Ⓐ at the title screen to start the game.

Assemble a robot out of three parts by lining up the lower parts so that the falling parts stack up on them. It doesn't have to be perfect (as you can see by the picture above). Just catch all the parts as they fall.

It's not easy defending the universe from evil aliens, but the pay is good! Line up your crosshairs with the alien spacecraft and press Ⓐ to blast them into bits. You must destroy several more spaceships as you reach the higher levels.

This cool Microgame has you dodging asteroids in your spaceship. Blast off with Ⓐ; release the button to drop down again. The later levels pit you against many more asteroids.

Dodge the fireballs that the alien bases fire at your ship in this exciting Microgame. Move your ship forward, backward, up or down as you avoid the incoming fire. You have to dodge several more fireballs as you progress through the game.

Rapidly press Ⓐ to make the little creature chomp the shapes. The faster you press Ⓐ, the faster you chomp.

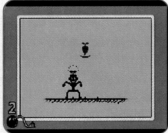

These Microgame$ are weird! In this one, move the man over to the small plant that sprouts up and press Ⓐ to pluck it from the ground. In later levels, you have to pluck up several plants.

This Microgame tests your hand-eye coordination. Press Ⓐ to make the lizard's tongue dart out and grab the heart circling in front of it. You have to lick several hearts at once as you progress through the game.

Selected Versions

The *Wario Ware, Inc. Mega Microgame$* icons on the right side of the Giant Treasure Chest in Treasure Square are selected versions of the four trial versions. These selected versions feature just one Microgame each, which you play over and over again. See how well you can do in each one.

Selected Version 1

After properly connecting your Game Boy Advance, punch the right-most *Wario Ware, Inc. Mega Microgame$* trial version icon on the right side of the Giant Treasure Chest in Treasure Square. Download the first selected version, then press Ⓐ at the title screen to start the game.

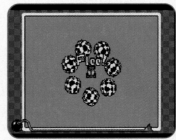

This is the "Flee" Microgame found in the first trial version. Move your little Indy car around and flee from the giant checkered balls that roll around trying to crush it. You have to dodge many more balls as you progress through the game.

Selected Version 2

After properly connecting your Game Boy Advance, punch the *Wario Ware, Inc. Mega Microgame$* trial version icon that's second from the right on the right side of the Giant Treasure Chest in Treasure Square. Download the second selected version, then press Ⓐ at the title screen to start the game.

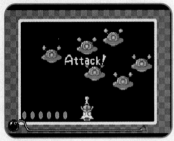

This is the "Attack" Microgame found in the second trial version. You must destroy the alien spaceships that fly from side to side overhead. More spaceships appear as you progress through the game, and you fail if you miss one shot.

This is the "Chomp" Microgame found in the fourth trial version. Press Ⓐ as fast as you can to chomp all of the shapes. As you can see from the screenshot above, the later levels have a whole lot of shapes to chomp.

Selected Version 3

After properly connecting your Game Boy Advance, punch the *Wario Ware, Inc. Mega Microgame$* trial version icon that's second from the left on the right side of the Giant Treasure Chest in Treasure Square. Download the third selected version, then press Ⓐ at the title screen to start the game.

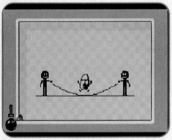

This is the rope-jumping Microgame found in the third trial version. Press Ⓐ when the rope lowers to jump it. You must jump the rope three times to pass each level. The rope turns faster as you progress, and your character makes shorter jumps.

Selected Version 4

After properly connecting your Game Boy Advance, punch the left-most *Wario Ware, Inc. Mega Microgame$* trial version icon on the right side of the Giant Treasure Chest in Treasure Square. Download the fourth selected version, then press Ⓐ at the title screen to start the game.

Modernist
Photographs

Modernist
Photographs

from the National Gallery of Canada

Ann Thomas

Ottawa, 2007

Modernist Photographs is the first in a series of publications focusing on selected masterpieces from the Photographs collection of the National Gallery of Canada.

The exhibition *Modernist Photographs from the National Gallery of Canada* is organized and circulated by the National Gallery of Canada.

Itinerary
National Gallery of Canada
4 May – 26 August 2007

The Rooms, Provincial Art Gallery Division, St. John's, Newfoundland and Labrador
14 January – 17 March 2008

Glenbow Museum, Calgary
18 October 2008 – 22 February 2009

Art Gallery of Hamilton
5 September – December 2009

National Gallery of Canada
Chief, Publications Division: Serge Thériault
Editors: Usher Caplan and Danielle Martel
Picture Editor: Andrea Fajrajsl
Production Coordinator: Anne Tessier

Copyright © National Gallery of Canada, Ottawa, 2007

Printed in Canada

ISBN 978-0-88884-829-1

Designed by Fugazi, Montreal. Typeset in Helvetica Neue
Printed on Astrolite Silk by Tri-Graphic Printing (Ottawa) Limited

Library and Archives Canada Cataloguing in Publication
National Gallery of Canada
Modernist photographs / Ann Thomas.
Exhibition catalogue.
Issued also in French under title: Photographies modernistes.
ISBN 978-0-88884-830-7

1. Photography, Artistic – Exhibitions. 2. Modernism (Art) – Exhibitions. 3. Photograph collections – Ontario – Ottawa – Exhibitions. 4. National Gallery of Canada – Exhibitions.
I. Thomas, Ann II. Title.

TR646.C3N37 2007   779.074'71384   C2007-986000-1

Distribution
ABC Art Books Canada
www.abcartbookscanada.com
info@abcartbookscanada.com

Cover
Franz Roh, *Untitled* (cat. 57)

Contents

Foreword

Modernist Photographs from the National Gallery of Canada is the first in a series of exhibitions and publications that will highlight the strengths of the National Gallery's world-class collection of photographs. International in scope, the collection illustrates the history of the medium from its beginnings until the present day. Launching this series in the year 2007 with an exhibition devoted to masterpieces of modern photography is particularly timely, as it not only celebrates the collection's fortieth year but also marks the hundredth anniversary of Picasso's creation of the modernist icon *Demoiselles d'Avignon*, a canvas that revolutionized the Western world's perceptions of what art could be in the twentieth century.

Modernist photographers explored the boundaries of their medium seeking to create a visual language that would proclaim its unique properties, represent the world about them from fresh perspectives, and express the power of abstract form. In so doing, they won an autonomous status for photography. Despite the art's intensely experimental bent, there was also an awareness of how photographic images from the past could reveal new possibilities to the modern sensibility, thus casting former practices in a different light while creating legacies for future generations of practitioners. The range and depth of the Gallery's collection has made it possible for Canadian as well as international visitors and scholars to enjoy this vital dialogue between past and present that continues between photographers even today.

The richness of the collection could not have been achieved without the support of many generous donors, who took on our mission to develop it as if it were their own. Dorothy Eidlitz's gift of sixty-nine gelatin silver prints in 1968 included the first modernist works to come into the Photographs collection, among them Charles Sheeler's sublime modernist masterpiece, *Side of White Barn*. Phyllis Lambert, Founding Director of the Centre Canadien d'Architecture / Canadian Centre for Architecture, contributed by dedicating additional funds from 1979 to 1988 for purchases at a critical time in the collection's history. Her generosity allowed for the acquisition of a number of the works represented in the exhibition and reproduced in this publication. As well, in 1982 she donated a major group of works by Walker Evans. The National Gallery is also home to the Lisette Model archive and an impressive selection of her photographs, donated in 1991 by the late Joseph G. Blum, Executor of the Lisette Model Estate, through the American Friends of Canada Committee (now the Council for American Canadian Relations). More recently, the Gallery has been fortunate to enjoy the support of Tomas Feininger, son of the modernist photographer Andreas Feininger, who, along with the Estate of Andreas Feininger, has promised the gift of a number of works to the National Gallery collection. To all our donors, we would like to offer sincere thanks.

Pierre Théberge, O.C., C.Q.
Director
National Gallery of Canada

Acknowledgments

An exhibition of this calibre would not have been possible without the unwavering support that I have received from Pierre Théberge, Director, National Gallery of Canada, David Franklin, Deputy Director and Chief Curator, and the National Gallery's Board of Trustees. Their ongoing encouragement made it possible for me to add many of the major works that now grace the walls of this exhibition to the collection, including Paul Strand's *Barn Gaspé*, and Alvin Langdon Coburn's *Vortograph*, among many others. A further debt of gratitude is owed to David Franklin for the idea of this series of exhibitions based on the collection and for his encouragement throughout the realization of the current exhibition. For his support over the years for the continuing presence of photographs in the galleries, I thank Daniel Amadei, former Director of Exhibitions.

As they say about the imminence of death, there is nothing like a brutal deadline to focus one's powers of concentration. My National Gallery colleagues who worked with me on this project laboured under the same relentless schedule of delivery dates – and they all came through with flying colours. My sincere thanks to the following: Lori Pauli, Assistant Curator, Photographs, for contributing her insight and expertise in authoring a significant number of catalogue entries (cat. 18, 24, 38–40, 52, 57, 67, and 76–79); editors Usher Caplan, to whom I am deeply grateful for his unswerving dedication to clear and accurate communication, Danielle Martel, for her careful attention to detail in the French edition, and Marcia Rodríguez, for contributing her critical eye to the finishing touches; Picture Editor Andrea Fajrajsl, who proved resolute and supernaturally good-natured in the face of an overwhelming task, and Andrea Dixon, who was tireless in her efforts to track down copyright holders. Serge Thériault, Chief of Publications, was, as always, extremely supportive at every stage of the production. Anne Tessier ably coordinated the publication schedule just as her exhibitions counterpart, Cindy Hubert, attended to the exigencies of the exhibition schedule. I would also like to thank Karen Colby-Stothart, Chief of Exhibitions, for her assistance, John McElhone, Photographs Conservator, Jacqueline Warren, Documentations and Storage Officer, and Louise Chénier, Administrative Assistant, for cheerfully bearing the stresses and strains that inevitably accompany such projects. Mark Paradis, Chief of Multimedia Services, and his team deserve special kudos for their contribution. To David Bosschaart, Design Services, I owe thanks for designing the exhibition in the true spirit of modernism.

For ably contributing to the publication and exhibition, I take this opportunity to acknowledge François Martin of Fugazi, who from his first design presentation made clear his understanding of the nature of modernism and the strength of his commitment to produce the finest possible exhibition catalogue; research assistant Katherine Stauble, a pillar of support, who checked facts, contacted various sources for information, and handled the ceaseless barrage of demands made upon her time; and David Mitchell, an art history student at McGill University, who exceeded the requirements of his summer internship by contributing careful research to many aspects of the project, but especially to the entries on Jaromír Funke, Marcel Mariën, Charles Sheeler, and Jindřich Štyrský.

Little could have been achieved without the help of my many colleagues in other institutions and cities: Jaroslav Anděl, Artistic Director, DOX, Prague; Vladimir Birgus, Head of the Institute of Creative Photography, Prague; Flip Bool, Senior Curator, Nederlands Fotomuseum, Rotterdam; Xavier Canonne, Director, Musée de la Photographie, Charleroi; Malcolm Daniel, Curator in Charge, Department of Photographs, The Metropolitan Museum of Art, New York; Antonín Dufek, Curator, Moravian Gallery, Brno; the photographer T. Lux Feininger and his son, Charles Feininger;

Frits Giertsberg, Head of Exhibitions, Nederlands Fotomuseum; Ryuichi Kaneko, Curator, Tokyo Metropolitan Museum of Photography; Alexander Lavrentiev, art historian (and grandson of Alexander Rodchenko); Satoshi Nakamura, Tokyo; Gael Newton, Senior Curator of Photography, National Gallery of Australia, Canberra; Nissan Perez, Senior Curator of Photography, The Israel Museum, Jerusalem; Margarita Tupitsyn, art historian; Matthew Witkowsky, Assistant Curator, Department of Photographs, National Gallery of Art, Washington, D.C.; and Steven Yates, Curator of Photography, Museum of Fine Arts, Santa Fe.

Photographs dealers, photographers, collectors, archivists, and librarians, along with others who responded to our requests for more precise provenance information, include Christopher Albanese, Stuart Alexander, Gordon L. Bennett, Nathalie Boulay, Adam Boxer, Robert Bourdeau, Ferdinand Brueggemann, Caroline Cohen, Jeremy Cox, Stephen Daiter, Michael Dawson, Rodney de Charmoy Grey, Shelley Dowell, Dawn Troy, Lauren Mang, Paul Hertzmann, Edwynn Houk, Charles Isaacs, Etsuro Ishihara, Paul Katz, Rudolf Kicken, Hans P. Kraus, Jr., Naomi Lyons, Lauren Mang, Anthony Montoya, David Peckman, Jill Quasha, Gerd (Gerhard) Sander, Fern Schad, Arturo Schwarz, Andrew Smith, Barry Singer, Nancy Thaler, Anne Tucker, and Stephen White.

Matthew Bown, Peter Bunnell, James Enyeart, Jamey Gambrell, Valerie Hillings, Christina Kiaer, Christopher Phillips, and the late Robert Rosenblum made valiant efforts to track down works pertinent to our research.

The assistance of the following individuals in providing in-text photographs for the catalogue has been invaluable: Jaroslav Anděl; Alena Bártová, Museum of Decorative Arts, Prague; Jennifer Belt, Art Resource; Lucy von Brachel, The Metropolitan Museum of Art; Jacklyn Burns, The J. Paul Getty Museum, Los Angeles; Brian Camp, Robert Koch Gallery, San Francisco; Xavier Canonne; Danielle Currie, Vancouver Art Gallery; Sue Daly, Sotheby's, London; Geneviève Defrance, Fonds Mercator, Brussels; Holly Frisbee, Philadelphia Museum of Art; Barbara Galasso, George Eastman House, Rochester; Ann Gonzalez, San Francisco Museum of Modern Art; Yaffa Goldfinger, Tel Aviv Museum of Art; Susan Grinols, Fine Arts Museums of San Francisco; Leanne Handrick, National Gallery of Australia; Sabine Hartmann, Bauhaus-Archiv, Berlin; Jennifer Ickes, New Orleans Museum of Art; Charles Isaacs; Gottfried Jäger; Joelle Jensen, Ubu Gallery, New York; Hinako Kasagi, Nagoya City Art Museum; Rajka Knipper, August Sander Archiv, Cologne; Robert Knodt, Museum Folkwang, Essen; Kathleen Kornell, The Cleveland Museum of Art; Alexander Lavrentiev; Luke Leonard, Throckmorton Fine Art, New York; Jessica Marx, Art and Commerce; Margaret McKee, The Museum of Fine Arts, Houston; Barbara Moore, Library of Congress; Satoshi Nakamura and Ryuichi Kaneko, Tokyo Metropolitan Museum of Photography; Lisa Nugent, Lotte Jacobi Collection, University of New Hampshire; Ellen Promise and Erin Schleigh, Museum of Fine Arts, Boston; Sebastien Robcis, World Picture News; Eric Rocca, Edwynn Houk Gallery, New York; Nathalie Roy, Centre Canadien d'Architecture / Canadian Centre for Architecture, Montreal; Ina Schmidt-Runke, Galerie Rudolf Kicken, Berlin; Kathryn Schuessler, Center for Creative Photography, The University of Arizona, Tucson; Tracey Schuster and Julio Sims, The Getty Research Institute; Piper Wynn Severance and Devin Flanigan, LACMA (Los Angeles County Museum of Art); Amy Snyder, Hirshhorn Museum and Sculpture Garden, Smithsonian Institution; Eileen Sullivan, The Metropolitan Museum of Art; Justin Tiernan and Joanna Fink, Alpha Gallery, Boston; Margarita Tupitsyn; Callie Vincent, Amon Carter Museum, Fort Worth; Ann and Jürgen Wilde and Stefanie Odenthal; Peter Zimmermann, Akademie der Künste, Berlin; and Stacey Zwald, Oakland Museum of California.

My thanks are also owing to Jean-Marie Fallu, editor of *Gaspésie*, and Miroslav Fajrajsl, for his Czech to English translation skills.

Ann Thomas
Curator, Photographs
National Gallery of Canada

Introduction

A variety of influences shaped the art of photography during the modernist period. Foremost among these was a wide-ranging and vigorous debate about the nature of art, beginning at the turn of the century and continuing into the 1920s. It was a debate that gave rise to a welter of movements – Cubism, Futurism, Precisionism, Dada, Surrealism, Expressionism, Constructivism, and numerous others – all of which attempted to redefine what art was and how it would reflect not only the look of the modern world but also the condition of modernity itself.[1]

Around the time that the first wave of twentieth-century *isms* was making itself felt in Europe, photography was enjoying an increased degree of acceptance as art, at least in the eyes of many influential practitioners and art critics. This acceptance was still by no means universal or unconditional, as can be seen from the uproar over Maurice Maeterlinck's catalogue essay for the 1907 *Exhibition of Pictorial Photographs*, held in Montreal that year. A number of conservative local artists took umbrage at the passage in the essay that referred to photography as an art form, and they insisted that the pages with the offending remarks be glued together.[2]

In spite of this kind of resistance, photographers such as Hugo Erfurth, Alfred Stieglitz, and Edward Steichen persisted in demonstrating how photography could be made more personally expressive and reveal the mark of human creativity. They also aimed to dispel the common belief that photography was merely mnemonic, documentary, and mechanical. They did so by replacing photography's high informational content and its purportedly mechanical and uniform appearance with soft-focus, painterly forms on textured papers, in the hope that it would thus take its place in the hierarchy of art, alongside painting, traditional printmaking, and sculpture. Frederick Evans's *A Pillar of Chartres* (fig. 1) – one of the first photographic prints to enter the National

Fig. 1   Frederick H. Evans, *A Pillar of Chartres*, 1906?, platinum print. National Gallery of Canada, Ottawa (21717)

Gallery of Canada's collection – and Edward Steichen's *Nocturne – Orangery Staircase, Versailles* (fig. 2) reflect the extraordinary intelligence, competence, and seductive power of Pictorialism at its best.

In the United States, Alfred Stieglitz championed Pictorialist photography as an art form under the rubric of the Photo-Secession. The movement was supported by an impressive infrastructure that included a prominent exhibition space, the Little Galleries of the Photo-Secession (also known as 291, named after its Fifth Avenue address in New York), consisting of several rooms devoted initially to contemporary photography and later to avant-garde European painting and sculpture as well. It also had its own handsomely illustrated journal, *Camera Work*, which featured contemporary Pictorialist photography, avant-garde art, and critical writings on photography.[3] The Little Galleries, *Camera Work*, and Stieglitz's eloquent tutelage of the movement resulted in the development of a critical vocabulary that not only gave form to the ideas surrounding the conception and creation of the photographs that were being exhibited and published, but also placed them in the context of current advances in the other arts.

The desire to achieve standing within the hierarchy of traditional art practice was sufficiently intense for Clarence H. White and his group of Pictorialist photographers to organize an exhibition for the Ehrich Art Galleries in New York titled *Old Masters of Photography*. Dedicated to an earlier generation of photographers, including Julia Margaret Cameron, Lewis Carroll, and David Octavius Hill and Robert Adamson, it was shown at the Albright Art Gallery in Buffalo in January and February of 1915.[4] This was a timely event that paid homage to the origins of Pictorialism and signalled the final stage of a movement now faced with a succession of *isms* that were rapidly redefining art and rendering inconsequential the Impressionist and Post-Impressionist painting it had sought to emulate.

It soon became evident to serious Pictorialist photographers that if they were to maintain their status as artists, they would need to re-examine the objectives of photography in light of the changes occurring in other media. The Pictorialists' struggle for recognition had not been in vain, however, as it resulted in a strongly articulated aesthetic against which a new generation could rebel – and rebellion, it would seem, was the *sine qua non* of modernism. Adventurous photographers, fresh from making

photographs for art's sake, took their next cue from the modernist credo of art for art's sake and now rallied to the call of photography for photography's sake. Following the same pattern of assertion and retreat that could be seen in the other arts, these photographers abandoned edge-softening, textured photographic papers and moved away from processes like gum bichromate, which gave their prints a more atmospheric appearance, or platinum, which endowed them with a greater delicacy and grace. Instead they began to explore the sharp delineation of form, even lighting, and the smooth, undifferentiated surface of gelatin silver paper.

Some photographers were quick to respond to the challenge, as two of the earliest examples of modernist photography in the National Gallery of Canada's collection demonstrate. Charles Sheeler's *Side of White Barn* (cat. 61), with its simplicity of composition, precise geometry, and neutral tonality, and Alvin Langdon Coburn's *Vortograph* (cat. 21), with its fracturing of form through light, both verge on the abstract and show how well photography could indeed respond to new currents – in these instances, Precisionist painting and Vorticism.

Coburn went from sublimely moody gum bichromate prints like *Trevi Fountain, Rome* (fig. 3) to the more neutral surface of gelatin silver paper for the exploding forms of his Vortograph images. In producing a type of image that was so radically new, and in so many respects antithetical to the spirit of Pictorialism, he made his intentions perfectly clear: "There was a notion at the time that the camera could not be abstract, and I was out to disprove this."[5] Coburn's move toward abstraction related to various intellectual currents he was responding to at the time he was making his Vortograph series. Paul Strand, on the other hand, attributes his and Charles Sheeler's awakening specifically to "understanding a painting like a Villon or a Braque – things in which there is an enormous amount of movement and no recognizable content as a whole."[6]

One of the strongest manifestations of the drive to redefine the vocabulary of expressive photography was the introduction of abstraction, and works such as those by Francis Bruguière, Lotte Jacobi, and Gyorgy Kepes (see cat. 17, 37, and 39) show just how far photographers were willing to depart from the naturalism of late nineteenth-century photography. For many photographers abstraction proved to be the most radical divergence from past practice.

Fig. 2 Edward Steichen, *Nocturne – Orangery Staircase, Versailles*, 1908, gum bichromate and platinum print. National Gallery of Canada, Ottawa (33361)

Fig. 3 Alvin Langdon Coburn, *Trevi Fountain, Rome*, 1905, gum bichromate print in two colours, heightened with watercolour. National Gallery of Canada, Ottawa (21496)

In the United States, the first stirrings of change were manifested in the Clarence H. White School, which had been the spawning ground of the American Pictorialists. While White himself was apprehensive about acknowledging that Cubism "or any similar ism" had helped to shape the new look in photography, he was willing to concede that modern art's proclivity for "picture construction" had done so.[7]

Alfred Stieglitz, who had been a Pictorialist when he originally led the charge in the battle for photography as art, and then later attempted to take photography out of the Pictorialist era into a more modern "straight" aesthetic – "idea photography," as he liked to call it – retained in his own work a half-symbolist, half-modernist aesthetic approach.[8] He was one of those photographers who even as they embraced abstraction could not totally abandon Pictorialism. His stirring untitled photographs of clouds made between 1922 and 1935 (see cat. 67) express some of the tension between his desire to capture the appearance of the world and his need to be modern.

Most photographers coming into their own in the 1920s, and especially those who were trained in a variety of media, did not feel as compelled to retain a connection with earlier photographic practice. Man Ray's irreverence toward the solemn protocols and conventions of photography and indeed of all artmaking of the past are blatantly evident in his work. If art had once been considered an activity involving the correct observance of pictorial laws and requiring the honing of certain technical skills, Man Ray set out to flout both of these premises. He did this, in the first instance, by simply placing random objects on a sheet of photographic paper and exposing the ensemble to a light source, apparently seeking to communicate nothing grander than the serendipitous effects of a primitive process, the results of which just happened to be delightful (see cat. 46). Likewise, in photographing the wood-and-plaster constructions in the Institut Poincaré for his *Mathematical Objects* series, he revelled in the banalizing of artistic purpose and in the gutting of the models' original meanings, recontextualizing them as objects of purely aesthetic interest (see cat. 47).

Photographs made in accordance with the tenets of Surrealism were often deliberately abrasive and grotesque. In his series depicting the female dolls he himself had fabricated, Hans Bellmer sought to etch the images of their often dismembered and contorted bodies and body parts into the viewer's imagination (see cat. 8). Disturbing in an even more elemental way are Frederick Sommer's photographs of his kabbalistically composed innards and body parts of poultry (see cat. 64).

In Europe the expression of modernism in photography was more pluralistic. Part of the reason is that there was no one dominant figure codifying and maintaining control over art photography as there was in the United States in the person of Alfred Stieglitz. In Europe a number of photographers wielded significant influence – Man Ray in France,

Fig. 4 Alfred Stieglitz, *A Snapshot: Paris*, 1911, printed January 1913, photogravure. National Gallery of Canada, Ottawa, Gift of Dorothy Meigs Eidlitz, St. Andrews, New Brunswick, 1968 (34999.126)

László Moholy-Nagy and Franz Roh in Germany, Alexander Rodchenko in the Soviet Union, Jaromir Funke and Jaroslav Rössler in Czechoslovakia – and they typically came out of a broad grounding that included painting, sculpture, and filmmaking (or, as in the case of Roh, art criticism). Moholy-Nagy, in his 1925 book *Malerei, Fotografie, Film*, showed a 1911 work by Stieglitz, *A Snapshot: Paris* (fig. 4), and captioned it: "The triumph of Impressionism, or photography misunderstood. The photographer has become a painter instead of using his camera *photographically*." By way of contrast, Moholy-Nagy offered a variety of other photographs that, in his view, better reflected the modern age, ranging from strictly scientific studies (macrophotographs of insects, x-rays, spectrographs) to commercial studio portraits, artistic photographs, and advertising photographs.

In urging photographers to re-examine the vocabulary of their art, Moholy-Nagy insisted that photography "has a field of its own, with its own laws governing its means, and that the point is to make use of these laws and to develop them wherever possible."[9] He also suggested that practical experiments be conducted in photography "in order to acquire the right finger-tip feel for the specific laws that govern its means." His examples included making photographs of structures and textures, recording the manifold effects of the play of light on different material surfaces (as he himself would do in his *Light-Space Modulator* photographs; see cat. 52), using mirrors and unusual lenses, and photographing "rare views, oblique, upward, downward, distortions, shadow-effects, tonal contrasts, enlargements, micro-photographs."[10]

In addition to the publication of Moholy-Nagy's *Malerei, Fotografie, Film*, other important initiatives in photography occurred in Germany in the late 1920s, including the 1929 *Film und Foto* exhibition in Stuttgart, organized by the Werkbund, and the publication during that same year of Franz Roh and Jan Tschichold's book *Foto-Auge*, in which the range if not the actual selections closely followed Moholy-Nagy's 1925 publication, encompassing photojournalism, medical photography, film stills, and photograms. The only substantial difference was that there were more Surrealist images in *Foto-Auge*. Werner Graf's more technically oriented book, *Es kommt der Neue Fotograf*, also published in 1929, demonstrated new ways of approaching composition in photography, to the point of trickery and mannerism, and achieved renown for its confir-

mation of a modernist aesthetic in photography. The message contained in all of these enterprises was essentially the same: new angles, negative images, and near abstractions were *de rigueur*, compositions needed to be dynamic, using strong diagonals and bold cropping wherever possible, and form had to prevail over content.

These dictates of modernist practice might have been less entrenched in photography in Czechoslovakia, where a wide range of experimentation was encouraged, but photography was nonetheless a thriving form of modern expression. Inspired by Cubism's explorations of form and Surrealism's plumbing of the psyche, it was celebrated, along with film, as a medium well suited to addressing the complexity of the modern world. The Czech art historian Jaroslav Anděl has noted that "in no other country was avant-garde photography so well developed and so multi-faceted as in Czechoslovakia in the 1920s and 1930s."[11]

While the exchanges among avant-garde photographers often crossed national borders (as with Man Ray and Funke, for example[12]), Czech modernism also spawned its own indigenous avant-garde photography groups – Anděl estimates that there were at least half a dozen movements active in the country.[13] Devětsil, founded in 1920, nurtured a strong ongoing dialogue between the various movements and raised discussions about the roles of all their members, including photographers and filmmakers. Czechoslovakia seems to have been relatively free of the hierarchization of the arts that stifled the growth of modernist photography in many European countries. Antonín Dufek has claimed that Czech art made its most significant contribution to Surrealism through photography.[14]

In the Soviet Union, Rodchenko's photographs from the 1920s energetically incorporated the Constructivists' and Suprematists' reduction of form to simple, dynamic, geometric configurations. Rodchenko also drew upon theories and technologies from outside the art world, creating an aesthetic that married dynamic form to contemporary means of mass communication. According to Alexander Lavrentiev, Rodchenko's library contained books relating to the "fourth dimension" in space, microscopy, and physical cosmology.[15]

While the course of modernist photography was closely tied to theories being proposed in the realms of painting and sculpture, the new photographic vision could not have taken the form it did, and

would never have become so dominant, had it not embraced the new technologies that were steadily emerging in the early part of the twentieth century. At the same time, it should be noted that, broadly speaking, technological innovations were embraced by photographers only when they actually provided interesting ways of seeing and recording the world. New cameras, like the 35mm Leica launched in 1925, were celebrated for their ease of handling. The Leica became almost emblematic of the modern woman photographer, who associated its portability and rapid action with a new-found freedom (see cat. 9). Advances in camera design and lens manufacturing permitted much faster exposure times, making possible the "decisive moment" images of Henri Cartier-Bresson. The flash bulb became commercially available in the 1920s, and was used by Brassaï in the 1930s to photograph in cafés and on the street at night, but it was Harold Edgerton's development of a sophisticated high-speed electronic flash unit in 1932 that was truly revolutionary, revealing for the first time the details of processes and events that are too rapid for the human eye to discern (see cat. 22).

As far as techniques were concerned, there were few that had not been tried out in the nineteenth century, albeit in a more random and less iconoclastic manner. The making of photograms, by placing objects on light-sensitive paper, was introduced into twentieth-century practice by Christian Schad, El Lissitzky, László Moholy-Nagy, Man Ray, Franz Roh,

and others, but went back to William Henry Fox Talbot, the inventor of the negative-positive process in photography (see fig. 5). Collage, a playful and irreverent application used in many late nineteenth-century family albums (see fig. 6), and montage were intrinsic to Dadaist, Surrealist, and Constructivist art and photography. In the early years of photography, photomontage had been associated with O.G. Rejlander and Henry Peach Robinson. Even Lewis Hine, the American photographer who documented child labour, had on at least one occasion experimented with the technique, in an unusual effort to create a composite portrait of the "typical" child labourer (see fig. 7), in the style of the pioneering British eugenicist Sir Francis Galton. The insouciant use of photocollage and photomontage in the modernist period was deliberately intended to unsettle the viewer, as in Marta Hoepffner's *On the Waves of Dreams* (cat. 34), and to provoke, as in John Heartfield's *Adolf the Superman Swallows Gold and Spouts Junk* (cat. 33).

Although photomicroscopy was a nineteenth-century technique developed largely in the service of scientific investigation, the renewed interest with which it was received by some modernist photographers was evidently a response to the search for fundamental structure and pure abstract form. While Laure Albin Guillot's splendidly crafted and luxuriously printed images added to the pure visual pleasure of looking at abstract form, as did Dain Tasker's pursuit of beauty through transparency in

Fig. 5 William Henry Fox Talbot, *Specimen of Lace*, c. 1839–1845, salted paper print. National Gallery of Canada, Ottawa (33487.19)

Fig. 6 Canadian, late 19th century, *Playing-card Portraits of Janie Butt, Joseph Fleming, Mary and Catherine Butt, Geraldine Bonner, and Three Unidentified Sitters*, c. 1870, albumen silver prints with watercolour and india ink. National Gallery of Canada, Ottawa (23896.14)

Fig. 7 Lewis Hine, *Composite Photograph of Child Labourers Made from Cotton-mill Children*, 1913, gelatin silver print. National Gallery of Canada, Ottawa (22903)

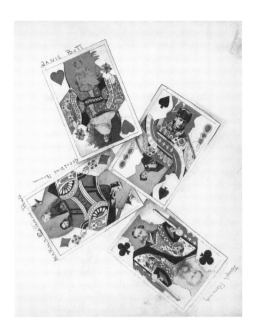

his positive x-ray of a lily (cat. 74), it was Carl Strüwe's photomicrographs that manifested the search for structure (see cat. 70).

Modernist photographs were not always made in response to the appearance of the world, however. In addition to the external pressures to change or to conform to new standards and models, there were also internal forces and individual experiences, as well as intuition. This was a more amorphous reality that ranged from personal discoveries to the making of images in the process of experimenting with tools or materials. It also involved being receptive to images made by other photographers, past and present. Often driven entirely by personal insight, this kind of artistic experience would also shape the direction of modernist photography. Eugène Atget's photograph of a window display of corset mannequins (cat. 5) might have been, to him, no more than the documentation of a building facade, but to the Surrealists images like this could evoke the unreal promises of dreams, stirring their sense of the serendipitous and the absurd. Walker Evans would find a different kind of inspiration in the work of Atget, one that came out of the photographer's structuring intelligence rather than the content of his images.

Modernist photographs sometimes addressed an even more elusive subject: the psychology of human behaviour and the expression of subconscious desires and dreams. The portrait and the nude were two subjects that especially lent themselves to the

expression of feelings about identity, relationships with others, and sexual desire. Hans Bellmer's photographs of the naked mannequins that he constructed are probably among the most extreme examples of psychological exploration in photography during the modernist period (see cat. 8). The human body was explored from a totally new perspective when photographers like Bellmer, Brassaï, and André Kertész (see fig. 8) looked at it from the fantasy-oriented and fragmented perspective of Surrealism. Faces might be blurred and distorted almost beyond recognition, their features cast in shadow or bleached out entirely by aggressive lighting, abandoning the notion of the portrait as an ennobling likeness and treating it instead as a vehicle for expressing a range of inchoate moods and emotions (see cat. 20 and 73).

Even though the modern period proved that photography, which had historically been associated with the recording of the external appearance of objects, places, and people, had the capacity to produce non-representational imagery, its practitioners continued to work in close proximity to the outside world, finding an expanded repertoire of subject matter in skyscrapers, bridges, planes, trains, machines, and factories. Generally speaking, it was not so much a question of what was photographed as how it was photographed. One exception to this was the subject that came to symbolize the age of modern photography in the late 1920s and early 1930s in both Germany and the United States: industry. From propeller shafts to factory smokestacks and from conveyor belts to boilers, it was celebrated in all of its manifestations.

During the period that preceded the Depression, and briefly again during the post-Depression years, the United States lived through a time of optimism about the progress of industry and the benefits of the machine. Paul Strand's close-ups of the internal mechanism of an Akeley movie camera (see fig. 16.1), Margaret Bourke-White's photographs for the Otis Steel Mills in Cleveland, Ohio, and for the Oliver Chilled Plow Company in South Bend, Indiana (cat. 12), and Charles Sheeler's views of the Ford Motor Company plant at River Rouge, are examples of industrial images that have greatly enriched the corpus of modern American photography. Many photographers were interested in the relationship between function and form in machinery, and were attracted by the slick, finely tuned precision of

modern manufacturing and the uniform, repetitive patterns of mass-produced objects. The towering forms of factory buildings, with their smoking chimneys, smelters and boilers, and complex networks of massive pipelines, apparently induced the same degree of passion that nineteenth-century painters had experienced in the face of epic landscapes. Photography had discovered the Industrial Sublime. The exhibitions *Machine Age* (1927) and *Machine Art* (1934), both held in New York, reflected the new sense of excitement and promise. Bourke-White believed that "any important art coming out of this industrial age will draw inspiration from industry" and that the "beauty of industry lies in its truth and simplicity."[16]

The principal exponent of industrial subject matter in Germany was Albert Renger-Patzsch. His views of architecture, factories, and machinery were seen with the same sharp and loving eye that he cast over the natural world. The New Objectivity style that he worked in favoured heightening the perception of the real rather than subverting it, placing great importance on the cool and meticulous rendition of details. Renger-Patzsch believed that photography provided the opportunity to "capture the magic of material things ... with a perfection beyond the means of painting."[17] He and his compatriot Karl Blossfeldt remained loyal to the subject of nature, adapting modernist ideals and the stylistic traits of the New Objectivity to render with precision and neutrality the forms of plants (see cat. 11 and 54). Carl Strüwe took this passion for the accurate and detailed description of natural forms to a new level of abstraction when he attached his camera to a microscope and sought to delineate the underlying patterns of nature (see cat. 70).

While many traditional subjects continued to be explored during the modern period, landscape proved to be of less interest to a generation of photographers whose work fed on the chaos and visual dynamics of the urban environment. Although not strictly a category of subject matter, the appearance of the everyday and the vernacular was particularly fascinating to modernist photographers, the most renowned among them being Walker Evans, who summed up his reasons for photographing simple wooden shacks, corrugated facades, and artless window displays (see fig. 9): "I lean toward the enchantment, the visual power, of the aesthetically rejected subject."[18] The "aesthetically rejected

Fig. 8 André Kertész, *Distortion No. 20*, 1933, printed before June 1976, gelatin silver print. National Gallery of Canada, Ottawa (31334)

Fig. 9 Walker Evans, *Photographer's Display*, c. 1936, gelatin silver print. National Gallery of Canada, Ottawa, Gift of Phyllis Lambert, Montreal, 1982 (19264)

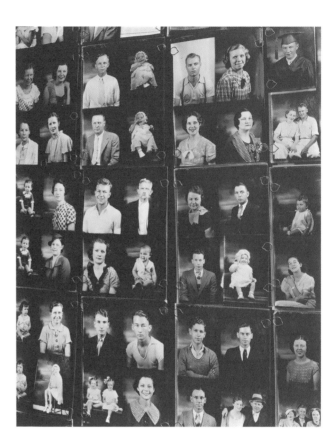

subject" also appealed to Margaret Watkins and Edward Weston, who would use common domestic items like a kitchen sink, a shower hose, or a bedpan in order to make some of their most memorable iconic images (see cat. 76, 77, and 79).

But nowhere was photography's involvement with the external world as contentious and oftentimes incendiary as in the realm of politics. It was here that clashes with authority occurred, when the propaganda machines of totalitarian regimes claimed the medium for their own purposes, and it was here that the proponents of social "content" stood opposed to the devotees of aesthetic "form."

In the Soviet Union, Alexander Rodchenko ultimately ran afoul of the political authorities, who monitored cultural activity as assiduously as they watched over potential dissidents in other areas. Along with the fate of certain Americans associated with the Photo League in the 1940s, the fall of the Russian avant-garde photographers constitutes one of the saddest tales in the history of modernist photography. Rodchenko's dynamic, truncated compositions and sharply angled views, made with great artistic conviction, incurred stinging criticism from Stalin's ideologues, who saw in Rodchenko's work the danger of fragmentation and disunity and "a departure from the proper balance between form and content."[19] Faced with the contemptuous comments of the new art experts – farmers, labourers, photojournalists – published in *Proletarskoe Foto*, and fully aware that greater censure would certainly follow, Rodchenko and seventeen of his colleagues, publicly capitulated in a tragic refutation of the artistic vision they had so passionately advocated. After being expelled in 1932 from the artists' union Oktjabr, which he had helped establish, Rodchenko announced remorsefully that he had learned his lesson and had now "plunged into photo-reportage and sports photography in order to cure myself from *stankovizm*" ("easelism," art-for-art's sake).[20]

In Germany that very same year, Nazi brownshirts went through the streets of Berlin ripping down poster versions of John Heartfield's *Adolf the Superman Swallows Gold and Spouts Junk* (cat. 33) and brawled with the young Communists who tried to stop them. In 1933 Heartfield fled to Prague; in 1938 he was on the run again and narrowly escaped to London.[21] In this instance, the Nazis were reacting specifically to the content of Heartfield's photocollages and not to the manner of presentation, but the

ferocity of their opposition to modern art in general would soon become apparent. In 1937 the government of the Third Reich commissioned an exhibition of so-called degenerate art ("entartete Kunst"), to publicly deride avant-garde painting and sculpture. Characterized by the art historian Stephanie Barron as "the most virulent attack ever mounted against modern art,"[22] the exhibition was part of a larger program by the Nazis to eliminate any cultural activity that diverged from their own romantic, *völkisch* ideal. In 1936 all of the available copies of August Sander's publication *Antlitz der Zeit* were seized and the plates for its production were destroyed because the portraits in it depicted ordinary citizens in a style that was realistic rather than idealizing, even showing examples of unemployed and handicapped people.

In the United States, most of the photographers who concentrated on social issues during the 1930s were either members of the Photo League, a left-wing organization based in New York, or were employed by one of the New Deal programs that hired artists to record the plight of the rural poor. While their photographs could be called documentary insofar as content was at least as important as form, many of these photographers departed from the more neutral position of their nineteenth-century forebears by implicitly advocating political and social change. The relatively temperate debates that took place among socially minded photographers in the United States, where formal explorations were far less radical than in Europe, arose out of the division between those who pursued the "fine print" ideal and those for whom content was supreme. Among the members of the Photo League there were individuals like Aaron Siskind who vehemently resisted the pressure to privilege content over craft. Photographers employed by the New Deal agencies sometimes had to contend with project supervisors who insisted on a strict adherence to photographic truth, meaning that the finished print was not allowed to depart in any way from what had been captured on the negative.

It was only in the late 1940s, however, that artistic freedom in the United States was challenged directly by the forces of political conservatism. Suspected of being a hotbed of Communist activity, the Photo League came under the scrutiny of the House Committee on Un-American Activities; monitoring of its members began in earnest, and in 1947 it was added to the Attorney General's list of subversive organizations. In 1949 the Photo League held its last exhibition. That same year, Lisette Model was placed under surveillance by the FBI as a suspected Communist.

By this time, modernism was already a cultural movement in decline, its momentum having been broken by the cataclysm of the Second World War and perhaps also by an inevitable exhaustion. For photography in particular, the modernist period had been one of significant advances. Viewed more clearly now in hindsight, modernist photography was more than just a rebellion against established pictorial conventions and accepted notions of beauty. It thrived on experimentation, and introduced a great array of new techniques and new kinds of subject matter. It was often socially engaged, playing a central role in the shaping of its own era. It evolved in close synchrony with the other arts of the period, both traditional and new, but also established an aesthetic that was entirely its own. It left a legacy of formal and conceptual innovation that would go on challenging future generations of photographers, as can be felt, for example, in the "dialogue" between the works of August Sander and Diane Arbus, of Albert Renger-Patzsch and Bernd and Hilla Becher, or of Walker Evans and Lee Friedlander. Most important of all, the modernist period in photography proved beyond doubt that the camera could be as powerful a tool of creative expression as any other in the history of art.

Note to the Reader

All dimensions – height × width in centimetres –
are of the image. If there is a border, the sheet size
is also noted. Inscriptions are handwritten by
the artist; annotations are by others, or are stamps.

Abbreviations

u.l.	upper left
u.c.	upper centre
u.r.	upper right
c.l.	centre left
c.	centre
c.r.	centre right
l.l.	lower left
l.c.	lower centre
l.r.	lower right
t.	along or at the top
b.	along or at the bottom
l.	left
r.	right
[...]	an erased or illegible portion of the inscription or annotation

1 Berenice Abbott
Springfield, Ohio 1898–1991 Monson, Maine
James Joyce 1926
Gelatin silver print, 30.5 × 26.9 cm
23878

Inscriptions **mount, l.r., *BERENICE ABBOTT***
Annotations **verso of mount, l.c., stamped, *PHOTOGRAPH / BERENICE ABBOTT***
Provenance **purchased from Jane Corkin Gallery, Toronto, 1980.**

Berenice Abbott is remembered for a range of contributions that she made to photography – her inspired photographic record of New York in the 1930s, her photographs illustrating scientific principles, her support of Eugène Atget's work, and her years of teaching photography at the New School in New York. She also has left us memorable portraits of celebrated literary and artistic figures of the 1920s, among them this bold portrait of James Joyce wearing an eye patch after one of his many eye operations. In contrast to most of the portraits of him, in which he gazes down in an apparent state of melancholy, here Joyce looks out over his left shoulder. Abbott greatly admired Joyce, and she had him sit for her on more than one occasion. The series of portraits of the writer wearing his eye patch is particularly engaging (see also fig. 1.1), not only for the way it captures the writer's vulnerability but also because the eye patch adds a strong dramatic touch. Abbott had a clear sense of how a portrait should not only capture the sitter's likeness but also communicate individual qualities revealed through expression and gesture. An intriguing self-portrait in the National Gallery of Canada's collection illustrates her interest in experimenting with new techniques, in this instance the use of a "distortion easel" of her own invention (fig. 1.2).

Abbott's first photographs were portraits. Having gained experience in Man Ray's portrait studio (after her return to Paris from a year-long sojourn in Berlin in 1923), she started to take her own photographs. A request from Peggy Guggenheim for a portrait sitting led to Abbott's establishing a studio in Paris in 1926. It was her work as a portraitist that enabled her to gain a reputation as a photographer. During the mid- to late 1920s her portraits of Parisian celebrities, along with those of Man Ray, adorned the walls of Sylvia Beach's famed Paris bookstore, Shakespeare and Company. They also formed part of two important exhibitions in Paris, the 1926 *Portraits photographiques* at the Galerie Au Sacre du Printemps and the 1928 *Premier Salon indépendent de la photographie*.[1] Speaking with an American journalist around the time of the latter exhibition, she shared her views on the principles that guided her practice: "A quick eye for drawing and a mountain of intuition are principal factors for a portraitist. Personally I strive for a psychological value, a simple classicism in portraits."[2]

Fig. 1.1 Berenice Abbott, *James Joyce, Paris*, 1926, gelatin silver print. The Metropolitan Museum of Art, New York, Purchase, Gifts in memory of Harry H. Lunn, Jr., and Anonymous Gifts, 1999 (1999.406)

Fig. 1.2 Berenice Abbott, *Portrait of the Artist as a Young Woman*, c. 1930, printed c. 1951, gelatin silver print. National Gallery of Canada, Ottawa, Gift of Dorothy Meigs Eidlitz, St. Andrews, New Brunswick, 1968 (20505)

Springfield, Ohio 1898–1991 Monson, Maine
Exchange Place 1933
Gelatin silver print, 23.7 × 6.2 cm
20507

Inscriptions   mount, l.r., *BERENICE ABBOTT*

Annotations   verso of mount, u.r., *221 / 14⅝ × 17*, c., *Exchange Place, N.Y. – 193*, c., stamped, *BERENICE ABBOTT / PHOTOGRAPH / 50 COMMERCE STREET / NEW YORK 14, N.Y.*

Provenance   Limelight Gallery, New York, bought by Dorothy Meigs Eidlitz, St. Andrews, New Brunswick, 1954; gift of Dorothy Meigs Eidlitz, 1968.

In 1921 Berenice Abbott moved from New York to Paris in order to study sculpture, an interest inspired in large part by earlier meetings with Marcel Duchamp and Man Ray in New York. Hired as a darkroom and studio assistant to Man Ray in his Paris portrait studio, Abbott found herself increasingly attracted to the medium of photography. In 1926 she established her own studio in Paris, where she made portraits of many of the prominent artistic and literary personalities of the day (see cat. 1). It was around this time that she became acquainted with the photographer Eugène Atget, whose haunting turn-of-the-century views of Parisian buildings, streets, and storefronts were to have a profound impact on her own development. Abbott also admired Atget's dedication to his work. After his death, she purchased his remaining glass-plate negatives and thousands of his prints, and she encouraged curators and scholars to recognize the contribution he had made to the history of photography.

In all likelihood it was Atget's photographs of Paris that inspired Abbott to return to New York in 1929 and to systematically chart its urban topography over the next ten years – from vertiginous skyscraper views to close-ups of architecturally nondescript storefronts (see fig. 2.1). This ambitious undertaking was eventually awarded funding through the WPA's Federal Art Project, and in 1939 a large selection of the photographs were published in the book *Changing New York*.

Exchange Place was an image that Abbott herself especially liked. "This photograph," she wrote, "always interested me; it was taken from Broadway, on about the tenth floor of a building that placed me as near as possible to looking straight down the street."[1] Exchange Place, located just south of Wall Street in the financial district of Manhattan, covers an area of about four blocks between Broadway and William Street. Its name is derived from the fact that it stands on the site of a seventeenth-century merchants' exchange; the street that Abbott refers to had previously been known as Oyster Pasty Alley, a path that once marked the way to British army fortifications. This particular print was exhibited at Helen Gee's Limelight Gallery in 1954 as part of a Christmas show, *Great Photographs*.

In creating her New York images Abbott worked with a large-format camera, probably an 8 × 10. In choosing to print just a narrow slice of the negative, she has accentuated the verticality and density of the view, and has underscored the way in which New York skyscrapers typically block the sun so as to create sharply contrasting areas of dark shadow and brilliant light.

Nightview, New York (fig. 2.2), made one year earlier, is another of Abbott's arresting images of the city in which she became a legendary figure in photography.

Fig. 2.1   Berenice Abbott, *Old Drug Store, Exterior, 46 Market Street, New York*, 1931, gelatin silver print. National Gallery of Canada, Ottawa, Purchased from the Phyllis Lambert Fund, 1981 (26640)

Fig. 2.2   Berenice Abbott, *Nightview, New York*, 1932, gelatin silver print. National Gallery of Canada, Ottawa, Gift of Dorothy Meigs Eidlitz, St. Andrews, New Brunswick, 1968 (20508)

3 Laure Albin Guillot

Paris 1879–1962 Nogent-sur-Marne, France

***Barley Root (Cross-Section),* plate XIX from *Micrographie décorative* before April 1931**

Photogravure, 27.4 × 21.5 cm

22369.19

Provenance **purchased from André Jammes, Paris, 1968.**

A genre of art photography known as decorative micrography emerged in Germany around the turn of the twentieth century, partly inspired by the publication of engraved micrographs of diatoms by the German protozoologist Ernst Haeckel. Decorative photomicrography flourished in Germany in the 1920s and 1930s in the hands of a number of practitioners whose works have entered into the history of twentieth-century photography. Although the French physician Alfred Donné had explored photomicrography as early as 1839, the genre was never as popular in France as it became in Germany. Laure Albin Guillot's photomicrographs are thus noteworthy not only for their sublimity of expression but also for representing the genre in France in the first half of the twentieth century.

Fascinated by the large collection of photomicrographs that she and her husband owned, Laure Albin Guillot began to focus her efforts on capturing their beauty in permanent form around 1930. In addition to working with popular subjects, including diatoms, she also transformed such unlikely objects as rhinoceros horns, buds of ash trees (fig. 3.1), and whale cartilage into motifs of visual fantasy. Her portfolio of photogravures, *Micrographie décorative*, a masterpiece of its kind, was printed and published by the distinguished firm of Draeger Frères in 1931. Founded in 1886, Draeger Frères had acquired a reputation for its innovative "Process No. 301," a method of gravure printing that they claimed was so lifelike as to be "startling." One reviewer of *Micrographie décorative* enthused: "Could any make-believe landscape hatched by the human brain ever equal, in fantasy, in poetry, in hallucinatory magic, the stirring architecture of crystallization? … What temple, what dream palace could bear comparison with a few grains of sand under the lens of a microscope?"[1]

Laure Meffredi began to practise photography in her late teens, not long after her marriage to Dr. Albin Guillot in 1897. Her first works were landscapes, and by the late 1920s she had ventured into the making of competent nude and portrait studies. *Nude Study* (fig. 3.2), another work by her in the collection of the National Gallery of Canada, probably dates from this period. Her photographs appeared regularly in the illustrated magazine *Vu* as well as in its rival publication *Photographie*.

In 1932 Albin Guillot was appointed director of the Archives Photographique d'Art et d'Histoire at the École des Beaux-Arts in Paris. Between 1936 and 1948 she produced photographic illustrations for several books, including Paul Valéry's *Narcisse*, Pierre Louy's *Chansons de Bilitis*, and Maurice Blain's *Illustrations pour les Préludes de Debussy*.

Fig. 3.1 Laure Albin Guillot, *Ash Bud (Cross-Section)*, before April 1931, gravure. National Gallery of Canada, Ottawa (22369.8)

Fig. 3.2 Laure Albin Guillot, *Nude Study*, c. 1925, gelatin silver print. National Gallery of Canada, Ottawa (39160)

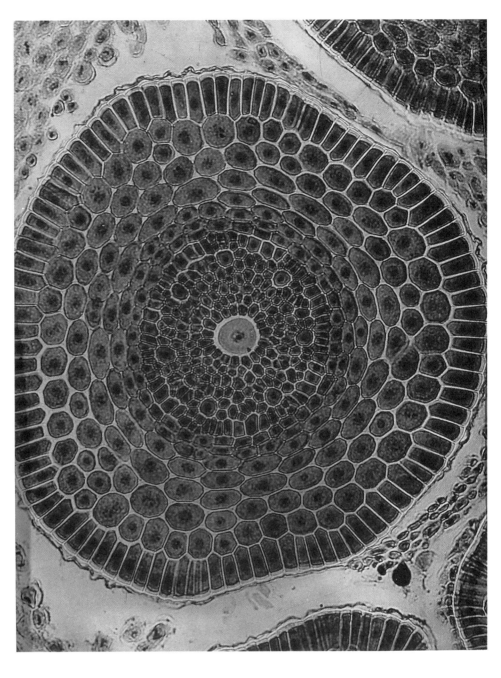

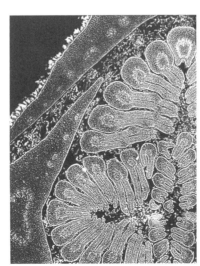

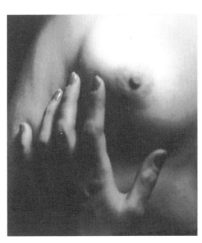

Mexico City 1902–2002 Mexico City

The Threshold 1947

Gelatin silver print, 24.4 × 19.4 cm

40067

Inscriptions   mount, l.r., *M. Alvarez Bravo / Mexico*

Annotations   verso of mount, l.c., *PF24955*

Provenance   Estate of Jack Lessinger, secretary to the Photo League, New York; Howard Greenberg Gallery, New York, 1988; bought by Thomas Walther, New York, 1989; purchased from Howard Greenberg Gallery, 1999.

Manuel Álvarez Bravo was born into an artistic family – his father was a writer, photographer, and amateur painter, and his grandfather had been a professional portrait photographer.[1] Forced to leave school at the age of thirteen because of his family's financial difficulties, he became a clerk in the Mexican Treasury Department, where he would continue to work in various capacities until 1931. He managed to further his interest in the arts, however, by enrolling in 1918 in music and painting studies at the Academia Nacional de Bellas Artes.

Álvarez Bravo came to maturity during the flowering of Mexico's artistic renaissance, and in a period in which photography was undergoing a burst of creative renewal throughout the world. His work, along with that of Tina Modotti, Águstin Jiménez, Emilio Amero, and Lola Álvarez Bravo (his first wife), reflects the new aesthetic concerns that were to give shape to Mexican modernism. While he was strongly affected by the epic imagery of the Mexican muralists José David Alfaro Siqueiros, Diego Rivera, and José Clemente Orozco, and by the paintings of the Mexican artist Rufino Tamayo, he was equally fascinated by the popular photography magazines of the period. In response to these combined influences, he ultimately aspired to create photographs that would express both his Mexicanness and his modernity. In 1923 he met the highly successful German-born Pictorialist photographer Hugo Brehme, and in October of that year he saw Edward Weston's photographs for the first time, at the Aztec Land Gallery in Mexico City.

Manuel Álvarez Bravo began his career in 1924, the same year that the Surrealist movement was launched in Europe with the publication of André Breton's first Surrealist manifesto. Throughout the following decade, he created his photographs in complete unawareness of the movement that would later adopt his work as emblematic of all it stood for. For Breton, Álvarez Bravo's photographs presented Mexico as "an inexhaustible register of sensations, from the most benign to the most insidious."[2]

The Threshold is one of Álvarez Bravo's cryptic, darkly sensual images of women. As in his iconic *Portrait of the Eternal* (fig. 4.1), there is a sense in it of the mysteriousness and vulnerability of the female body. All that we see of a human figure in *The Threshold* are the lower legs of a woman standing at the entrance to a room. Her bare feet rest on a paved floor, where large puddles spill into each other. In an eloquent gesture of avoidance, the woman's toes curl upward and away from the puddles. Natural light transforms this otherwise banal moment by falling like a spotlight on the scene. The light strikes the topmost puddle with a bright downward band, drawing the viewer's eye to the threshold, while the successive pools are etched in luminous outline. Álvarez Bravo was attuned to the way in which light both reveals and conceals, and he uses it here to focus our attention on the inscrutable drama being played out.

Although he clearly took pleasure in exploiting the mysterious suggestiveness inherent in black-and-white photography, Álvarez Bravo could also produce images like *Striking Worker Assassinated* (fig. 4.2) that are disturbingly direct. The enigmatic quality evident in this image was to become increasingly pronounced in his work after 1938.

Fig. 4.1   Manuel Álvarez Bravo, *Portrait of the Eternal*, 1935, gelatin silver print. Courtesy of Throckmorton Fine Art, New York

Fig. 4.2   Manuel Álvarez Bravo, *Striking Worker Assassinated*, 1934, gelatin silver print. National Gallery of Canada, Ottawa (20516)

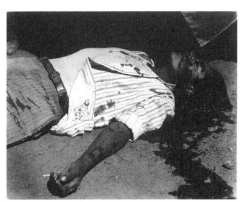

5 Eugène Atget

Libourne, France 1857–1927 Paris

Boulevard de Strasbourg, 10th Arrondissement, Paris 1912

Gelatin silver print, 22.5 × 17.7 cm

21114

Inscriptions   **verso of mount, u.c.,** *Bd de Strasbourg, c., #379*

Annotations   **mount, l.r.,** *261*

Provenance   **purchased from The Museum of Modern Art, New York, 1970.**

From 1898 until the year of his death, in 1927, Eugène Atget photographed the architecture of Old Paris, in the wake of the dramatic transformation that had occurred under Baron Haussmann's extensive modernization of the city in the mid-nineteenth century. It was in his comprehensive recording of the facades of surviving historic buildings that he happened to capture so many storefronts, inadvertently becoming a pioneer in the photography of store windows and their mannequins and merchandise (see fig. 5.1). But beyond merely documenting the storefront displays, his photographs show a fascination with the interplay between the reflections on the glass windows and the objects behind them. This would sometimes result in a mingling of Atget's own reflected image in the window or door – his camera on a tripod also visible – with the figures of the curious store employees peering out at the photographer. In *Au Bon Puits* (fig. 5.2) his silhouette is discernible in the lower-right door pane.

Unschooled in art, Atget nevertheless possessed a special talent for creating a visual narrative of the times he lived in. His abilities may have been due in part to his training as an actor at the Conservatoire d'Art Dramatique between 1879 and 1881. The difficulty of balancing his military service with his schooling proved an impediment to his progress, and this along with the handicap of having features that were "too large and discordant, and … ruled by a contracted intensity of will" limited him to being a bit-player with a touring company in the provinces.[1] Indulging his love of art whenever he was resident in Paris, Atget visited exhibitions with his friend the actor André Calmettes. It is possible that in so doing he encountered photographs exhibited in one of the Salons and was inspired to pick up a camera. While the precise date that Atget started to photograph is unknown, it is generally thought to be around the late 1880s. In 1892 he opened a photographic studio in Paris and began to supply artists with landscape, plant, and architectural views that could be used by them as *aides-mémoire* in their work. He also provided the service of photographing their paintings.[2]

In the early decades of the twentieth century, as marketing and advertising became increasingly aggressive and inventive, more and more photographers discovered the appeal of store windows and their reflections as subject matter. The absurd nature of many store displays, with their blank-faced mannequins (or truncated parts thereof – heads, torsos, legs) standing in for human models, caught the attention of Surrealist artists, who saw them as "found objects." Atget's *Boulevard de Strasbourg*, made in 1912, was reproduced along with two other photographs by him in a 1926 issue of *La Révolution surréaliste*; this particular image accompanied a story titled "Rêves" by the Surrealist author Marcel Noll.[3] As in many Surrealist creations, the connection between text and image remains loose, and the meaning to be extracted from their relationship is left largely to the reader's imagination. One could guess that the corsets in the window perhaps tie in with the protagonist's romantic dream fantasies about the king's daughter. The appeal of this image to avant-garde artists was made evident again by its appearance in Franz Roh and Jan Tschichold's influential 1929 book *Foto-Auge*. Roh must have been attracted to Atget's subject, as there is nothing in the picture's straightforward framing to have warranted its inclusion as an example of novel composition.

Fig. 5.1   Eugène Atget, *Avenue des Gobelins*, 1925, gelatin silver print. National Gallery of Canada, Ottawa (21227)

Fig. 5.2   Eugène Atget, *Au Bon Puits, 36 Rue Michel-le-Comte, 3rd Arrondissement*, 1901, printed later, albumen silver print. National Gallery of Canada, Ottawa (29134)

6   Herbert Bayer

Haag, Austria 1900–1985 Montecito, California

Metamorphosis **1936**

Gelatin silver print, 25.7 × 34 cm, sheet 27.9 × 35.3 cm

20536

Inscriptions   l.r., *Bayer 36*; verso, l.l., *Trial Proof*, l.c., *(fotoplastik) "Metamorphosis"*, l.r., *Bayer 1936*

Annotations   verso, l.l., *CC. 97*, l.r., *1000–*

Provenance   purchased from Stephen White's Gallery of Photography, Los Angeles, 1980 (Phyllis Lambert Fund).

Herbert Bayer moved from his native Austria to Germany after the First World War. From 1921 to 1923 he attended the Bauhaus in Weimar, where he studied mural painting and design under Paul Klee and Wassily Kandinsky. In 1924 he began to explore photography as an expressive medium and as a design element in his commercial work. By the end of the 1920s Bayer was working as the director of the Dorland Design Studio in Berlin and at the same time was experimenting with photographic techniques that would radically alter the documentary function of photographic images and thus change perceptions about the purported realism of the photograph. His photographic manipulations included the construction of scenes as well as the use of montage and collage to render the photograph a completely artificial object. László Moholy-Nagy's concept of *fotoplastiken*, which divorced the photograph from its origins as an ostensibly faithful reproduction of nature, appealed to Bayer's sense of innovation and creativity. By 1936 he had embraced this idea fully, creating a series titled *fotoplastiken*. Bayer claimed that the term *fotoplastik* signified for him the "plastic quality that dominates in these images." To make them, he would first construct various three-dimensional objects, which he then arranged as in a still life. He would carefully light these arrangements and photograph them. The resulting prints were touched up and airbrushed, and then they themselves would be photographed. It was from these final negatives that the *fotoplastiken* were produced.[1]

Bayer took pains to distinguish this elaborate technique from simple photomontage. Whereas photomontage refers to the projection and integration under the enlarger of several separate photographic negatives into one final image, Bayer stressed that his process involved setting up the scene with different elements before the photographic image was made.

Metamorphosis not only succeeds in making the photograph an image detached from naturalism and visible reality but also manages to subvert the traditional boundaries between still life and landscape by combining the two genres in one image. The creation of a dreamlike topography of spheres, cubes, cones, and oblongs through which the viewer is compelled to travel before reaching the familiar landscape of trees, sky, water, and horizon line conforms with the Surrealist notion of harnessing dream states and incorporating them into art. Other images in the series of eight that constitute the *fotoplastiken* portfolio, such as the *Self-portrait* (fig. 6.1), go beyond the transformation of reality to the creation of the grotesque.

Bayer also staged figures in uncommon outfits and poses to achieve a surreal or dreamlike mood, as in *Knight with Flowers* (fig. 6.2), in which he posed Friedrich Voredemberge-Guidewart in a medieval visor during a visit to a Swiss castle owned by the art patron Madame de Mandrot.

Fig. 6.1   Herbert Bayer, *Self-portrait*, 1932, gelatin silver print. Collection of the Center for Creative Photography, The University of Arizona, Tucson

Fig. 6.2   Herbert Bayer, *Knight with Flowers*, 1930, printed later, gelatin silver print. National Gallery of Canada, Ottawa (29158)

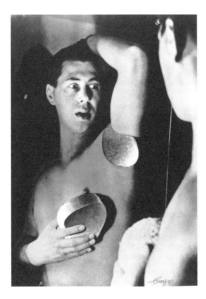

London 1904–1980 Broadchalke, England
Marlene Dietrich c. 1935
Gelatin silver print, 24.6 × 19.4 cm, sheet 25.4 × 20.3 cm
20804

Inscriptions   u.l., from negative, *B23-12*

Annotations   verso, c., *Beaton*, c., *Magazine*(?), l.r., *22*

Provenance   Arts et Métiers graphiques, Paris; unknown Swiss photographer; bought by Rodney de Charmoy Grey, Geneva, c. 1976; gift of Rodney and Cozette de Charmoy Grey, 1979.

Inspired by the boldness and innovation of modern art, the leading fashion photographers of the 1930s produced some of the most creative and elegant photographs the industry has ever known. Cecil Beaton belonged to this talented group, and was no doubt the most theatrically inclined among them. He was at his best when photographing celebrities, and he went to great lengths to present them with elegance and aplomb, as is demonstrated by this photograph featuring the German-American actress and singer Marlene Dietrich.

The world of fashion is predicated on the notion of newness and a constantly changing cast of ideal types, but at the same time it depends heavily on the revival of the past. Styles in the 1930s harked back to classical Greek and Roman models of beauty, which in large part explains the inclusion of classical sculptures as props in the fashion photographs of Beaton, Horst P. Horst, and George Hoyningen-Huene. The white plaster bust that Dietrich is shown nestling up against here is suggestive of the classical model, while the choker around the neck and the wavy hairdo allude to an eighteenth-century female type. The narcissistic aspect of fashion modelling is referred to in the partial resemblance between Dietrich and the plaster likeness she is affectionately caressing. The flowers are signature elements of Beaton's – he claimed to like using them to "set-off" the model's features. Beaton's photographs are among the earliest examples of the fashion industry using film stars to model their wares.[1]

Two variant photographs from the same sitting (figs. 7.1 and 7.2) not only reveal Beaton's method of working but also illustrate his attention to detail – changing the model's pose, circling the model and the prop with his camera, and capturing numerous views of the set-up. The physical effort required to move around the posed subject would not have been onerous for Beaton, as he frequently used a hand-held roll-camera. He worked intensely, however, often producing as many as thirty exposures in an hour of shooting.[2]

Beaton's penchant for creating elaborate settings for his models, using props and backdrops that he would find or create on his own, was heavily influenced by his passion for the theatre and his occasional work as a stage designer. Although his involvement in photography had modest beginnings, starting as a hobby in the early 1920s, by the 1930s it had evolved into a full-fledged and celebrated career.

Fig. 7.1   Cecil Walter Hardy Beaton, *Marlene Dietrich with Mannequin*, c. 1935, gelatin silver print. George Eastman House, Rochester

Fig. 7.2   Cecil Walter Hardy Beaton, *Marlene Dietrich with Mannequin*, c. 1935, gelatin silver print. National Portrait Gallery, London

Kattowitz, Germany 1902–1975 Paris

Untitled, from *La poupée* 1934, printed 1936

Gelatin silver print, 7.7 × 11.7 cm

40981

Provenance   Sotheby's, London, bought by Paul M. Hertzmann, Inc., San Francisco, 18 May 2000, lot 178; purchased from Paul M. Hertzmann, Inc., 2002.

Hans Bellmer left Kattowitz in 1923 when his domineering father enrolled him in the Technical University of Berlin. Unhappy about being forced into a career path that did not suit him, Bellmer rebelled by adopting a bohemian lifestyle and befriending a circle of artists that included Otto Dix, George Grosz, and the brothers Wieland and Helmut Herzfelde. Establishing himself in Berlin, he worked as an illustrator and typographer, and in 1926 opened a design agency.

In 1933, in protest against the formation of the Hitler government, Bellmer closed his design agency, and soon after he began the construction of his first doll. The art historian Sue Taylor has determined, from written records and from photographs documenting its fabrication, that the doll (now lost) was made out of a combination of moulded flax fibre, broomsticks or dowel rods, and glass eyes, with other elements added later (see fig. 8.1).[1] Bellmer's inspiration for the doll arose out of a convergence of several personal experiences in 1931 and 1932. These included the discovery that Margarete Schnell, his wife of three years, had contracted tuberculosis; the arrival in Berlin of his attractive seventeen-year-old cousin Ursula Naguschewski from Kassel; and the receipt of a trunk full of his childhood toys sent to him in Berlin by his mother. Most significant of all, however, was his viewing, along with his wife, cousin, and brother, of Offenbach's operatic version of *The Tales of Hoffmann* in 1932, directed by Max Reinhardt at Berlin's Grosses Schauspielhaus. In the opera's first act, Hoffmann is tricked by the evil maker of a pair of magic eyeglasses into falling in love with an automaton named Olympia, who is ultimately dismembered.

The constructing of mannequins and automatons was not unique to the work of Bellmer. Bellmer's interest in creating dolls was piqued by Oskar Kokoschka's replication of his former lover, Alma Mahler, in mannequin form.[2] In 1918 the artist issued precise orders to the Berlin doll-maker Hermine Moos for the construction of a doll that would capture her likeness. Kokoschka's letters containing the specifications of the anatomical details were published in 1925 in the periodical *Kunstlerbekentniss*; Bellmer read the letters and was fascinated by them.[3] Other photographers inspired by mannequins and dolls include Umbo, Werner Rohde, Lisette Model, and Ralph Steiner.

In 1934 Bellmer published *Die Puppe*, a book of ten photographs of his doll along with an introductory essay. He sent a copy to Ursula Naguschewski, who was by then studying at the Sorbonne, asking her to deliver it, along with a letter, to André Breton. Breton published eighteen photographs of the doll in the December 1934 issue of *Minotaure*.

Extracted from the 1936 French version of Bellmer's book, *La poupée*, these intimate and delicately toned prints (see also fig. 8.2) display a compelling tension between the elegance and playfulness of the composition and the violence of the subject matter. By the time the 1936 edition appeared, Bellmer had moved on to producing a new and even more bizarre doll articulated with ball-and-socket joints. In 1938 he established himself permanently in France.

Fig. 8.1   Hans Bellmer, *The Doll*, c. 1934, gelatin silver print. The Metropolitan Museum of Art, New York, Ford Motor Company Collection, Gift of Ford Motor Company and John C. Waddell, 1987 (1987.1100.261)

Fig. 8.2   Hans Bellmer, *Untitled,* from *La poupée,* 1934, printed 1936, gelatin silver print. National Gallery of Canada, Ottawa (40980)

Frankfurt am Main 1899–1998 New York
Self-portrait in Mirrors, Paris 1931
Gelatin silver print, 26.6 × 30.3 cm
20873

Inscriptions l.l., *ILSE / BING / 1931*

Annotations verso of mount, c.r., inverted, *33½%*, l.r., *Self portrait in mirrors / Paris 1931 / 1* (circled)

Provenance purchased from Witkin Gallery, New York, 1977.

Also known as *Self-portrait with Leica*, this image of the photographer in the act of capturing her own image encapsulates the energy and excitement that marked the entrance of women into the field of modernist photography. While there are examples of women working as photographers in the nineteenth and early twentieth centuries, it was the rise of photojournalism in the 1920s and 1930s that inspired a significant number of women to take up the camera and compete with men for magazine assignments. Since the dawn of modernism heralded the prospect of new avenues of creativity and employment for women, this image of Bing looking through the lens of her Leica and into her reflection in a mirror is particularly poignant. It is a complex and engaging picture with the mirror reflecting back both the action of Bing photographing herself and the presence of another mirror in the background, which in turn gives us a profile view of the photographer. This faceted representation of female identity addresses some of the pivotal issues surrounding its characterization – notions of objectivity versus subjectivity and of internal focus versus external focus being just two among many others.

It is evident from the number of self-portraits that Bing made with the camera, starting with one from her adolescence in 1913 and continuing through various images made in the 1930s and later, that this act of self-affirmation was important to her. It is informative to compare this composition with another frame clearly taken during the same self-portrait session in which Bing confronts the mirror unobscured by the camera body and appears somewhat more tentative (fig. 9.1).

Introduced in 1925, the Leica was a camera closely associated with the modernist movement in photography. As Lotte Jacobi's self-portrait with her earlier and more cumbersome camera demonstrates (fig. 9.2), the Leica's great advantage was its portability and unprecedented rapidity of exposure. Although the tripod is much in evidence in this image, the Leica even permitted dispensing with it and gave photographers the option of engaging more intimately and spontaneously with the world around them. To this extent, the self-portrait of a female photographer with a Leica in the 1920s could be construed as a declaration of independence and a determination to engage as intensely in the modern world as did their male counterparts.

Bing's decision to devote her career to photography was to a large degree inspired by an exhibition of photographs that she saw in Frankfurt that included the work of the American-born photographer Florence Henri. Bing became a great admirer of Henri's assertively modernist style of photography, which, incidentally, often employed mirrors as pictorial motifs. In 1929 Bing moved to Paris, where Henri was based at the time.

Bing enjoyed a successful career as a photojournalist. In 1929 she contributed picture essays to *Das Illustrierte Blatt* (a supplement of the *Frankfurter Illustrierte* newspaper), and later had her work published in *Vu*, *Arts et Métiers Graphiques*, and *Le Monde illustré*. More important, her photographs were featured in a number of exhibitions during the 1930s in Europe and the United States. They appeared regularly at the Galerie de la Pléiade in Paris alongside the work of other members of the photographic avant-garde. In New York her work was included in *Modern European Photography: Twenty Photographers* at the Julien Levy Gallery in 1932 and in Beaumont Newhall's groundbreaking *Photography 1839–1937* at the Museum of Modern Art in 1937.

Fig. 9.1 Ilse Bing, *Self-portrait with Leica*, 1931, gelatin silver print. Courtesy Edwynn Houk Gallery, New York

Fig. 9.2 Lotte Jacobi, *Self-portrait*, c. 1930, gelatin silver print. Currier Museum of Art, Manchester, New Hampshire, Gift of Bernadette Hunter (1986.11.1.3)

10 Ilse Bing

Frankfurt am Main 1899–1998 New York

New York 1936

Gelatin silver print, 18.9 × 28.3 cm

40667

Inscriptions   l.l., *ILSE BING / 1936*

Annotations   verso of mount, c., *ILSE / BING / 1936 / N.Y. / Staten Island*

Provenance   purchased from Galerie Berinson, Berlin, 2001.

The ability to capture contrasting juxtapositions in nature is one of the alluring characteristics of photography and just one of its aspects that attracted twentieth-century artists to it. The play of formal opposites of broad silhouettes and complex linear details in dynamic relationship to one another characterizes this image by Ilse Bing. Her first serious encounter with the medium was photographing the neoclassical architecture of Friedrich Gilly (1772–1800) for her doctoral dissertation in art history. Bing abandoned her academic interests in favour of a career in photography, and her passion for buildings and architectural form is evident in many phases of her photographic work. For one of the commissions she periodically undertook as an architectural photographer, she produced a series of photographs of a newly constructed home for the elderly in Frankfurt in 1930, a perfect integration of her direct modernist vision with a style of architecture that accentuated simplicity and functionalism (see fig. 10.1). Responding to the low, horizontal, understated quality of these buildings by making well-crafted but quiet prints, Bing adjusted her printing style to complement the environment in which she was working.

Settled in Paris in the 1930s, Bing found in the city a rich reservoir of subject matter for photography, capturing everything from the Eiffel Tower at night to the crumbling walls of buildings from the *ancien régime*. Her night views show silhouetted buildings with intense punctuations of light.

New York, made on her first visit to the United States, in 1936, is a triumph of contrapuntal composition. Solids and voids, verticals and horizontals, and dynamic lines converge and criss-cross, creating a tightly structured image that captures the energy and excitement of the city. Bing was at her best when her subject gave her the opportunity to play with a variety of complex perspectives and forms, and on her 1936 visit the city seems to have done just this, permitting her to create some of her most eloquent and masterful images. A photograph titled *New York, the Elevated, and Me* (fig. 10.2), taken during the same visit, shows Bing using a similar compositional structure with multiple viewpoints and converging perspectives.

The ability to record the interplay of complex structures with informality and rapidity (conditions central to photographic creation in the modern age) but also with precision was facilitated by Bing's use of the Leica camera, introduced in 1925 and embraced by a number of photographers for the spontaneity it permitted.

In 1940 Bing returned to New York, settling there permanently after she and her husband had been interned briefly in Paris as "enemy aliens" by the Vichy government.

Fig. 10.1   Ilse Bing, *Detail of the Entrance Hall Stairs of the Budge Foundation Old People's Home, Frankfurt am Main, Germany*, 1930, gelatin silver print. Canadian Centre for Architecture / Centre Canadien d'Architecture, Montreal

Fig. 10.2   Ilse Bing, *New York, the Elevated, and Me*, 1936, gelatin silver print. New Orleans Museum of Art, Museum purchase through the National Endowment for the Arts Matching Grant (81.49)

11   Karl Blossfeldt
Schielo, Germany 1865–1932 Berlin
Valeriana alliariifolia (Valerian) **1915–1925**
Gelatin silver print, 29.7 × 11.8 cm
36996

Inscriptions   verso, l.c., *Valeriana alliariifolia / Baldrian / Junger Spross in 8 Facher Vergrosserung*

Annotations   verso, u.l., *55/K75*, l.l., *X2201*

Provenance   acquired from Blossfeldt estate by Ann and Jürgen Wilde; bought by Werner Bokelberg; purchased from Hans P. Kraus, Jr., Inc., New York, 1993.

After the appearance of his first publication, *Urformen der Kunst*, in 1928, Karl Blossfeldt's photographs of plant forms were acclaimed simultaneously by the Surrealists and by the followers of the New Objectivity movement. While the former appreciated them for how they endowed ordinary subjects with a compelling strangeness, the latter responded to their crisp definition and neutrality. Both Franz Roh and Walter Benjamin wrote at length about the relationship between Blossfeldt's precisely documented images of plants and the formal concerns of contemporary German art. While the impact of these images on the art of the time is unarguable, what is of equal interest is how they connected to a wider exploration of architectonic form and its place in art and nature (see fig. 11.1).

Nowhere is the complex beauty of branching systems in plants made as sharply visible as in Blossfeldt's photographs (see fig. 11.2). The clarity of expression that we find in his work was in no small measure related to his mastery over the technical realization of the image. A self-taught photographer, Blossfeldt worked as an apprentice sculptor in the Art Ironworks and Foundry in Magdesprung from 1882 to 1884. This experience and his subsequent study of painting and sculpture from 1884 to 1890 at the Unterrichtsanstalt des Kunstgewerbemuseums in Berlin inspired in him a respect for craftsmanship. As far as his study of plant forms is concerned, the formative years of training were those of 1890–1896, which he spent as a scholarship student under Moritz Meurer in Rome. Around 1890 he produced his first plant photographs with a homemade plate camera. Under Meurer's tutelage Blossfeldt not only absorbed the idea that the origins of all forms in art are derived from nature but also learned, on trips with him in Italy, Greece, North Africa, and Egypt, how to collect and preserve plants. It was this body of specimens that provided Blossfeldt with a source of subject matter for the rest of his life.[1]

Valeriana alliariifolia is a typical example of Blossfeldt's work: magnified by a factor of eight, the specimen is placed centrally in front of a neutral background, its silhouette and volumes expressed through a middle range of tones. The simplicity of structure gives this image a singular beauty – the solid forms of the structure playing against the negative forms of its background, and the forking articulation of its structure repeating from the solid stem upwards to the more delicate shoots. Insistence on smooth surfaces, attention to detail in the rendering of the newly budding leaves, and symmetry are the features of this image that draw attention to precise relationships and structures in the form. The neutral background heightens the specificity of the object in a way that can still be identified in the morphological and typological imagery of the German artist couple Bernd and Hilla Becher.

From 1926 until his death, in 1932, Blossfeldt worked as an independent photographer, studying the forms of plants and contributing to *UHU*, *Atlantis*, *Photographische Correspondenz*, and *Das Deutsche Lichtbild*, among others. His photographs were exhibited for the first time in Berlin at the Galerie Nierendorf in 1928, and they were to have a strong impact on the local art community. They were exhibited again in 1929 at the Zwemmer Gallery in London and at the *Film und Foto* exhibition in Stuttgart. Apart from an exhibition shortly after his death, once again at the Zwemmer Gallery, his work was rarely shown again until 1975, when Ann and Jürgen Wilde, owners of the Blossfeldt archives, exhibited it in their gallery in Cologne.

Fig. 11.1   Karl Blossfeldt, *Azorina vidalii*, 1915–1925, gelatin silver print. Karl Blossfeldt Archiv – Ann and Jürgen Wilde, Zülpich, Germany

Fig. 11.2   Karl Blossfeldt, *Valeriana alliariifolia*, 1915–1925, gelatin silver print. Karl Blossfeldt Archiv – Ann and Jürgen Wilde, Zülpich, Germany

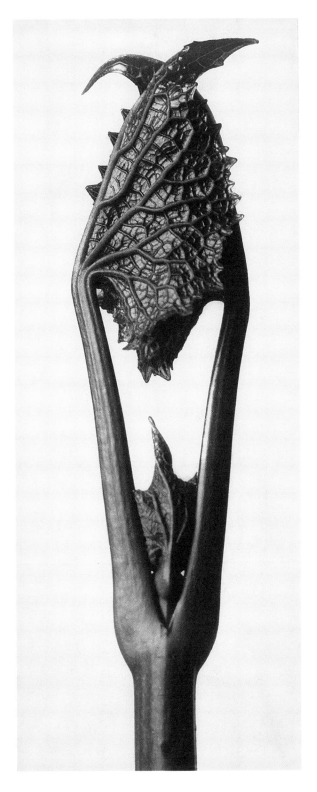

New York 1904–1971 Stamford, Connecticut

Plow Blades, Oliver Chilled Plow Company 1929

Gelatin silver print, 33.4 × 23.3 cm

20972

Annotations   verso of mount, u.c., stamped, *A / MARGARET BOURKE-WHITE / PHOTOGRAPH*, u.c., typewritten on label, *Plow Blades / Oliver Chilled Plow Company*

Provenance   Edward Weston; Christel Gang; acquired by Seymour Stern, Ottawa, from Christel Gang on her death, 1960s; Seymour Stern's widow, Elizabeth Stern; purchased from Elizabeth Stern, 1979 (Phyllis Lambert Fund).

Margaret Bourke-White's career as a woman photographer is without parallel in the first half of the twentieth century. She photographed in iron foundries, served as a war photographer during the Second World War, and photographed from scaffolding 800 feet above the ground on building construction sites. In short, she operated without restraint in what at the time would have been considered a "man's world." In addition, during the first half of the 1930s she ran a financially successful photographic studio in New York. Entrepreneurial, fearless, and gifted, she also descended into the depths of mineshafts, flew in the cockpits of B-47 bombers, and photographed in the Soviet Union, Germany, India, South Africa, and Korea during times of political upheaval, war, and repression. Although she witnessed the collapse of the fortunes of many of America's powerful industrialists in the Crash of 1929, and photographed the devastation experienced in 1934 by drought victims of the Dust Bowl in the American West, her work of the 1930s predominantly reflects the energy of a country with a burgeoning economy.[1]

Margaret Bourke-White was born in 1904 to Joseph White, an engineer and designer who was employed in the printing industry, and Minnie Bourke, an independent-minded woman who taught blind children to read.[2] From the age of seventeen to twenty-four Bourke-White's attention was focused on post-secondary school studies – enrolling at Columbia University in 1921, taking courses at the Clarence H. White School of Photography at Columbia,[3] and finally in 1927 graduating with a degree in biology from Cornell University.[4] During her senior year Bourke-White worked as a photographer for the school newspaper and received commissions to photograph people's homes.[5] Upon graduation she decided to pursue a career in photography, and by the age of twenty-six she was the financially secure owner of the Bourke-White Studio, housed in the newly erected Chrysler Building in New York.

The initial switch in Bourke-White's work from a Pictorialist approach to abstract modernism resulted from a conversation that she had with the photographer Ralph Steiner in late 1927 or early 1928, in which he urged her to adopt a sharper focus.[6] Bourke-White heeded Steiner's advice and delivered her industrial photographs in the sharp-focus aesthetic now widely associated with modernist images of machinery. In the present example, by deciding to photograph the plow blades just before they were to be painted red, she opted for the expression of a highly reflective metallic surface and emphasized uniformity and repetitive arrangement through the play of light. Projects like those for the Otis Steel Mills in Cleveland, Ohio, and for the Oliver Chilled Plow Company in South Bend, Indiana, represented a major point in the development of her career and led to her photographing other industrial operations when she travelled to Germany and the Soviet Union in June 1930. *Propeller Shafts for Steamship, Borsig Locomotive Works, Germany* (fig. 12.1) and *Assembling Generator Shell, USSR* (fig. 12.2) are two examples of her industrial images made outside the United States. That same year, Bourke-White was lured to New York by the publishing tycoon and founder of Time Inc., Henry R. Luce, who was impressed by what he had seen of her work and hired her to photograph for his new publication, *Fortune* magazine.[7] Images from the Oliver Chilled Plow Company project were included in an essay titled "Unseen Half of South Bend" that appeared in *Fortune* in March 1930.[8]

Fig. 12.1   Margaret Bourke-White, *Propeller Shafts for Steamship, Borsig Locomotive Works, Germany*, 1930, gelatin silver print. National Gallery of Canada, Ottawa, Purchased from the Phyllis Lambert Fund, 1979 (20974)

Fig. 12.2   Margaret Bourke-White, *Assembling Generator Shell, USSR*, 1930, gelatin silver print. National Gallery of Canada, Ottawa, Purchased from the Phyllis Lambert Fund, 1979 (20973)

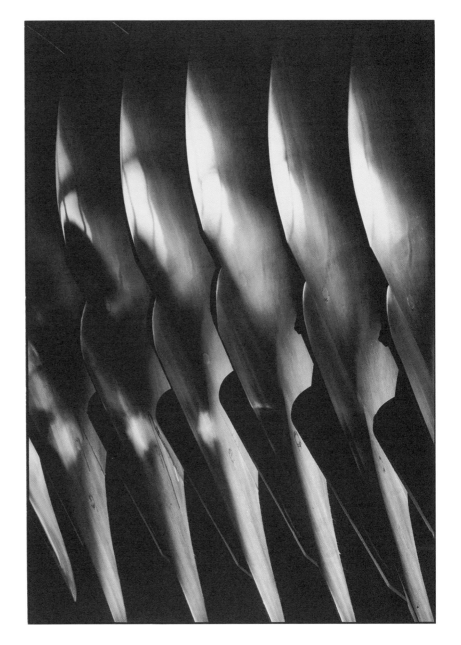

New York 1904–1971 Stamford, Connecticut
George Washington Bridge 1933
Gelatin silver print, 34.2 × 22.1 cm, sheet 34.5 × 22.6 cm
41282

Inscriptions   mount, l.r., *Bourke / White*

Annotations   verso, c., *26*; verso of mount, u.c., stamped, *A MARGARET BOURKE-WHITE PHOTOGRAPH*, l.c., *#26 Geo. Washington Bridge*, l.c., *PF43624H*

Provenance   St. Louis, Missouri, thrift shop, bought by Linda Hartman, c. 1997; e-Bay auction, bought by Lee Gallery, Winchester, Massachusetts, c. 1999; bought by Howard Greenberg Gallery, New York, 2001; purchased from Howard Greenberg Gallery, 2003.

This 1933 photograph of the George Washington Bridge by Margaret Bourke-White is a quintes-sentially modernist work. Its soaring dynamic and clean-lined abstract composition illustrate beautifully the aesthetic and structures of the engineering technology of the period. Designed by the Swiss-American engineer Othmar H. Ammann, and completed in 1931, the George Washington Bridge connected Fort Lee, New Jersey, to Upper Manhattan, across the Hudson River. Its 3,500-foot-long main span made it one of the longest single-span suspension bridges in the world. The Port of New York Authority, which held jurisdiction over the bridge, commis-sioned Bourke-White to photograph it along with a number of other large structures around the city, mainly tunnels and bridges, for a story in *Fortune* magazine.[1]

Bourke-White composed her view of the bridge in such a way that all of the structural elements – towering arches, slightly sagging cables, vertical wires – and even the non-structural streetlights function harmoniously in the picture, expressing an apparent lightness and delicacy belying the subject's real properties of massiveness and strength. By avoiding the flat predictability of a sym-metrical composition, choosing instead to exaggerate the perspective and take the photograph from an off-centre angle, Bourke-White was able to emphasize the bridge's dynamism, achieving precisely what she was commissioned to do – to produce images of "engineering miracles."[2]

The years prior to the Great Depression were marked by a spirit of optimism about the progress of industry and the benefits of the machine. Exhibitions such as *Machine-Age Exposition*, held in New York in 1927, and *Machine Art*, organized by the Museum of Modern Art in 1934, reflected the sense of excitement and promise with which these developments were received. When asked one time about her views on industry and art, Bourke-White replied in a telegram: "Believe any important art coming out of this industrial age will draw inspiration from industry, because industry alive, vital…. Industrial subjects close to heart of life today…. Beauty of industry lies in its truth and simplicity."[3] Her photograph of the Chrysler Building gargoyle (fig. 13.1), with its streamlined metallic form arching out over the city against a background of skyscrapers, captures this sense of optimism about industry.

Along with the more generic paintings of the soaring forms of bridges and factory chimneys by American painters like Joseph Stella and Francis Criss, there are other iconic bridge photographs that date from around the same period as Bourke-White's monumental *George Washington Bridge* image, including Edward Steichen's view of the same site (fig. 13.2) taken from a slightly different vantage point in 1930, a year before the bridge opened. Walker Evans had made a series of photographs of the Brooklyn Bridge in 1929, the most effective of which were taken from below it, expressing its rugged and massive strength.

Fig. 13.1   Margaret Bourke-White, *Chrysler Building*, 1930, gelatin silver print. George Eastman House, Rochester

Fig. 13.2   Edward Steichen, *The George Washington Bridge, New York*, 1930, gelatin silver print. Fine Arts Museums of San Francisco, Museum Purchase, M.H. de Young Memorial Museum (54122)

14 Brassaï

Brassó, Hungary 1899–1984 Nice, France
Portrait of Janet 1932
Gelatin silver print, 18 × 23.6 cm
30825

Annotations   verso, u.l., *11*, l.c., *CEL 49*, l.r., inverted, *1932 / Paris*, l.r., *Photo Brassai / Reproduced in 'Minotaure' / in a photomontage by Dali*

Provenance   Francis F. Dobo, brother-in-law of the model's sister, New York; purchased from Francis F. Dobo, 1990.

Born Gyula Halász in the Transylvanian town of Brassó in 1899, Brassaï adopted his pseudonym ("of Brassó") in the early 1930s while living in Paris. After serving in the Austro-Hungarian cavalry in 1917–1918, he attended the Academy of Fine Arts in Budapest. In 1920 he went to Berlin, where he worked as a correspondent for Hungarian newspapers and fell in with the artists László Moholy-Nagy, Oskar Kokoschka, and Wassily Kandinsky. A brief sojourn in Brassó in 1922 convinced him to stay abroad, and two years later he moved permanently to Paris. There he encountered members of the expatriate Hungarian community as well as artists, poets, and writers attached to the Surrealist movement, such as Michel Seuphor, Robert Desnos, Raymond Queneau, and Henri Michaux. It is also certain that Brassaï and André Kertész met and that the latter's work had a decisive influence on Brassaï's famous night photographs of Paris, made between 1930 and 1934.

Portrait of Janet instantly associates Brassaï with the abandon of bohemian Paris. Like Atget, Brassaï could be considered a *flâneur* of sorts, prowling the streets of the city to find his images. Unlike Atget, he did this most often under the cover of night and focused his attention not on empty streets or *ancien régime* facades but on demimonde society (see fig. 14.1). In the present image we have a woman with her eyes closed and her head thrown back as if in a kind of sexual ecstasy. The photograph attracted the attention of the Surrealist painter Salvador Dalí, who chose to include it in a photocollage that he published in *Minotaure* in 1933.[1]

Fantasy played a large role in the making of this photograph. The model, Janet Fukushima, was related by marriage to the brother of Frank Dobo, the original owner of the photograph. She was not Brassaï's lover, nor was she a woman of the night, as might be supposed from the context of Brassaï's many depictions of prostitutes in his 1932 publication *Paris de nuit* (see fig. 14.2).

Fig. 14.1   Brassaï, *Bijou at the Bar de la Lune, Montmartre, Paris*, 1932, gelatin silver print. National Gallery of Canada, Ottawa (37013)

Fig. 14.2   Brassaï, *Prostitute, Rue de la Reynie*, c. 1931–1932, gelatin silver print. National Gallery of Canada, Ottawa (30828)

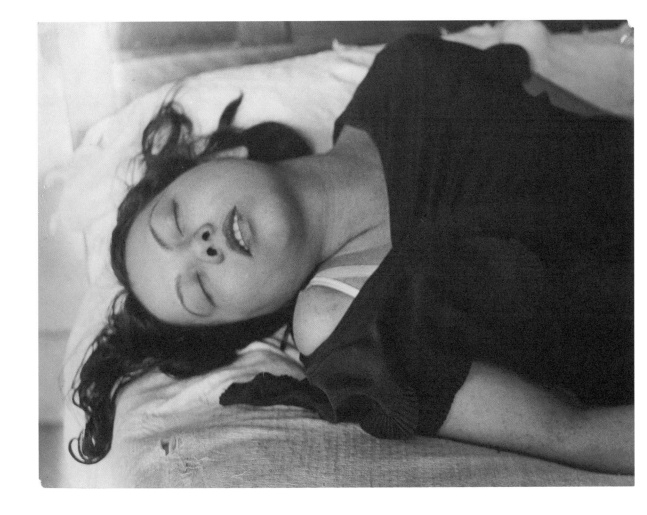

15   Brassaï

Brassó, Hungary 1899–1984 Nice, France

Nude c. 1932, printed c. 1950

Gelatin silver print, 37.5 × 48.9 cm, sheet 40.8 × 49.9 cm

41559

Annotations   verso, u.r., *Nu / minotaure – début années trente*, c., *Nu. 102*, c.r., *50 × 40*, l.l., *VB054CGB NU 102*, l.c., stamped, *Photographie BRASSAÏ / © copyright Gilberte Brassaï / Tous droits réservés*, l.r., *Nu*, l.r., *2/30*, l.r., *Tirage par l'auteur*

Provenance   Gilberte Brassaï, Paris; purchased from Edwynn Houk Gallery, New York, 2005.

Photographer, author, sculptor, draughtsman, and filmmaker, Brassaï was a man of many talents, all of which he managed to give expression to at different points in his life, moving from one medium to another with great fluidity, if not always with the same degree of dexterity. Like most of his photographs of nudes, this work dates from the period 1931–1934, shortly after his having taken up photography seriously. This was also when he was busy photographing Paris's demi-monde for his much-acclaimed 1932 publication *Paris de nuit*. As Anne Tucker points out, Brassaï adopted three different approaches to the nude during this period; close-ups of the essential sculptural forms of the torso, combined drawings and photographs of elements of the torso, and partially clad full-length figures.[1] It is the first two bodies of work that represent Brassaï's most successful attempts to depict the female form through photography.

The present photograph was one of four Brassaï nudes that appeared in the Surrealist journal *Minotaure* in 1933.[2] The images selected for publication were evidently those that were considered "most capable of transforming our perceptions of the human figure, and most open to metaphoric or Surrealist reading."[3] The group as a whole, consisting of twenty works, can be viewed simultaneously as abstractions and as erotically evocative images. In conversation with Picasso in 1943, Brassaï described them as having been done "entirely in curving lines and contours, in 'roundings'" (see fig. 15.1). He also likened the female body to a "sort of vase, or musical instrument, or fruit."[4]

Most of the recent critical responses to this group of Brassaï's nudes have focused on the psychoanalytical notion of doubling, with the female torso functioning simultaneously as an erotic object and as a Medusan threat.[5] Writing about the fetishistic aspect of Surrealist nudes in general, and referring specifically to this nude by Brassaï, Hal Foster makes the observation that "these nudes are cropped or otherwise manipulated in a way that turns the female body into a semi-penile form, a near fetish-image."[6] Dawn Ades notes that in another of the photographs from this group "the image never settles into one reading."[7] This ambiguity is characteristic of the sculptural nudes. However, those from the series known as *Transmutations*, in which Brassaï has covered the surface of the body with intensely drawn patterns in applied pigment (see fig. 15.2), are not so much ambiguous as static. Concealing the body by "clothing" it with geometric shapes, Brassaï renders it less human and less prone to association with other anatomical forms.

But to what extent was Brassaï committed to the Surrealist platform of reawakening the subconscious, extolling the fantastic, and elevating the accidental? Brassaï's answer would most likely have been, not at all. Brassaï, like his compatriot André Kertész, rejected any attempt to situate his work within the Surrealist "framework." Interviewed by the British photographer Tony Ray-Jones in 1970, he claimed that although he had worked with Surrealists for years, he did not like Surrealism because he was "very objective." "But," he went on to say, "they like my photographs. They found a kind of surrealism in my pictures even though I was objective…. I was opposed to their ideas but I was friends with them all anyway."[8]

Fig. 15.1 Brassaï, *Nude*, 1934, gelatin silver print. Musée National d'Art Moderne, Centre Georges Pompidou, Paris

Fig. 15.2 Brassaï, *Femme-Fruit*, from *Transmutations*, 1934–1967, gelatin silver print. Musée National d'Art Moderne, Centre Georges Pompidou, Paris

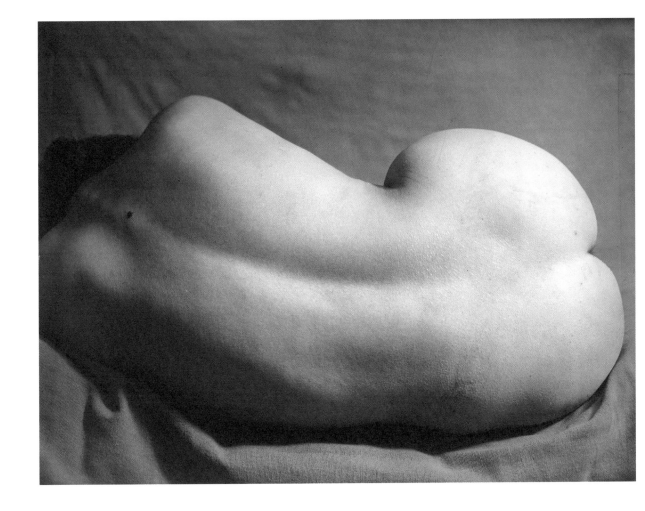

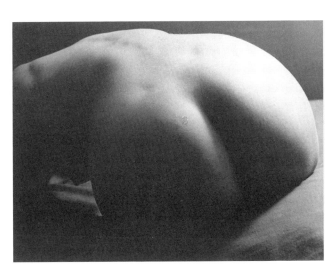

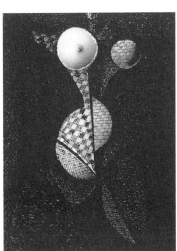

16   Anton Bruehl
Hawker, Australia 1900–1982 San Francisco
Crankshaft with Pistons 1929
Gelatin silver print, 34.5 × 27.6 cm, sheet 35.4 × 27.8 cm
35941

Annotations   verso of mount, c., stamped, *ANTON BRUEHL / Bruehl*
Provenance   purchased from Houk Friedman Gallery, New York, 1991.

The machine as a subject in photography goes back to the mid-nineteenth century when the photographer C.M. Ferrier submitted salted paper prints of various objects including steam hammers, a locomotive engine, and agricultural implements to be published in the *Reports by the Juries* commemorating the Great Exhibition of 1851 at the Crystal Palace.[1] In the twentieth century the capture of precise detail, smooth surface texture, and pristine luminosity were made possible through the introduction of the gelatin silver process, which seamlessly matched the subject matter and its medium of delivery. Without this technical development, it is unlikely that photographers would have been able to give expression as they did to their modernist impulse to record industrial forms and surfaces – Paul Strand, for example, in his iconic Akeley movie camera image (fig. 16.1), or Margaret Bourke-White in her photographs of propeller shafts and plow blades (see cat. 12). Commissioned by Cadillac to produce high-definition images of the insides of their automobile engines for a brochure for the 1930 New York Auto Fair, Bruehl recorded the bobbing piston heads in a dynamic contrapuntal arrangement that affirmed the mechanical nature of the object.[2]

Crankshaft with Pistons is one of the most animated and exquisite images in all of Bruehl's oeuvre. The photographer framed his view so that the curiously anthropomorphic piston heads recede and converge dramatically in sharp perspective. Although the machine is shown in a static phase, the composition captures the arrangement of the pistons in such a dynamic way as to suggest potential propulsion and sound. Clearly dazzled by the play of light on the reflective steel surface, Bruehl has succeeded in making the object look lustrous and magical. This photograph and *Boat Hull*, from about 1937 (fig. 16.2), are key images for the connection that they make between Bruehl the photographer and Bruehl the engineer.

Born in Hawker, Australia, on 11 March 1900, Anton Bruehl came to his love of photographing things mechanical by way of an early interest in the structure and order that underlie the design and function of mechanized objects. Cameras – both the manufactured and homemade varieties – were familiar to Bruehl from childhood on. He immigrated to the United States in 1919, settling in New York, where he worked as an electrical engineer for several years. In 1923 he viewed an exhibition of photographs by students of the Clarence H. White School at the Art Center in New York.[3] The experience was a revelation for Bruehl, and he apparently requested a leave of six months from his employer in order to pursue his own photography. By 1924 he was enrolled at the Clarence H. White School, where he soon after became an instructor. In addition to this period of training with Clarence H. White, out of which a close but brief friendship developed (White died in 1925), Bruehl worked as an assistant to the New York studio photographer Jessie Tarbox Beals (1871–1942).[4] Bruehl and his brother Martin established a photographic studio in 1927, which they ran until 1966.

Bruehl's contribution to advertising photography was not limited to making high-quality images but extended into innovation in the process of colour photography. Bruehl collaborated with Fernand Bourges in producing colour images in the early 1930s, and the very successful results of their work together have been credited with elevating the standards of colour reproduction.[5]

Fig. 16.1   Paul Strand, *Double Akeley, New York*, 1922, gelatin silver print. San Francisco Museum of Modern Art, The Helen Crocker Russell and William H. and Ethel W. Crocker Family Funds purchase

Fig. 16.2   Anton Bruehl, *Boat Hull*, c. 1937, gelatin silver print. National Gallery of Australia, Canberra

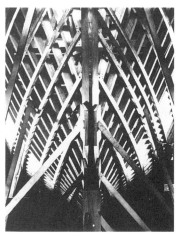

17 Francis Bruguière

San Francisco 1879–1945 London

Cut-Paper Abstraction 1929

Gelatin silver print, 23.8 × 18.7 cm

40571

Inscriptions   mount, l.r., *Francis Bruguiere*

Annotations   verso of mount, u.l., *CLEA*[...]

Provenance   Rosalinde Fuller, the artist's model and companion; Galerie Michèle Chomette, Paris; purchased from Paul M. Hertzmann, Inc., San Francisco, 2001.

A painter, filmmaker, and photographer, Francis Bruguière enjoyed experimentation in all media. Along with Alvin Langdon Coburn and Paul Strand, he wanted to introduce a radically new vocabulary of form into photography by breaking away from its documentary and narrative conventions. Bruguière was aware of the new developments in art. His paintings, with their emphasis on planar surfaces, fragmentation, and abstraction of form, reveal the influence of Cubism (see fig. 17.1). During an extended stay in New York in 1905–1906, Bruguière became caught up in the excitement being generated around photography. In 1903 Alfred Stieglitz had launched the influential publication *Camera Work*, and in 1905 he opened his Little Galleries of the Photo-Secession. It was here that issues surrounding photography and modern art were discussed and, most important, the medium of photography was shown and critiqued within the context of modernist practice.[1] Unfortunately Bruguière had to end his sojourn in New York after receiving news that his wealthy San Francisco banking family had lost its entire fortune in the 1906 earthquake. In order to earn a living he now became a professional portrait photographer.

Although Bruguière started out as a Pictorialist photographer and was a member of the Photo-Secession (exhibiting with them in the 1910 International Photo-Secession exhibition at the Albright Art Gallery in Buffalo, New York), his greatest passion was always for painting. As he expressed it: "Photography remained for certain sunny days when my other experiments palled, and a new idea for light and shade, an idea which could best be preserved by camera and lens, occurred to me."[2] The years between 1906 and his return to New York in 1919, when he would establish a studio in Manhattan, were marked by continuing experimentation in photography that included the making of multiple exposures. The idea of introducing a "fourth dimension" into photographs was very much in the air during this period, with articles by Max Weber, Charles Caffin, and Alvin Langdon Coburn appearing in *Camera Work* and *Photograms of the Year*.[3]

Bruguière's experimentation with lighting in his photographs may well have related to his involvement with Thomas Wilfred's "color organ" in 1921. The colour organ synchronized musical scales with lights, and the resulting projections were fluid abstract forms, which Bruguière photographed to illustrate an article on this phenomenon by Stark Young in a 1922 issue of *Theatre Arts*. In Bruguière's description of it, this was "photographing unadulterated light as form."[4]

Cut-Paper Abstraction is from a series of abstractions titled *From Beyond This Point*, in which Bruguière explored dynamic form, geometricized shapes, and light (see also fig. 17.2). Although Cubist in character, the volumes represented in these images are often suggestive of the shapes of parts of the human body. In the present image, the luminous semi-spherical forms in the background suggest breasts or buttocks. Conversely, a series of multiple exposure nudes that Bruguière made around 1926 are strongly reminiscent of his abstractions.

Fig. 17.1   Francis Bruguière, photograph of his own painting, c. 1930, gelatin silver print. George Eastman House, Rochester, Museum Collection

Fig. 17.2   Francis Bruguière, *#32*, c. 1930, gelatin silver print. George Eastman House, Rochester, Gift of Rosalinde Fuller

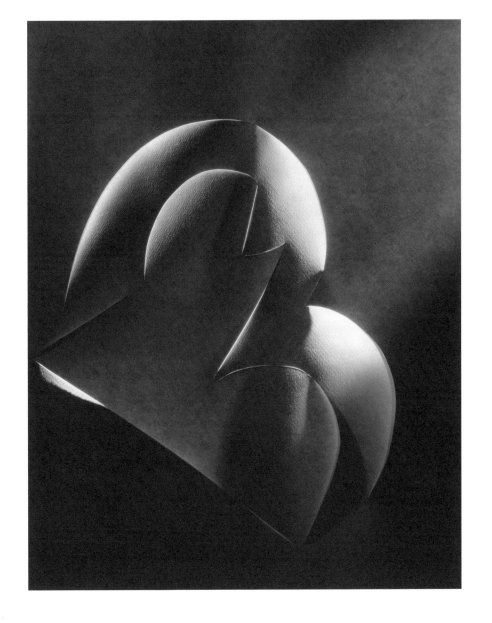

Chanteloup, Seine-et-Marne, France 1908–2004 Céreste, France
Valencia, Spain 1933, printed before 1947
Gelatin silver print, 16.5 × 24.2 cm
28594

Annotations   verso, c.l., *HB* (crossed out), c., *A*, c., *is E18*, c.r., *T4872–35/35*, l.c., ← *5⅞″* →, l.c., stamped, *REPRODUCE ONLY ON CONDITIONS: / (1) CREDIT MUST BE GIVEN TO / HENRI CARTIER-BRESSON / (2) PHOTOGRAPH MUST NOT BE ALTERED BY TRIMMING*

Provenance   Monroe Wheeler, New York; purchased from Jane Corkin Gallery, Toronto, 1984.

Raised in a wealthy Paris household, Henri Cartier-Bresson enrolled in a private art school in 1927 and also studied under the Cubist sculptor and painter André Lhote. At the same time he steeped himself in European art and literature and began to associate with a number of Surrealists. He furthered his studies at Cambridge in 1928–1929, and did his military service in France in 1930. In 1931 Cartier-Bresson went to the Ivory Coast, where he lived in the bush and contracted a fever that nearly killed him. During that year in Africa he was shown a photograph by the Hungarian photographer Martin Munkácsi (*Black Boys Ashore, Lake Tanganyika*), which so profoundly impressed him that he decided to give up painting and pursue photography instead.

In 1932 Cartier-Bresson purchased his first Leica, a light and versatile camera with a 50mm lens that had been introduced in 1925. It gave him the freedom of movement he wanted, as well as a certain degree of anonymity and the ability to capture fleeting events instantaneously. He knew very well that spontaneity was the key to his art, and would later sum up his work stating: "I was there and this is how life happened to me at that moment."[1]

In the early 1930s he travelled widely in Europe and photographed in many cities. The photograph *Valencia, Spain* was made during a trip to Spain in 1933. Later that same year it was included in Cartier-Bresson's first solo exhibition, at the Julien Levy Gallery in New York.[2] In this image, a young boy balances himself against a tarred wall, with his head thrown back and his eyes rolled upward, as if in a kind of ecstatic trance. No other visual clues are provided to help us make sense of the scene, which loses its mysteriousness only after we learn that the boy has just thrown a ball into the air and is waiting for it to fall. An even more surreal moment is captured in another photograph from the same trip, *Roman Amphitheatre, Valencia, Spain* (fig. 18.1), which calls to mind the haunting and disorienting painted landscapes of De Chirico.

This print of *Valencia, Spain* was acquired by the National Gallery of Canada in 1984 along with twenty-three other Cartier-Bresson prints, all of which had been used to illustrate the catalogue that accompanied the Museum of Modern Art's 1947 retrospective of his work. A number of the prints are stamped on the verso as being courtesy of *Revue Verve*, *Harper's Bazaar*, and Braun et Cie, indicating that they had been used by magazine and book publishers in the late 1930s and early 1940s.

Fig. 18.1   Henri Cartier-Bresson, *Roman Amphitheatre, Valencia, Spain*, 1933, printed before 1947, gelatin silver print. National Gallery of Canada, Ottawa (28595)

19   Henri Cartier-Bresson

Chanteloup, Seine-et-Marne, France 1908–2004 Céreste, France
Madrid, Spain **1933, printed before 1947**
Gelatin silver print, 16.5 × 24.2 cm
28593

Annotations   verso, u.r., *615*, c.l., *T4872–35/35*, c. A, c., *is E4B*, c., *HB* (crossed out), c., stamped, *REPRODUCE ONLY ON CONDITIONS: / (1) CREDIT MUST BE GIVEN TO / HENRI CARTIER-BRESSON / (2) PHOTOGRAPH MUST NOT BE ALTERED BY TRIMMING*, l.c., ← 5⅞" →, l.r., *P.31*

Provenance   purchased from Jane Corkin Gallery, Toronto, 1984.

The vitality of Henri Cartier-Bresson's images lies not only in the photographer's exceptional ability to seize a particular moment in time when several elements converge to form a curious, witty, and often surreal visual spectacle, but also in his talent for structuring space and form with great eloquence. Like Walker Evans and André Kertész, he is among those photographers of the first half of the twentieth century who introduced new approaches to photography but did not depart entirely from depicting the world as it is (see fig. 19.1).

Cartier-Bresson apparently did not enjoy darkroom work, preferring to be out on the street shooting. Although it is tempting to speculate that these photographs might be some of the last works printed by Cartier-Bresson himself, the information regarding when precisely he stopped printing is contradictory. While he claimed, on the one hand, that he no longer printed for himself after the 1933 Julien Levy Gallery exhibition in New York, he also stated that he did not use professionals until after the Second World War.[1] It was in 1947 that Cartier-Bresson, along with Robert Capa, David Seymour ("Chim"), George Rodger, and others founded Magnum Photos and started having their prints made there. This may very well have been the point at which Cartier-Bresson stopped making his own prints. He certainly never emphasized the "fine print" aesthetic – on the contrary, he mocked what he considered the overly fastidious and precious attention accorded to it in the marketplace. Yet there is a vitality to these prints that matches that of the imagery, leading one to suspect that it was the photographer who made them.

In addition to demonstrating Cartier-Bresson's exceptional ability to capture the right moment, *Madrid, Spain* displays his sophisticated grasp of composition, combining random movement and static forms. The foreground captures an apparently chaotic massing of children; some of them seem to be aware of the photographer and his camera, while the others remain rapt in their activity. The action is set against a modernist backdrop that evokes at one and the same time the stark white facade of a Le Corbusier building and the rectangular rhythms of a Mondrian painting. *Madrid, Spain* also conveys the special visual exchange that occurs between the photographer and the strangers he engages with. One is struck by the same feature in his *Alicante, Spain* (fig. 19.2). Both of these photographs attest to the remarkable mental as well as physical gymnastics required of Cartier-Bresson in order to create his most powerful images.

Fig. 19.1   Henri Cartier-Bresson, *Hyères, France*, 1932, printed before 1947, gelatin silver print. National Gallery of Canada, Ottawa (28590)

Fig. 19.2   Henri Cartier-Bresson, *Alicante, Spain*, 1933, printed before 1947, gelatin silver print. National Gallery of Canada, Ottawa (28588)

20   Paul Citroen

Berlin 1896–1983 Wassenaar, Netherlands

Lotti Weiss, Basel 1926

Gelatin silver print, 14.6 × 10.1 cm

29748

Annotations   verso, u.r., *II*, u.r., *Lotti Weiss / Basel / 1926*, l.l., *80.10.13.7*, l.l., *Paul Citroen*

Provenance   purchased from Prakapas Gallery, New York, 1987.

Despite Paul Citroen's decision to ultimately abandon photography for painting, his photographic portraits are among the most intimate and emotionally resonant works made during the modernist period. Like many of his contemporaries, Citroen began his artistic career as a painter. He studied art at various institutions, including the Brandenburg Academy (Studien Ateliers für Malerei und Plastik) in Berlin and the Bauhaus in Weimar, where he studied under Johannes Itten and Georg Muche. In photography, however, he was largely self-taught. In his early years he worked at Der Sturm, a Berlin bookshop and gallery owned by the writer and musician Herward Walden, where he was exposed to avant-garde art and befriended the Dadaists Richard Huelsenbeck, George Grosz, Walter Mehring, and the brothers Wieland and Helmut Herzfelde.

The subject of the present photograph was a young woman named Lotti Weiss, with whom Citroen had formed a friendship when he was at the Bauhaus. Her brother, Geza Weiss, a Berlin actor and amateur photographer who would also take up portrait photography after fleeing Germany for the Netherlands in 1933, is believed to have collaborated with Citroen in the making of a series of portraits of Lotti in Basel in 1927.[1] That may be close to when this portrait was taken, but given the slightly earlier date and the distinctive manner of composition and lighting it more likely was made by Citroen alone.

An almost spectral image of a woman's profile emerging from darkness in a blurred silhouette, this portrait of Lotti contrasts with the more pedestrian views of her taken around the same time (see fig. 20.1). Not only does it oppose the conventional notion of the portrait as a faithful likeness, but it also counters the idea of detached interest, the principal tenet of the New Objectivity movement. This reduction of the human countenance to broad tonal planes can also be seen in other portraits by Citroen (see fig. 20.2)

Paul Citroen was born of Dutch parents in Berlin. His interest in photography may have sprung from his lifelong friendship with Erwin Blumenfeld, but he did not start to photograph seriously until the mid-1920s, after he had completed three years of study at the Bauhaus in Weimar. While he would not have undertaken formal studies in photography there (it did not appear on the curriculum until 1929), he would have come into contact with László Moholy-Nagy, whose unusual self-portrait photograms evidently impressed him (see fig. 20.3). Citroen's interest in photography can be seen as early as 1923, in his famous photocollage *Metropolis*, made from photographs, postcards, and fragments of type.

During the period 1925 to 1927, when Citroen made this portrait of Lotti Weiss, he was running a portrait studio in Berlin with the German photographer Umbo (Otto Umbehr) and also travelling frequently to Basel, where he met Weiss and her brother Geza. From 1928 to 1935 Citroen worked in Amsterdam as a freelance portrait photographer, but in the late 1930s he returned to painting. An influential teacher, he founded and directed the Nieuwe Kunstschool from 1933 to 1937 and later taught at the Academie voor Beeldenden Kunsten in the Hague.

Fig. 20.1   Paul Citroen, *Lotti Weiss*, July 1927, gelatin silver print. Prentenkabinet, Universiteitsbibliotheek Leiden (PK-F-RPC.1946)

Fig. 20.2   Paul Citroen, *Portrait of Let*, 1931, gelatin silver print. National Gallery of Canada, Ottawa (23910)

Fig. 20.3   László Moholy-Nagy, *Self-portrait, Berlin*, 1925, gelatin silver print. George Eastman House, Rochester, Museum Purchase, ex-collection Sybil Moholy-Nagy

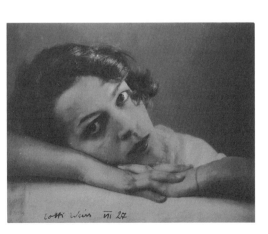

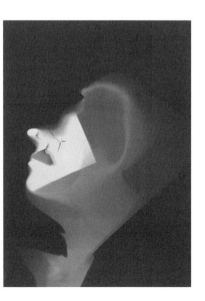

21 Alvin Langdon Coburn

Boston 1882–1966 Colwyn Bay, Wales
Vortograph **1917**
Gelatin silver print, 27.6 × 20.3 cm
41656

Inscriptions   mount, l.r., *Alvin Langdon Coburn*

Provenance   gift of the artist to Leonard Arundale, London; his grandson, Leon Arundale, London; Christie's, London, bought by Edwynn Houk Gallery, New York, May 2003; purchased from Edwynn Houk Gallery, 2005.

Alvin Langdon Coburn's Vortographs are among a handful of landmark images in modernist photography. Along with Alfred Stieglitz's *Paula* of 1889 and *The Steerage* of 1907, Christian Schad's 1917 Schadographs, Paul Strand's white picket fence of 1917 (fig. 68.1) and views of the Akeley movie camera (see fig. 16.1) from the early 1920s, and perhaps a few others, the Vortographs situate photography squarely within the modernist canon. These are images that participate fully in modernity and do not merely hint at it. What makes Coburn's Vortograph an iconic image in twentieth-century art is not only its fragmentation of a solid object into a gemlike array of exploding pulses and facets of light, but also its propulsion of photography onto a new plane of abstract expression.

A nonconformist, Coburn had an eye for making striking images and superb prints almost from the start of his career, as exemplified in *Mission, San Fernando Valley* (fig. 21.1), from 1911. He was considered something of a prodigy, receiving praise for his photographs from Stieglitz at the age of twelve. Independently wealthy, he was able to concentrate on the aesthetic aspect of his art more than most of his contemporaries. One year before he made his series of Vortographs, Coburn published an article in which he challenged his readers to consider a radically new application of photography to the making of art, one that would "throw off the shackles of conventional representation and attempt something fresh and untried" and even be "impossible to classify, or to tell which was the top and which was the bottom!"[1]

Between October 1916 and January 1917 Coburn turned his attention to doing just this. In collaboration with his friend the Vorticist poet Ezra Pound he constructed an apparatus consisting of three fragments of Pound's shaving mirror and placed it around his camera lens. The effect was to create an image that fragmented the objects in front of the lens into a complex cluster of intersecting planes and shafts of light. Coburn's Vortographs were greeted with outrage when eighteen of them were exhibited for the first time in 1917 at the Camera Club in London.

As radical as these images might have appeared, there is evidence that Coburn was exploring the nature of abstract form even earlier, in photographs such as *New York from Its Pinnacles* and *The Thousand Windows, New York* (fig. 21.2), both from 1912. In these images Coburn adopted a radical vantage point, aiming his camera down at the streets from the tops of the city's skyscrapers, creating a perspective that he described as Cubist. It has been suggested that Coburn's *Thousand Windows* influenced the work of the artist Wyndham Lewis and was probably the source of the latter's 1914 watercolour drawing *New York*. While Coburn's prints constitute the only known use of the Vortoscope for photographs, it is believed that Pound introduced the device to Fernand Léger, who apparently used it in the making of his film *Ballet mécanique* in 1923–1924. Coburn also used the Vortoscope to portray Pound (fig. 21.3).

Coburn's experiments with Vortographs did not last long. Within a few months he abandoned them and returned to making more conventional images. He became increasingly interested in mysticism and comparative religion.

Fig. 21.1   Alvin Langdon Coburn, *Mission, San Fernando Valley*, 1911, gum bichromate and platinum print. National Gallery of Canada, Ottawa (21500)

Fig. 21.2   Alvin Langdon Coburn, *The Thousand Windows, New York*, 1912, printed later, gelatin silver print. George Eastman House, Rochester, Gift of Alvin Langdon Coburn

Fig. 21.3   Alvin Langdon Coburn, *Ezra Pound*, 1917, printed later, gelatin silver print. George Eastman House, Rochester

22 Harold Edgerton
Fremont, Nebraska 1903–1990 Cambridge, Massachusetts
Milk Drop Coronet 1936, printed later
Gelatin silver print, 45.8 × 36.5 cm, sheet 50.6 × 40.7 cm
38458

Inscriptions   verso, l.c., *HAROLD EDGERTON*
Annotations   verso, l.r., *46/90*, l.r., *3602.2046*
Provenance   gift of the Harold and Esther Edgerton Family Foundation, Santa Fe, New Mexico, 1997.

Driven by a curiosity to know how objects look in all their phases of acceleration and change, Harold Edgerton developed a technology that enabled him to capture a moving subject with bursts of light fired in rapid succession on a single sheet of film. In so doing, he made a unique contribution to the history of photography and the representation of movement. His highly graphic depiction of the coronet of a milk splash is but one of his many photographs that have achieved iconic status.

Through his knowledge of electrical engineering and his fascination with technology Edgerton shortened the duration of the intense flashes of light, thus arresting action in a high-speed sequence of split seconds. This was an achievement that nineteenth-century photographer-scientists like A.M. Worthington and Étienne-Jules Marey had aspired to before him.

As important as this technical knowledge was to the creation of these images, the status that they enjoy today is also due to Edgerton's flair for visual presentation. While his never-before-seen views were dramatic simply by virtue of their content – finches fighting in mid-air (fig. 22.1), a football at the moment it is kicked, an apple being pierced by a bullet – Edgerton also had a talent for theatrical composition. In his 1957 colour photograph of a milk splash (fig. 22.2) he deliberately used a red plate so as to make the explosion of the drop all the more graphic. In fact, Edgerton has always been perceived as part-artist, part-scientist, and part-magician.

Milk Drop Coronet captures our imagination on a number of levels. Formally, it is an arresting image graced with a simple elegance. It satisfies our curiosity about what is invisible to the human eye, and it provokes thought about the surprising similarities of forms that can appear in disparate parts of the natural world. The photographic historian Beaumont Newhall selected *Milk Drop Coronet* for inclusion in the Museum of Modern Art's first photography exhibition, in 1939, and a variant was used to illustrate D'Arcy Wentworth Thompson's scientific investigations into the morphology of small water-borne organisms.

Edgerton learned the rudiments of photography from an uncle, and at the age of fifteen he bought his own Kodak folding camera from his savings. Recognition of Edgerton's contribution to the world of art and photography followed shortly after his strobe-flash photographs were published for the first time in various science and photography magazines. In 1933 and 1934 his photographs were shown at the annual Royal Photographic Society exhibition in London. In 1941 he was the recipient of an award from the Franklin Institute in Philadelphia for the invention of a high-speed motion picture camera that "increased knowledge in the fields of pure and applied science."[1]

Fig. 22.1   Harold Edgerton, *Fighting Finches*, 1936, printed later, gelatin silver print. National Gallery of Canada, Ottawa, Gift of the Harold and Esther Edgerton Family Foundation, Santa Fe, New Mexico, 1997 (38456)

Fig. 22.2   Harold Edgerton, *Milk Drop Coronet*, 1957, printed 1983?, dye coupler print. National Gallery of Canada, Ottawa, Gift of the Harold and Esther Edgerton Family Foundation, Santa Fe, New Mexico, 1997 (38489)

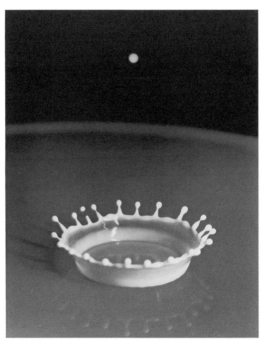

St. Louis, Missouri 1903–1975 New Haven, Connecticut
Manhattan 1928 or 1929
Gelatin silver print, 8.6 × 12.4 cm
30735

Annotations   verso of mount, c., stamped, *PHOTOGRAPH / WALKER EVANS / 179 COLUMBIA HEIGHTS / BROOKLYN,*
l.l, WE–10

Provenance   purchased from Prakapas Gallery, New York, 1990.

"Stare," Walker Evans once said. "It is the way to educate your eye. Stare, pry, listen, eavesdrop. Die knowing something."[1] Evans brought to photography a penetrating, complex, and subtle visual intelligence. He left behind a powerful body of photographs that range from precisely seen abstractions like *Manhattan*, through stirring portraits of sharecropper families and subway passengers, to images of vernacular architecture and objects. *Manhattan* may at first be startling, for it seems radically different from the more familiar documentary works by which this artist has come to be known. It represents a three-year period in the late 1920s and early 1930s when Evans was introducing strongly angled views and abstraction into his images, experimenting with an approach to seeing and recording the world that was more European modernist than American.

In *Manhattan*, Evans has taken an ordinary urban view of elevated railroad tracks and iron girders seen against a background of pavement and transformed it into a complex and dynamic lattice of lines and textures. He has achieved this by holding his camera in a strongly angled position and rejecting the traditional perspective of the viewer who stands upright before a lateral horizon. Photographing this elaborate interplay of lines and surfaces under an even light, Evans has also captured the important details of rivets and sprockets that punctuate the diagonal beams and attach the rods to the vertical bars on the right-hand side. The repetition of these circular forms sets up a rhythm within an otherwise planar and static arrangement.

Although Evans would soon reject the more formalist vision of European modernist photography, seeing it as a distortion of the world rather than a clarification of it, he always remained sensitive to how the slightest shift in a photographer's viewpoint alters the sense and structure of the image. He is best known for his photographs of vernacular American architecture and for the images of rural poverty that he produced in the 1930s for the Farm Security Administration, and his work is generally associated with the documenting of urban and small town America.

Manhattan is therefore an unusual work for Evans, undoubtedly inspired by his 1926–1927 stay in Europe, an experience that was reinforced by his acquaintance with two young Germans, the painter Hanns Skolle and the architect Paul Grotz. Grotz, an advocate of the new unadorned modernist style in architecture, apparently lent Evans his Leica camera, and he later recalled that Evans was attracted to the cultural life of Berlin, in particular German film and architecture. The sharply angled perspective and the emphasis on dynamic geometrical shapes that we see in *Manhattan*, as well as in other works (see fig. 23.1), are certainly reminiscent of the experiments made by German photographers, particularly those associated with the Bauhaus.

This photograph is significant not only because it is a rare example of Evans working in an abstract manner but also because it encourages us to look with renewed interest at our everyday surroundings (see also fig. 23.2).

Fig. 23.1   Walker Evans, *New York City*, c. 1928–1929, gelatin silver print. National Gallery of Canada, Ottawa (30734)

Fig. 23.2   Walker Evans, *Wall Street Windows*, c. 1929, gelatin silver print. The J. Paul Getty Museum, Los Angeles

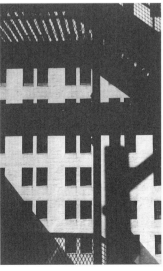

St. Louis, Missouri 1903–1975 New Haven, Connecticut
Subway Portrait **1938–1941**
Gelatin silver print, 12 × 18.5 cm, sheet 20 × 25.2 cm
19428

Annotations   verso, l.l., *1588*, l.c., stamped, *Walker Evans / VI 116*, l.r., *11*
Provenance   gift of Phyllis Lambert, Montreal, 1982.

Walker Evans is best known for the spare, lyric photographs of sharecroppers that he made for the Farm Security Administration in the middle of the Great Depression. His career lasted over five decades, during which he made thousands of photographs of a range of subjects that encompassed Victorian architecture, the Brooklyn Bridge, road signs, tools, pedestrians, and subway passengers. With their seemingly neutral and unsentimental style, his photographs documented life in mid-century America and paved the way for a generation of photographers who would similarly reject artiness and aestheticism in favour of a direct, dispassionate presentation of reality.

Evans spent the larger part of his childhood first in St. Louis, Missouri, and then in a suburb of Chicago. When his parents separated, he moved with his mother to New York. In 1926 he went to Paris to study literature at the Sorbonne, and while there he also spent some time working at the famous Nadar photography studio. He was back in the United States by 1928, living in Greenwich Village among a circle of writers that included Hart Crane and James Agee. Evans had originally dreamed of becoming a writer too, but he now began making photographs. A decade later, in 1938, his achievement was acknowledged by the Museum of Modern Art in a retrospective exhibition and an accompanying publication, *Walker Evans: American Photographs*. Evans went on to work briefly as a staff writer for *Time* magazine, and then embarked on a twenty-year career as a photographer and writer for *Fortune*. In 1965 he was offered a professorship at Yale University, where he taught until his death in 1975.

Between 1938 and 1941 Evans surreptitiously made a large number of portraits of passengers in the New York subway. He took these photographs with a camera that was hidden inside his coat and controlled by means of a shutter-release cable threaded through the sleeve. Evans thus photographed all of his subjects without their knowledge, framing his portraits of them in a somewhat haphazard way. The poor lighting in the trains and the small, crowded spaces posed special difficulties – not to mention the fact that then, as now, it was illegal to take pictures in the subway.

The project resulted in over 600 negatives, out of which 89 photographs were eventually selected by Evans for publication. For reasons that have never been entirely clear, the photographs were held back and not published until 1966, in a book titled *Many Are Called* that accompanied an exhibition at the Museum of Modern Art. A slightly enlarged version of the book was issued by the Metropolitan Museum of Art and Yale University Press in 2004 to coincide with the centenary of the New York subway system.

In the present image, two older women are seated underneath a sign that identifies the terminal stations of the Lexington Avenue line. The woman on the left is staring upward distractedly, while her companion seems to be addressing her. In other frames the women are caught in a variety of poses, and the difficulty that Evans had in controlling the framing is obvious (see figs. 24.1–3).

One of Evans's inspirations for his subway portraits was Daumier's *Third-Class Carriage* (fig. 24.4).[1] Other artists who used New York subway passengers as subjects around this same period included the painters Reginald Marsh and Mark Rothko and the printmaker Ellen Simon. As Sarah Greenough has observed, the subway had become "a ripe subject for the socially committed artist … a symbol of the 1930s, a counterpoint to the skyscraper imagery of the 1920s."[2]

Fig. 24.1–3   Walker Evans, *Subway Portraits*, 1938–1941, gelatin silver prints. The J. Paul Getty Museum, Los Angeles

Fig. 24.4   Honoré Daumier, *The Third-Class Carriage*, c. 1863–1865, oil on canvas. National Gallery of Canada, Ottawa (4633)

25 Gertrude Fehr
Mainz, Germany 1895–1996 Lausanne
Process of Transformation c. 1930
Gelatin silver print, 27 × 29.8 cm
35920

Annotations verso, u.l., *20*, c., *7*

Provenance purchased from Prakapas Gallery, La Jolla, California, 1991.

The motif of newspaper pages and headlines is not unusual in German photography of the 1920s and 1930s, often appearing in photomontages such as this work by Gertrude Fehr. Given the greater number and wider distribution of newspapers in Europe during the first decades of the twentieth century and their central role in keeping the populace informed, it is not difficult to appreciate the excitement that they generated in a region with turbulent politics and also with significant increases in literacy. As Europe moved toward war, for the second time in the century, news, newspapers, and photojournalism were sources of tremendous interest. At the same time, the energetic, readymade graphics that a newspaper page provided would have been highly seductive to the photographer. We see this in S. Friedland's photomontage *Die Käufliche Presse*, which appeared in the influential 1929 publication *Foto-Auge*, predating Fehr's image.[1] Heinz Hajek-Halke created a similar photomontage in 1928 (fig. 25.1).

The vertiginous, hallucinatory drama of *Process of Transformation* has a strong counterpart in another Fehr photomontage in the National Gallery of Canada's collection, *Street Vendor*, from about 1940 (fig. 25.2), in which the shrill excitement of the news announcer is the central theme. In their meshing of formal concerns with an interest in contemporary issues, both of these works capture the conditions of Europe between the wars.

Gertrude Fehr was born in 1895 in Mainz. From 1918 to 1921 she studied photography at Eduard Wasow's studio in Munich, and in 1922 she established a portrait studio in nearby Schwabing. In 1933 she moved to Paris with her husband, the painter Jules Fehr. They established a school of photography called Publiphoto on the Rue Simon Derem. Around this time Fehr began to experiment with solarization and to work with the superposition of negatives. She specialized in portraits of theatre personalities, and it seems that her sense of theatricality was not limited to these sittings but in fact was an underpinning of much of her work. Perceiving a stiffness in some photographic portraits, she once stated that a photograph should be the result of "inspired inspiration" and "not a warrant for arrest."[2]

Fig. 25.1 Heinz Hajek-Halke, *Angst*, before 1928, gelatin silver print. Heinz Hajek-Halke Collection, Agentur Focus, Hamburg

Fig. 25.2 Gertrude Fehr, *Street Vendor*, c. 1940, printed after 1975, gelatin silver print. National Gallery of Canada, Ottawa (35869)

26 Andreas Feininger
Paris 1906–1999 New York
Cities Service Building, New York c. 1945
Gelatin silver print, 33.3 × 24.8 cm, sheet 35.3 × 27.8 cm
41993

Inscriptions verso, l.r., *Andreas Feininger*
Annotations verso, l.l., *T 2/5*, l.c., *2281*
Provenance gift of the artist's son, Tomas Feininger, Quebec City, 2007.

Andreas Feininger's work as a photographer covered a wide spectrum, from landscape and architectural photography, to portraiture, to the macrophotography of leaves and insects. What unified it was an attraction to the organizing principles behind natural and man-made forms. Within each area of interest there were certain recurring motifs to which he was especially attracted. In portraiture, he selected close-ups of the faces of workers wearing goggles, visors, and masks as they used their instruments. In architecture, he was drawn to the dynamic graphic forms of fire escapes, with their play of horizontal and vertical lines, which he often placed in the foreground as a framing device. Featured in several of his views of New York, they supply a readymade composition of complex geometry, as *Cities Service Building, New York* demonstrates. Berenice Abbott's *Exchange Place* (cat. 2) is a similarly structured vertical composition of silhouetted masses and slivers of light. With its extreme downward view, however, Abbott's photograph conveys an almost claustrophobic compression of space, while Feininger's upward view leads us out into the open sky.

Feininger's photographs of buildings, street facades, and urban vistas constitute some of his best work. Having worked as an architect, he understood these subjects well. Feininger's early interest in architecture was probably a result of his contact with the architect Walter Gropius at the Bauhaus in Weimar, where he enrolled in 1922 at the young age of sixteen. He began his formal studies in architecture in 1925 at the Bauschule in Weimar, and he continued them at the Staatliche Bauschule in Zerbst in 1927–1928. After practising as an architect in Dessau and Hamburg from 1929 to 1931, Feininger left for Paris in 1932 to work in Le Corbusier's studio. In 1933 he moved to Stockholm, where he remained active in architecture for a brief time. By 1936, however, he had switched completely to working in photography. The employment restrictions imposed on foreign residents in Sweden in the late 1930s led Feininger to leave for the United States. In 1939 he arrived in New York, together with his wife and son, and settled there. He soon found work as a photojournalist for the Black Star Picture Agency and was subsequently employed on a retainer for *Life* magazine.

Feininger came from a family that was steeped in the knowledge and practice of art. His father, Lyonel Feininger, was an influential painter and had taught at the Bauhaus in Weimar for several years. T. Lux Feininger (see cat. 27), one of Andreas's two younger brothers, was a photographer who was noted for his informal photographs of Bauhaus students, faculty, and productions, and it was his initial fascination with cameras in his teens that is said to have inspired Andreas.

Cities Service Building, New York is one of Andreas Feininger's many photographs of New York skyscrapers (see figs. 26.1 and 26.2). Before moving to New York he had already published a number of instructional books on photography, as well as his first book devoted to a city, *Stockholm*, published in 1936. He went on to publish several books on New York architecture.

Fig. 26.1 Andreas Feininger, *New York 1941 – Looking SSE from RCA Tower towards Brooklyn and Brooklyn Bridge*, 1941, gelatin silver print. George Eastman House, Rochester, Gift of the photographer

Fig. 26.2 Andreas Feininger, *Truck Alley between Michigan and Wabash Avenues*, 1941, gelatin silver print. National Gallery of Canada, Ottawa, promised bequest of Gertrud Feininger, New York (2007.0315.4)

27   T. Lux Feininger

born Berlin 1910

By the Sea 1928

Gelatin silver print, 23.6 × 17.9 cm (irregular), sheet 24 × 17.9 cm

29749

Inscriptions   verso, l.c., *Lux Feininger / Zum Meer*

Annotations   verso, l.l., *26* (circled) *Feininger 6*, l.l., *1928*

Provenance   purchased from Prakapas Gallery, New York, 1987.

By the Sea is typical of Lux Feininger's snapshot approach to photography. Here he has photographed his subjects (his brother Laurence, in the middle, and two friends) either with their backs to the camera or partly obscured, breaking every rule for successful picture taking that the manufacturers of cameras and photographic supplies outlined in their manuals. Reminiscent of much avant-garde photography of the 1920s and 1930s, this image, like his iconic portrait of Clemens Röseler (fig. 27.1), is taken from an elevated position, exaggerating the photographer's distance from his subject and focusing attention more on the formal arrangement of the group than on the identities of the individuals. On other occasions Feininger's subjects were posed above him, again affording the opportunity to explore a foreshortened angle (see fig. 27.2). This style is characteristic of the work of Feininger and the group of artists at the Bauhaus who made photographs. Adopting a playful approach to the technology and optics of the medium, they attached little importance to print quality and pre-visualization. They also revelled in the optical surprises that resulted from this more informal approach – oddly angled views, truncated figures, and distorted features.

Unlike his brother, Andreas Feininger, Lux only began to receive recognition for his photographic work in the 1980s. The neglect of Lux as a photographer was due partly to a general lack of knowledge about this body of work, dating mostly from the 1920s through the 1940s, and partly to the fact that his reputation was mainly that of a painter. The sons of the Bauhaus instructor and painter Lyonel Feininger, both Andreas and Lux pursued careers in art. Even before entering the Bauhaus in Dessau in 1926, Lux had been taking a camera with him wherever he went. Many of his photographs from the late 1920s record various activities at the school; a notable series chronicles Oskar Schlemmer's theatre piece *Mensch im Raum*, for which the balconies and roofs of the Bauhaus buildings provided the stage settings.

Feininger's youthful rebelliousness during his Bauhaus years may have led him to a particular choice of subject matter, but in 1928 the remarkably competent images he was producing caught the eye of the photographer Umbo (Otto Umbehr, formerly a student at the Bauhaus in Weimar), who encouraged him to sign up with the recently established Berlin agency Dephot. In 1929 Feininger was selected to exhibit his work in the prestigious *Film und Foto* exhibition in Stuttgart. During the period that Feininger was taking photographs he continued to paint and exhibit as an artist.

Fig. 27.1   T. Lux Feininger, *Clemens Röseler*, c. 1928, gelatin silver print. The Metropolitan Museum of Art, New York, Ford Motor Company Collection, Gift of Ford Motor Company and John C. Waddell, 1987 (1987.1100.476)

Fig. 27.2   T. Lux Feininger, *Members of the Bauhaus Orchestra* (*Josef Tokayer, Liesel Henneberger, Waldemar Alder*), 1931, gelatin silver print. Bauhaus-Archiv, Berlin

Vienna 1895–1990 Brewster, New York
Wilhelm Furtwängler's Hand 1930?
Gelatin silver print, 6.5 × 10.5 cm
29852

Annotations   l.r., blind stamped, *Trude Fleischmann / WIEN LEBENDORFERSTR.3*; verso, u.l., *Wilhem / Furtwanglers hand*, u.r., *photo*, u.r., stamped, *TRUDE FLEISCHMANN / 127 WEST 56th STREET / NEW YORK, N.Y.*

Provenance   Prakapas Gallery, New York, bought by Paul Katz, North Bennington, Vermont, c. 1986; purchased from Paul Katz, 1987.

The hand was a popular motif in European photography of the 1920s and 1930s (see fig. 28.1). Shown isolated from the rest of the body, it acquires a symbolic weight that has been interpreted differently by various scholars. In an article exploring in particular the subject of the hand in German photography of the period, Rosalind Krauss refers to it as representing the extension of technology, namely the camera. In the more banal world of German commercial photography at the time, the hand was often treated as an instrument of genius, power, and supreme creativity. *Wilhelm Furtwängler's Hand* appears to be more closely linked with this latter notion of the heroic genius. A delicate, tightly structured image that has the kind of attraction that exquisitely seen and realized daguerreotypes possess, it was probably taken at the same time as a full portrait of Furtwängler (fig. 28.2).

Like Lisette Model, Trude Fleischmann was born into an upper-middle-class family in Vienna. At the age of eighteen she went to Paris to study painting. Soon after, she returned to Vienna to apprentice to a photographer and finally to establish her own portrait studio in 1920. Fleischmann's clientele included Viennese socialites as well as writers, painters, architects, and musicians, among them Karl Kraus, Oskar Kokoschka, Adolf Loos, Bruno Walter, and Alban Berg. In 1939 Fleischmann, like many other European artists of Jewish extraction, fled the continent and went to the United States. She settled in New York, where she worked as a portrait photographer. A few years after her arrival there she made a powerful portrait of her compatriot Lisette Model (fig. 28.3). In 1969 she took up residence in Lugano, Switzerland.

Fig. 28.1   Jindřich Hatlák, *Study – The Hands of J. Nusl*, 1930s, gelatin silver print. Private collection

Fig. 28.2   Trude Fleischmann, *Wilhelm Furtwängler*, 1930, pigment print. The Metropolitan Museum of Art, Gilman Collection

Fig. 28.3   Trude Fleischmann, *Lisette Model*, 1943, gelatin silver print. National Gallery of Canada Library and Archives, Ottawa, Lisette Model fonds

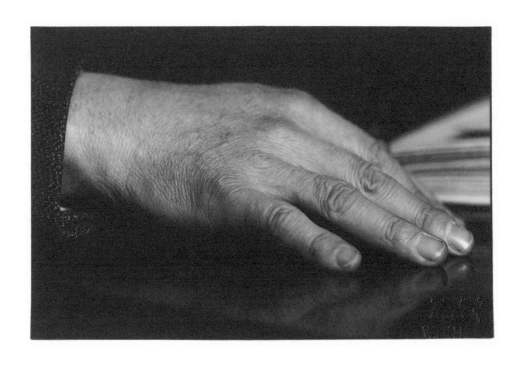

FURTWÄNGLER

Annotations   verso of mat backboard, c., typewritten on label, *165 WJP: LID(?) Jaromir Funke / Untitled (Tribuna) / 1927 / 9.0 × 11.3*

Provenance   purchased from Jane Corkin Gallery, Toronto, 1989.

Objects held a special fascination for Jaromír Funke, even unremarkable objects such as books, magazines, and newspapers, or simple panes of glass (see fig. 29.1). Within a shallow, carefully lit stage he would play with the density or transparency of their surfaces, composing them in such a way as to create a lively play of light and dark. In an article published in 1925 he wrote:

> It is necessary to make progress, step by step, in the arrangement of objects: to advance very carefully and circumspectly so that every compositional defect can become distinct and clear to its author, be explained and, at the same time, removable in the next picture. The composition of objects is management of objects…. Still life is the most distinct path and opportunity for absolutely perfect management of objects, so that individual elements can complement one another and each of them serves the other towards a more distinct depiction, with its outline as well as with its total shape.[1]

The simple graphic power of this studied composition of folded newspapers, their front pages arranged at various angles to each other within a shallow space, challenges the conventional notion of the still life. Instead of displaying a group of different objects with different textures, the photographer here restricts himself to things of uniform shape and graphic character. Funke was a reflective artist who formulated theories around his practice, and who often published his writings alongside his images. It is tempting to believe that in this work he was essentially testing the dynamic potential of the picture plane. The fact that he chose to feature the covers of an arts and letters journal to make this photograph, however, does suggest that he is also making a statement about the importance of art in life.

Funke began to photograph intensively in 1920 while studying law. His first photographs were in the soft-focus style that led to his participation in international camera club salon exhibitions, including some in Canada.[2] Soon, however, Funke became more interested in the innovative approaches to the medium that related to Cubism, Constructivism, and Surrealism. Though he rejected processes such as gum bichromate and bromoil, which subordinated photographic particularity to the soft edges associated with traditional printmaking, there is a quality of softness to this print that suggests that it represents the photographer's transition from Pictorialism to modernism. The exploration of light became increasingly important to Funke, resulting in complex arrangements of transparent objects that produced an intense interplay of light and shadow (see fig. 29.2).

In the 1930s Funke turned his interest toward social documentary photography, recording the lives of the rural poor of Czechoslovakia. He did not, however, abandon experimental photography, but worked simultaneously on *Time Persists*, a series of Surrealist urban photographs. He also pursued an active teaching career. He died in a Prague hospital in 1945 when emergency surgery he was due to receive could not be administered because of an air raid.[3]

Fig. 29.1 Jaromír Funke, *Composition*, 1927–1929, gelatin silver print, silver bromide. The Cleveland Museum of Art, John L. Severance Fund (1986.38)

Fig. 29.2 Jaromír Funke, *Composition IV*, 1927–1929, gelatin silver print. Museum of Decorative Arts, Prague (GF-1.777)

Catalogue

84

30 Sid Grossman
New York 1913–1955 New York
Black Christ Festival, Panama 1945
Gelatin silver print, 26.1 × 28.6 cm
22391

Annotations   verso, l.l., *TR: 13.9–78*, l.r., on dry-mount tissue, *Grossman / Black Christ Festival / Panama 1946*, l.r., *SG XIV*

Provenance   purchased from Visual Studies Workshop, Rochester, New York, 1979.

Sid Grossman took a series of photographs of the Black Christ Festival while he was stationed with the United States Army Air Corps in Panama in 1945–1946, serving in the Air Force Public Relations section.[1] In October 1945 he visited Portobelo, a town with a predominantly Catholic population located near the middle of the north coast of the isthmus, along the Caribbean Sea. It is here that the Black Christ Festival is celebrated once each year, in a tradition that is believed to date back to the seventeenth century. The most eagerly anticipated moment of the festivities is the carrying of the "Nazarene," a life-size wooden effigy of Christ in the form of a Black man, through the streets of Portobelo. On the 21st of every October, between 8 o'clock in the evening and midnight, the sculpture is hoisted on the shoulders of celebrants who carry it out of the church of San Felipe and into the waiting crowds.

In this photograph, Grossman has recorded an extraordinary moment in the pageant, capturing the tension and excitement of the ceremony, and the serendipitous instant when the tightly clasped hands around the supporting poles form, in the center of the picture, a symbolic ring suggestive of the wreath of thorns that crowned Christ. The straining bearer on the right of the image becomes a modern-day Christ figure. As in most religious festivities of this kind, the lighting of votive candles and the arousal of religious fervour result in an atmosphere that is both visually dramatic and emotionally charged. Grossman took this photograph using a hand-held press camera, deliberately exploiting blurred movement and the intense effects of flash to capture the thrilling, mysterious mood of the celebration.

Grossman's interest in communities of differing cultural backgrounds dates back to when he joined the Film and Photo League in the early 1930s.[2] In 1936 Grossman and a fellow member, Sol Libsohn, spearheaded the formation of a breakaway group for still photography that would be called the Photo League. Grossman was a driving force behind many of the educational activities of the Photo League and also participated in several of its "Feature Groups," composed of members who, under the direction of one of them, systematically documented the street life and architecture of working-class neighbourhoods in Manhattan. He participated in the Chelsea group in 1938 and 1939 and also undertook an extensive documentary project in Harlem in 1939 under the auspices of the WPA's Federal Art Project (see fig. 30.1).

Grossman was in charge of the Photo League from 1938 to 1949. In 1947 the Attorney General of the United States blacklisted the League on suspicion that it was a Communist organization. This step was taken as a result of covert investigations made by the FBI into the lives of many of the League's members, including Grossman. Despite the League's valiant efforts to rally its members in the face of charges of subversion, it slowly dissolved. After being placed on the black-list, Grossman found it increasingly difficult to address social issues in his photographs, and he gradually turned to more formal and less threatening subjects. He resigned from the League in 1949. One of his last projects documenting street life was his series of photographs of the San Gennaro Festival in New York in 1948 (see fig. 30.2), where he once again captured the fervent mood of a community celebration.

Fig. 30.1   Sid Grossman, *Swimming Pool, Colonial Park, Harlem*, c. 1938–1939, gelatin silver print. National Gallery of Canada, Ottawa (28653)

Fig. 30.2   Sid Grossman, *San Gennaro Festival, New York*, 1948, gelatin silver print. National Gallery of Canada, Ottawa (22393)

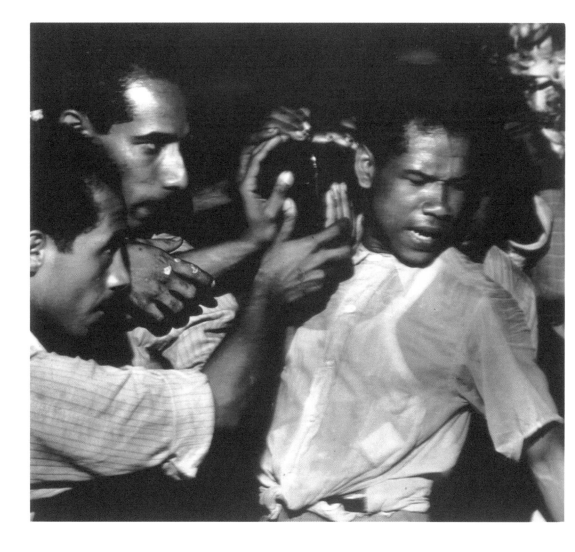

31   John Gutmann

Breslau, Germany 1905–1998 San Francisco

San Francisco Celebrates World's Fair 1939

Gelatin silver print, 19.6 × 19.1 cm

28640

Inscriptions   verso, l.r., *John Gutmann*

Annotations   verso, u.r., *324,6*, l.l., *S.F. celebrates World Fair*, l.l., *1931*, l.c., *JG.255.Y*

Provenance   bought from the artist by Fraenkel Gallery, San Francisco, 1984; purchased from Fraenkel Gallery, 1984.

Like many of his contemporaries in photography, John Gutmann came to the medium with the training of a painter. When he moved to the United States in 1933, in flight from Nazi Germany, he was struck by the cultural differences between Europe and America and illustrated these impressions by making photographs. *San Francisco Celebrates World's Fair*, part of a series begun in 1934 called *The Automobile in the U.S.A.*, applies Gutmann's painterly eye for graphic detail to his experience of the New World's thriving automobile culture, its frontier mentality, and its extroverted nature (see also figs. 31.1 and 31.2).

Gutmann's artistic journey began with painting, which he studied under Otto Müller at the Staatliche Akademie für Kunst und Kunstgewerbe in Breslau. Graduating from there in 1927 he went on to further studies in Breslau and Berlin. His first exhibition of paintings and drawings was held in Berlin in 1927. Possibly looking for a way to earn a living as a photojournalist, Gutmann turned to photography in 1933 and within a short time obtained a contract with Presse-Photo, an agency he continued to work for until 1936. Between his photojournalism assignments for numerous American illustrated magazines and his teaching at San Francisco State College, Gutmann was able to make a living, but he still pursued his artistic career. He exhibited his drawings and watercolours at the Paul Eder Gallery in San Francisco in 1935, and in 1941 he was given a solo exhibition of his photographs, titled *Wondrous World*, at the M.H. de Young Memorial Museum, also in San Francisco.[1]

Fig. 31.1   John Gutmann, *"Yes, Columbus Did Discover America!" San Francisco*, 1938, printed c. 1974, gelatin silver print. San Francisco Museum of Modern Art, Bequest of John Gutmann

Fig. 31.2   John Gutmann, *Pop Advertising, San Francisco*, 1939, gelatin silver print. San Francisco Museum of Modern Art, Purchased through a gift of Amy McCombs and Frederick Currier

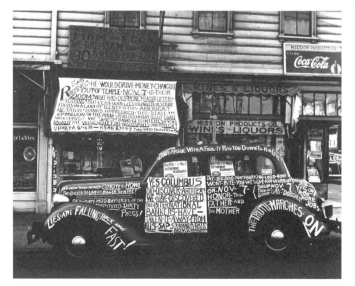

Berlin 1898–1983 West Berlin

Vile Gossip 1932

Gelatin silver print, 33.1 × 29.6 cm (irregular)

29353

Annotations   verso, c., stamped, *H. HAJEK-HALKE / Experimentelle Fotografie / für Presse und Werbung / WASSERBURG-BODENSEE*, c., typewritten on label, *"Üble Nachrede". / 2 verschiedene Belichtungen ein* (that word crossed out) *nacheinander (also 2 Negative) auf / ein Papier*, c., *Hajek-Halke (Fotoforme) / aus Ausstellung Subjektive / Fotografie im Amerikahaus*

Provenance   purchased from Prakapas Gallery, New York, 1986.

Born in Berlin, Heinz Hajek-Halke received his early education in Argentina. He returned to Berlin with his family around 1910. From 1915 to 1916 he studied at the Königliche Kunstschule Berlin, and was then called to serve in the First World War. Returning from duty, he continued his studies and worked as a copper engraver, designer, and editor until 1923. The following year he began to work as a photographer.

The female body was the subject of a significant part of Hajek-Halke's artmaking. A montage of a street scene with three men standing on the outspread nude torso of a woman, *Vile Gossip* is a disturbing image for the way in which the female body has become the surface of the paved road. If in this instance the photographer's message is intended to criticize the subjugation of women, it also has a context in another genre of imagery in which the female body was seen to represent Mother Earth. This notion was not only popular in the 1920s and 1930s, but can be traced back to the latter part of the nineteenth century. Franz Roh explored the relationship of the female body to the landscape in several photomontages (see fig. 32.1).

One of at least three variant images, *Vile Gossip* was made from the superposition of two negatives onto a sheet of photographic paper. This was a technique often used by Hajek-Halke and other photographers of the period, in which two or more negatives would be used interchangeably with others to produce completely different pictures. The method is exemplified in another photomontage by Hajek-Halke, *Autumn* (fig. 32.2).

This print of *Vile Gossip* was exhibited in Amerikahaus in Munich in 1951 as part of Otto Steinert's important exhibition *Subjective Photography*. In an essay in the exhibition catalogue, J.A. Schmoll gen. Eisenwerth refers to it and another Hajek-Halke work, *Heimat der Matrosen*, as examples of the "use of the nude photograph in montage for surrealistic allusions of a covertly sarcastic nature."[1] Hajek-Halke was so adept at photomontage that he was asked by the Nazi ministry of propaganda in 1933 to manipulate documentary photographs for them, which he evidently refused to do.[2]

Although Hajek-Halke worked as a freelance photographer and photojournalist for many years, he remains best known for his expressive work and for his activity as a teacher at the Hochschule für Bildende Künste in Berlin, where one of his many students was the German photographer Dieter Appelt.

Fig. 32.1   Franz Roh, *Untitled* (*Nude in Park Landscape; Daphne II*), c. 1922–1928, gelatin silver print. Courtesy Kicken, Berlin

Fig. 32.2   Heinz Hajek-Halke, *Autumn*, c. 1932, gelatin silver print. Heinz Hajek-Halke Collection, Agentur Focus, Hamburg

Berlin 1891–1968 East Berlin

Adolf the Superman Swallows Gold and Spouts Junk before August 1932

Gelatin silver print, 33 × 24.1 cm, sheet 35.4 × 24.6 cm

22863

Annotations   verso, u.r., *4* (circled), c.r., *Heartfield / "Adolph the Superman ...*, l.r., *SGJH2A*

Provenance   **purchased from Visual Studies Workshop, Rochester, New York, 1979.**

John Heartfield's photomontages of the 1930s are among the most striking expressions of political satire in the twentieth century. While Max Beckmann, Otto Dix, and George Grosz generally attacked the complacency and corruption of the rich and powerful, Heartfield pointedly attacked the political leadership of the Weimar Republic and the Third Reich.

Along with Hannah Höch and George Grosz, Heartfield was among the first artists to recognize how photographic images taken out of their context could be recomposed and used to subvert their original intention. In *Adolf the Superman Swallows Gold and Spouts Junk*, which first appeared as an illustration in the socialist weekly *Arbeiter Illustrierte Zeitung* in July 1932,[1] Hitler's head has been taken from a photograph of him addressing a crowd in Berlin's Lustgarten in April of that year (fig. 33.1). Heartfield has cleverly placed the head above a chest X-ray – possibly his own – and has turned the esophagus into a column of gold coins. A swastika substitutes for a heart. The theme of Hitler and money, a reference to the financial support that the Nazi party received from wealthy industrialists, was a subject that Heartfield addressed in other images as well (see fig. 33.2). The National Gallery of Canada's print was made for a 1938 exhibition at the Photo League in New York, from the original photomontage but without the caption that had accompanied the magazine's photogravure reproduction.

The power of Heartfield's art lies less in his ability as a photographer than in his gift for recognizing how to transform the photographs made by others. In creating his photocollages and photomontages he had recourse to a supply of images that he used as source material. On occasion he would hire a photographer to produce a specific image; at other times he would search in picture archives.[2] David Evans has described his working method as follows:

> Typically, Heartfield first made a pencil sketch of an idea, often after discussions with his brother. He undertook the picture research, but a photographer did the original image making, as well as the copying and printing to size, following his instructions. The combination was Heartfield's work, but someone else often did the retouching.[3]

Born in Berlin, Helmut Herzfelde anglicized his name in 1916 at the end of his military service. He studied painting and drawing, beginning in 1905 in the studio of Hermann Bouffier and ending in 1911 at the Kunstgewerbeschule in Munich. Although very much involved with the Dada movement and a close collaborator of George Grosz, Heartfield turned to commercial art studios to find work from 1911 to 1919. It was through the contacts he made at this time that he entered into the theatre world and the publishing industry. From 1921 to 1923 he was the art director for Max Reinhardt's Deutsches Theater in Berlin. He enjoyed a close relationship with his brother Wieland, for whom he worked as an illustrator at Malik Editions from 1924 to 1933. In 1924 he joined the newly formed Rote Gruppe, the association of Communist artists in Berlin.

Being both a Communist and a Jew, as well as a visible critic of the Nazis, Heartfield decided to leave Germany when Hitler came to power in 1933. He moved to Prague, and during his five years there participated in several local exhibitions that resulted in protests from the German embassy and the confiscation of some of his works. He fled Prague in 1938, making his way to England, where (like many German refugees) he was interned in a camp for a period at the start of the Second World War. After the war he settled in East Berlin and worked mainly as a stage designer.

Fig. 33.1   Unknown, *Hitler Speaking in the Lustgarten, Berlin, April 4, 1932*, 1932, gelatin silver print. Stefan Lorant Collection, Research Library, The Getty Research Institute, Los Angeles (920024)

Fig. 33.2   John Heartfield, *The Meaning of the Hitler Salute: Little Man Asks for Big Gifts / Motto: Millions Are Behind Me!*, from *AIZ* XI:42 (16 October 1932), frontispiece, photoengraving. Akademie der Künste, Berlin, Kunstsammlung Heartfield (217)

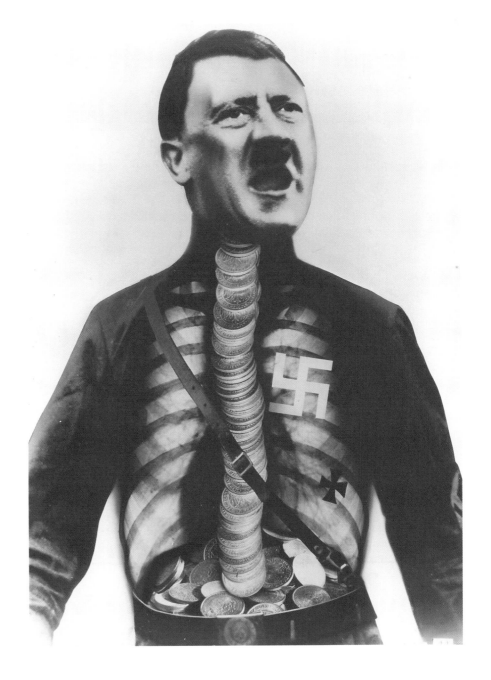

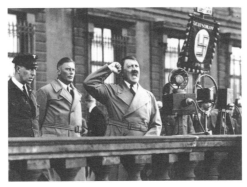

DER SINN DES
HITLERGRUSSES:

MILLIONEN
STEHEN
HINTER MIR!

Kleiner Mann bittet um große Gaben

Pirmasens, Germany 1912–2000 Lindenberg, Germany

On the Waves of Dreams 1935

Gelatin silver print collage, 12.6 × 17.9 cm

39769

Annotations verso, c., stamped, partly covered by label, *Marta Hoepffner / FRANKFURT/M / PHOTO* [...] *IK / Marta Hoepffner / HOFHLIM A. TAUNUS*, l.c., *Traum 3*, l.c., printed on label, *Marta Hoepffner / Eichendorffweg 56/58 / 7993 Kressbronn / Bodensee*, b., *Das Illustrierte Blatt 1935*

Provenance acquired from the artist by Adam Boxer, New York, c. 1995; purchased from Charles Isaacs Gallery, Malvern, Pennsylvania, 1998.

On the Waves of Dreams is the second collage in the series *Tonight I Dreamed (A Stroll over the Waves of Consciousness)*. The suite of seven images (see also fig. 34.1) describes the descent of a woman into a dream state. As she slips into a hallucinatory world of semi-consciousness, sleep transports her into a realm of unimagined beauty and terror where, fully released from her earth-bound condition, she drifts among the stars, faces monsters, and is brought back to consciousness by her mother. *On the Waves of Dreams* shows her having fallen asleep and her bed floating on a swelling ocean.

Published in *Das Illustrierte Blatt* in March 1936, this series of photocollages was made by Marta Hoepffner when she was a young artist influenced by Dada and Surrealist thinking. In the accompanying text she refers to the experience of the dream as a state of heightened sensation and remarks on the fluid boundaries between sleep and dream:

> Beyond the mysterious border of sleep, our "I" encounters a new, unfamiliar land. Here the laws of sensible reality hold no sway. Gravity is thrown over – we float and fly. Beings approach us that our conscious minds insist cannot exist. Events break over us, and vainly we urge ourselves to remain calm, wish to be convinced of their impossibility. The deeper we sink into the purple depths of the dream, the more accustomed to it we become, the more viscerally we experience joy and pleasure.[1]

Hoepffner's observations are highly reminiscent of what Breton and other Surrealists like Crevel and Desnos anticipated and experienced from the dream exercises and hypnotic trances they practised. Hoepffner's association with the Dadaist Hugo Ball suggests that she would have been familiar with Breton's manifesto and the Surrealist interest in transcending the boundaries of consciousness through dreams. Her title for this work, *On the Waves of Dreams*, could be a direct reference to Aragon's *Une vague de rêves*.

Collage was considered by the Surrealists to be an ideal medium for juxtaposing disparate objects, thus creating a new, unexpected "reality." And photocollage was an especially popular choice of medium – seen in the work of Hannah Höch, John Heartfield, Jindřich Štyrský, Georges Hugnet, and others – because it could even more potently subvert and transform reality.

Though she presented a number of solo exhibitions from 1949 to the late 1970s, Hoepffner is little known outside of Germany. She was born in Pirmasens, south of Frankfurt, in 1912.[2] In 1929 she encountered the work of the Dadaist co-founder and writer Hugo Ball and was much influenced by it. That same year she enrolled at the Kunstschule Frankfurt, where she studied painting, printmaking, and photography under Willi Baumeister. In 1934, the year following her graduation from the Kunstschule, she was involved in the founding of the Ateliers für Werbefotografik in Frankfurt. A self-portrait made in 1941 (fig. 34.2) shows her interest in the use of photomontage.

Fig. 34.1 Marta Hoepffner, *Passage through the Otherworldly Realm*, 1935, gelatin silver print. Private collection

Fig. 34.2 Marta Hoepffner, *Self-portrait in Mirror*, 1941, gelatin silver print. Los Angeles County Museum of Art, The Audrey and Sydney Irmas Collection (AC 1992.197.69)

35 Horst P. Horst

Weissenfels, Germany 1906–1999 Palm Beach Gardens, Florida
Electric Beauty **1939, printed later**
Gelatin silver print, 24.3 × 19.3 cm, sheet 35.3 × 27.7 cm
41643

Inscriptions   u.r., from negative, *4617-5*; verso, c., *Horst*

Annotations   verso, l.c., *PF 23184*, l.c., stamped, *HORST ©*

Provenance   purchased from Howard Greenberg Gallery, New York, 2005.

Daring forays into foreshortened perspectives, dream imagery, and surreal juxtapositions of objects revitalized modernist advertising and fashion photography. The best fashion photography of the 1920s and 1930s in Europe and the United States was elegant, witty, and stylish, and often included clever borrowings from the repertoire of masterpieces of Western painting. Photographers such as Horst, George Hoyningen-Huene, Edward Steichen, Cecil Beaton, Erwin Blumenfeld, and Herbert List, to mention but the most renowned, left us images that went far beyond their original purpose of grabbing attention for the latest fashion creations. These photographers not only understood the principles of carefully crafted composition and seductive presentation, but also created a highly original theatre-based set of conventions for the posing and lighting of their models.

Born in Weissenfels, Germany, in 1906, Horst Paul Albert Bohrmann changed his name to Horst P. Horst in 1943, three years after he had moved to the United States. He did this in order to ensure that he would never be associated with Hitler's private secretary and head of the Nazi party chancellery, Martin Bormann, a coarse and brutal man whom Horst abhorred. In the mid-1920s Horst attended the Kunstgewerbeschule in Hamburg, studying painting and preparing to become an architect. He then moved to France, where he worked for some years as an apprentice to Le Corbusier. Visiting a friend at *Vogue* magazine in Paris, he was invited into the studio, where his latent interest in photography was piqued. This experience led to his move from architecture into fashion photography. Between 1935 and 1940 Horst commuted between the *Vogue* studios in Paris and New York.

Electric Beauty dates from 1939, the year in which Europe entered the Second World War. With its backdrop relating to Hieronymus Bosch's *Temptation of Saint Anthony*, it goes beyond a depiction of the more surreal aspects of the fashion industry to communicate a sense of impending menace. The photograph shows a woman seated under a lamp undergoing a beauty treatment that entails having her face covered by a heat mask with one small breathing hole. Electrical cords snake around her entire body. She holds an electric nail buffer in one hand and steadies the overhead lamp with the other. One of her legs is lathered with hair-removing cream, and the other rests in a tub of soapsuds. The analogy to the Bosch figures that animate the backdrop is not all that far-fetched, and the same may be said with regard to a variant view showing the model without the mask (fig. 35.1).

Mainbocher Corset (fig. 35.2), thought to be the last photograph that Horst made before the outbreak of war, is a fine companion piece to *Electric Beauty*, reinforcing a mood of eeriness. Horst enjoyed friendships with both Schiaparelli and Dalí, who had introduced Surrealism into the world of fashion, and though he did share many of their predilections, he claimed to have only once consciously made a fashion photograph that reflected the Surrealist aesthetic (presenting a piece of Cartier jewelry).[1] *Mainbocher Corset* nevertheless suggests a strong indebtedness to Dalí's sense of arrested moment, flat lighting, empty space, and inexplicable relationships between objects.

Fig. 35.1   Horst P. Horst, *Electric Beauty* (variant), 1939, gelatin silver print. Horst Archive

Fig. 35.2   Horst P. Horst, *Mainbocher Corset, Paris*, 1939, printed later, gelatin silver print. National Gallery of Canada, Ottawa (41644)

Loutzk, Ukraine 1899–1976 Moscow
The Shower 1935
Gelatin silver print, 49.6 × 34.9 cm; sheet 49.8 × 39.7 cm
35078

Annotations   verso, l.l., *IGNATOVITCH I*

Provenance   the artist's widow; purchased from Prakapas Gallery, New York, 1990.

Boris Ignatovich's back view of a naked young man hosing down a line-up of similarly naked men explores an unusual subject in an unconventional manner. It differs radically from Ignatovich's more typical photographs of smiling rural peasants and of earnest workers and the products of their labours. Having no reformist message and being strongly atmospheric, it departs from the style of the party-line photographs required by the Soviet propaganda machine. Its fascination with physical culture and the ideal body calls to mind German, Italian, and also Soviet paintings from the 1930s. As Christopher Wilk has observed, it was during the modernist period that "images of sports men and women, dancers and gymnasts, swimmers and sunbathers … were everywhere, shown in mass-circulation magazines and in newsreels, in design publications, in art galleries and in public exhibition spaces."[1]

The Shower indicates what Ignatovich's work might have been like had he enjoyed the liberty to photograph what he wished. Here he uses several rule-breaking and highly effective pictorial strategies to arouse our curiosity. The principal figure is seated with his back to the viewer; the photograph is shot into the light, thus thrusting the dominant foreground figure into semi-silhouette; the tableau of spindly male figures (who are similarly facing away from the viewer) is separated by a veil of steam. The effect of all this is a diminishing of the far background to the point where it has almost disappeared, and a compression of the layers of information in-between. Unlike Alexander Rodchenko's *The Pair* (fig. 36.1), in which two young pioneers clad in bathing suits gaze optimistically outward, Ignatovich's "New Man" is like a figure set in a mirage.

Ignatovich and Rodchenko came to photography from very different backgrounds. While Rodchenko was steeped in art and art schooling, Ignatovich's introduction to the medium was through journalism. He first moved to Moscow from the Ukraine in 1921 to edit various magazines, and then a year later established himself in Leningrad for a three-year period, working in the same capacity with a group of satirical magazines. By the time he returned to Moscow he had also become a skilled photojournalist. It was in 1927, however, when the magazine *Bednota* was publishing many of his photographs, that he began to think seriously about formal and aesthetic issues in photography, particularly in relation to the subject matter of post-revolutionary Russia – machinery, industry, and workers.[2]

Despite their divergent backgrounds, Ignatovich and Rodchenko had a great deal of respect for each other. Both were members of the artists' union Oktjabr, established in 1928. Within their circle and in various publications both men promoted experimental photography, and both also worked for the lavishly illustrated *USSR in Construction*, which despite its rank propagandistic vision could boast one of the most interesting avant-garde layouts of the time for a picture magazine.

In the late 1920s the cultural climate became increasingly restrictive. It was decreed that photography, like all the visual arts, had to serve the working people as "ideological propaganda" and support the "production and immediate organization of … collective everyday life."[3] Along with other photographers, Ignatovich and Rodchenko were bullied into increasing the informational content of their images. Finally both came under attack from their colleagues in Oktjabr for embracing a foreign aesthetic and for being too avant-garde and too bourgeois. Rodchenko was expelled from the union in January 1932.[4] Ignatovich remained a member until the union itself was disbanded, in April of the same year.

Fig. 36.1   Alexander Rodchenko, *The Pair*, 1932, gelatin silver print. Private collection

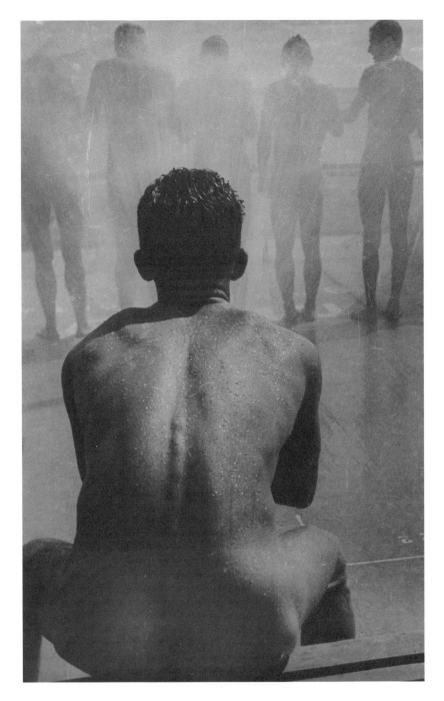

Thorn, Germany 1896–1990 Concord, New Hampshire
Untitled **1946–1955, printed 1979**
Palladium print, 23.6 × 18.8 cm, sheet 30.5 × 25.4 cm
38524

Inscriptions l.r., *Lotte Jacobi*; verso, b., *Palladium print made by Carlos Richardson under my supervision Lotte Jacobi*

Provenance acquired from the artist by Robert Bourdeau, Ottawa, c. 1984; purchased 1997.

Like Eugène Atget and Helmar Lerski, Lotte Jacobi's first ambition was to make her mark in the theatre. Although her experience with acting in 1914 amounted to not much more than a brief flirtation,[1] she carried her love of performance into her photography when in 1927 she began making portraits in her father's photographic studio in Berlin (for one of her self-portraits, see fig. 9.2). Among the many personalities whose likeness she captured were the German stage and film performers Peter Lorre, Hans Albers, and Lotte Lenya. These portraits were done with a flair for the dramatic moment that often obliged her to crop the image radically in order to eliminate any distracting backgrounds. Jacobi also photographed dancers such as Claire Bauroff, Mary Wigman, Alex von Swain, and Liselotte Felger. Her dance photographs are among the most captivating images ever made of performers executing difficult, gravity-defying movements. Sadly, Jacobi's successful career as a portrait and dance photographer in Germany came to an abrupt halt in 1935 when, as a Jew, she decided to emigrate and settle in New York, leaving behind thousands of her negatives.

Jacobi's reputation in photography is based largely on three bodies of work: the portraits, the dance photographs, and the "Photogenics." The last-mentioned works were made during a period of about nine years from 1946 to 1955. In their pursuit of pure abstract form, these photographs differ radically from the concentration on subject matter that we see in the portraits of celebrities and scenes of dancers in action. At the time that she started on the Photogenics, Jacobi and her sister were running their own photographic studio in New York, and initially one gets the impression that she made them as a diversion from her commercial work. Jacobi herself claimed that the idea of the Photogenics came from Leo Katz, a New York artist and teacher with whom she and her ailing husband took an art class in the mid-1940s.[2] These works were made without a camera. Pieces of glass, cellophane, and scrolled paper were placed in direct contact with the light-sensitive photographic paper, which was then exposed to a moving light source. This produced subtle delineations of the passage of light as it penetrated a variety of media. Unlike photograms, in which objects are exposed to a stationary source of illumination – a method Jacobi thought was too static – the Photogenics are particularly delicate and yet have a strong graphic presence.[3] Starting out as a set of variations on the theme of abstraction in photography, these images show Jacobi's ability to make eloquent and harmonious compositions using just line and light (see fig. 37.1). They also display a talent for creating memorable images out of the most basic materials.

The original Photogenics were made as gelatin silver prints. In 1979, seeing the potential for enhancing the delicacy of the images by producing them as palladium prints, Jacobi hired Carlos Richardson to make a new series from her negatives. As the print in the National Gallery of Canada's collection demonstrates, the use of palladium (as also with the more common platinum process) produces a more refined gradation of mid-tones. While the intent of the Photogenics was quite different from that of the dance photographs, the two groups of images are in some ways closely related. In both bodies of work, the curves of movement are animated by light that is exquisitely subtle and at the same time theatrical (see fig. 37.2) For all the rigorous requirements that go into their making, the Photogenics retain a spontaneity and freshness of vision that Jacobi valued above all.

Fig. 37.1 Lotte Jacobi, *Photogenic*, 1947–1955, gelatin silver print. Lotte Jacobi Collection, University of New Hampshire, Durham

Fig. 37.2 Lotte Jacobi, *Pauline Koner, Dancer*, c. 1937, gelatin silver print. Lotte Jacobi Collection, University of New Hampshire, Durham

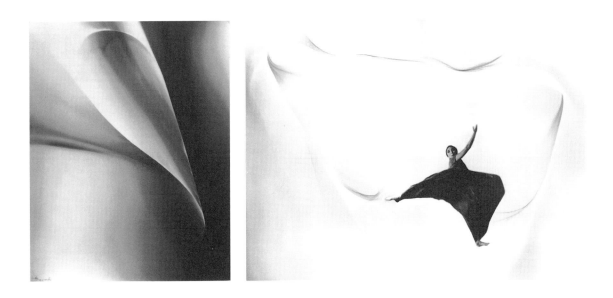

Frankfurt am Main 1897–1973 Newtown, Pennsylvania
Alfredo (Freddo) Bortoluzzi **1928**
Gelatin silver print, 22.3 × 15.2 cm
40575

Inscriptions   verso, c., *Margrit Fischer / 1928*

Annotations   verso, l.l., *RK-83-54*, l.l., *P8309172*

Provenance   acquired from Thomas Walther by Howard Greenberg Gallery, New York, 1998; purchased 2001.

A student at the Bauhaus in Dessau from 1926 to 1928, Grit Kallin-Fischer would have been aware of László Moholy-Nagy's experiments with photography as well as the photographic portraits made by his first wife, Lucia Moholy. She would also have come into contact with many influential artists of the period, including Paul Klee, Josef Albers, and Wassily Kandinsky. Although photography was not formally part of the Bauhaus curriculum until 1929, many students and professors began experimenting with it several years earlier.

In this portrait of her fellow Bauhaus student Freddo Bortoluzzi (see also fig. 38.1), Kallin-Fischer has accentuated the sinuous curve of his elongated neck by photographing him in profile and shirtless. Bortoluzzi's face is white with stage make-up, and small flecks of the face paint have collected on his bare chest. The unusual vantage point and ingenious use of space are typical of photographs produced at the Bauhaus in the late 1920s.

Kallin-Fischer frequently arranged the limbs of her subjects into angles and curves in her tautly composed portraits. In a self-portrait (fig. 38.2) made in the same year as the photograph of Bortoluzzi, Kallin-Fischer's reclining body extends in a strong diagonal across the picture plane. Her arms are placed in opposite directions across her chest, and her awkwardly turned right hand extends the bending line of the counter-diagonal. A cigarette sits between two fingers of her left hand, poised dramatically above her lips, while her right hand rests on the floor.

Grit Kallin-Fischer, born Margrit Vries, began her art studies in Marburg in 1911 with the painter Karl Doerbecker, and then studied with Lovis Corinth in Leipzig from 1915 to 1917. After the First World War she moved to Berlin, where she met the musician Marik Kallin, whom she married in 1920. The couple moved to London but their marriage did not last long. In 1926 Kallin-Fischer returned to Germany, enrolling as a student at the Bauhaus in Dessau. Two years later she went back to Berlin to work as a photographer for the magazine *Gebrauchsgraphik*. In 1933 she married Edward L. Fischer, a fellow Bauhaus student, with whom she moved to the United States in 1934. In 1937 she and Fischer commissioned Walter Gropius and Marcel Breuer, two Bauhaus architects, to design a home and studio for them in Newtown, Pennsylvania. Kallin-Fischer later worked as a sculptor and graphic artist with Hermann Hubacher and Marino Marini, and travelled frequently to Europe.[1]

Freddo Bortoluzzi was born in Karlsruhe, Germany, in 1905. His parents were both Italian – his father a craftsman, his mother a designer. As a young man Bortoluzzi studied at the Staatliche Akademie der Bildenden Künste and then at the Bauhaus from 1927 to 1930. He later worked as a set designer and choreographer in France and Germany. Bortoluzzi died in 1995 in Peschici, Italy.

Fig. 38.1   Grit Kallin-Fischer, *Alfredo Bortoluzzi*, 1927–1928, gelatin silver print. Bauhaus-Archiv, Berlin, Gift of Bortoluzzi, 1993

Fig. 38.2   Grit Kallin-Fischer, *Self-portrait*, c. 1928, gelatin silver print. Bauhaus-Archiv, Berlin

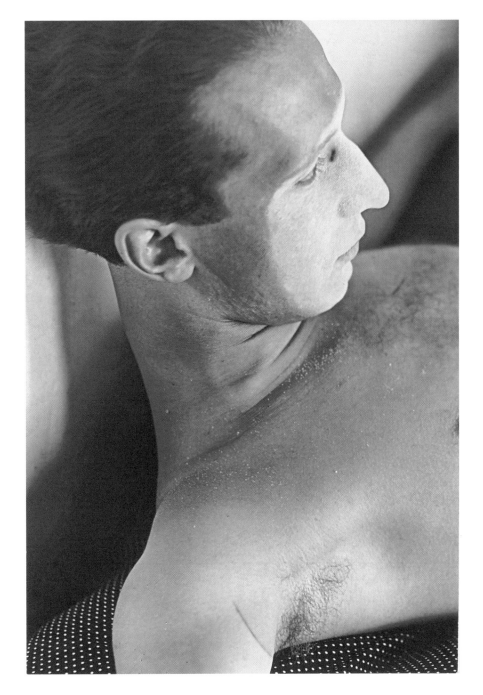

39 Gyorgy Kepes
Selyp, Hungary 1906–2001 Cambridge, Massachusetts

Light Abstraction c. 1940

Gelatin silver print, 35.3 × 27.9 cm

40550

Annotations   verso, u.l., *GK 219*, l.l., *5/2/19*

Provenance   acquired from the artist by James Prestini and Jesse Reichek, Chicago, 1943; transferred to Creators Equity Foundation; Stephen Daiter Gallery, Chicago, c. 1998; purchased from Stephen Daiter Gallery, 2001.

Gyorgy Kepes studied painting at the Royal Academy of Fine Arts in Budapest from 1924 to 1928. During this period he became associated with Munka ("Work Circle"), a group of artists and writers who introduced him to the art and ideas of the Suprematists, the Futurists, and the Constructivists. It was also as a student that Kepes made his first photograms. In 1930, at the invitation of a fellow Hungarian artist, László Moholy-Nagy, Kepes moved to Berlin, where the two began a fruitful collaboration on a variety of design projects. In 1936 he joined Moholy-Nagy in London, and in 1937 he again followed his peripatetic mentor, this time to Chicago, in order to teach at the New Bauhaus and set up its Light and Colour department. The New Bauhaus survived only one year, though Moholy-Nagy was quickly able to reconstitute it as the Institute of Design. By 1946, however, Kepes had moved on and accepted a position at the Massachusetts Institute of Technology, as a professor of visual design. He would later establish MIT's Center for Advanced Visual Studies and serve as its first director, from 1967 to 1972. Throughout his long teaching career he also remained active as a painter, photographer, designer, and writer.

The present work, which is thought to have been made around 1940, demonstrates Kepes's strong sense of graphic design (see also figs. 39.1 and 39.2). Using various tools such as prisms, mirrors, paper cut-outs, and a light box, he explored the elements of space, line, and form in his photographic images. Like Moholy-Nagy, Man Ray, Franz Roh, and others, Kepes also experimented with other photographic techniques in addition to the photogram, including negative printing and solarization. In 1944 he published his theories about the perception of space in the two-dimensional image in an influential book titled *The Language of Vision*.

Fig. 39.1   Gyorgy Kepes, *Untitled*, n.d., gelatin silver print. Courtesy Alpha Gallery, Boston

Fig. 39.2   Gyorgy Kepes, *Twin Forms*, 1943, gelatin silver print. Courtesy Alpha Gallery, Boston

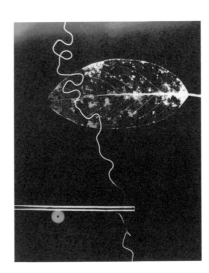

40 André Kertész

40 André Kertész

Budapest 1894–1985 New York

Fork, Paris 1928

Gelatin silver print, 7.5 × 9.2 cm, sheet 8.5 × 10.6 cm

31336

Inscriptions   verso, c., *A. Kertesz / 1928*

Provenance   purchased from David Mirvish Gallery, Toronto, 1978.

André Kertész's long career in photography began as a youthful hobby that he pursued with great enthusiasm during hours off from his job as a clerk at the Budapest stock exchange. In 1925 he moved to Paris and soon met many of the artists and intellectuals who frequented the Café du Dome, a gathering place for newcomers to the city. Among the friends that he photographed were Piet Mondrian, Marc Chagall, Berenice Abbott, Tristan Tzara, and Lajos Tihanyi. *Mondrian's Glasses and Pipe* (fig. 40.1), one of Kertész's famous early still lifes, functions also as a portrait of the artist, not only in its depiction of some personal objects that stand in for their owner, but also in the seemingly offhand but in fact careful arrangement of these objects on a stark white table-top that projects diagonally into a black background – a subtle allusion to Mondrian's pursuit of geometrical abstraction in his paintings.

Kertész was one of the first photographers to exploit the creative possibilities offered by the recent introduction of the 35mm camera. As early as 1928 he was using his first Leica, taking special advantage of its light weight and small size, which allowed him to work unobtrusively in the streets of Paris, nimbly capturing what the Soviet writer Ilya Ehrenburg described as "the moment of truth."

Fork, Paris, made by Kertész in 1928 with his newly acquired Leica, is a deceptively simple and at the same time graphically powerful image. Kertész selected and purchased the fork at a department store and methodically worked out the perfect placement of its tines along the edge of a white plate. The strong lighting creates a deep shadow that is almost as substantial as the fork itself. When the photograph was exhibited at the *Premier Salon indépendent de la photographie* in 1928, the writer Pierre Bost singled it out in his review as "moving in its purity" and "the only work that gave me the impression of being a real work of art."[1] The photograph went on to appear in several popular French and German magazines in 1929 and 1930, and was even used in an advertisement for cutlery (fig. 40.2). The National Gallery of Canada's version is one that was produced on postcard stock – an inexpensive method of printing photographs that was common at the time.

In 1936 Kertész was invited to the United States to work on assignment as a photographer for the Keystone Agency. Although he worked mainly for magazine publishers like Condé Nast from the 1940s to the 1960s, he continued to make photographs for himself up until his death in 1985. These "private" or "sentimental" photographs, as he described them, display the quiet romanticism that infuses much of his work. At the same time, Kertész's photographs are filled with a subtle wit, a keen sense of timing, and a lively appreciation of the absurd.

Fig. 40.1 André Kertész, *Mondrian's Glasses and Pipe, Paris*, 1926, printed c. 1970–1979, gelatin silver print. National Gallery of Canada, Ottawa, Gift of the American Friends of Canada Committee, Inc., 1995, through the generosity of Mr. and Mrs. Noel Levine (37864)

Fig. 40.2 Advertisement from *Die Dame* (Berlin), November 1929

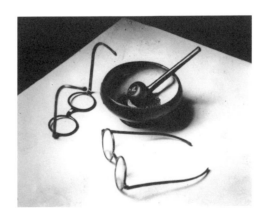

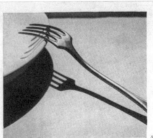

Dresden, Germany 1892–1970 Birkenwerder, German Democratic Republic

Self-portrait **1931**

Gelatin silver print, 30 × 23.8 cm

30355

Annotations   verso, u.r., *A954* (boxed), c., *75* (circled), c., stamped, *Prof. Edmund Kesting*, l.l., *Gallerie Vheurming*(?) /

Zeigr / Werke Von Edmund Kesting / RMG #781.33, l.r., *RMG #781.33*

Provenance   purchased from Jane Corkin Gallery, Toronto, 1989.

Kesting explored his own image with a passion that bordered on the obsessive. Through his trademark use of multiple exposure he heightened the viewer's expectation, naive though it might be, that some hidden truth was being revealed. His self-portraits often prominently include creative instruments such as paintbrushes, cameras, or violins, representing the artistic well-springs of his own life. This self-portrait communicates a playful ambiguity about the nature of visual representation: the artist has photographed his face as it is being crafted into a painted likeness. A ghostly, disembodied hand bearing a paintbrush appears to lightly touch the face near the one visible, wide-open eye. The painter's pale hand, supposedly conjuring an image into being, obscures most of the rest of Kesting's face.

The basic questions that rush to the viewer's mind when looking at this work are both philosophical and technical. What is the artist conveying to us about himself? Why does a paintbrush enjoy such a defined presence in a photographer's self-portrait? And finally, faced with the logistics of the pose, how does the hand relate to the artist's face? Close scrutiny of the vibrant and moody surface of this Kesting print reveals that the photographer, an arch illusionist, used a photomontage technique to introduce the hand with the brush. Kesting not only photographed himself in a variety of poses but also made variant croppings of this image, as in the print in the collection of the Los Angeles County Museum of Art (fig. 41.1).

Kesting was an artist of his time, and the self-portrait was a popular genre among Expressionist painters in Germany and Austria during the first three to four decades of the twentieth century. Within this corpus containing the works of many artists, Max Beckmann's and Otto Dix's extraordinary self-portraits come to mind. But it is Karl Schmidt-Rottluff's half-length frontal self-portrait of 1920 (fig. 41.2), showing the artist gripping a bunch of brushes in one hand while a brush in the other hand paints his forehead, that resonates most strongly as a comparison with this Kesting self-portrait. For Kesting, being an artist of his time meant that he would not only explore both the internal and external world but that he would also experiment with a variety of media, including photography. As an artist fully alert to the changing ideas surrounding picture-making and medium, visual expression and psychological insight, Kesting's self-portrait is also a portrait of an era.

Fig. 41.1   Edmund Kesting, *Self-portrait*, c. 1925, gelatin silver print. Los Angeles County Museum of Art, The Audrey and Sydney Irmas Collection (AC 1992.197.78)

Fig. 41.2   Karl Schmidt-Rottluff, *Self-portrait*, 1920, oil on canvas. Nationalgalerie, Staatliche Museen zu Berlin

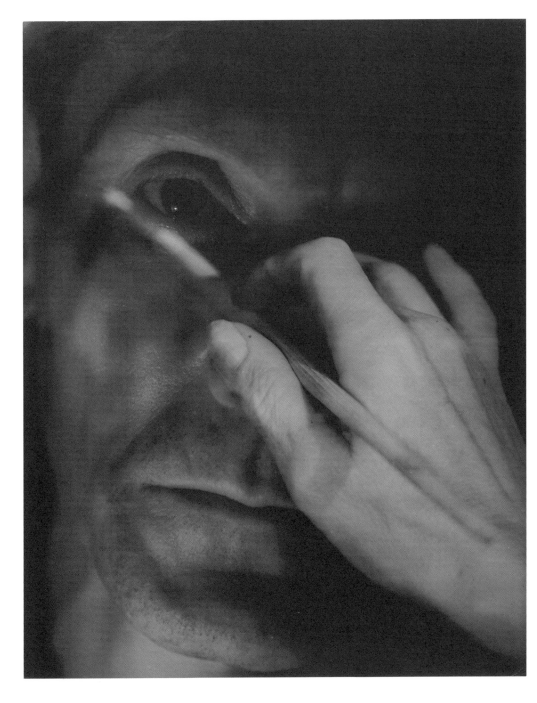

Latvia 1895–1938 Soviet Union
Let Us Fulfill the Plan of the Great Projects 1930
Gelatin silver print, with gouache, 15.6 × 11.4 cm
36854

Provenance   purchased from Walker, Ursitti, and McGinniss, New York, 1993.

Gustav Klutsis was a fighter with a Latvian riflemen detachment in 1917, defending the Bolshevik government. He went to Moscow in 1918 to study at VKhUTEMAS, the state-run art school, and came into contact with Kazimir Malevich and Alexander Rodchenko. *Dynamic City* (1919), a photomontage, and *Electrification of the Entire Country* (1920), a maquette for a poster, were, according to him, the first Soviet photomontages. Prior to producing photograph-based imagery he experimented with painting textured canvases. He also made three-dimensional structures under the tutelage of Antoine Pevsner and Naum Gabo.

While the technique of photomontage was not entirely new, the application of it to political ends by Klutsis, Rodchenko, El Lissitzky, and John Heartfield was. Enthusiastic about the role that art could play in a revolutionary society, Soviet avant-garde artists combined aesthetic innovation with a social message. "Photomontage," Klutsis wrote, "appeared on the 'left' front of art at the time when non-objectivity lost its meaning. For agit-art one needed realistic representation."[1] The photographic element in Klutsis's photomontages of the 1920s, and in this image from 1930 in particular, provided an immediate and convincing way to communicate the rise and empowerment of the masses.

Of all of Klutsis's graphic images made for the thirteenth anniversary of the October Revolution, including drawings for agitprop kiosks, book covers, and posters, *Let Us Fulfill the Plan of the Great Projects* and a later variant, *Male and Female Workers All to the Election of the Soviets*, are the best-known works. The main reason for the prominence of this particular image, which appears in all states of its evolution – source photograph, collage, maquette, printer's proof, finished poster, and lithographic print (fig. 42.1) – is its exceptional graphic quality.

This particular version of *Let Us Fulfill the Plan of the Great Projects* is a maquette. Despite its small scale and preparatory nature, it has a very strong presence. The raised open palm of a hand, placed diagonally in the composition, dominates over a mass of workers' heads and a sea of identical but smaller raised hands. The outstretched, affirming gesture of the hand is the anchor of the composition, its diagonal orientation no less than its repetition supplying a dynamic graphic power to the image. The hand that serves as the leitmotif here is Klutsis's own, demonstrating, according to Tupitsyn, his identification with the masses.[2] Lissitzky similarly used his own hand in a photomontage (fig. 42.2), albeit for an image that was more personal than political.

Klutsis's profound belief in art as an instrument of social change is evident in his work of the 1920s, in which he portrays the masses as a vigorous force in control of their collective future. In spite of his sympathetic sentiments, however, Klutsis (like other artists at the time) faced a demanding public as well as political watchdogs who proved hard to satisfy.

An age-old technique in the making of propaganda art is to deify powerful individuals by making them dominate in size over the scene in which they are shown. This is precisely what Klutsis did when he made a number of images glorifying Lenin in the 1920s. But his enlargement of the leader's figure in relation to his surroundings was not as extreme as it became in the 1930s, when he virtually dedicated his career to the aggrandizement of Stalin. *Let Us Fulfill the Plan of the Great Projects* is Klutsis's last inspired work on the theme of the new Soviet society. Apart from the irony that issues from contemporary views on the progress of that society, there remains the more tragic fact of Klutsis's death by execution eight years later.

Fig. 42.1   Gustav Klutsis, *Fulfilled Plan, Great Work*, 1930, lithograph, printed in colour. The Museum of Modern Art, New York, Purchase Fund, Jan Tschichold Collection (00357.37)

Fig. 42.2   El Lissitzky, *The Constructor (Self-portrait)*, c. 1924, lithograph and gelatin silver print. Private collection, Switzerland / Courtesy Kicken, Berlin

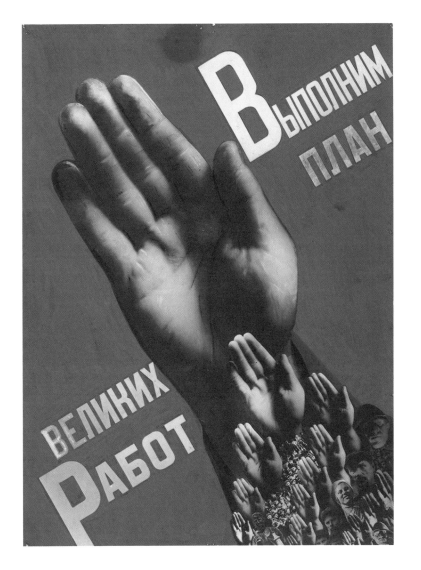

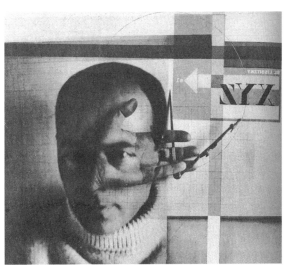

43 Dorothea Lange
Hoboken, New Jersey 1895–1965 San Francisco
White Angel Breadline 1933, printed c. 1945
Gelatin silver print, 34 × 26.5 cm, sheet 35.3 × 27.9 cm
41560

Annotations   verso, c., stamped, *PHOTOGRAPHY BY / DOROTHEA LANGE / 1163 EUCLID AVENUE / BERKELEY /*

CALIFORNIA, l.r., *DL-CAL-E*(?)*B-1413*

Provenance   given to Arvid Anderson by a friend of the artist; purchased from Edwynn Houk Gallery, New York, 2005.

White Angel Breadline is considered to be Lange's first street photograph. Made during the Depression, in the early 1930s, it captures the desperate plight of the unemployed and destitute who were becoming increasingly visible on the streets in large American cities. With tens of millions of unemployed, cities became refuges for job-hunting, displaced people. Early in 1933 Lange became aware of the lines forming outside a soup kitchen that was visible from the window of her studio on Montgomery Street in downtown San Francisco and gradually felt compelled to photograph it. "I looked down as long as I could," she recalled many years later, "and then one day I said to myself, 'I'd better make this happen.'"[1]

Several other croppings of *White Angel Breadline* exist, some of them placing the emphasis on the man in the front by omitting almost everything else, and others enlarging the view to include even more of the background (figs. 43.1 and 43.2). What is striking about this particular cropping – the one that Lange considered the most successful – is the extraordinary way in which the formal composition of the image is balanced with its narrative. Lange focuses the viewer's attention on just one individual in the crowded pen of people lining up for food. This is the figure of a man who, from the evidence of his clothing and dishevelled appearance, has been down and out for some time. Clutching a tin cup, and apparently lost in thought, he leans on one of the wooden railings that crosses the lower quarter of the picture diagonally. His eyes are shielded from the camera's view by the brim of his battered hat, and he has his back to the crowd. He emerges out of this dark sea of men by virtue of his counter-positioning, accentuated by the light that falls on his hat, his cup, and his clasped hands. With Lange's spotlighting of critical details, her composing of the central character slightly left of centre, and her establishment of strong tensions between the vertical and diagonal elements, she has created an image that is theatrical in presentation and engaging in terms of its content. In this regard, it is reminiscent of Alfred Stieglitz's *The Steerage* (fig. 43.3), an image that Lange surely was familiar with. As a number of art historians have pointed out, Lange has struck a brilliant balance here between a collective portrait of humanity and an individual portrait of a person.

It is clear from Lange's most important photographs that she was not a documentary photographer in the strictest sense of the word, searching as she always did for the one image within the sequence, or, alternatively, the detail within that one image that expressed the narrative in its most eloquent form. Therese Heyman points this out in her description of Lange's working method: "Someone working intuitively, as Lange did, would have taken many exposures of the same event, and we know she did here. It wasn't until later that she was actually able to say that, of all the negatives she made here, this one best represents what she wanted."[2]

Lange's *White Angel Breadline* and *Migrant Mother* (cat. 44), along with Arthur Rothstein's 1936 photographs *Steer Skull, Pennington County South Dakota*, and *Fleeing a Dust Storm, Cimarron County, Oklahoma*, are among the quintessential images of the Depression era, but they also occupy a place in the larger history of photographic image-making that makes us turn our attention to the circumstances of everyday as opposed to ideal life.

Fig. 43.1 Dorothea Lange, *White Angel Breadline, San Francisco*, 1933, gelatin silver print. The Dorothea Lange Collection, Oakland Museum of California, City of Oakland, Gift of Paul S. Taylor

Fig. 43.2 Dorothea Lange, *White Angel Breadline, San Francisco*, 1933, gelatin silver print. The Dorothea Lange Collection, Oakland Museum of California, City of Oakland, Gift of Paul S. Taylor

Fig. 43.3 Alfred Stieglitz, *The Steerage*, 1907, printed 1915, photogravure. National Gallery of Canada, Ottawa, Gift of Rosemary Speirs, Ottawa, 1997, in memory of Alan John Walker, Toronto (39132)

Migrant Mother March 1936, printed c. 1950–1959

Gelatin silver print, 33.1 × 26 cm

37848

Inscriptions l.c., *For Charlie Rotkin / from Dorothea Lange*

Provenance acquired from the artist by Charles E. Rotkin, 1963; Neikrug Gallery, New York; purchased from Howard Greenberg Gallery, New York, 1995.

Plagiarized, reworked as a leitmotif for social causes, appropriated as an object of deconstruction for at least one contemporary artwork, and the subject of numerous analyses, Dorothea Lange's *Migrant Mother* has exercised great power over the human imagination. In spite of all the attention it has received, it remains an intense and beautiful image that relates to its time and yet imparts universal meaning. Known also as *Migrant Madonna* for its obvious references to Renaissance religious paintings, this image demonstrates Lange's brilliance as a picture-maker and a portraitist. Her early training in studio portraiture, including a stint with Arnold Genthe in New York, gave her an assurance when faced with composing her subjects in less formal settings.

By the early 1930s Lange had started to work for government aid agencies, documenting in photographs the plight of migrant workers and the conditions under which they were living and working. In August 1935 she took a job with the federal Resettlement Administration as a photographer-investigator, and it was in this capacity that she made her iconic *Migrant Mother*. Lange selected this image of a mother with three of her eight children from a series of five negatives that she made of Florence Thompson and four of her children on a cold, wet March day in a migrant pea-picking camp outside San Francisco. She later recalled the encounter with the woman and her family: "I saw and approached the hungry and desperate mother, as if drawn by a magnet. I do not remember how I explained my presence or my camera to her, but I do remember she asked me no questions."[1]

Seeing *Migrant Mother* in the context of the other images in the series (fig. 44.1, for example), it is clear that Lange wanted to make a photograph that would tell a story and mobilize the public to respond to the plight of these dispossessed people. The impact of the publication of two of the images in the *San Francisco News* (neither of them the classic image) was immediate: Federal Emergency Relief Administration funds were diverted to build two emergency migrant camps and to provide food for the pea-pickers.

Every element in *Migrant Mother* suggests a series of self-conscious decisions regarding aesthetic arrangement and narrative structure. The dynamic lines of the composition create a complex and dramatic interplay of tangible forms. The accents of light draw attention to the mother's tentative gesture of touching her face with her hand, to the expression of anxiety etched in her furrowed brow, and to the vulnerability of the two children whose backs are turned away from the photographer. With shoulders abutting, and the older children's heads nestling into and against the mother's frame, *Migrant Mother* is a pyramid of connected bodies forming a rhythmic tableau of gesture and presenting, albeit only symbolically, an indestructible defense against the outside world.

The many known prints of this image range greatly in quality and were made at various different times. The most interesting comparison is between the J. Paul Getty's print (fig. 44.2), created in the same year as the negative, and prints from a later date, such as the one in the collection of the National Gallery of Canada. Lange's attempt to hide the thumb visible in the lower-right corner of the Getty print was regarded by Roy Stryker, manager of the Resettlement Administration's photodocumentary project, as tampering with fidelity and undermining the credibility of his operation. With his unshakeable belief in photography's truth-telling powers, Stryker failed to understand that Lange was above all a picture-maker who accorded greater value to the narrative power of pictures than the alleged neutral authority of the camera.

Fig. 44.1 Dorothea Lange, *Migrant Mother*, March 1936, gelatin silver print. The Dorothea Lange Collection, Oakland Museum of California, City of Oakland, Gift of Paul S. Taylor

Fig. 44.2 Dorothea Lange, *Human Erosion in California* (*Migrant Mother*), March 1936, gelatin silver print. The J. Paul Getty Museum, Los Angeles

45 Helmar Lerski
Strasbourg 1871–1956 Zurich
Untitled, from *Metamorphosis through Light* 1936
Gelatin silver print, 29 × 23.1 cm, sheet 29 × 23.3 cm
40581

Inscriptions l.l., *LERSKI*

Annotations verso, c., *579*, l.l., *ARK-1500-OM*, l.c., *Ki 9203087*, l.r., *P9203087*

Provenance Lerski estate; Galerie Rudolf Kicken, Cologne; private collection, United States; Christie's, New York; purchased from Kicken, Berlin, 2001.

Helmar Lerski once wrote: "The portrait gains meaning not through a 'true-to-life' surface similarity, but rather through the movement of inner life, as reflected in a given expression, in other words, by making the invisible visible. The static principle means stagnation and death. Movement is life. Art means: to animate."[1] This close-up profile view is part of a series of 175 photographs made by Lerski of a model who posed for him on the rooftop of his studio in Tel Aviv in 1936 for a project he titled *Verwandlungen durch Licht* (*Metamorphosis through Light*). Although extreme close-up views and sharp angles had become a standard element in the portrait photographer's vocabulary in Germany in the 1920s and 1930s, Lerski's approach was unique because of the theatrical way in which he lit and posed his subjects and his habit of taking a great many views in a single sitting. The eccentrically spiritual dimension of his work might seem, at first, to distance him from the avant-garde art of his time, although together with his theatricality it in fact aligns him in some ways with the Expressionists.

Lerski always considered his *Metamorphosis through Light* series to be his most important body of work. He said that with it he wanted to "prove that the photographer can create freely, according to his inner being, in the same way as the painter, the printmaker, and the sculptor."[2] Even in the portraits that he made outside this series, depicting a wide variety of individuals, Lerski usually aimed to express the "inner life" (see figs. 45.1 and 45.2).

It is not surprising to learn that Lerski, like Eugène Atget, had pursued a career in the theatre prior to becoming a photographer. He was born Israel Schmuklerski in Strasbourg, France. His father had arrived there from Poland, and in 1876 the family settled in Zurich. In 1893 Lerski went to the United States to study acting and to perform in German theatre productions in Chicago and New York. He changed his name to Helmar Lerski in 1896. It was around 1911, when he was still living in the United States, that Lerski, whose wife was a professional photographer, started to take photographs of fellow actors. Encouraged to continue in his efforts by the German portrait photographer Rudolph Dührkoop, Lerski abandoned the stage for photography and went on to produce his renowned studies of the human face that sought to represent the universal inner life of people from all walks of life.

By 1915 Lerski had returned to Europe, settling in Germany, where August Sander was in the middle of compiling his monumental typology of the face of mankind. In 1931, two years after the appearance of Sander's *Antlitz der Zeit*, Lerski published his *Köpfe des Alltags*, which has been described as presenting "very extraordinary faces of very ordinary people."[3] That same year Lerski made his first trip to Palestine, in the hope of eventually producing a book that was to be titled "Jüdische Köpfe" ("Jewish Heads"). These photographs appeared in a 1933 magazine series titled *Zeugnisse unserer Zeit* (*Documents of Our Time*), but the book was apparently never realized.[4]

In 1932 Lerski and his wife decided to move to Palestine, where they lived for sixteen years before going back to Zurich. In addition to undertaking *Metamorphosis through Light* and a photographic series on hands during this period, Lerski returned to filmmaking, which had been his principal occupation between 1916 and 1928.[5]

Fig. 45.1 Helmar Lerski, *Charwoman*, 1928–1931, gelatin silver print. George Eastman House, Rochester, Museum Purchase

Fig. 45.2 Helmar Lerski, *Beggar from Saxony*, 1928–1931, gelatin silver print. Museum Folkwang, Essen

Rayograph **1922**
Gelatin silver print, 23.9 × 17.8 cm
19202

Inscriptions   mount, l.r., *Man Ray 1922*

Annotations   verso of mount, t., *1 / Rayographie Man Ray 1922*, c.l., *8* (crossed out) *tir* [..] *de Noaille* [..], c., ← *11 cm* →, c., ← *20 cm* →, l.c., *3629* (circled and crossed out), l.r., stamped, *ORIGINAL*

Provenance   acquired from the artist by Arturo Schwarz, Milan, 1970; purchased from Arturo Schwarz, 1982.

Although Man Ray had made photographs before coming to Paris, nothing he had ever done with a camera excited his interest in quite the way the Rayographs would. In a letter of 5 April 1922 to his American patron Ferdinand Howald, he wrote: "I have freed myself from the sticky medium of paint, and am working directly with light itself."[1] In many respects, Man Ray's Rayographs are a fitting example of the avant-garde's desire to renew the language of art through invention and experimentation. They also are an illustration of the Surrealists' obsession with transforming everyday objects through the making of art. Man Ray claimed that his first Rayographs were produced in his darkroom in Paris purely by accident. Finding an unexposed sheet of paper in the developing tray, he placed on top of it several darkroom objects – a thermometer, a glass funnel, and a beaker. He then turned on the overhead light, and, as he would later recall, "before my eyes an image began to form."[2] He had created his first "cameraless photograph."[3]

The history of the making of cameraless photographs, which would come to be called photograms, starts not with Man Ray, however, but with the British scientist, cryptologist, and photographer William Henry Fox Talbot, who experimented with placing ferns, fossils, and pieces of lace directly onto light-sensitized paper, which he then exposed to the sun. Man Ray claimed to be ignorant of Talbot's efforts as well as those of an artist much closer to his time, Christian Schad, who started exposing scraps of paper and fabric on photographic paper in 1917. What was special about the cameraless photographs by Man Ray, László Moholy-Nagy, and other photographers who began such experiments in the 1920s was the intent to subvert the traditional view of photography as a vehicle of information.

Serendipity has played an important role in art as much as in other areas of human investigation and creativity, but to the Dadaists and Surrealists it was almost a credo. In cameraless photography Man Ray saw an opportunity to exploit the element of chance at the same time as realizing his objective of making automatic images. Ironically, the Rayograph technique launched him into a period of intensely creative activity in which the mind and hand of the author are quite evident. Man Ray's darkroom became a kind of dimly illuminated cave in which he created dream images out of moving shadows and bursts of light. Cut off from the outside world, he explored the patterns that resulted from differing degrees of opacity and translucency in various objects, including crystals and prisms, and experimented with a moving light source in order to obtain an impression of an object's three-dimensionality.

In the present example, the prisms, with their sharp-edged geometric forms and brilliant luminosity, are set off against the soft-edged organic-looking shapes in the upper part of the composition. The tight bundles of hair – or are they dustballs? – appear to float in the space, their highlights giving them an airy, mobile, almost playful presence. As one writer has observed, the Rayographs show a "total lack of gravity."[4] The present image is closely related to several others that Man Ray made probably around the same time using the identical prisms and hair-like substances (see figs. 46.1 and 46.2).

The annotation on the verso of the National Gallery of Canada's print suggests that it may have been owned at one time by Charles and Marie-Laure de Noailles, who were keen supporters and patrons of the Surrealists.

Fig. 46.1   Man Ray, *Rayographie* (*Rayogram*), 1922, gelatin silver print. Tel Aviv Museum of Art, Gift of Peggy Guggenheim, Venice, through the America-Israel Cultural Foundation, 1954

Fig. 46.2   Man Ray, *Rayograph*, 1923, gelatin silver print. The Museum of Modern Art, New York, Gift of James Thrall Soby (117.1941)

Man Ray 1922

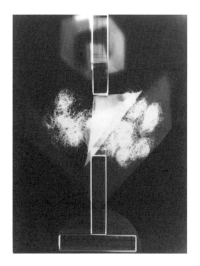

47   Man Ray
Philadelphia 1890–1976 Paris
Mathematical Object 1936
Gelatin silver print, 23 × 29.7 cm
19203

Annotations   verso, u.l., *154* (circled), l.l., *MR8*, l.r., *Man Ray*, and stamped, *Reproduction interdite / sans autorisation écrite / de l'ADAGP / 9 et 11, rue Berryer / Paris – 8ieme / 924-03-87*, l.r., *– MAN RAY – Paris*, and stamped, *Man Ray – 8 rue / du Val de Grace / Paris – 5e FRANCE / DANTON 92-25*

Provenance   purchased from Prakapas Gallery, New York, 1982.

Man Ray first encountered the mathematical constructions housed in the dusty cases of the Institut Poincaré in Paris in the company of his artist friend Max Ernst some time in 1934 or 1935.[1] The objects photographed by him in the mid-1930s were constructed of wood, metal, and plaster, and were created to illustrate algebraic equations. Understanding absolutely nothing about their mathematical significance, Man Ray reveled in the opportunity to photograph these "readymades." In 1963 he wrote: "The formulas accompanying the mathematical objects meant nothing to me, but the forms themselves were as varied and authentic as any in nature. The fact that they were man-made was of added importance to me."[2]

Several of the *Mathematical Objects* images were included in the exhibition *Man Ray: Peintures et objets* at the Galerie des Cahiers d'Art in November 1935, and the card announcing the exhibition featured a witty drawing by Max Ernst that alluded to Man Ray's involvement with these objects (fig. 47.1). Some of the actual constructions from the Institut Poincaré were included in the *Exposition surréaliste d'objets* at the Galerie Charles Ratton in May 1936. The exhibition also included natural objects, interpreted natural objects, and Readymades. In conjunction with the exhibition, Christian Zervos published a special issue of *Cahiers d'Art* (no. 1–2, 1936) devoted to the object and its place in Surrealist art.[3] Twelve of the photographs from the *Mathematical Objects* series were reproduced in this issue, along with essays by Zervos and Breton on Surrealism and the object.

In many ways, the *Mathematical Objects* can be seen as a distillation of Man Ray's early interest in the problem of abstraction, mathematical logic, and the Surrealist concern with rendering absurd the algebraic concept of rational equivalence. The series is also a rare photographic realization of the Surrealist interest in the found object, and it also has significance because it served as a point of departure for a series of paintings called *Shakespearean Equations* that Man Ray executed between 1948 and 1954.[4] A selection of these paintings was shown in an exhibition at the Copley Galleries in Beverley Hills, California, from December 1948 to January 1949. After initially substituting poetic titles such as *Pursued by Her Hoop* and *Death of the Paper Favor* for the original mathematical titles, Man Ray renamed the series *Shakespearean Equations* and named the individual works after Shakespearean plays.[5] The image from the series that the National Gallery of Canada owns a print of was once titled *Surface minima d'Enneper*.[6] It was the source for the painting *Twelfth Night* in the Hirschhorn Museum (fig. 47.2).

Fig. 47.1   Max Ernst, collage, invitation announcement for *Man Ray: Peintures et objets*, Galerie Cahiers d'Art, November 1935

Fig. 47.2   Man Ray, *Shakespearean Equation: Twelfth Night*, 1948, oil on canvas. Hirshhorn Museum and Sculpture Garden, Smithsonian Institution, Gift of Joseph H. Hirshhorn, 1972

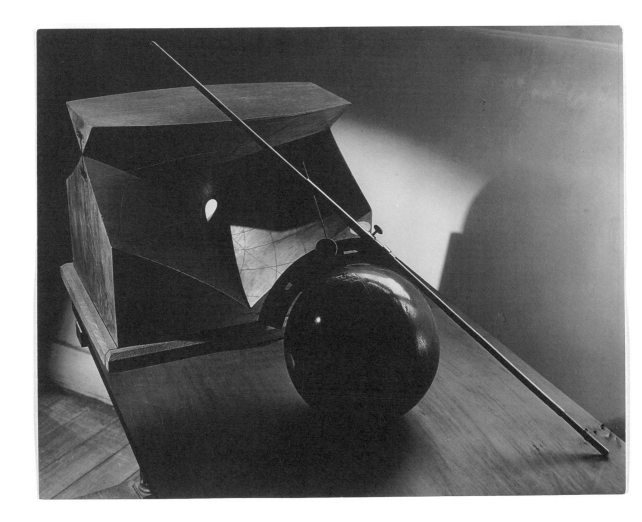

Antwerp 1920–1994 Brussels
Stairs **1949**
Gelatin silver print, 7 × 5 cm
28771

Inscriptions   verso, u.c., *Marcel Marien / 1949*

Annotations   verso, c., ← *11 cic.* → */ 5 cm / ti 100*, l.l., *50* (circled), l.c., *MARIEN 1*

Provenance   purchased from Prakapas Gallery, New York, 1985.

Marcel Mariën was introduced to the Belgian Surrealist author Paul Nougé and the painter René Magritte at the early age of seventeen. He became deeply engaged in Surrealism, eventually challenging André Breton's authority within the movement. Along with other Belgian Surrealists, including Magritte, he called for a "greater independence and vigour of [Surrealism's] Belgian manifestation."[1]

While perhaps best known for his literary work – poems, essays, and the publishing of writings by his fellow Surrealists – Mariën also produced paintings, drawings, and sculptures, as well as photographs and films. His photographs were occasionally embellished with texts or made into collages or fantastic pictorial set-ups of found and constructed objects. Recognition of his talent as a Surrealist poet came early when in 1937 he was invited to participate in the exhibition *Surrealist Objects and Poems* in London.

Mariën was conscripted into the Belgian army and was a prisoner of war in Germany in 1940–1941. On his return to Belgium after his release he began to devote much of his time to publishing and writing. Although he would continue to be preoccupied with the serendipitous and the erotic until the end of his life, Mariën rarely used the term "Surrealist" to describe his work after 1947, on account of its association with Breton.

There appear to be few surviving examples of Mariën's photographs from before the mid-1950s. *Stairs*, from 1949, presents us with a pair of disembodied shoes that seem to be ascending a staircase of their own accord. It is a picture that seems at first glance to belong to the world of spirit photography, but for the absence of the requisite floating ghostlike shapes that characterize this genre. With its playful, poetic animation of the inanimate, this image, like its close variant from about the same period (fig. 48.1), subverts the usual expectation that a photograph is a record of reality, no more and no less. Mariën, a Surrealist by inclination even if he did not sub-scribe to André Breton's strict definition of the movement, would have argued that what is depicted here is indeed reality, but a reality of his own making. Since the Surrealists set out to make art that overturned the established codes of representation, it followed that once Mariën took up pho-tography he would reject the accepted view of how the world should be pictured in photographs. In the late 1930s, in a similar vein, he had created versions of everyday objects distorted so as to be subversive both in appearance and in function (see fig. 48.2).

Although Mariën's later photographs remained playful and irreverent, they frequently resorted to the use of obvious visual shock effects, mocking revered works of art and flaunting pornographic imagery. In 1954 he launched the journal *Les lèvres nus*, in which he published works by promi-nent Belgian Surrealists and Situationists, among them Guy Debord.[2] In the catalogue that accompanied a 1993 survey of contemporary Belgian artists, Michel Baudson described Mariën's studio as "the nerve centre of his ironic activities."[3]

Fig. 48.1   Marcel Mariën, *L'esprit de l'escalier*, 1948, gelatin silver print. Collection of Xavier Canonne, Belgium

Fig. 48.2   Marcel Mariën, *L'introuvable*, 1937, gelatin silver print. Private collection, Brussels

49 Lisette Model

Vienna 1901–1983 New York

Promenade des Anglais, Nice **7 August 1934, printed c. 1940–1949**

Gelatin silver print, 34.2 × 27.6 cm

29041

Inscriptions verso of mount, t., *Lisette Model*, t., *Promenade des Anglais Nice*

Annotations verso of mount, b., *CLM 1083.60 / 500*

Provenance Lisette Model estate; purchased from Sander Gallery, New York, 1985.

Although small in stature Lisette Model was a mighty figure in photography in New York, from the time of her arrival there in the late 1930s until her death in the early 1980s. She was widely revered as a photographer and as a teacher. This striking image of a lounging, stony-faced man staring at the photographer from his chair on the Promenade des Anglais was taken in the mid-1930s, when Model was living in Nice. It is an example of the uncompromising and witty approach to photography that helped create her American legend.

Lisette Model was born Elise Amelie Felicie Stern into a prosperous Viennese family that lost its wealth during the First World War. She moved to Nice in 1924, where her mother had settled after being widowed. In 1933 she abandoned her dreams of a concert career and turned to the visual arts, studying drawing and painting briefly with André Lhote and photography with Rogi André. By 1934 she had decided to become a professional photographer, and the following year she met her husband-to-be, the painter Evsa Model.

In 1934 she began a series of photographs of visitors to the Côte d'Azur who frequented the boardwalk in Nice. These were the images that riveted attention on Lisette Model when she first arrived in New York, in 1938. American photographers like Ansel Adams and Ralph Steiner had never before seen photographs that were so boldly expressive of emotion while bordering on the satirical. Though they were sometimes judged to be lacking in technical polish – according to the standards of American photographers – her images were undeniably powerful. Model was soon offered an assignment by the influential art director of *Harper's Bazaar*, Alexey Brodovitch, to produce a comparable series of portraits on Coney Island, and Ralph Steiner, the picture editor at *PM*, published a selection from the *Promenade des Anglais* series.

As a political refugee in the United States, Model was cautious about what she revealed concerning her European experience, and so she never let it be known that the *Promenade des Anglais* photographs were originally made to illustrate an article on labour strife in Nice and were published in February 1935 in the left-leaning French magazine *Regards*.

In the present photograph from the series there is a strong sense of confrontation between photographer and subject, arising from the seeming closeness of their encounter. Part of this impression was in fact created in the darkroom. Two uncropped images from the original negatives (figs. 49.1 and 49.2) indicate that the expression on the man's face was probably more one of curiosity than of hostility, as it would have been less obvious to him that he was the main object of attention. Using her 2¼ × 2¼ Rolleiflex, held at waist level for viewing, Model gradually moved closer in but still maintained a certain distance. Later, in the printing of the final image, she manipulated the composition through severe cropping and tilted the paper holder to exaggerate the foreshortening of the figure, effectively intensifying the dramatic tension.

Fig. 49.1 Lisette Model, *Promenade des Anglais, Nice*, 7 August 1934, full-frame enlargement by Justin Wonnacott from original negative, 1989. Lisette Model fonds, National Gallery of Canada Library and Archives, Ottawa

Fig. 49.2 Lisette Model, *Promenade des Anglais, Nice*, 7 August 1934, full-frame enlargement by Justin Wonnacott from original negative, 1989. Lisette Model fonds, National Gallery of Canada Library and Archives, Ottawa

Karolinenthal, district of Prague 1894–1989 Zurich
Franz Roh **1926**
Gelatin silver print, 39.3 × 30.1 cm
29152

Inscriptions   verso of mount, l.l., *Franz Roh / 1926*, l.r., *Lucia Moholy*

Provenance   Galerie Rudolf Kicken, Cologne; purchased from Sander Gallery, New York, 1985.

One of the most innovative European avant-garde portrait photographers, Lucia Moholy was associated with the teachers and students of the Bauhaus, although she was never formally connected to the school. Like the artists around her, she believed that visual images should extend the parameters of visual perception. Moholy did not make "psychological portraits," but her portraits are riveting and unconventional for the way in which they capture individual presences under sometimes excruciatingly ordinary conditions.

Moholy (born Lucia Schulz) studied philosophy, philology, and art history at the University of Prague. She was introduced to photography by her husband, László Moholy-Nagy, whom she married in 1921, a year after she had moved from Prague to Berlin. She collaborated with him on the early photograms, one of which was a joint self-portrait (fig. 50.1). She also made architectural photographs and portraits, and taught for a period of time. In 1933, like many of her contemporaries, she fled Germany, settling in England, where she continued to photograph and teach. By that time she and László Moholy-Nagy had parted ways.

The present photograph is a portrait of the German art historian, critic, and photographer Franz Roh blinded by light. Seen from close up and tightly framed, his face appears as a composite of planes, lines, and geometric shapes, and his expression reveals discomfort and inwardness. Roh was an influential figure in avant-garde German art in the 1920s, and was a co-editor of the 1929 publication *Foto-Auge*, thereby helping to define what was currently understood as cutting-edge photography.

There would seem, at first, to be some irony in the depiction of Roh with his eyes closed, as if he wished to shut out the world around him. However, it is reasonable to assume that Moholy purposely intended this image of pensive inwardness to convey a sense of Roh's deeply intellectual nature. In another striking portrait by her in the National Gallery of Canada's collection, *Lily Fischel* (fig. 50.2), a young woman is portrayed in profile, with a lock of hair falling forward over her brow and casting a shadow. Both of these images present a radical view of portraiture, and through their accenting of formal elements both suggest an emotional detachment of the photographer from her subjects.

László Moholy-Nagy interpreted her portraits as striving for neutrality. The two portraits by avant-garde photographers that appeared in his 1925 book *Malerei, Fotografie, Film* were by them. Hers was of Julia Feininger, the wife of a friend and Bauhaus colleague, though it carried only the generic title *Portrait*. In the accompanying caption we learn more about what she was striving for, at least from László Moholy-Nagy's viewpoint: "An attempt at an objective portrait: the individual to be photographed as impartially as an object so that the photographic result shall not be encumbered with subjective intention."[1] There is no doubt that on a formal level a dialogue was taking place between the portraits of these two photographers during their time together, as can be seen in a comparison of Lucia Moholy's portrait of Franz Roh and a portrait by László Moholy-Nagy titled simply *Head* (fig. 50.3).

Fig. 50.1   László Moholy-Nagy and Lucia Moholy, *László and Lucia, Double Portrait*, 1923, from original negative in the Estate of Moholy-Nagy. Bauhaus-Archiv, Berlin (F8666)

Fig. 50.2   Lucia Moholy, *Lily Fischel*, c. 1928–1932, gelatin silver print. National Gallery of Canada, Ottawa (30733)

Fig. 50.3   László Moholy-Nagy, *Head*, c. 1926, gelatin silver print. The Museum of Modern Art, New York, Anonymous gift (505.1939)

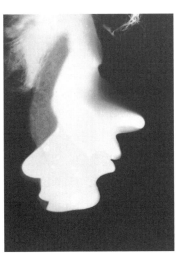

Borsod, Hungary 1895–1946 Chicago
Photogram c. 1925
Gelatin silver print, 12.1 × 12.8 cm
19204

Annotations   verso, u.r., *51* (circled) *80.4.5.11*

Provenance   William Larson, photographer; purchased from Prakapas Gallery, New York, 1982.

László Moholy-Nagy's passion for art transcended the boundaries of medium. His reputation as a pioneer in modernism and as a contributor to the influential avant-garde New Vision was based on his experimental, enquiring, and often conceptual approach to artmaking. He went beyond his own practice of painting, printmaking, sculpture, photography, and film to devote himself to teaching and writing. During the period that he taught at the Bauhaus he published a landmark book on the relationship between film, painting, and photography. Painting and lithography were the media through which Moholy-Nagy explored the infinite range of compositions in two-dimensional abstraction, while sculpture, film, and photography allowed him to experiment with light and movement in the expression of three-dimensional abstraction.

Moholy-Nagy turned to the making of art as a result of his war experience. He enrolled as a law student at the University of Budapest in 1913, but a year later was called up to serve in the Austro-Hungarian army on both the Russian and the Italian fronts. He was hospitalized for shell shock and injuries, and it was during his convalescence that he took up drawing. Although his ideas about art were to change radically in the next few years, by the end of his life he returned to the expressionistic style of drawing with which he had started.

Moholy-Nagy created his first photograms in 1922, as a "diagrammatic record of the motion of light."[1] He claimed to have been completely unaware of similar works produced by Christian Schad, Man Ray, and El Lissitzky. Moholy-Nagy's photograms of the 1920s closely parallel his early lithographs (see fig. 51.1). The Suprematist elements of cross, circle, and diagonal line can be seen in some of his "transparency" paintings (see fig. 51.2), which display a similar handling of abstract form. Also evident in the photograms of this time are the grid components that appear in his *Light-Space Modulator* of 1930 (cat. 52).

The manipulation of planes, the effects of transparency, and the use of cut-paper constructions remain constant from the early to the later photograms, but the unmodulated backgrounds and static compositions gradually give way to more fluid and bolder compositions. From 1923 onward the imagery becomes more complex. The post-1930 work includes more curvilinear, Arp-like shapes, and often more technically manipulated light effects, with the occasional appearance of a grid. The present photogram clearly belongs to the 1922–1928 period, as can be seen from its references to Suprematist composition, its luminosity, its extremely subtle tonal gradations, and the inclusion of unusual objects – gauzy, grid-like, and wheel-like (the last perhaps an eggbeater) – all of which contribute to the work's fascinating complexity.

Fig. 51.1   László Moholy-Nagy, *Geometric Composition*, 1923, colour lithograph on wove paper, with japan paper borders. National Gallery of Canada, Ottawa (18110)

Fig. 51.2   László Moholy-Nagy, *A IX*, 1923, oil and graphite on canvas. San Francisco Museum of Modern Art, Gift of Sibyl Moholy-Nagy

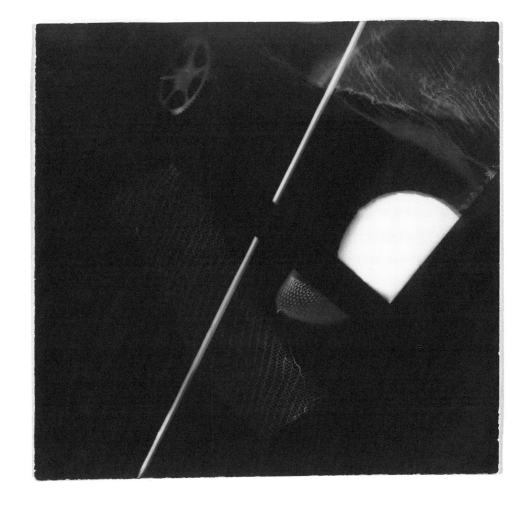

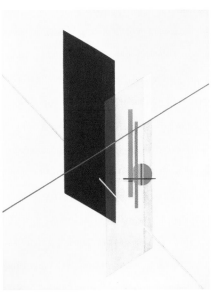

Borsod, Hungary 1895–1946 Chicago

Light-Space Modulator 1930

Gelatin silver print, 27.2 × 20.8 cm, sheet 30.2 × 23.4 cm

40572

Inscriptions   verso, t., *l. moholy-nagy / das lichtrequisit (1922–1930)*

Annotations   verso, c., *11*

Provenance   Otto Eisler, architect and friend of the artist; Sotheby's, London, bought by Paul M. Hertzmann, Inc.,

San Francisco, 18 May 2000, lot 165; purchased from Paul M. Hertzmann, Inc., 2001.

During the years that László Moholy-Nagy was teaching at the Bauhaus in Weimar and Dessau, from 1923 to 1928, he became obsessed with the idea of designing and constructing a motorized kinetic sculpture that would be able to produce complex light effects. At the very time that he was experimenting with photography and photograms, he dreamed of an apparatus that would allow him to go beyond using light as a tool for making art on paper and turn it into an artistic medium in itself. This was a pursuit that meshed well with the ongoing technical work required for the staging and lighting of the Bauhaus's own theatre productions, and also was in keeping with the general emphasis on the integration of technology and industrial design into the school's curriculum.

After leaving the Bauhaus in 1928, Moholy-Nagy entered an intense period of activity as a freelance designer in Berlin, working on book covers, posters, advertisements, and stage and costume designs. In 1929 he was invited to provide the stage design and lighting for the Berlin State Opera's production of *The Tales of Hoffmann*, and working on this commission may have been what inspired him to revive his design for a light sculpture and bring it to fruition. Collaborating closely with an engineer named István Sebök (see fig. 52.1), he completed the construction of what he would call, at first, his *Light Prop for an Electric Stage*. One of its earliest showings was at the Werkbund exhibition held at the Grand Palais in Paris in the summer of 1930.[1] During that same year he documented it in action in a six-minute film titled *A Lightplay: Black White Grey*. Some observers considered the film to be more successful than the object filmed, and Moholy-Nagy regretted that "for most people the beauty of … its emotional penetration had not been revealed."[2]

In addition to filming the sculpture, which later came to be called the *Light-Space Modulator*, Moholy-Nagy also photographed it. As with the film, the photographs take full advantage of the effects of light bouncing off the gleaming surfaces and have a beauty of their own apart from their documentary significance. In fact, it is obvious from the present photograph that Moholy-Nagy's primary interest was not in the factual record; he has moved in too close for that, obscuring our view of the top and bottom and focusing instead on the abstractions of light and their interactions with the geometric forms of the machine. In another of his photographs of the *Light-Space Modulator*, seen from a different angle (fig. 52.2), the camera is again sharply tilted so as to create a dynamic effect. In neither photograph do we actually get a very clear sense of the operation of the various components – rotating glass spiral, sliding metal ball, perforated metal discs and screens, light bulbs, and an exposed motor and gear mechanism at the base. Moholy-Nagy was more interested in conveying the textural and sculptural qualities of the work and less concerned with documenting it or trying to show how it worked.

The original *Light-Space Modulator*, which is a little over 1.5 metres high, is now housed in the collection of the Busch-Reisinger Museum at Harvard University. Two replicas are in the Bauhaus-Archiv in Berlin.

Fig. 52.1   István Sebök, *Construction Drawing for László Moholy-Nagy's Light Prop for an Electric Stage*, 1930, pencil on tracing paper, stamped. Bauhaus-Archiv, Berlin

Fig. 52.2   László Moholy-Nagy, *Light-Space Modulator*, 1930, gelatin silver print. The J. Paul Getty Museum, Los Angeles

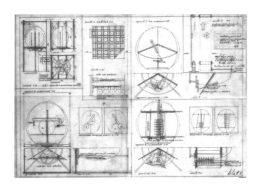

New York 1896–1958 Laguna Beach, California

Knife and Cheese 1922, printed later

Platinum print, 12.2 × 9.6 cm, sheet 12.7 × 10.2 cm

35924

Inscriptions   l.r., *Paul Outerbridge Jr.*

Provenance   Van Deren Coke collection; purchased from Prakapas Gallery, La Jolla, California, 1991.

One of the twentieth century's most influential advertising photographers, Paul Outerbridge, Jr., did his early training in art and theatre. He studied aesthetics and anatomy from 1915 to 1917 at the Art Students League in New York, beginning his career as a stage designer and painter before studying under Alexander Archipenko from 1923 to 1924. Outerbridge's modernist appreciation of the purely formal value of objects and his elegant sense of design, which later dominated at the expense of any other consideration, clearly served the style and purposes of the major American fashion magazines of the time. *Vogue*, *Vanity Fair*, and *Harper's Bazaar* were his main clients from 1922 to 1925. He also had corporate clients such as Pyrex and Ide.

Knife and Cheese, like Outerbridge's iconic *Ide Collar* (fig. 53.1), transcends the limits of illustration to become a work of art by virtue of its rigorous composition and stunning graphic power. Outerbridge's most important photographs were made from about 1920 until 1929, which was the period when he started to concentrate on improving the carbro-colour process. Outerbridge brought his experience of working in the theatre to his photographs. He was a master of elevating the banal to the sublime. In all of his images of ordinary objects that he made for advertising – cracker boxes, shirt collars, milk bottles, eggs, cups, light bulbs, machine parts – he devoted exacting attention to form and light, and above all to the geometry of the composition. By choosing to realize this image as a platinum print, he further emphasized the particularity of form and the subtlety of light.

Outerbridge left the United States in 1925 for Europe, working in London, Paris, and Berlin over a four-year period. In Paris he met Man Ray, George Hoyningen-Huene, and Berenice Abbott, and opened his own studio in 1927. In 1928–1929 he was employed as an assistant film director in Berlin. On his return from Europe he opened a studio in Monsey, New York, which remained in operation until 1943, and worked for various magazines, mainly in the fashion business. Despite the serious reception that his work received in avant-garde art circles (he participated in the 1928 *Premier Salon indépendent de la photographie* in Paris and the 1929 *Film und Foto* exhibition in Stuttgart), his direction on his return to New York from Europe became increasingly oriented toward commerce.

Fig. 53.1   Paul Outerbridge, Jr., *Ide Collar*, 1922, gelatin silver print. The Metropolitan Museum of Art, Ford Motor Company Collection, Gift of Ford Motor Company and John C. Waddell, 1987 (1987.1100.462)

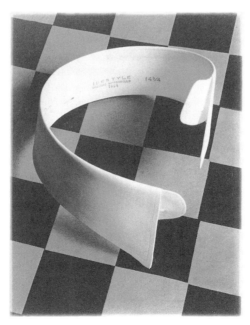

54 Albert Renger-Patzsch
Würzburg, Germany 1897–1966 Wamel bei Soest, Federal Republic of Germany
Agave attenuata 1928
Gelatin silver print, 22.8 × 16.8 cm, sheet 23 × 17.1 cm
36750

Annotations **verso: u.l.,** *20– / Agave attenuata,* **u.r., stamped,** *Jede Reproduktion / verboten,* **u.r., stamped,** *Phot. A.*
Renger-Patzsch / BAD-HARZBURG, **l.l.,** *RKP9201009*

Provenance **purchased from Galerie Rudolf Kicken, Cologne, 1992.**

When Albert Renger-Patszch wrote about "seeing the world anew" he was not simply advocating an experimental approach to the observation and recording of the world, like his fellow Bauhaus and New Vision photographers, but was referring rather to a rediscovery of familiar things through an increased sensitivity to the object itself and a more truthful capturing of its essence. He took great pleasure in photographing both constructed and natural objects that displayed an intricate geometry and observed with precision the fundamental structure of plants and crystals and their patterns of growth and complex surface detailing. Renger-Patzsch was convinced that what he saw as the inherent properties of the photographic medium – fidelity to detail, precision, clarity, and objectivity in the transmission of information – should be respected, as should the integrity of the objects before the lens. What he perceived as revolutionary about the medium of photography in his time was not that it could alter perceptions about space and representation through the photographer's manipulation of perspectival viewpoints and juxtapositions, but that a renewal of art could occur through a more rigorous examination of the object itself. Renger-Patzsch related to a classical model of beauty, while Moholy-Nagy, Franz Roh, and T. Lux Feininger, if they considered the notion of beauty at all, saw it as residing in an exciting new relationship between observer and subject.

It comes as no surprise that Renger-Patzsch's post-secondary school education was in chemistry, at the Technische Hochschule in Dresden from 1919 to 1921. He brought to his observation of the natural world a scientific sense of order and precision and an artist's sense of wonder, transforming the plants he photographed from specimens to objects of awe. Writing in 1928, Hugo Sieker pinpointed what it was that made Renger-Patzsch an artist rather than a scientist – "his pursuit of the charm of earthly things, his ability to force even the most accidental and transient phenomena into pictures that are superbly organized, balanced, and structured."[1] In "Joy before the Object," an essay Renger-Patzsch wrote celebrating photography and nature, he emphasized the need for the photographer to take joy in the object and to "become fully conscious of the splendid fidelity of reproduction made possible by his technique."[2]

Agave attenuata, a close-up of the leafing structure of a cactus plant, celebrates symmetry and order. It represents natural form as a source of wonder. This emphasis on close observation can be seen also in Renger-Patzsch's photographs of mineral specimens. In all of his photographs, ranging from plants to architecture, landscape, and industrial subjects, he focused on the revelation of structure (see figs. 54.1 and 54.2).

Self-taught in photography, Renger-Patzsch went on to become head of the photography department at the Folkwang-Archiv in Essen from 1921 to 1924, where he was a colleague of Ernst Fuhrmann, also a photographer of natural objects. A member of the Werkbund, he showed fourteen works in the *Film und Foto* exhibition in Stuttgart in 1929, including *Agave attenuata*. Two of his photographs were included in the 1929 publication *Es kommt der neue Fotograf!* by Werner Gräff. From 1927 to 1940 Renger-Patzsch photographed principally for industry, producing extraordinary images of machinery and the architecture of factory interiors.

Fig. 54.1 Albert Renger-Patzsch, *Fan Vaulting, St. Mary's Church, Danzig,* 1928, gelatin silver print. National Gallery of Canada, Ottawa, Purchased from the Phyllis Lambert Fund, 1980 (32714)

Fig. 54.2 Albert Renger-Patzsch, *Sempervivum,* 1928, gelatin silver print. National Gallery of Canada, Ottawa (36748)

St. Petersburg, Russia 1891–1956 Moscow
Portrait of My Mother 1924, printed c. 1940–1969
Gelatin silver print, 28.5 × 20.1 cm
37214

Annotations   verso: u.c., *14* (circled), u.c., *Фото А. М. Родченко. 1924 год. / "ПОРТРЕТ МАТЕРИ" / Если можно, то для обложки*, c., *Překlad: / Je-li to možné – použit na obálce! / První fotografie A.M. Rodčenko / Maminka (1924)*, l.c., stamped, *univ. prof. ing. lubomir linhart / praha 2 – nové město, ladova č. 7 / telefon 29 54 28*, l.c., *← 12,3 cm →, pozor! jen šiři obrázku – označeno / japonský ofset*, l.l., stamped, *A-19* (boxed), l.r., stamped and handwritten, *ČTENÍ / O SSSR / č. '1/651' / str* (boxed)

Provenance   Lubomir Linhart, professor of engineering and friend of the Rodchenko-Stepanova family, Prague; Vladimir Birgus; bought by Howard Greenberg Gallery, New York, early 1990s; purchased from Howard Greenberg Gallery, 1993.

Alexander Rodchenko's father was a railway construction worker and his mother a washerwoman. He took this portrait of his mother as she was holding one of her reading-glass lenses close to her eye, intently poring over a newspaper. This touching portrayal of Olga Yevdokimovna was made shortly after she had first learned to read. Clearly moved by the sight of his mother's absorption in the newspaper, Rodchenko captured several views of her on this occasion. The present photograph is the most famous of the images in the sequence. Severely cropped from the more encompassing view seen in the original negative (fig. 55.1), it focuses our attention on Olga's expression of intense concentration. Although it is to the uncropped image that we must turn in order to see what she is in fact doing, it is the cropped version that truly qualifies as a portrait because of the emphasis on the face and its expressive features. Olga furrows her brow with the effort of taking in what she is reading. The hand and the circular frame of the one eyeglass become the focal point of the composition. This is a portrait as much suffused with feeling as Rodchenko's charming photograph of his daughter Varvara in the bathtub (fig. 55.2). *Portrait of My Mother* appeared on the cover of the October 1927 issue of *Sovetskoe Foto*, with the uncropped version inside.[1]

Rodchenko was born in a small apartment above the stage of a St. Petersburg theatre where his father was employed in a variety of jobs, from caretaker and props man to walk-on actor. Early in the new century Rodchenko's family moved to Kazan, and from 1910 to 1914 he attended the Kazan School of Art. Within a year of moving to Moscow in the spring of 1915 he was already exhibiting his drawings with such notable avant-garde artists as Kazimir Malevich and Vladimir Tatlin, both of whom would influence his work.[2] In 1918 he taught at the Proletkul't school. During the early 1920s he was on the governing body of INKhUK (Institut Khudozhestvennoi Kul'tury, the Institute of Artistic Culture) and taught at VKhUTEMAS, where he was appointed professor and dean of the faculty of metalwork.

Rodchenko's earlier paintings, posters, and constructions explored the abstract values of form and space. They were progressive and lively. But portraits were almost entirely absent from his repertoire before the 1920s. When he started to make his own photographs in the early 1920s – as opposed to simply incorporating existing photographs in his photomontages and collages – a new world of expression was opened for him. Instead of reducing people to formal ciphers, he began to see human engagement as an important element in all of his photographic portraits. This was true when he was portraying famous cultural figures such as Vladimir Mayakovsky and Osip and Lili Brik no less than when he was portraying members of his family or even strangers. The qualities of intimacy and playfulness are most evident, however, in his portraits of his mother, his daughter, and his wife, the painter Varvara Fedorovna Stepanova.

Fig. 55.1   Alexander Rodchenko, *Mother Reading*, 1924, gelatin silver print from glass negative (broken in 1930s). Private collection

Fig. 55.2   Alexander Rodchenko, *Morning Wash*, 1930, printed posthumously c. 1980–1989, gelatin silver print. National Gallery of Canada, Ottawa (36993)

St. Petersburg, Russia 1891–1956 Moscow
Courtyard 1926
Gelatin silver print, 28.6 × 20 cm
35880

Annotations   verso, stamped, c., *ФОТО / РОДЧЕНКО*

Provenance   purchased from Walker, Ursitti, and McGinniss, New York, 1991.

Coming to maturity in the midst of a political and cultural revolution, Alexander Rodchenko played a central role in the redefinition of art in the emerging Soviet Union. The modernist revision of artistic values took many forms, from Cubism and Futurism to Constructivism and Surrealism, and varied from country to country. The two central issues to emerge in Russian avant-garde art in the first decades of the twentieth century were the exploration of abstract form and the relationship of the picture plane to representation.

Rodchenko acquired his first camera in 1923 and immediately began making use of it as a tool for creative expression. He had already been incorporating other people's photographs into his collages from about 1919, but now he was capturing images directly from the world around him. By 1924 he had found a bold and dynamic style of his own. His photographs would eventually form as integral a part of his legacy as his paintings, books, posters, and collages.

Courtyard, Moscow comes from a larger body of photographs of urban subjects made by Rodchenko during the latter half of the 1920s. An intriguing composition of complex geometry, it is one of several views taken from the balcony of the family's apartment[1] through the changing seasons of winter, spring, and summer (see also figs. 56.1 and 56.2). With its oval modules intersected and edged with a delicate and precise filigree of tree branches, it exemplifies Rodchenko's strong formal structuring of images. The radical tilts, dramatically foreshortened figures, and vertiginous repetitions of architectural features in the foreground bring dynamism to an otherwise static subject. Extreme perspectival viewpoints, such as aerial and worm's-eye views, were trademarks of Rodchenko's style. The emboldened sense of deep perspective in this picture relates back to the brief period in 1918 when he was making small wood and card constructions in the style of his mentor Vladimir Tatlin. There is undoubtedly also the influence of contemporary Russian cinema and theatre, for which he would produce designs well into the 1930s. Rodchenko's photographs were not so much about the transformative values of art as they were a perspective on reality that was vigorous, new, and, to his mind, more "true" than a slavish adherence to photographic veracity.

By 1928 the political climate had become inhibiting and even dangerous for experimental artists like Rodchenko. As a founding member of the editorial board of *Sovetskoe Foto*, he could significantly influence its content, and he encouraged the publication of works that reflected some of the radical innovations in European photography of the time. When his choice of photographs for publication – and his own photographs – came under attack from the more conservative elements within *Sovetskoe Foto*,[2] he defended his position on the role of photography in modern society:

> The photograph represents a new and rapid instrument for description of the world: given its possibilities, it ought to be trying to show the world from different points, it ought to be teaching us to look from all sides. But at this point "the psychology of the navel," with centuries of authoritarianism behind it, clashes with the modern photographer.[3]

Fig. 56.1   Alexander Rodchenko, *Courtyard in Winter, Moscow*, 1928, printed posthumously c. 1980–1989, gelatin silver print. National Gallery of Canada, Ottawa (36991)

Fig. 56.2   Alexander Rodchenko, *Courtyard*, 1928–1930, gelatin silver print. San Francisco Museum of Modern Art, Collection of the Prentice and Paul Sack Photographic Trust

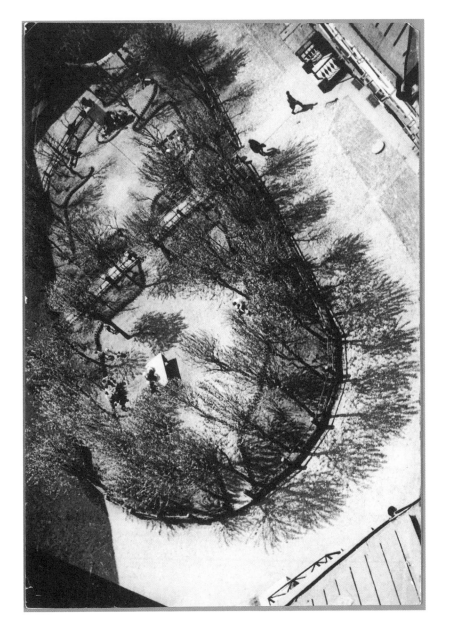

57   Franz Roh
Apolda, Germany 1890–1965 Munich
***Untitled* 1922–1928**
Gelatin silver print, 18.2 × 24 cm
41135

Annotations   verso, u.l., stamped, *dr. franz roh / münchen 39 / pickelstrasse 11 / telefon 60277*, u.l., stamped, *NACHLASS FRANZ ROH*, u.l., *85279* (circled), l.r., *#1040*

Provenance   private collection, Italy; Emilio Bertonati; purchased from Galerie Priska Pasquer, Cologne, 1993.

Critic, art historian, and photographer, Franz Roh belonged to a circle of artists, including Max Ernst, Willi Baumeister, George Grosz, László Moholy-Nagy, Jan Tschichold, and Kurt Schwitters, who in the years following the First World War were searching for new forms of expression. An interest in creating "automatic" and "objective" images led many of these artists to explore photography. In the early 1920s, evidently unaware of the "light drawings" that had been made by a number of photographic pioneers in the nineteenth century, and probably also unaware of each other's contemporary experiments, Christian Schad, El Lissitzky, Man Ray, and László Moholy-Nagy independently arrived at the discovery of the photogram process, which involved placing objects directly onto sensitized sheets of paper and then exposing them to light.

In this untitled photogram made by Roh, we see the outlines of four objects: two combs, a light bulb, and what appears to be a loupe. The smaller comb, at the lower left, is overlapped by the light bulb and partly blurred by it. In writing about the work of Moholy-Nagy in 1930, Roh provided his own description of the photogram technique:

> The objects are put on sensitive paper. They are left a short space or long space of time, held close or at a distance, exposed to intense or subdued light, to a mobile or fixed light: the results attained appear like weird spheres of light, often of marvellous transparency, that seem to penetrate space. Sublime gradations, from gleaming white through a thousand shades of grey down to deepest black, can be produced thus. And by intersection either extreme nearness or the most distant distance is suggested.[1]

Franz Roh studied at universities in Leipzig, Berlin, and Basel, and gained his doctorate from the University of Munich in 1920, where he concentrated on seventeenth-century Dutch painting and served for several years as Heinrich Wölfflin's assistant. He came to be best known for his 1925 book on modern European painting, *Nach Expressionismus*, in which he coined the term "magic realism" (though not with the popular meaning it would later acquire). He took up photography in the early 1920s, trying out a wide variety of other experimental techniques, including solarization and negative printing (see fig. 57.1). It was only around the end of the decade that he began to show some of his photographs and to write about photography. Following the 1929 *Film und Foto* exhibition in Stuttgart, he and Jan Tschichold co-edited the now legendary book *Foto-Auge*, which included an essay by Roh and seventy-six photographs that were representative of the contents of the exhibition.

Roh's experimental photography and his writings about non-objective art were apparently what led to his imprisonment at Dachau for several months in 1933. Under the Nazi regime he was forbidden to publish or to exhibit his work. After the war he returned to teaching at the University of Munich. His photographs were generally unknown until the publication in 1978 of Emilio Bertonati's book about experimental photography in the period of the Weimar Republic.[2]

Fig. 57.1   Franz Roh, *Untitled*, c. 1930, vintage gelatin silver print. Ubu Gallery, New York / Galerie Berinson, Berlin

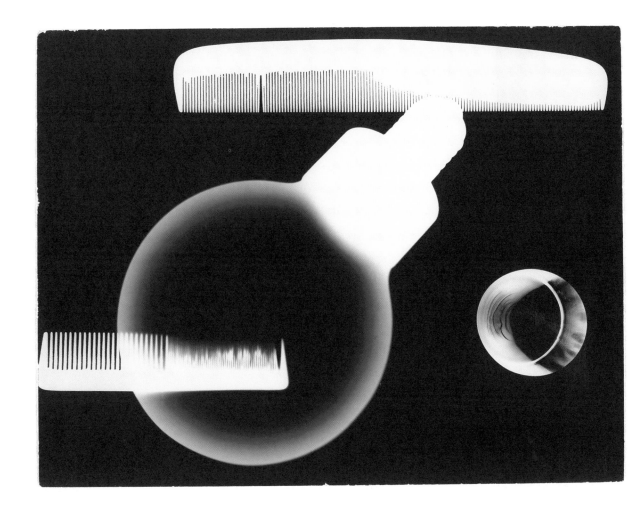

Bremen, Germany 1906–1990 Worpswede, Federal Republic of Germany

Woman with Veil 1931

Gelatin silver print, heightened with paint, 8.6 × 6.8 cm

40666

Annotations   mount, u.l., *58*, l.l., *6,7 – 8,7*, l.l., *56/2*; verso of mount, l.c., *W. ROHDE / P8809039 RK*

Provenance   purchased from Kicken, Berlin, 2001.

Rohde's portraits are among the most fascinating of his images. Whether photographing strangers, friends, or himself, he was constantly aware of the interplay between the face and the mask. Although Expressionist painting may have been responsible to a large degree for his interest in the relationship between appearance and psychological reality, there is also a certain element of theatricality in Rohde's photographs that owes its origins to his work in the fashion industry. This involvement with the image-conscious world of women's fashion accounts for the numerous photographs of intact and broken wax mannequin heads (see fig. 58.1), of masks, and of fashion models with cool, impenetrable gazes. Along with his series of self-portraits showing him either parading as a clown or removing a mask from his face (see fig. 58.2), *Woman with Veil* is one of his most compelling images.

Rohde's interest in photography first emerged in 1927 when he was a student at the Kunstgewerbeschule Burg – known as the Burg – in Halle an der Saale. Rohde was encouraged by the photographer Hans Finsler, and found photography to be the ideal form for him because it allowed him to experiment while still producing recognizable images, a necessity if he was to avoid his conservative father's wrath. His father, George Karl Rohde, a decorative painter and stained-glass maker, was critical of so-called free painting. He owned the large-format camera with which Rohde made his first self-portraits and the portraits of Renata Bracksieck, the woman who would become his wife and business partner.

In 1929 Rohde stayed in Paris for six months. There he established lifelong friendships with the photographers Marianne Breslauer and Paul Citroen, and also met Erwin Blumenfeld and Umbo, who were at the centre of European modernist photographic practice in the 1920s and 1930s. In the spring of 1929 Rohde's photographs were shown for the first time at the Museum Folkwang in Essen and at the Kestner-Gesellschaft in Hanover. Most significant, however, was his inclusion in the landmark *Film und Foto* exhibition that took place in Stuttgart later that year.[1]

During the 1930s Rohde photographed models for whom Bracksieck designed clothes. It is possible that *Woman with Veil* was made in the course of this work, though it is equally possible that it arose out of a general fascination with the masking of the face. The motif of the veiled woman was popular among artists of the period, as can be seen in paintings by Egon Schiele and Otto Dix and photographs by Gertrud Arndt, Umbo, Edward Steichen, and Lisette Model.

Although Rohde continued to enjoy success in Germany over the next four years, the dark shadow of the Third Reich that eclipsed the careers of so many promising artists and intellectuals would eventually fall over his professional and creative activities. At the Burg, shortly after an exhibition of forty of Rohde's photographs, government officials fired the director Gerhard Marcks along with thirteen teachers and confiscated numerous works of art. Rohde tried to obtain an exemption under the racial purity and political allegiance legislation of September 1933, but this effort was unsuccessful and his career effectively came to an end.

Fig. 58.1   Werner Rohde, *Wax Head*, 1928, gelatin silver print. F.C. Gundlach Foundation, Hamburg

Fig. 58.2   Werner Rohde, *Self-portrait with Mask*, 1928, gelatin silver print. F.C. Gundlach Foundation, Hamburg

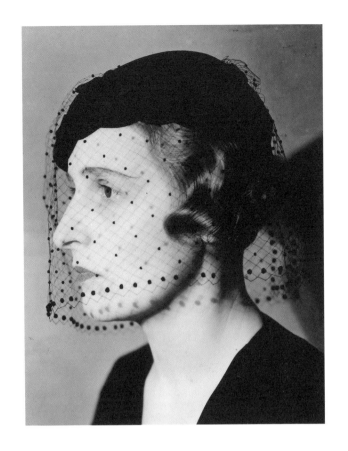

59 Jaroslav Rössler

Smilov, Czechoslovakia 1902–1990 Prague

Untitled **1930**

Gelatin silver print, 21.6 × 15.8 cm

35916

Inscriptions   **verso, c., *Rössler / 30 Paris***

Annotations   **verso, l.l., *4674.1180 / 154005***

Provenance   **Rössler estate; purchased from Jane Corkin Gallery, Toronto, 1991.**

It is possible that the original inspiration for Jaroslav Rössler's decision to experiment with light and to produce his cameraless images came from his having seen a selection of Man Ray's Rayographs in *Zivot*, one of the journals of the avant-garde Czech group Devětsil, in December 1922.[1] This was also the year that Man Ray published his portfolio of Rayographs, *Les champs délicieux*, in Paris. Or it may be that Rössler first saw the Rayographs when they were exhibited in Prague in 1923 at the *Modern Art Bazaar*, an exhibition organized by Devětsil.[2] Rössler made this untitled photogram in Paris in 1930.

Rössler was one of several influential modernist photographers who were based in Prague; his compatriots included Jaromír Funke, Josef Sudek, and Karel Teige. Rössler apparently started making photograms in 1925 or 1926, but their present whereabouts are unknown.[3] Rössler's work with photograms was a natural extension of his fascination with the phenomenon of light. A photogram that he made in 1929 used only cigarette smoke as the image-forming object (fig. 59.1).

In contrast to Rössler's richly intricate *Light Constructions* (see fig. 59.2), this work seems radically simple. The suggestive power of open scissors, ready to cut, placed at the edge of a sheet of paper, produces a charged image that takes the photogram beyond its obvious Surrealism to a level of psychological expression. On this level of sophisticated play with the symbolic nature of the object, it is on a par with Man Ray's Rayographs using thermometers, keys, a magnifying glass, and an astrolabe.

Rössler was a reclusive individual but nevertheless enjoyed being in the vanguard of experimentation. He has been credited with having made the "first known Constructivist photograph in Europe" by 1919 or 1920.[4] During the period 1923–1924 he made photomontages and collages. In Paris in 1927 he worked out a method of placing a mirror prism in front of a camera lens to create multiple views in the same image.[5] The apparatus he invented for this purpose, which sounds rather like a version of the Vortoscope, was apparently offered to the MGM motion picture studio, but there is no indication that they ever responded.[6]

Rössler's work was shown in a group exhibition in Paris in 1924. A major factor in strengthening if not shaping his vision was his association with Devětsil, a group established in 1920 by avant-garde artists, architects, writers, and theoreticians who shared left-wing political views and aligned themselves with cultural trends in Moscow, Paris, Budapest, Warsaw, and various centres in Germany. Rössler was a member of Devětsil from 1923.

Fig. 59.1   Jaroslav Rössler, *Smoke*, 1929, gelatin silver print. Museum of Decorative Arts, Prague (GF-152)

Fig. 59.2   Jaroslav Rössler, *Untitled*, 1929, gelatin silver print. Courtesy Robert Koch Gallery, San Francisco

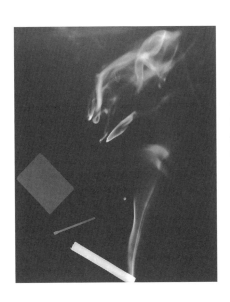

Herdorf, Germany 1876–1964 Cologne
Heinrich Hoerle **1928, printed before 1938**
Gelatin silver print, 61 × 48.4 cm
30222

Annotations l.l., blind stamped, *AUG. SANDER / KOLN / LINDENTHAL*

Provenance the artist's son, Gunther Sander; his son, Gerhard Sander; purchased from Sander Gallery, New York, 1989.

August Sander was born in Herdorf, a village in the mining and farming district of the Westerwald, east of Cologne. He had early hopes of becoming a painter, but owing to his family's limited financial resources he had to spend the first eight years of his working life as a miner. A formative moment in Sander's life was his encounter with a landscape photographer, which led to the pursuit of a practical career that also provided an outlet for creative expression. Sander opened his first photographic studio in Linz, Austria, in 1902. In 1910 he moved to Cologne.

Heinrich Hoerle (1895–1936) was one of the founding members of the group of artists known as the Cologne Progressives. This portrait of Hoerle formed part of "Menschen des 20. Jahrhunderts" ("People of the Twentieth Century"), an epic undertaking by Sander in which he systematically photographed the faces of people who represented various strata of German society – peasants and professionals, as well as the insane and destitute. The notion of a visual model of social hierarchy was not new; Hans Sachs's sixteenth-century publication *The Book of Trades* ranked humans in a vertical social order according to the work they performed, with the clergy at the top and peasants and the "four fools" at the bottom.[1] Sander replaced the Renaissance model of social order with an evolutionary cycle, beginning with those who lived and worked close to nature, such as peasants, farmers, and villagers, proceeding to tradesmen, artisans, and members of the bourgeoisie, and culminating with professionals, artists, and intellectuals before concluding with nomads and gypsies, circus people, and the ill, insane, and disabled. The final portrait was a death portrait.

First conceived around 1910, the project was to have consisted of over 600 photographs issued in forty-eight portfolios of about twelve photographs each. The National Gallery of Canada's collection contains an extremely rare set of one portfolio titled *Der Bauer* ("The Farmer"). In its twelve images – the earliest of them dating from 1911 – it establishes the primary human archetypes from which, in Sander's view, all of society originated (see fig. 60.1). Hoerle's portrait belonged to a grouping of "Painters," which also included a photograph of him at his easel, drawing a portrait of the boxer Hein Domgörgen (fig. 60.2). With its unblinking scrutiny of facial contours and its emphasis on structure, Sander's portrait of Hoerle exemplifies the tenets of the New Objectivity, an avant-garde movement that began in Germany and sprang out of a revolt against the soft-focus and sometimes formulary aesthetic of the Pictorialist movement. It favoured objectivity, precision, and the exploration of new ways of looking at familiar subjects.

Because Sander's approach to portraiture and to class divisions eschewed both the sentimental and the heroic, it did not meet with the approval of officials representing the Third Reich. In 1936, copies of *Antlitz der Zeit* (published in 1929, and intended as an introduction to "People of the Twentieth Century") were seized and the printing plates destroyed. Unlike Lerski's *Köpfe des Alltags* series, which took an intensely subjective and dramatic approach to universalizing all human types through expressions of suffering and melancholia, and unlike photographs favoured by the Nazis, depicting the ideal type as heroic and Aryan, Sander's photographs presented his subjects with an uncompromising matter-of-factness. Weimar painters relied heavily on satire and caricature to present searing comments on society, but Sander borrowed very lightly from them, using contextual props and exaggeration only as needed. No matter how much of a theory Sander attempted to construct around his portraits, they remain objects of intense presence and intelligibility in and of themselves.

Fig. 60.1 August Sander, *The Wise One, the Shepherd*, 1913, printed 1927, gelatin silver print. National Gallery of Canada, Ottawa (19725.4)

Fig. 60.2 August Sander, *Heinrich Hoerle Drawing a Portrait of the Boxer Hein Domgörgen*, 1932, gelatin silver print. Die Photographische Sammlung / SK Stiftung Kultur, Cologne

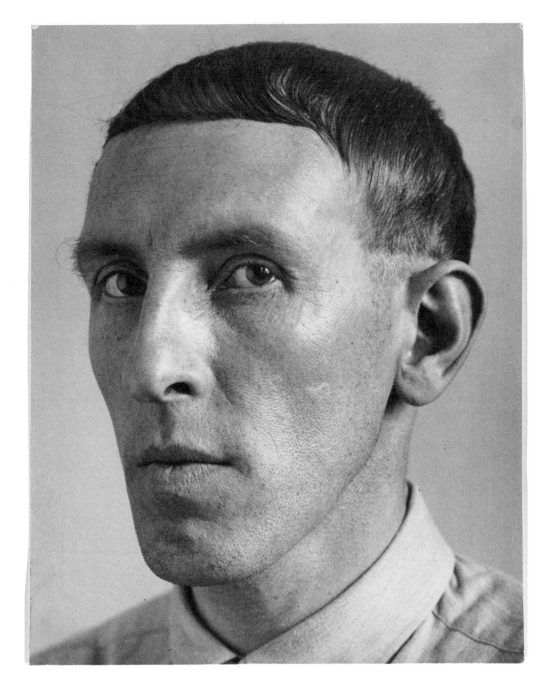

Philadelphia 1883–1965 Dobbs Ferry, New York
Side of White Barn 1916–1917
Gelatin silver print, 19.3 × 24.3 cm, sheet 20.3 × 25.3 cm
32988

Provenance   acquired from the artist by Dorothy Meigs Eidlitz, St. Andrews, New Brunswick; gift of Dorothy Meigs Eidlitz, 1968.

Although Charles Sheeler is remembered mainly as a painter and as a central figure in the Precisionist movement, his achievements in photography are no less significant. Sheeler attended the Philadelphia School of Industrial Art from 1900 to 1903, focusing on industrial design, and then studied painting at the Pennsylvania Academy of the Fine Arts from 1903 to 1906. He formed a close friendship with Morton Schamberg that would last until Schamberg's premature death in 1918. After a year-long sojourn together in Europe from 1908 to 1909, during which the two aspiring young artists immersed themselves in the art of the past as well as in new developments such as Cubism, Sheeler and Schamberg returned home determined to break new ground in American art. In 1913 Sheeler showed six paintings in the famous Armory Show in New York. By this time he had also begun to work in commercial photography, specializing in architectural subjects, as a means of supporting his activities as a painter.

Side of White Barn (also known as *Pennsylvania Barn* and *Bucks County Barn*) is part of a large body of drawings, paintings, and photographs of barns that Sheeler made over the years. Around 1910 Sheeler and his friend Schamberg began renting a Shaker-style country house in Doylestown, Bucks County, Pennsylvania. After several years of summers and weekends there, he began to take an interest in drawing and photographing the barns that dotted the surrounding farmland. Along with his interior views of the house itself (see fig. 61.1), the barn photographs were, in the words of Gilles Mora, his first "consciously aesthetic photographs."[1]

Sheeler's own retrospective dating of *Side of White Barn*, in a letter to Beaumont Newhall, was "about 1915." Theodore E. Stebbins, Jr., and Norman Keyes, Jr., have argued for a slightly later date, based on the photograph's stylistic affinities to drawings such as the well-known *Barn Abstraction* from 1917 (fig. 61.2), which is similarly "spare and abstract, completely lacking in three-dimensionality or incidental detail."[2] According to Stebbins and Keyes, Sheeler produced numerous variant croppings of *Side of White Barn*, experimenting "with the subtlest nuances of tone and composition, adjusting each edge as he sought a perfect image."[3]

Another seemingly related work is Sheeler's 1918 watercolour painting *Bucks County Barn* (fig. 61.3). We know that later in his career Sheeler would use photographs directly as sources for his paintings. While there is no evidence of literal copying in this instance, the similarities are certainly intriguing, and there is no reason to preclude the possibility that Sheeler looked at the photograph while working on the watercolour.

Side of White Barn has earned its iconic status in the history of American modernist art because of its exquisitely fine translation of the architectural forms of a vernacular structure into a work of art. Its close cropping removes the extraneous surrounding details and draws the viewer's attention to the simple elegance and materiality of the barn, with an emphasis on the rhythmic repetition of verticals and horizontals in the partitioning of the facade. The interplay of rectangles foreshadows Paul Strand's *Barn, Gaspé* (cat. 69), made two decades later. What might seem at first to be a contradiction between the sophisticated modernist style and the plain, utilitarian subject is in fact a perfect illustration of the simplicity that Le Corbusier was aiming for in architecture and the geometric rigour that Mondrian sought in painting.

Fig. 61.1   Charles Sheeler, *Doylestown House – Stairs from Below*, 1917, gelatin silver print. The Metropolitan Museum of Art, New York, Alfred Stieglitz Collection, 1933 (33.43.343)

Fig. 61.2   Charles Sheeler, *Barn Abstraction*, 1917, black conté crayon on paper. Philadelphia Museum of Art, Gift of Louise and Walter Arensberg

Fig. 61.3   Charles Sheeler, *Bucks County Barn*, 1918, opaque watercolour and black chalk on paper. Philadelphia Museum of Art, A.E. Gallatin Collection

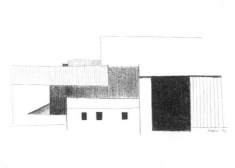

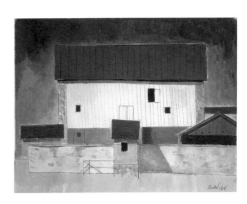

Wakayama Prefecture, Japan 1890–1944 Japan
Untitled c. 1940
Gelatin silver print, 24.1 × 29.5 cm
39996

Inscriptions   verso, c.l., signed in Japanese
Provenance   the artist's son; Zeit-Foto, Tokyo, 1984; purchased from Zeit-Foto, 1999.

The Japanese Pictorialist photographer Shinzo Fukuhara believed that photographs could express spirituality by the introduction of the simple responsiveness of a haiku poem into the capturing of the image:

> With nothing more complicated than clicking the shutter as soon as the moment strikes you, you can take your photo in almost one-tenth of a second. When the moment strikes you it is as if your heart has melted and become one with nature…. The artistic boundaries of photography, I think, are no different from those of poetry.[1]

Indeed, this untitled still life by Shimamura Hōkō has the simplicity and immediacy of a haiku, as do the two images by Hisano Hisashi and Sakata Minoru illustrated here (figs. 62.1 and 62.2). The inert body of a fish flopped onto a large block of ice can, on one level, be considered a curious and mundane choice for the subject of a picture, but on another level it proves to be astonishingly rich in visual detail. The photographer succeeds in communicating to the viewer the way in which the smooth-surfaced, dense, and irregular block of ice acts as a distorting mirror of sorts, transforming the reflections of the surrounding light and shadow into undulating abstract shapes. The transparency of the ice reveals the presence of a sea urchin embedded in the lower-left corner. The silvery surface of the fish, isolated against a simple dark background, also reflects light, which animates its form and texture.

Born in the Wakayama prefecture, into a family whose fortune was made in the production of _sake_, Shimamura seems to have been only peripherally involved in the family business.[2] His involvement in photography spanned over thirty years, beginning with his establishing the Meikô Photography Circle in 1909.[3] His work was considered good enough to be published in the _Japan Photographic Annual_ for 1925–1926.[4] At this time Shimamura was incorporating the soft-focus aesthetic into his imagery. But at some point between the mid-1920s and 1940 he discovered the sharp-focus, clean-angled aesthetic of the Western modernist photographers. This change may have resulted from his seeing the 1931 touring version of the _Film und Foto_ exhibition, which went to Tokyo and Osaka,[5] or may have stemmed from his familiarity with the avant-garde Zoei Shudan group, formed in 1937 out of the Naniwas Shashin Club, of which he was a member, and the Tanpei Shashin Club.

The choice of Shimamura's unconventional subject matter for a still-life picture is an expression of the growing interest in Japan in Surrealism. In 1937 the _Overseas Surrealism_ exhibition organized by Takaiguchi Shuzo and the poet Yamanaka Chiruu exerted an enormous influence on Japanese artists, triggering "another boom in still-life photography," as one writer described it.[6] Takaiguchi Shuzo's 1938 book _Kindai Geijutsu_ ("Modern Art") also helped to introduce Surrealism into Japan.

Other published works by Shimamura reveal an interest in still life, flower studies, and landscape. While they all display the same strong sense of design, they better fit the description of his work as reflecting "traditional Japanese tastes."

Fig. 62.1   Hisano Hisashi, _Untitled_, 1930s, gelatin silver print. Private collection

Fig. 62.2   Sakata Minoru, _Untitled_, c. 1937–1939, gelatin silver print. On deposit at Nagoya City Art Museum, Japan

63 Aaron Siskind
New York 1903–1991 Providence, Rhode Island
Untitled 1938
Gelatin silver print, 31 × 26 cm
37254

Inscriptions   verso of mount, u.l., *Aaron / 230 / N.Y*, u.r., *from: Dead End: / The Bowery*, c.r., *Ret. O Siskind*

Annotations   verso of mount, c.l., stamped, *Photograph by AARON SISKIND / '1938'*, l.l., *961 / 2*, l.r., *AS.115*, l.r., *5* (circled)

Provenance   acquired from the artist's estate by Robert Mann Gallery, New York, 1993; purchased from Robert Mann Gallery, 1994.

Aaron Siskind's earliest ambition was to be a poet, and in order to earn a living he took a job for a time as an English teacher in New York's public school system. Like many other young intellectuals in the 1930s, Siskind was attracted to socialist politics, and in 1932 he became a member of the Film and Photo League, an active, left-leaning organization that gave its members the opportunity to express their social views through their films and photographs and offered support in the form of classes, informal lectures, and collective critiques. With no other training than this, Siskind went on to become one of the most accomplished American photographers of his time.

In 1935 the Film and Photo League splintered into two factions, and the following year the photography branch reconstituted itself as the Photo League. Siskind transferred his allegiances to the new Photo League, and soon after he instituted its first "Feature Groups." In this capacity, he organized, participated in, and presided over projects in which Photo League members produced documentary photographic essays based on their explorations of specific neighbourhoods and sites in Manhattan. Among the early projects undertaken were *Portrait of a Tenement* (1936) and *Dead End: The Bowery* (1938). The present photograph, an untitled work, was made as part of *Dead End: The Bowery*. According to the photographic historian Carl Chiarenza, it was in this series that Siskind found his true subject and his visual vocabulary: "Evidence of man's mark-making, in its full range of forms, is the element most consistently present throughout Siskind's life work."[1]

This particular image from the series speaks of a human absence. Like Robert Frank's poignant photograph of a closed suitcase lying on a blanket on a Paris sidewalk, Siskind's more sombre image, centred on an open suitcase framed by deep shadows, reminds us of lives lived on public thoroughfares. It evokes a feeling of homelessness, and yet it is uncommonly beautiful, with its resonance of dark and light and its detailing of the objects that lie within this rich play of chiaroscuro.

From his early Photo League images of people seen in the context of their neighbourhood, to his purer, less narrative explorations of space and line in architecture and the human body, Siskind displayed an unequalled mastery of abstract form. Whether photographing the facade of a building (fig. 63.1) or the remnant of a torn poster on a wall (fig. 63.2), he succeeded in bringing to the viewer an appreciation of simple geometric elegance. It comes as no surprise that his work was especially esteemed by many of the New York painters of his generation, such as Barnett Newman, Adolph Gottlieb, Franz Kline, and Willem de Kooning.

It was inevitable that Siskind's interest in form would one day lead to clashes with his Photo League colleagues, who were committed to the primacy of content. Early in 1941, after exhibiting his *Tabernacle City* photographs, he found himself being challenged in a group discussion. Unable to justify his subject matter on political grounds or to defend himself against charges of "being too arty," Siskind finally quit the League.[2]

Fig. 63.1 Aaron Siskind, *Tabernacle City*, 1935, printed before March 1965, gelatin silver print. National Gallery of Canada, Ottawa (32904)

Fig. 63.2 Aaron Siskind, *New York 62*, 1976, gelatin silver print. National Gallery of Canada, Ottawa (37093)

64 Frederick Sommer
Angri, Italy 1905–1999 Prescott, Arizona
Chicken Parts 1940
Gelatin silver print, 24.2 × 19.2 cm
29327

Inscriptions   verso of mount, u.l., *Negative #91 1940*, c., *Frederick Sommer*
Provenance   purchased from Laurence Miller Gallery, New York, 1986.

Diversity of subject matter and a highly experimental approach to the photographic process are two of the defining characteristics of Frederick Sommer's photographs. Although his images exploit ways of seeing and printing that are peculiar to the medium of photography, Sommer's perception of his evolution as an artist was that he owed as much to the influence of the paintings of Paul Cézanne and Max Ernst as to the photographs of Alfred Stieglitz and Edward Weston.

Chicken Parts postdates his meeting with Weston in 1936, an encounter that led to Sommer's use of a large-format camera and the adoption of a sharp-focus aesthetic. It was during the following four years, when Sommer began to apply himself seriously to photography,[1] that the inspiration of Surrealist imagery made itself apparent in his work. While photographers like Wols and Weston certainly approached the subject of death in their photographs, neither confronted the subject of mutilation and decay with the same compulsive interest as Sommer.

This image, in which Sommer has displayed and recorded chicken anuses and organs with an unsettling mix of scientific orderliness and fetishistic obsessiveness, is part of a body of work that he created in the late 1930s and early 1940s in which glistening entrails, organs, coyote cadavers, and a human limb are the subject of his unwavering curiosity (see figs. 64.1 and 64.2). The photographic historian Van Deren Coke regarded it as the most important work of Sommer's career. In fact, the fetishistic sorting out and rephrasing of the bits of human and animal anatomy, presented on the one hand like biological specimens and on the other like shamanistic charms, suggests that there is a collective significance underlying this group of photographs.

Although Sommer's work falls chronologically into the context of American Surrealism – a later phase of the movement – its connections with European Surrealist thought can be seen in its affinities to the writings of Georges Bataille. The latter's 1930 essay "Mouth," for example, plays irreverently with the notion of debasement of the human form by suggesting that a rotation from the vertical axis to a horizontal one would alter the human eye/mouth relationship to the eye/anus relationship of four-legged animals.[2]

Although it is doubtful whether Sommer's work came directly from any such theoretically constructed notions – he was too much of a mystic – it certainly exploits the same set of ambiguities. By contemplating a grouping of animal parts that evoke the human mouth, eye, and vagina, the viewer is forced to transgress a number of rational boundaries and confront a mixture of emotions ranging from attraction to repulsion. The fastidious printing of these images, which is undoubtedly the result of Weston's influence, makes them at once more beautiful and more grotesque. As Keith Davis has noted:

> For Sommer, every photograph was an explicitly handmade thing. On several occasions, he carefully etched his negative to add weight and tone to his final image. His work in the darkroom (gently bleaching specific areas of a print with Farmer's reducer) and in the studio (meticulously spotting dry-mounted prints to connect and extend tonal relationships) also testifies to his application of drawing skills to the making of photographs.[3]

Sommer contributed, along with Breton, Duchamp, Man Ray, and others, to the 1940s avant-garde magazine *View*. He was the only photographer whose work was included in *Le surréalisme en 1947*, an international Surrealist exhibition at the Galerie Maeght in 1947.

Fig. 64.1   Frederick Sommer, *Chicken Entrails*, 1939, gelatin silver print. San Francisco Museum of Modern Art, Gift of Brett Weston

Fig. 64.2   Frederick Sommer, *Coyote*, 1945, gelatin silver print. San Francisco Museum of Modern Art, Purchased through gift of Richard and Pamela Kramlich

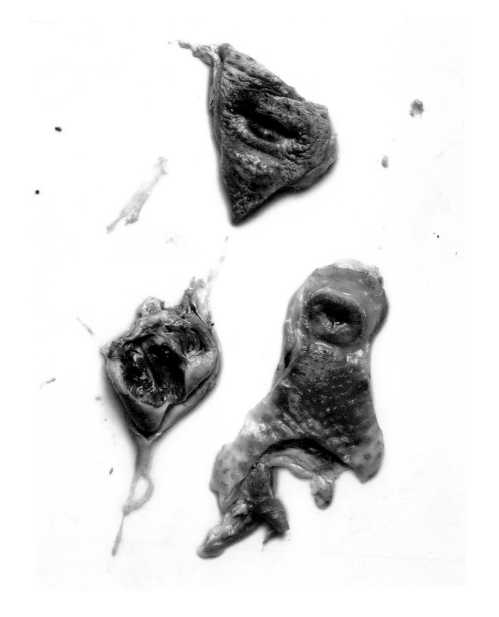

Luxembourg 1879–1973 West Redding, Connecticut

Sunburn, New York 1925

Gelatin silver print, toned, 24 × 19.4 cm, sheet 25 × 20 cm

40068

Inscriptions   verso, l.c., *34*, l.c., *Sunburn*

Annotations   verso, u.c., stamped, *PHOTOGRAPH BY STEICHEN / 80 WEST 40th STREET / NEW YORK*, c., stamped, *COPYRIGHT / Conde Nast Publications, Inc.*, l.c., *PF 22738*

Provenance   Joanna Steichen; Howard Greenberg Gallery, New York, 1998; purchased from Howard Greenberg Gallery, 1999.

Created when Steichen was chief photographer for Condé Nast Publications, *Sunburn, New York* stands out from his more conventional portraits of socialites and celebrities that appeared in *Vanity Fair* at the time. A closely cropped study of the face of a young woman staring unflinchingly into the lens of the camera, it reflects the emotional intensity that Steichen seemed so compelled to express in his portraits but rarely achieved. Commenting later in life on his iconic *J.P. Morgan, New York* (1903), he noted that it had taught him that a portrait "must get beyond the universal self-consciousness that people have before the camera." *J.P. Morgan* and *Sunburn* are both moody and intense images, but they differ significantly in the degree of closeness between the photographer and his subject. The former is a dramatically lit, frontal, three-quarter-length seated portrait. *Sunburn* is a close-up view of a young woman's face that appears as a disembodied element precariously balanced in the centre of the picture space, evocative of a Brancusi bronze. Dark hair and the sombre background frame the sitter's oval-shaped face, with its finely sculpted features.

According to Joanna Steichen, who was the photographer's last wife, the model in *Sunburn, New York* was either a temporary assistant in Steichen's studio or someone who visited him there.[1] In fact, the implications of Steichen making a portrait with such intense and apparently intimate overtones at this time are far more intriguing than the assumption that he was only interested in her tanned face. Aside from revealing his ambivalence about making portraits for the consumption of *Vogue* and *Vanity Fair* readers, this work relates strongly to Alfred Stieglitz's photographic portraits of Georgia O'Keeffe and to Paul Strand's of Rebecca Salsbury. Steichen was unstinting in his praise of Stieglitz's series, produced over a period of twenty years, from 1917 to 1937; he described it as "the most comprehensive and intimate portrayal of a single person that has ever been realized by the visual arts."[2]

Stieglitz's images of O'Keeffe from 1918 to 1922 are radical compositions that go beyond the standard head-and-shoulders format, closing in on the features of the face and thus expressing intimacy (see fig. 65.1). Similarly, there are images from Strand's series of portraits of Rebecca taken around 1923 (see fig. 65.2) where the face fills the frame in a way that points forward to *Sunburn, New York*. Steichen was attracted to the idea of creating an extended portrait through a series of photographs. He once wrote: "To imagine that a visual artist in any medium could condense a complete portrait into one picture is putting a strain on logic."[3] Yet he himself never undertook to make such a series.

From the very accomplished Pictorialist photography he produced in the first decade of the twentieth century, which included experimentation with colour photographs using the Autochrome process, Steichen turned in the 1920s to "straight" photography and to making fashion photographs. His use of photography for commercial ends created a rift between him and Stieglitz. From 1947 to 1962 Steichen was curator of photographs and director of the department of photography at the Museum of Modern Art in New York.

This toned contact print of *Sunburn, New York* is probably one of Steichen's "guide prints," intended for use by him and his printer, Rolf Petersen, in their best-quality work from his negatives.

Fig. 65.1   Alfred Stieglitz, *Georgia O'Keeffe*, 1918, platinum print. The Metropolitan Museum of Art, New York, Gift of Georgia O'Keeffe through the generosity of The Georgia O'Keeffe Foundation and Jennifer and Joseph Duke, 1997 (1997.61.25)

Fig. 65.2   Paul Strand, *Rebecca, New York*, c. 1923, palladium print. The Metropolitan Museum of Art, New York, Gift of Marilyn Walter Grounds, 1989 (1989.1135)

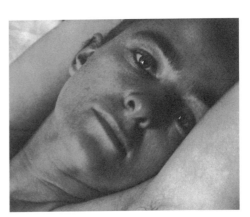

66 Ralph Steiner
Cleveland, Ohio 1899–1986 Hanover, New Hampshire
Nude and Mannequin 1931
Gelatin silver print, 19 × 23.8 cm, sheet 20.5 × 25.4 cm
30000

Inscriptions   verso of mount, c., *Ralph Steiner / 1931 / neg / 1931 / print*
Annotations   verso of mount, c.l., *CS-V21*, c.l., 9⅝ × 7¾, l.c., *orig neg. damaged*
Provenance   Caroline Steiner; purchased from Prakapas Gallery, New York, 1988.

Ralph Steiner first began taking photographs as a teenager growing up in Cleveland. He studied chemical engineering at Dartmouth College, but what he wanted above all was to be a creative artist. Although he had little formal exposure to art or art history, he gradually acquired an appreciation for it on his own.[1] Steiner was eventually able to incorporate his science education into his practice as a photographer: the chemistry and physics he studied at Dartmouth helped him to work through certain technical problems in photography. A year spent at the Clarence H. White School of Photography in New York in 1921–1922 gave him a fundamental understanding of the principles of composition.

An early photograph of a street scene in New York (fig. 66.1) was probably made when Steiner had just completed his year at the school. His apparent interest here in exaggerated angles suggests an affinity with some of his European and Russian contemporaries, but the soft focus belies a stronger Pictorialist influence at this point. After gaining experience working in a photogravure printing establishment, Steiner turned to photojournalism and advertising. He also made films, two of which – *H2O* (1929) and *Café Universal* (1934) – are generally regarded as significant landmarks in American avant-garde filmmaking. A retreat at the artists' colony in Yaddo in the late 1920s gave Steiner the opportunity to reflect on the direction he wanted to take. Out of this came works such as *American Rural Baroque* (fig. 66.2) and *Nude and Mannequin*.

Nude and Mannequin is an unusual photograph not only in the context of Steiner's oeuvre but in American photography during this period. Although reminiscent of Edward Weston's *Civilian Defense*, made a decade later and also uncharacteristic of its creator, Steiner's work enters into a dialogue with contemporaneous European avant-garde photography. By juxtaposing a life-size wooden mannequin with a nude female it recalls Man Ray's playful series titled *Mr. and Mrs. Woodman* and anticipates the rather more sinister photographs of dolls by Hans Bellmer (see cat. 8).

In a letter to Margaret Bourke-White written probably a year before the making of *Nude and Mannequin*, Steiner expressed his desire to make a photograph of a nude that would be radically different, but said he was apprehensive about hiring a "regular model who would think I was either mad … or making dirty post cards." He appealed to Bourke-White to pose for him.

> I have another brainstorm that I am excited about. I'll make you a proposition: you said something about my photographing you. When you come this trip I'll take a series of portraits of you – some with your camera – perhaps against an industrial background – which would be swell for publicity…. Now in exchange – I have two jointed wooden figures life size, and I want to do a lot of pictures of them with a nude for contrast. Sections of the body with the corresponding section of the figures. I think that they'll be the most startling nudes ever done.[2]

Steiner's suggestion was evidently rejected, as there is no evidence that Bourke-White ever posed for him.

Some fifty years later, Steiner downplayed the significance of this image in a letter to his dealer, Eugene Prakapas. Writing in a somewhat jocular tone, he claimed that it was all about rebelling against his Puritan upbringing – "a youthful indiscretion; probably an attempt to get back at my parents who'd not encouraged me to go to the nearby Cleveland Art Museum because they had NAKID ladies on the wall."[3]

Fig. 66.1   Ralph Steiner, *New York*, c. 1920, palladium print. National Gallery of Canada, Ottawa (26749)

Fig. 66.2   Ralph Steiner, *American Rural Baroque*, 1928, gelatin silver print. National Gallery of Canada, Ottawa, Gift of Benjamin Greenberg, Ottawa, 1982 (19065)

Hoboken, New Jersey 1864–1946 New York
Equivalent 1929
Gelatin silver print, 11.8 × 9.1 cm
41561

Annotations   verso of secondary mount, l.l., *Equivalent 1929 / For Dorothy Brett / Stieglitz* (almost erased), l.r., *NY-AS-1153*, l.r., *167-A*

Provenance   acquired from the artist by Georgia O'Keeffe, New Mexico; given in kind to O'Keeffe's agent, Doris Bry, New York; purchased from Edwynn Houk Gallery, New York, 2005.

In his various roles as publisher, art dealer, mentor, and groundbreaking photographer, Alfred Stieglitz was undoubtedly the central figure in American modernist photography. Raised in a well-to-do, cultured household on Manhattan's Upper East Side, he set out to study engineering at the Technische Hochschule in Berlin in 1882. His interests quickly shifted to photography, and by the time of his return to the United States in 1890 he had committed himself to promoting it as a fine art. To that end he organized the Photo-Secession in 1902, with Gertrude Käsebier, Edward Steichen, and Clarence H. White among its founding members. The following year he began publishing *Camera Work*, a magazine that shaped the ideals of an entire generation of artistic photographers. From 1905 until his death he ran a series of art galleries, beginning with the Little Galleries of the Photo-Secession, in which he championed the work of prominent contemporary artists and photographers from Europe as well as the United States. His long association with the painter Georgia O'Keeffe, who became his second wife, resulted in the creation of an extensive series of photographic portraits and studies of her made over a span of two decades.

Stieglitz began photographing clouds in 1922, and over the next fifteen years, during summers spent at his family's country house at Lake George, New York, the subject evolved into one of his great passions. Part of the motivation was the sheer technical challenge. At the outset he used a cumbersome 8 × 10 view camera, which proved an awkward tool for capturing the fleeting movements of the clouds rolling across the hills. In the time that it took him to load the film holder and expose the film, the view that had caught his attention in the first place was likely to have shifted. Stieglitz was a fastidious craftsman, and a hit-and-miss approach would not have been to his liking. As soon as he switched to a 4 × 5 Graflex camera, in 1923, the cloud studies, though smaller, became livelier and more expressive.

As early as 1923 Stieglitz stated that his studies of clouds were also a way to "put down my philosophy of life."[1] After 1925 he began titling these works *Equivalents*, meaning that the images could also be taken as representing various subjective states, feelings, and emotions.[2] The present work, dark and dense with rippled cloud formations (like many of the cloud studies made between 1929 and 1935) is perhaps reflective of upheavals Stieglitz was experiencing in his private life.[3]

Stieglitz exhibited his cloud photographs in ever-changing sequences, selecting images made in different years and placing them in arrangements that have often been described as "musical." In fact, before settling on the term *Equivalents*, he had presented some of the early groupings under titles such as *Music – A Sequence of Ten Cloud Photographs* and *Clouds in Ten Movements*.[4] By the time of his death, in 1946, there were over 300 mounted cloud photographs in his collection. A comparison with the one other example illustrated here (fig. 67.1), made around 1930, offers just a hint of the wide range of expression conveyed in the series as a whole.

Fig. 67.1   Alfred Stieglitz, *Equivalent*, c. 1930, gelatin silver print. National Gallery of Canada, Ottawa (41925)

New York 1890–1976 Orgeval, Yvelines, France

Rock, Port Lorne, Nova Scotia 1919

Gelatin silver print, 24.3 × 19.5 cm

33309

Inscriptions   verso, c., *Rock, Port Lorne 1914 / Paul Strand AK*

Annotations   verso, u.r., #37, c., stamped and handwritten, *L 77.037*

Provenance   David Mirvish Gallery, Toronto; purchased 1979 with the assistance of a grant from the Government of Canada under the terms of the Cultural Property Export and Import Act.

Paul Strand had two formative experiences as a young man that would influence his decision to become a photographer. As a high school student, he had the good fortune to study with the American documentary photographer Lewis Hine. Hine was Strand's art teacher at the Ethical Culture School in New York in 1907, and under his guidance the young Strand learned of the existence of Alfred Stieglitz's Little Galleries of the Photo-Secession. It was there that Strand would encounter some of the finest photography being made in the United States, and would be party to lively discussions about the nature and direction of the medium. Stieglitz not only showed examples of the most progressive photography but also integrated painting, sculpture, and various forms of contemporary printmaking into his exhibition program. Both Hine and Stieglitz were pivotal figures in the development of photography: Hine provided the foundations upon which twentieth-century American documentary photography would be based, and Stieglitz spearheaded the movement to have photography accepted on an equal basis among the arts. Strand also made contact with members of the New York Camera Club, which he joined at the age of eighteen. It was through the club that he learned a variety of non-silver processes – gum, carbon, and platinum. Although his involvement with Pictorialism was brief, it laid the foundation for a profound understanding of the subtle and complex relationship between the language of technique and the expression of meaning.[1]

The second crucial experience for Strand came in 1913, when the now legendary Armory Show was held in New York, exposing him to some of the most radical art of the day and leading him to explore the boundaries of abstraction in his own photographs. Strand's drive toward increasing abstraction is manifested not only in the striking images published in the last issue of *Camera Work*, in June 1917 (see figs. 68.1 and 68.2), but also in his refusal to give them either descriptive or metaphorical titles. The generic title *Photograph* indicated that the meaning he wished to communicate was confined to the image in and of itself.

In 1919, after his release from the army, Strand undertook a three-week trip to Nova Scotia in the company of his old school friend Herbert Seligmann, a writer and social activist. By this time his vision had already been shaped by what he had seen in some of the most radical art of his time. *Rock, Port Lorne, Nova Scotia* reduces natural forms to strong diagonals and geometric shapes. It mixes anthropomorphism and abstraction, recalling the elegant simplicity of Brancusi's work in sculpture, which he would undoubtedly have seen at Stieglitz's gallery. Writing later about his trip to Nova Scotia and the photographs he took there, he acknowledged the influences that were shaping his vision: "I couldn't have done the rocks without having seen Braque, Picasso, Brancusi."[2]

Fig. 68.1   Paul Strand, *Photograph*, before June 1917, photogravure. National Gallery of Canada, Ottawa, Gift of Dorothy Meigs Eidlitz, St. Andrews, New Brunswick, 1968 (34999.168)

Fig. 68.2   Paul Strand, *Photograph*, before June 1917, photogravure. National Gallery of Canada, Ottawa, Gift of Dorothy Meigs Eidlitz, St. Andrews, New Brunswick, 1968 (34999.170)

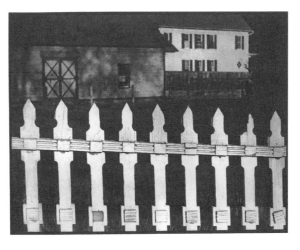

69 Paul Strand
New York 1890–1976 Orgeval, Yvelines, France
Barn, Gaspé 1936
Platinum print, varnished, 12.4 × 15.7 cm
41146

Inscriptions verso of mount, l.l., *VIN/PLAT / 1st / class – P.S. 815A FII X*

Provenance Paul Strand Archive, Millerton, New York; Galerie Zur Stockeregg, Zurich, 1984; purchased from Galerie Zur Stockeregg, 2003.

The present work is one of only two known prints of Paul Strand's *Barn, Gaspé*. It shows the facade of a barn, enlivened by an arrangement of doors and windows that Strand has carefully orchestrated into a play of verticals and horizontals, with dark and light solids and voids.[1] The picture reminds us of Strand's accomplishments as a photographer of abstract forms in the period 1915 to 1919, when he made close-up photographs of bowls, picket fences, and other objects, evincing an interest in the paintings of Braque and Cézanne. For all the elegant structuring, precise framing, and deliberate accentuation of geometry that we witness, this is a work that nevertheless remains rooted in the vernacular subject matter of the barn. It is a photograph that demonstrates Strand's ability to communicate the material, social, and atmospheric reality of a subject along with the fundamental abstract structure of what he is seeing.

Strand made two visits to the Gaspé Peninsula in the province of Quebec, in the summers of 1929 and 1936.[2] Up until the year of the first trip, he had confined his engagement with the landscape to close-ups of plants, rocks, and driftwood. These were essentially formal studies, seen with an exacting eye and executed with great mastery. In the early summer of 1929, on a visit to Alfred Stieglitz at his Lake George home, Strand made his first attempt to photograph the landscape as a whole, capturing the relationship between land, sky, and farm buildings. Stieglitz, who claimed Lake George as his own photographic subject, rebuffed Strand's efforts. Strand subsequently destroyed his Lake George negatives and headed off on his first trip to the Gaspé. In view of Stieglitz's territorial response, the remoteness and unfamiliarity of the Gaspé must have held a special attraction for Strand. One of the representative works from this earlier visit is *Percé Beach, Gaspé* (fig. 69.1), a picture that speaks to the unity of land, sky, weather, and people at work.

It is often assumed that the most desirable print of any work by Strand from 1915 to 1940 is in the form of a platinum print. This was not how Strand approached printmaking, however, as he sought out a correspondence between the formal expression and the ideas and feelings contained within the image. All of Strand's 1929 Gaspé images, for example, were printed in gelatin silver, a process that he felt was more suited to rendering the cool northern light:

> When I went up to the north to Gaspé in 1929, I couldn't print my pictures on platinum paper. I felt that, photographically speaking, though platinum was a much superior paper, it was the wrong paper. The north is cold, the colour that best showed this was something with a black overtone.[3]

The 1936 Gaspé images, on the other hand, were all printed at least once in platinum. It may be that Strand chose the platinum process for the rendering of houses and barns because he was setting out to describe physical surfaces, such as the weathered wood of this barn, rather than atmosphere and a precise quality of light. Strand's choice of process in his Gaspé works reveals the high degree of importance he placed upon the relationship between content and form.

A rigorous printmaker, Strand made very few prints of any given image, which is why they are quite rare. In the 1960s, however, he did make gelatin silver enlargements of a selection of the 1936 Gaspé images (see fig. 69.2). More contrast in tone and dramatic in mood, these later prints tend to be radical reinterpretations of the original works.

Fig. 69.1   Paul Strand, *Percé Beach, Gaspé*, 1929, printed c. 1945, gelatin silver print. National Gallery of Canada, Ottawa (41145)

Fig. 69.2   Paul Strand, *Fox River, Gaspé*, 1936, printed 1960s, gelatin silver print. National Gallery of Canada, Ottawa, Purchased 1979 with the assistance of a grant from the Government of Canada under the terms of the Cultural Property Export and Import Act (33312)

70   Carl Strüwe

Bielefeld, Germany 1898–1988 Bielefeld, Federal Republic of Germany

Forms of Movement and Structure **1930**

Gelatin silver print, 24 × 18.4 cm

41849

Inscriptions   verso, c., *Carl Struwe*, c., *Schildhof 12* (crossed out, beside the stamped and also crossed out "AM LOTHBERG 3")

Annotations   verso, c., stamped, *CARL STRUWE / BIELEFELD / DITFURTHSTR. 39c*, c., stamped *URHEBERRECHTLICH / GESCHUTZT. COPYRIGHT BY / CARL STRUWE / BIELEFELD, AM LOTHBERG 3* (crossed out after comma) / *NACHDRUCK NUR MIT VERMERK: FOT. STRUWE / BIELEFELD*, c., stamped *FORMEN DES / MIKROKOSMOS*, l.l., *ARK-010503*, l.l., *Formen des Mikrokosmos / "Bau und Bewegungsformen" / Eine Station der Blutsbahn in Menschenkorper Kapillargefasse 100.1*, l.r., *P0305040*

Provenance   purchased from Galerie Thessa Herold, Paris, 2006.

The present work is a rare example of a photomicrographic print by Carl Strüwe in a public collection outside of the Kunsthalle Bielefeld, which houses his archive. Although it is difficult to identify the original subject with any precision, the beauty of its rhythmic forms and intricate patterns clearly appealed to the photographer. The truncated composition that we see here is characteristic of most photomicrographic images. In a less typical photomicrograph, Strüwe has arranged a large number of diatoms (unicellular algae) to form a lively pattern (fig. 70.1).

Born in Bielefeld, in the Nordrheim-Westfalen region of Germany, Strüwe worked as a graphic designer for the publishing and advertising industries and as a lithography teacher before turning his talent to photography in the early 1920s.

Strüwe's fascination with entomological and botanical forms studied under a microscope was fuelled by the new visual order proposed in the hand-drawn illustrations of the symmetries and abstract intricacies of organisms by the German protozoologist Ernst Haeckel. *Kunstformen der Natur*, a collection of engravings of Haeckel's drawings and micrographs, was extremely popular in its day (see fig. 70.2), and even though they were not photographic they served as a source of inspiration for Strüwe (who refers to them with reverence in his 1954 *Formen des Mikrokosmos*) and for many other photographers in the early decades of the twentieth century. Haeckel's name and work were repeatedly invoked as representing a desirable standard of accomplishment in articles that appeared in German magazines on photomicrography in the 1920s and 1930s. The term that most aptly describes the kind of imagery that Haeckel's work inspired is "decorative photomicrography," a style epitomized by the French photographer Laure Albin Guillot's seductive 1931 album of photogravures, *Micrographie décorative* (see cat. 3). Decorative photomicrography was accorded special attention in Germany, where it became a subject of study for art students.

In addition to Strüwe, other German photographers who adopted this subject matter included Alfred Ehrhardt (1901–1984), Herbert Schürmann (1908–1982), Anton Stankowski (1906–1999), Ernst Fuhrmann (1866–1956), and August Kreyenkamp (1875–1950). While these photographers shared an appreciation of photomicrography, they did not all approach it from the same philosophical viewpoint. Some were drawn more to the biomorphic and spiritual aspect of photographing organisms up close, while others saw the artistic use of the microscope as subverting the worship of technology as an end in itself. As the critic and photographer Franz Roh expressed it: "Finally, we capture the world of the microscope, not just for scientific reasons, but also with elemental amazement at the wondrous forms of the microcosm."[1]

Fig. 70.1   Carl Strüwe, *Prototype of Individuality* (*Single Cells of Diatoms*), 1933, gelatin silver print. Kunsthalle Bielefeld

Fig. 70.2   Ernst Haeckel, *Thalamophora, Foraminifera*, plate 2, engraving, from *Kunstformen der Natur* (Leipzig and Vienna: Verlag des Bibliographischen Instituts, 1904). Blacker-Wood Library of Biology, McGill University, Montreal

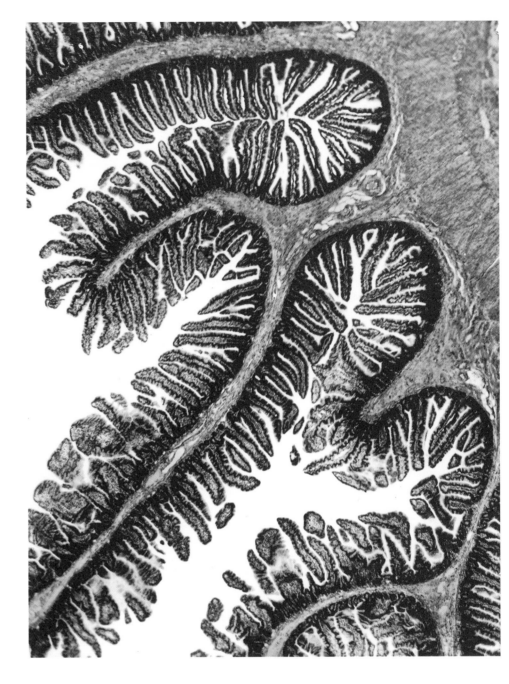

Čermná, Bohemia 1899–1942 Prague
Mirror with Hat 1934
Gelatin silver print, 9 × 8.5 cm, sheet 9.4 × 8.9 cm
36745

Annotations   verso, c., *10*; mount, c., *X*; verso of mount, c., stamped and handwritten, *jako žádná přilba ... 'IX'*, l.l., *P8403003*

Provenance   purchased from Galerie Rudolf Kicken, Cologne, 1992.

Like mirrors themselves, representations of mirrors invite close examination of the reflections that lie within their frames. The mirror in Jindřich Štyrský's *Mirror with Hat*, however, while initially drawing attention by virtue of its brilliance, refuses to yield a clear image. Its indistinct reflection of a mere blur of ground and trees leaves us not with a redoubled conviction of the reality of things seen but rather with a sense of the fleeting and insubstantial nature of experience. Not only does the mirror seem to address emptiness, but the chair and the hat on the cupboard behind the mirror also indicate a human absence. The Czech art historian Karel Srp has observed that in front of Štyrský's lens

> utilitarian articles become personal fetishes. Stripped of all connection with their surroundings, they enter the inner space of his mind, where they merge with it and change into a polysemic symbol.... Štyrský particularizes, rips fragments out of their context, monumentalizes details.[1]

Štyrský's work as a whole was inspired by two avant-garde movements that one would normally think of as antithetical: Poetism, which, as its name implies, privileged poetic over mundane forms, and Artificialism, a movement that privileged man-made over natural forms. Štyrský's art involved the careful arrangement of found objects into poetically expressive compositions. In *Mirror with Hat*, the use of the mirror could be an illustration of Štyrský's understanding of Artificialism, which has been described as a "mirror without an image."[2] The photograph was first shown in an exhibition of Surrealist works at the Mánes Gallery in Prague in 1935, as part of a series of thirty-eight images collectively titled *Man with Blinkers* (see also fig. 71.1).[3] The photographs' original titles, which were intended, as Štyrský's put it, to "underscore their suppressed meaning," are now unfortunately lost.[4] *Man with Blinkers*, along with a seventy-three part series of photographs called *Frog Man* (see fig. 71.2), received a great deal of attention from reviewers of the exhibition.[5] Six years later, in 1941, not long before Štyrský's death, Jindřich Heisler used a selection from these two series of photographs to accompany his poetic texts in a volume titled *Na jehlách těchto dní* ("On the Needles of These Days"), which was published clandestinely by Edice Surrealismu.[6]

Jindřich Štyrský was also a painter, stage designer, illustrator, and writer. In 1917, at the age of eighteen, he began working as a teacher, in accordance with his father's wishes for him. Three years later he enrolled at the Academy of Fine Arts in Prague, and he continued his studies there until 1923. He joined the Czech avant-garde group Devětsil, where he espoused the tenets of Poetism. From 1925 to 1929 he lived in Paris, and by the late 1920s he was assimilating Surrealist motifs and themes. From 1930 to 1933 Štyrský co-edited and contributed to the Prague *Erotic Review*. He was known for his articles on Surrealism, Artificialism, and psychoanalysis, as well as for his studies of Rimbaud and the Marquis de Sade. Štyrský worked closely with the painter Toyen (Marie Čermínová), who was also his lifelong partner.[7]

Fig. 71.1 Jindřich Štyrský, *Untitled*, from the *Man with Blinkers* series, 1934, gelatin silver print. Museum of Decorative Arts, Prague (GF-1734)

Fig. 71.2 Jindřich Štyrský, *Untitled*, from the *Frog Man* series, 1932, gelatin silver print. Museum of Decorative Arts, Prague (GF-1719)

Kolín, Bohemia 1896–1976 Prague
Portrait of My Friend Funke 1924
Gelatin silver print, 28.5 × 22.6 cm
29022

Provenance　Van Deren Coke, San Francisco; bought by Sander Gallery, New York, 1985; purchased from Sander Gallery, 1985.

Jaromír Funke and Josef Sudek's lives were closely connected at the time of the making of this portrait. Events that took place contemporaneously indicate that the two men shared a common nonconformist streak that frequently landed them in trouble. In 1924, the year this photograph was made, they co-signed a damning review of the work of a fellow member of the Prague Photography Club and were consequently expelled. Along with several other photographers, they then founded the Czech Photographic Society, an organization from which they would also eventually be ejected for their lack of initiative and involvement.

These two strong-willed individuals, who were key figures in the Czech avant-garde movement, could not have emerged from more disparate backgrounds. Funke came from a well-to-do and cultured family. He began studying medicine and then switched to law before taking up photography. Sudek's origins, by contrast, were humble. The son of a house painter, he studied bookbinding at the Royal Bohemian Trade School in Kutna Hora beginning at the age of twelve. On active service during the First World War, he lost his right arm in combat and as a result was forced to abandon his apprenticeship as a bookbinder. In spite of his disability, Sudek took up photography in 1917 and formally studied it at the Prague Graphic Arts School from 1922 to 1924.

Prague in the 1920s was a flourishing cultural centre, with all of the most radical manifestations of contemporary thought and culture in evidence. From the imports of Cubism, Surrealism, Constructivism, and New Objectivity to home-grown Poetism, all the new currents in art converged there. Apart from a period in the 1940s when he experimented with Surrealist-inspired imagery, Sudek responded most keenly to the spirit of Poetism, the movement that celebrated "the art of life, the art of being alive and living life."[1] For Sudek, Poetism was in effect a "non-movement" that gave him the freedom to express only that which moved him. Because of his disability and his use of a large-format camera, his work demanded considerable physical exertion, and it is certain that when he ventured out to take photographs he would have wasted little time or energy pursuing the dreams of others.

Sudek's photographs typically reflect private, soulful, and exquisitely seen glimpses of the world around him (see figs. 72.1 and 72.2). With their insistence on the personal, they seem to be related to the sometimes brittle and fractious modernist vision in only a few instances, of which *My Friend Funke* is one. Leaning into the left side of the picture space, Funke appears as if caught in mid-stride by the camera. His frame fills the photograph, and his profile casts a dramatic shadow on the background, giving the portrait an energetic resoluteness.

Fig. 72.1　Joseph Sudek, *View from a Window*, c. 1940, carbon print. National Gallery of Canada, Ottawa (30753)

Fig. 72.2　Joseph Sudek, *Labyrinth on My Table*, 1967, gelatin silver print. National Gallery of Canada, Ottawa (41540)

73 Maurice Tabard
Lyon 1897–1984 Nice

Monsieur Gardé 1931

Gelatin silver print, 22.7 × 17.1 cm

36689

Inscriptions   mount, l.l., *tabard 31*

Annotations   verso of mount, u.r., *3* (circled), c., stamped, *MAURICE / TABARD / PARIS*, c., *1931*, c., *Portrait*, c., *Mr. GARDE*, l.l., *7*, l.c., stamped, *PHOTO / Maurice / TABARD / PARIS*, l.c., stamped, *31–16*

Provenance   acquired from the artist by Robert Shapazian, Los Angeles; Paul Walther, New York; Jill Quasha, New York, c. 1989; bought by Adam Boxer and Gerhard Sander, New York, 1991; purchased from Sander Gallery, New York, 1992.

Like Man Ray, Jaroslav Rössler, László Moholy-Nagy, and other European photographers of the period, Maurice Tabard was attracted by photography's promise of extending the parameters of human vision and image-making by means of new lenses, controlled lighting, and innovative processing techniques. Tabard evidently enjoyed friendships with Philippe Soupault, René Magritte, and Man Ray, and he has been described by some writers as having been connected to the Surrealist movement, but in fact the influence that Surrealism had on his work was fairly superficial. While his fascination with what Rosalind Kraus has termed the "reversibility of the photograph" may contain references to the notion of the subconscious, there is also a strong decorative element in his compositions that tends to undermine any psychological reading. He clearly avoided straight depictions of "reality" and was deeply engaged in the expression of the realm of fantasy, but the high degree of consciousness and technical experimentation in his work and his insistence on the basic geometry of visual structure suggest a greater affinity with the practices of the New Vision. From the manipulation of light through controlled illumination, to darkroom techniques such as burning, dodging, and solarization (see fig. 73.1), Tabard was using many of the standard methods of the New Vision. It is mainly in his photomontages that the tangential effects of Surrealism can be felt.

Tabard's work can be divided into several large groupings – fashion photographs, commercial photographs, portraits, and photographs intended for personal expression. This head-and-shoulders portrait of a certain Monsieur Gardé appears to belong to the last of these categories. It is believed that Gardé, who was photographed by Tabard on several occasions, was a dancer. A photomontage portrait, combining a half-length with the close-up of the face reversed (fig. 73.2), dates from the same period. Tabard learned a great deal about lighting and the establishment of mood from his friend Carlos Baca-Flor, a portrait painter. He probably also acquired some knowledge of conventional studio lighting methods during his short period of employment at the Bachrach Studios in Philadelphia in the early 1920s.

By submerging half of the face in total darkness, Tabard has achieved a striking, almost Grand Guignol sense of the dramatic in this portrait. The oppositions of light and dark – or, more generally, of reversal – that exist within this image are to be found elsewhere in various permutations in Tabard's imagery.[1]

Fig. 73.1   Maurice Tabard, *Untitled*, 1942, gelatin silver print. National Gallery of Canada, Ottawa (30966)

Fig. 73.2   Maurice Tabard, *J'ai la tête à l'envers*, 1931, gelatin silver print. New Orleans Museum of Art, Museum purchase, 1977, Acquisition Fund Drive (77.45)

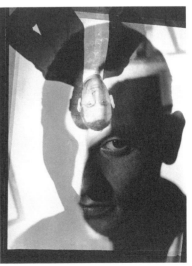

74 Dain Tasker
Beloit, Wisconsin 1872–1964 Oceanside, California
Lily – An X-ray 1930
Gelatin silver print, 29.6 × 24.5 cm
39167

Inscriptions   mount, l.l., *Lily – An X-Ray*, l.r., *Dr. Dain L. Tasker 30*

Annotations   verso of mount, l.l., *GORDON L. BENNET COLLECTION*

Provenance   antique store, Pasadena, California, bought by Christopher Albanese, Antiquario, San Francisco, c. 1990; bought by Gordon L. Bennett, San Francisco, c. 1995; purchased from Gordon L. Bennett, 1998.

The late nineteenth and early twentieth centuries witnessed extraordinary new developments in science, some of which had an impact not only on what we know about the nature of matter but also on how we picture it. These developments prompted the British biologist and mathematician D'Arcy Wentworth Thompson to reflect in 1917 that we had come "to the edge of a world of which we have no experience, and where all our preconceptions must be recast."[1] In many ways, modernist photography was an attempt to come to terms with this new world and to discard existing preconceptions in view of several extraordinary late nineteenth-century discoveries, such as X-rays, radium, and X-ray diffraction crystallography. The revelation that there were forms of radiation in the electromagnetic spectrum other than visible light capable of producing images stimulated the human imagination. Two decades after the discovery of radiography in 1896, excitement about the aesthetic potential of this new imaging process was palpable. But in spite of Moholy-Nagy including several reproductions of X-ray images in his influential 1925 modernist publication *Malerei, Fotografie, Film*, the practicalities of artists actually creating radiographs rather than borrowing those made for medical purposes was as remote as it is today. Unlike the microscope, which had been relatively accessible to artists, X-ray equipment was prohibitive for a variety of reasons not exclusively related to cost. Artists' interest in radiographic imagery has consequently most often taken the form of reproducing existing medical X-rays or incorporating their stylistic elements into their photographic images.

Dr. Dain Tasker's awareness of the aesthetic attraction of radiography and his access as a medical doctor to X-ray equipment was thus a rare occurrence. His use of radiography to make a telling and formally beautiful image finds its context in an earlier history of scientists producing X-ray images, albeit with a decidedly aesthetic motivation. Although Josef Maria Eder and Eduard Valenta set out to produce a guide to the making of radiographs in their 1896 publication *Versuche über Photographie mittelst der Röntgen'schen Strahlen*, the results were a set of fifteen exquisite photogravures made from X-rays (see fig. 74.1).[2] The radiography of Tasker's *Lily*, however, unlike Eder and Valenta's images of human anatomy and skeletal structures of fish, frogs, and rabbits, or the many radiographs by others of the chambered nautilus shell showing its internal logarithmic growth pattern (see fig. 74.2), has no scientific justification. A very simple process of dissection could have revealed its anatomy.

With the most minimal elements of line and the subtlest range of densities and transparencies, Tasker describes in this print of a radiograph a botanical form that artists have celebrated for centuries. The scientist-artist has transcribed the simple elegance of the lily's internal structure through graduated tonalities of the pistil and the relative densities of the petals that surround it.

The Hungarian critic Ernö Kallai, writing in 1928, praised the "wondrous chiaroscuro structures of a simple X-ray." He also summed up the strength of images like Tasker's *Lily* when he wrote:

> Photographic realism captures nature without problematic obscurity, without petit bourgeois sentimentality; simply with the clear and knowingly serene eyes of modern intelligence. And yet we experience its pictures as miracles of an absolutely unrestricted, mysteriously silent, and blindingly precise revelation of the real.[3]

Fig. 74.1   Josef Maria Eder and Eduard Valenta, *Radiographs of Frogs in Anterior and Posterior Positions*, photogravure, from *Versuche über Photographie mittelst der Röntgen'schen Strahlen* (Vienna: Halle, 1896). Ezra Mack, New York

Fig. 74.2   Joseph Bernard Polak, *Nautilus Pompilius*, c. 1923, radiograph. From *Wendingen* (Amsterdam) 5th ser., no. 8–9 (1923), Schelpennummer ("Shell issue")

"Lily - an X-Ray"   Dr. Dain L. Tasker 30

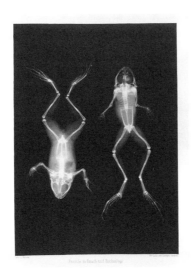

75   John Vanderpant
Alkmaar, Netherlands 1884–1939 Vancouver
Rhythm (Cauliflower) **1936**
Gelatin silver print, 25 × 19.7 cm
41633

Inscriptions   mount, l.l., *"Rhythm" (Cauliflower)*, l.r., *Vanderpant*

Provenance   Tom Jacobson; Christies, New York, bought by Barry Singer Gallery, Petaluma, California, 13 October 2000; purchased from Barry Singer Gallery, 2005.

John Vanderpant's photographs are typically Canadian modernist, in that while his style evolved from quintessential Pictorialism to modernism he never entirely abandoned the softness and warmth of the earlier movement for the clean-edged, cooler aesthetic of what would broadly come to be known as the New Vision (see fig. 75.1). Vanderpant did not begin to introduce geometric forms and abstract compositions into his photography until 1929, and even then, as Sandra Shaul notes, "the persistent soft focus, the use of tonal paper, and significant retouching at the time of printing, mark him as an artist that always had one foot firmly anchored in the early precepts of Pictorialism, as did his use from time to time, even as late as 1935, of poetic titles."[1]

Born in Alkmaar in the Netherlands, John Vanderpant was a student of literature and the history of language. He started to work as a photojournalist in 1910.[2] In 1911 he married Catharina over de Linden and immigrated to Canada. Settled in New Westminster, British Columbia, he opened a commercial portrait studio at the end of the First World War. While he was initially happy to run this successful operation and to participate in international camera club salons, Vanderpant's artistic interests became increasingly discriminating. By 1926, when he opened the Vanderpant Galleries at 1216 Robson Street with Mortimer Lamb, he was orienting his activities to a much wider circle than the camera club. And by 1928 he was actively withdrawing from showing his work in Pictorialist salons.[3]

Rhythm (Cauliflower) is one of several images made by Vanderpant over the course of about five years that show the internal and external structures of various plant forms (see fig. 75.2). In so doing he was photographing subject matter explored by well-known American and European photographers of the 1920s and 1930s such as Edward Weston and Imogen Cunningham in the United States and Karl Blossfeldt and Albert Renger-Patzsch in Germany. These works were made during a period when Vanderpant was questioning his earlier attachment to the sentimental imagery of the camera club aesthetic: "More than ever I am convinced that back to purity, to photography for photography's sake employed by a mind rich in artistic vision – either creative or selective – is the only way out of that rut of sentimentality and process faking."[4]

In this image Vanderpant has selected a section of the plant that reveals an interesting pattern of curved shapes and clusters of textures, as well as a strong contrast between the smooth fibrillar surface of the plant's stem and the dense activity of the florets. As Charles Hill has pointed out, the plants depicted in these images held little meaning for Vanderpant, but rather offered the opportunity to make a statement about the extraordinary patterns created in nature that allowed for the expression of line, form, and emotion. *Rhythm (Cauliflower)* is an image that shows Vanderpant at the peak of his powers as an art photographer, incorporating what he learned about form from photographers like Weston and Cunningham and preserving the integrity of his belief that photographs should be expressive of emotion.[5]

Fig. 75.1   John Vanderpant, *Colonnades on Parade*, c. 1926, gelatin silver print. National Gallery of Canada, Ottawa (41966)

Fig. 75.2   John Vanderpant, *Untitled (Curvature)*, 1933–1934, gelatin silver print. Vancouver Art Gallery, Acquisition Fund (VAG 90.68.38)

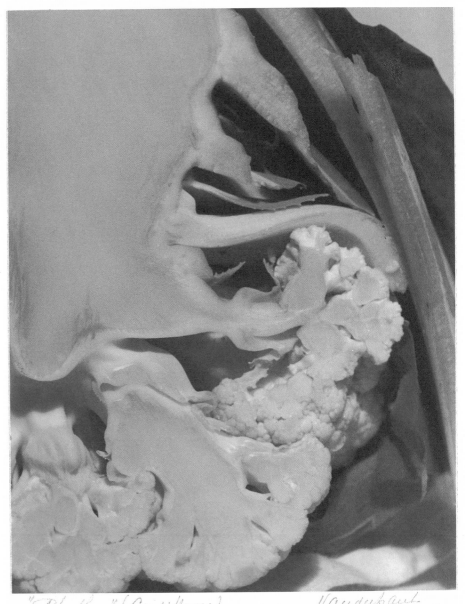

"Rhythm" (Cauliflower)   Vandepaul

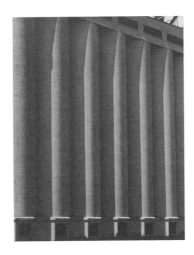

76   Margaret Watkins
Hamilton, Ontario 1884–1969 Glasgow
Domestic Symphony 1919
Palladium print, 21.2 × 16.4 cm
20627

Inscriptions   mount, l.l., *Margaret Watkins 1919.*

Provenance   Joseph Mulholland, neighbour of the artist, Glasgow; Light Gallery, New York, early 1980s; purchased from Light Gallery, 1984.

Margaret Watkins grew up in Hamilton, Ontario, where she studied art and music. Her extended family lived in Scotland, and she made a number of visits there with her parents. In 1915 she moved to Boston, where she worked as a studio assistant to the Pictorialist photographer Alice Boughton. By 1916 Watkins had settled in New York, taking classes at the Clarence H. White School of Photography (she had been a summer student there as early as 1913). In 1917 she became a teacher at the school, and later its registrar; among her students were Anton Bruehl, Paul Outerbridge, Jr., Ralph Steiner, and Margaret Bourke-White. Watkins was also an active member of the Pictorial Photographers of America (founded by Clarence H. White and others), and she helped organize exhibitions at the Art Center, the PPA's home on East 56th Street. Some of Watkins's most significant photographs were made for commercial advertisements. In keeping with White's credo that photographs should be both beautiful and practical, she worked on assignments for the Macy's chain of department stores and for the Fairfax and J. Walter Thompson advertising agencies.

In 1928 Watkins went to Glasgow to visit her aging aunts. From there she travelled to France, Germany, and the Soviet Union, and her photographs from this journey show that she was continuing to experiment and innovate. On returning to Scotland she decided to put off her trip home to New York in order to look after her aunts. She made an effort to remain active in Glasgow, photographing dock workers, entering competitions, and making abstract images that she hoped to sell to carpet and tile manufacturers, but she could no longer count on advertising contracts or the support of friends and colleagues. At the outbreak of war in 1939 she again put off her departure. In the end she chose to stay in Scotland permanently, spending the rest of her life more or less as a recluse.

Domestic Symphony was made while Watkins was working at the Clarence H. White School. Like her more famous *Kitchen Sink* (fig. 76.1), it is a still life grouping set in an ordinary household kitchen. In both of these works the subjects are seen almost in isolation, and the kitchen context is hardly acknowledged. Our attention is drawn across the image from right to left by the sinuous curve of the drainboard as it sweeps over the edge of the sink. Three eggs resting on the drainboard echo the curving forms of the counter and sink, while a dishtowel anchors the entire composition. Although some critics complained that the subject was banal and that none of the individual elements stood out, they were clearly missing the point. These were not photographs "about" eggs, or a dishtowel, or a sink; if anything they were about design. They illustrate precisely Watkins's strength as an advertising photographer and also reveal the qualities that mark her as a modernist.

Fig. 76.1   Margaret Watkins, *The Kitchen Sink*, c. 1919, palladium print. National Gallery of Canada, Ottawa, Purchased 1984 with the assistance of a grant from the Government of Canada under the terms of the Cultural Property Export and Import Act (20629)

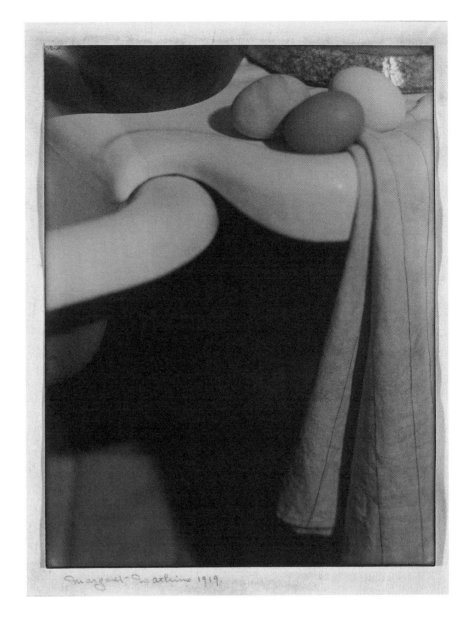

Margaret Watkins 1919.

Hamilton, Ontario 1884–1969 Glasgow
Still Life – Shower Hose 1919
Gelatin silver print, 21.2 × 15.9 cm
20628

Inscriptions   mount, l.l., *Margaret Watkins 1919*

Provenance   Joseph Mulholland, neighbour of the artist, Glasgow; Light Gallery, New York, early 1980s; purchased from Light Gallery, 1984.

Reacting to the view that Marcel Duchamp's *Fountain* of 1917 (fig. 77.1) was not art but merely plumbing, Beatrice Wood famously observed: "The only works of art America has given are her plumbing and her bridges."[1] That a common, mass-produced item – and, of all things, one that belonged in the bathroom – could be presented as art, or even simply treated as a subject of art, is a quintessentially modernist notion. This beautifully achieved image of an ordinary shower hose was made by Margaret Watkins in 1919, six years before Edward Weston's now famous photograph of a toilet (fig. 79.1) and more than ten years before his photograph of a bedpan (cat. 79).

Many of Watkins's photographs are still lifes that combine carefully selected objects so as to create an overall design. In *Still Life – Shower Hose* a somewhat primitive and glamourless object has been transformed into a pattern of concentric circles set against a grid of vertical lines. In another photograph from about the same period, *Design – Angles* (fig. 77.2), a breadknife set on a book breaks up the picture plane into a series of dark and light triangles. In both cases, the repetition of similar forms is what lifts the objects out of their ordinariness, infusing the entire image with a visual lyricism.

Working on assignment for various advertising agencies, Watkins was often required to photograph ordinary items such as blocks of cheese, dishes, soap, gloves, or glassware. As editor of a special issue of *Pictorial Photography in America* she contributed her own statement on the subject of advertising and photography, pointing out that through careful attention to design and composition photographers were able to heighten the allure of ordinary manufactured products: "Stark mechanical objects revealed an un-guessed dignity: commonplace articles showed curves and angles which could be repeated with the varying pattern of a fugue."[2]

Fig. 77.1   Marcel Duchamp, *Fountain*, 1950 (replica of 1917 original), porcelain urinal. Philadelphia Museum of Art, Gift (by exchange) of Mrs. Herbert Cameron Morris, 1998

Fig. 77.2   Margaret Watkins, *Design – Angles*, 1919, gaslight silver chloride print. Amon Carter Museum, Fort Worth, Texas (P1983.41.3)

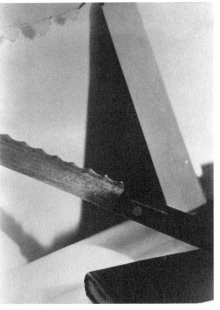

Highland Park, Illinois 1886–1958 Carmel, California
***Christel, Glendale* 1927**
Gelatin silver print, 24 × 18.5 cm
33693

Inscriptions   mount, l.l., *E W 16/50*, l.r., *Edward Weston / 1927*

Annotations   verso of mount, u.l., *SSM / 1927*, l.l., by Christel Gang, *My back by E.W. / C.G.*

Provenance   Christel Gang; acquired by Seymour Stern, Ottawa, from Christel Gang on her death, 1960s; Seymour Stern's widow, Elizabeth Stern; purchased from Elizabeth Stern, 1979 (Phyllis Lambert Fund).

Edward Weston's first camera, a Kodak No. 2 Bulls-Eye, was given to him in his mid-teens by his father. In 1911, at the age of twenty-five, Weston opened his first commercial studio in Tropico, California (later to become part of the city of Glendale). Until about 1922, his photographs were in the Pictorialist style, with even lighting, soft focus, and subjects often inspired by literature. Gradually he began to experiment with portraits of friends and colleagues, photographing them in the sharply angled corners of an attic room or with bold rectangular shadows forming a modern backdrop. His commercial portraits, while technically competent, reflected none of this experimentation.

A memorable encounter with Stieglitz in New York in 1922 reinforced Weston's desire to break free and pursue a more creative path. The following year he left his wife and three younger sons and moved to Mexico with Tina Modotti and his eldest son. Apart from a number of trips back to California, he remained there until November 1926. Stimulated by the Mexican artistic renaissance, he began exploring unconventional subjects and finding new ways of looking at traditional ones.

Christel Gang, the model in this photograph, was born in Germany in 1892 and arrived in San Francisco with her mother in 1906.[1] She eventually settled in Los Angeles, where she ran her own secretarial company. When she and Weston first met in the summer of 1925, at an exhibition of his photographs, she was already an ardent admirer of his work and asked if he would photograph her. The two soon became lovers, and were to remain lifelong friends. A lively and intelligent woman, Gang moved in circles that included many of Weston's own acquaintances, including the filmmaker Sergei Eisenstein, the critic and poet Sadakichi Hartmann, the dancer and writer Ramiel McGehee, and the Japanese-American photographer Tazio Kato.

The present work is one of two photographs of Gang made in 1927 that Weston himself especially prized (for the other, see fig. 78.1). At the time that he was photographing her, he wrote in one of his daybooks: "A start has been made. C. has a body of exaggerated proportions. To overstate her curves became my preoccupation. The ground glass registered sweeping volumes which I shall yet record more surely."[2] Gang's exceptionally elongated back, as depicted in Weston's photographs, indicates something of those "exaggerated proportions." The torso is almost rectangular in form. By instructing Gang to drop her head forward, and then by tightly cropping the image, Weston was able to concentrate on the back alone. It was his belief that each part of the body could be photographed in such a way as to reveal its quintessence. Unlike the romantic and often sentimental nude studies still being made by Pictorialist photographers around the same time, this stark and radically modern study is a perfect example of how Weston endeavoured to open our eyes to the underlying formal beauty of familiar things through the use of unconventional vantage points and sharp focus.

As a token of gratitude to Gang for modelling for the two nude studies, Weston gave her a print of one of the images. She in turn made a gift of it to the filmmaker Sergei Eisenstein. On learning of this, Weston generously offered to provide her with a replacement, but could not remember which version she had received from him. To clarify the matter, he drew two sketches for her in a letter, illustrating the two different views of her back (fig. 78.2), and asked her to specify which one she wanted. The photograph in the National Gallery of Canada is the print that Weston made for Gang to replace the one she had given away.

Fig. 78.1   Edward Weston, *Nude, Los Angeles*, 1927, gelatin silver print. The J. Paul Getty Museum, Los Angeles

Fig. 78.2   Edward Weston, letter to Christel Gang, 7 October [1931?]. Christel Gang fonds, National Gallery of Canada Library and Archives, Ottawa

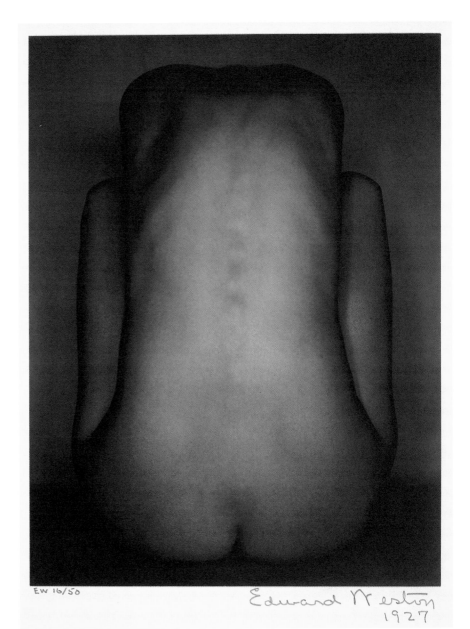

EW 16/50

Edward Weston
1927

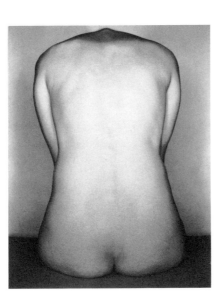

EDWARD WESTON
CARMEL-BY-THE-SEA
CALIFORNIA

Your description of nude was not
clear: the drawing plain enough, but
you marked what really were legs,
"arms." Which one is it of these two.
⬜←legs ⬜←arms ?

Highland Park, Illinois 1886–1958 Carmel, California
Bedpan 1930
Gelatin silver print, 24 × 14.6 cm
33694

Inscriptions   verso, u.c., *Bed Pan*; mount, l.l,. *E.W. 18/50*, l.r., *Edward Weston 1930*

Provenance   Christel Gang; acquired by Seymour Stern, Ottawa, from Christel Gang on her death, 1960s; Seymour Stern's widow, Elizabeth Stern; purchased from Elizabeth Stern, 1979 (Phyllis Lambert Fund).

One of Edward Weston's artistic goals, as expressed in his 1927 daybook, was to "present objectively the texture, rhythm, form in nature, without subterfuge, or evasion in technique or spirit."[1] This dictum applied not only to his interest in things like vegetables, rocks, or shells, but also to his treatment of various manufactured objects whose forms he considered no less attractive. *Bedpan*, like another famous photograph, the 1925 *Excusado, Mexico* (fig. 79.1), shows Weston moving close in to his subject, filling the picture space in a way that is breathtaking in its audacity and yet utterly simple. His straightforward approach strips away any possible narrative interpretation in order to distill the object's very essence.

Weston intuitively understood the sculptural dimension of light, and this was how he was able to transform the most ordinary objects into icons. Fully aware of the classical reverberations in his work, he once remarked that the *Excusado* reminded him of the famous Winged Victory of Samothrace, a headless Greek statue.[2] He also knew that *Bedpan* could be compared with Brancusi's sculptures, such as *Princess X* (fig. 79.2) or *Bird in Space*, both of which he had seen when visiting Walter Arensberg in 1930.[3]

To photograph the bedpan Weston first placed it inside a cardboard box so that it could easily be stood on one end. The glossy white sheen of the enamel contrasts with the box's dark recesses, and our attention is thus drawn to the pronounced curves. The basin swells at the top, where it seems like the chest of a bird, and the handle soars to the right, looking as if it were the neck of a headless swan. Weston himself once spoke in almost anthropomorphic terms of the bedpan's "stately, aloof dignity."[4]

During the early 1930s, Weston became associated with the circle of photographers known as Group f/64. The name was a reference to the smallest aperture setting on large-format cameras, providing maximum depth of field and maximum sharpness but requiring long exposure times, and hence immobile or nearly immobile subjects – a technical way of saying that they favoured landscapes and still lifes over photojournalism and documentary photography. By this period Weston had abandoned the softer platinum print for the stronger contrast and light-reflecting qualities of gelatin silver. Along with other members of f/64, including Ansel Adams, Willard Van Dyke, and Imogen Cunningham, Weston valued the precision of contact printing on glossy paper and learned to exploit the dramatic potential of the sharply focused black-and-white gelatin silver print.

Fig. 79.1   Edward Weston, *Excusado, Mexico*, 1925, printed before July 1969, gelatin silver print. National Gallery of Canada, Ottawa (33649)

Fig. 79.2   Constantin Brancusi, *Princess X*, 1915–1916, polished bronze on limestone block. Philadelphia Museum of Art, The Louise and Walter Arensberg Collection, 1950

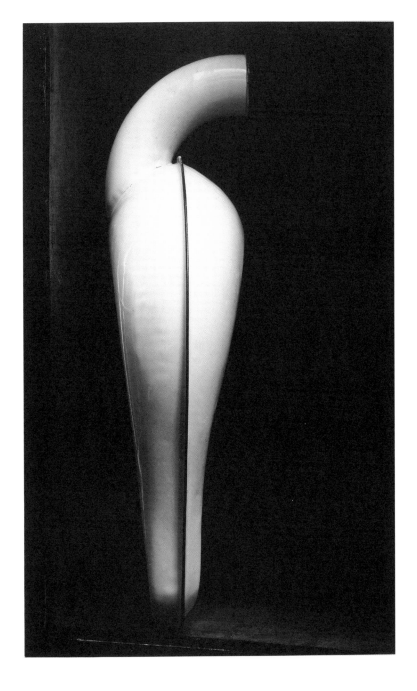

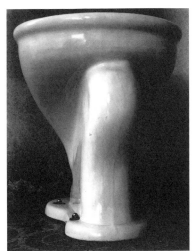

Notes

Introduction

1   Charles Harrison defines modernization as "a range of technological, economic and political processes associated with the Industrial Revolution and its aftermath" and modernity as "the social conditions and modes of experience that are seen as the effects of these processes." Charles Harrison, *Modernism* (Cambridge: Cambridge University Press, 1997), p. 6.

2   Lilly Koltun, "Art Ascendant, 1900–1914," in *Private Realms of Light: Amateur Photography in Canada, 1839–1940*, ed. Lilly Koltun (Markham, Ont.: Fitzhenry & Whiteside, 1984), p. 44.

3   *Camera Work*'s first issue appeared in 1903. As Jonathan Green notes: "Stieglitz demanded that the plates serve as more than a record of what was being produced in the photographic world; they had to interpret fully the spirit and quality of the original print." Jonathan Green, *Camera Work: A Critical Anthology* (New York: Aperture, 1973), p. 11.

4   Bonnie Yochelson, "Clarence H. White, Peaceful Warrior," in *Pictorialism into Modernism: The Clarence H. White School of Photography*, ed. Marianne Fulton (New York: Rizzoli, 1996), p. 50. The exhibition consisted of copy prints made by Alvin Langdon Coburn.

5   Alvin Langdon Coburn, "The Future of Pictorial Photography," *Photograms of the Year*, 1916, pp. 23–24, quoted in Nancy Newhall, "Alvin Langdon Coburn – The Youngest Star," in *Alvin Langdon Coburn: Photographs, 1900–1924*, ed. Karl Steinorth (Zurich: Stemmle, 1998), p. 41.

6   Naomi Rosenblum, "Paul Strand: The Early Years, 1910–1932" (Ph.D. diss., City University of New York, 1978), p. 67, citing an interview with Strand, 6 July 1975.

7   Pictorial Photographers of America, *Annual Report* (National Arts Club, 1918), p. 14, quoted in Yochelson, "Clarence H. White, Peaceful Warrior," p. 68.

8   Stieglitz's grip on American photography loosened when new and influential players entered the field. He was hypersensitive to any implied criticism of his work and any seeming irreverence toward his new rules of correct photographic form. When Charles Sheeler referred to Stieglitz's platinum prints on view at the Anderson Galleries in 1923 as "precious" and compared one of his landscapes to a painting by Andrea Mantegna, Stieglitz was greatly offended and relations between the two men remained frosty for some time.

9   László Moholy-Nagy, "Photography Is Manipulation of Light," in Andreas Haus, *Moholy-Nagy: Photographs and Photograms*, trans. Frederic Samson (New York: Pantheon, 1980), p. 47.

10   Ibid., p. 48.

11   Jaroslav Anděl, "Modernism, the Avant-Garde, and Photography," in Jaroslav Anděl et al., *Czech Modernism, 1900–1945* (Boston: Bulfinch Press, 1989), p. 87.

12   Antonín Dufek, "Imaginative Photography," in Anděl et al., *Czech Modernism*, p. 123.

13   Anděl, "Modernism, the Avant-Garde, and Photography," p. 87.

14   Dufek, "Imaginative Photography," p. 124.

15   Alexander Lavrentiev, "On Priorities and Patents," in *Aleksandr Rodchenko*, ed. Magdalena Dabrowski et al. (New York: Museum of Modern Art, 1998), p. 55.

16   Telegram from Bourke-White to Roberts Everett Associates, 17 October 1930, quoted in Vicki Goldberg, *Margaret Bourke-White: A Biography* (Reading, Mass.: Addison-Wesley, 1987), p. 89.

17   Albert Renger-Patzsch, "Ziele," *Das Deutsche Lichtbild* (1927), translated as "Aims," in *Photography in the Modern Era: European Documents and Critical Writings, 1913–1940*, ed. Christopher Phillips (New York: Metropolitan Museum of Art, 1989), p. 105.

18   "The Thing Itself Is Such a Secret and So Unapproachable," interview with Walker Evans in *Image* XVII:4 (December 1974), p. 18, reprinted from the *Yale Alumni Magazine*, February 1974.

19   Leah Dickerman, "The Propagandizing of Things," in *Aleksandr Rodchenko*, ed. Dabrowski et al., p. 88.

20   Ibid., p. 89

21   David Evans and Sylvia Gohl, *Photomontage: A Political Weapon* (London: Gordon Fraser, 1986), p. 49; Peter Selz, *Photomontages of the Nazi Period: John Heartfield* (New York: Universe Books, 1977), p. 15.

22   Stephanie Barron, ed., *Degenerate Art: The Fate of the Avant-Garde in Nazi Germany* (Los Angeles: Los Angeles County Museum of Art, 1991), p. 9.

Cat. 1

1   Hank O'Neal, with commentary by Berenice Abbott, *Berenice Abbott: American Photographer* (New York: McGraw-Hill, 1982), pp. 11–12. The 1926 exhibition opened on 8 June and ran for two weeks. Included were portraits of James Joyce, Jean Cocteau, Sylvia Beach, and André Gide, among others. The 1928 exhibition opened on 24 May and ran to 7 June.

2   Ibid., p. 13.

Cat. 2

1   Hank O'Neal, with commentary by Berenice Abbott, *Berenice Abbott: American Photographer* (New York: McGraw-Hill, 1982), p. 30.

Cat. 3

1   Roger Brielle, "Laure Albin Guillot ou la science féerique," *Art et Décoration: Revue mensuelle d'art moderne* LX (July–December 1931), p. 165.

Cat. 4

1   Susan Kismaric, *Manuel Álvarez Bravo* (New York: Museum of Modern Art, 1997), p. 20.

2   André Breton, "Souvenir du Mexique," *Minotaure* 6th year, 3rd ser., no. 12–13 (May 1939), pp. 38–39, translated by Geoffrey MacAdam as "Memory of Mexico," *Review: Latin American Literature and Arts*, no. 51 (Fall 1995), p. 10.

Cat. 5

1   James Borcoman, *Eugène Atget 1857–1927* (Ottawa: National Gallery of Canada, 1984), p. 17.

2   Maria Morris Hambourg, "A Biography of Eugène Atget," in *The Work of Atget*, ed. John Szarkowski and Maria Morris Hambourg (New York: Museum of Modern Art, 1981–1985), vol. 2, p. 11.

3   *La Révolution surréaliste*, no. 7 (15 June 1926), p. 6.

Cat. 6

1   The process is described in a letter by Bayer to Tim Gidal in 1977, quoted in Udo Hartmann, "The Eye of Herbert Bayer," in *Photography at the Bauhaus*, ed. Jeannine Fiedler (Cambridge, Mass.: MIT Press, 1990), p. 67.

Cat. 7

1 *The International Center of Photography Encyclopedia of Photography* (New York: Crown, 1984), pp. 58–59.

2 Ibid.

Cat. 8

1 Sue Taylor, *Hans Bellmer: The Anatomy of Anxiety* (Cambridge, Mass.: MIT Press, 2000), p. 24.

2 Ibid., p. 32.

3 Ibid., p. 58.

Cat. 11

1 Jürgen Wilde, "Blossfeldt, Karl," in *Contemporary Photographers*, ed. Colin Naylor (Chicago: St. James Press, 1988), pp. 79–81.

Cat. 12

1 Stephen Bennett Phillips notes that industrial production from 1919 to 1929 doubled in the United States and that this thriving economy "supported the construction of factories, skyscrapers, bridges, dams and tunnels over that decade." Stephen Bennett Phillips, *Margaret Bourke-White: The Photography of Design, 1927–1936* (New York: Phillips Collection in association with Rizzoli, 2003), p. 10.

2 Sean Callahan, *The Photographs of Margaret Bourke-White* (New York: New York Graphic Society, 1972), p. 5.

3 Phillips, *Margaret Bourke-White*, p. 14.

4 Ibid., p. 18.

5 Callahan, *The Photographs of Margaret Bourke-White*, p. 29.

6 Phillips, *Margaret Bourke-White*, p. 23.

7 Luce had seen a portfolio of her industrial photographs published in the rotogravure sections of several Midwestern newspapers. Callahan, *The Photographs of Margaret Bourke-White*, p. 29.

8 *Fortune*, March 1930, pp. 52–57.

Cat. 13

1 The photograph was published in "Port of New York Authority," *Fortune*, September 1933, pp. 22–31.

2 Letter to Bourke-White from *Fortune*'s associate editor, Ralph McAllister Ingersoll, 13 January 1933, quoted in Stephen Bennett Phillips, *Margaret Bourke-White: The Photography of Design, 1927–1936* (New York: Phillips Collection in association with Rizzoli, 2003), p. 183.

3 Telegram to Roberts Everett Associates, 17 October 1930, quoted in Vicki Goldberg, *Margaret Bourke-White: A Biography* (Reading, Mass.: Addison-Wesley, 1987), p. 89.

Cat. 14

1 *Minotaure* I:3–4 (1933), p. 77.

Cat. 15

1 Anne Wilkes Tucker, with Richard Howard and Avis Berman, *Brassaï: The Eye of Paris* (Houston: Museum of Fine Arts, 1999), p. 86.

2 They served as illustrations for Maurice Raynal's article "Variété du corps humain," in *Minotaure* I:1 (1933), pp. 41–44, alongside anonymous French nineteenth-century photographs of nudes and drawings by Seurat and Renoir. Several playfully erotic drawings by Picasso, under the heading "Une anatomie," also appeared in this issue of *Minotaure*.

3 Tucker, *Brassaï*, p. 86.

4 Brassaï, *Picasso and Company*, trans. Francis Price (Garden City: Doubleday, 1966), p. 69.

5 Hal Foster, "Violation and Veiling in Surrealist Photography: Woman as Fetish, as Shattered Object, as Phallus," in *Surrealism: Desire Unbound*, ed. Jennifer Mundy (London: Tate, 2001), p. 203.

6 Ibid.

7 Quoted in Tucker, *Brassaï*, p. 73.

8 "Brassaï: Talking about Photography," *Creative Camera*, April 1970, p. 120, quoted in Tucker, *Brassaï*, p. 71.

Cat. 16

1 *Reports by the Juries on the Subjects in the Thirty Classes into Which the Exhibition Was Divided* (London: Spicer Brothers, 1852). The official title of the exhibition was *Exhibition of the Works of Industry of All Nations*.

2 Gael Newton, Curator of Photographs, National Gallery of Australia, was kind enough to bring this brochure to my attention (correspondence, 28 March 2004).

3 David Travis, *Photographs from the Julien Levy Collection: Starting with Atget* (Chicago: Art Institute of Chicago, 1976), p. 34.

4 Beals was born in Hamilton, Ontario. She is reputed to have been the first woman press photographer. Turner Browne and Elaine Partnow, *Macmillan Biographical Encyclopedia of Photographic Artists & Innovators* (New York: Macmillan; London: Collier Macmillan, 1983), p. 41.

5 "Bourges … developed a process for creating a color transparency made of thin acetate sheets coated with light sensitive emulsions which were dyed and sandwiched together with glass. Condé Nast Engravers used these extremely fine color transparencies as guides and, with hand work, made the printing plates in a painstaking process which resulted in some of the finest color reproductions ever made." Joe Deal, "Anton Bruehl," *Image* XIX:2 (June 1976), p. 2.

Cat. 17

1 Ideas about abstraction were being discussed in *Camera Work* (see issue no. 31). In an essay on the "Fourth Dimension from a Plastic Point of View," Max Weber summed up his view of abstraction as a "consciousness of a great and overwhelming sense of space-magnitude in all directions at one time … somewhat similar to color and depth in musical sounds." Quoted in James Enyeart, *Bruguière: His Photographs and His Life* (New York: Knopf, 1977), p. 14.

2 Enyeart, *Bruguière*, p. 8.

3 Coburn's essay in *Camera Work* in 1911, "The Relation of Time to Art," was concerned with the role that time played in photography. See Enyeart, *Bruguière*, p. 15.

4 Enyeart, *Bruguière*, p. 57.

Cat. 18

1 Henri Cartier-Bresson, *The Europeans* (New York: Simon & Schuster, 1955).

2 Cartier-Bresson kept a handwritten list of the photographs that he sent to Levy in 1933. Number 60 in it is described as "enfant jouant mur goudronné Valence" (child playing tarred wall Valence). See Agnès Sire, "L'histoire," in *Documentary & Anti-Graphic Photographs by Cartier-Bresson, Walker Evans, & Alvarez Bravo*, ed. William Ewing and Agnès Sire (Gottingen: Steidl, 2004), p. 23.

Cat. 19

1 Agnès Sire, "The Story," in *Documentary & Anti-Graphic Photographs by Cartier-Bresson, Walker Evans, & Alvarez Bravo*, ed. William Ewing and Agnès Sire (Gottingen: Steidl, 2004), p. 29.

Cat. 20

1 Flip Bool, "Joint Camerawork," in *Paul Citroen (1896–1983)*, ed. Flip Bool et al. (Amsterdam: Focus, 1997), p. 28.

Cat. 21

1 Alvin Langdon Coburn, "The Future of Pictorial Photography," *Photograms of the Year: The Annual Review of the World's Photographic Art* (London: Illiffe; New York: Philosophical Library, 1916), p. 23.

Cat. 22

1 Gus Kayafas, ed., *Stopping Time: The Photographs of Harold Edgerton* (New York: Abrams, 1987), p. 154.

Cat. 23

1 Quoted in Jerry L. Thompson, *Walker Evans at Work* (New York: Harper & Row, 1982), p. 161.

Cat. 24

1   See Leslie Katz, "Interview with Walker Evans," *Art in America*, no. 59 (March–April 1971), p. 86.

2   Sarah Greenough, *Walker Evans: Subways and Streets* (Washington, D.C.: National Gallery of Art, 1991), p. 17.

Cat. 25

1   Franz Roh and Jan Tschichold, ed., *Foto-Auge: 76 Fotos der Zeit / Oeil et photo: 76 photographies de notre temps / Photo-eye: 76 photos of the period* (Stuttgart: Akademischer Verlag F. Wedekind, 1929), plate 62. Facsimile editions of this book were issued by several publishers in the 1970s.

2   Quoted in Walter Boje, "Auf Brettern, die die Welt bedeuten," in *Gertrude Fehr: Fotografien seit 1918* (Munich: Münchner Stadtmuseum, 1980), p. 7.

Cat. 29

1   Jaromír Funke, "On Modern Photography," English translation in *Jaromír Funke: Pioneering Avant-Garde Photography (1896–1945)* (Brno: Moravská Galerie, 1996), p. 149.

2   Milan Chlumsky, "Jaromír Funke," in *Encyclopedia of Twentieth-Century Photography*, ed. Lynne Warren (New York: Routledge, 2006), vol. 1, p. 577. From 1923 Funke took part in "exhibitions of amateur photography in Czechoslovakia and abroad (about 60 salons)" as well as "most of the exhibitions of modern photography in Czechoslovakia." Antonín Dufek et al., *Czechoslovakian Photography: Jaromír Funke / Jaroslav Rössler* (London: Photographers' Gallery, 1985), p. 10. Of particular interest from a Canadian perspective are *The Toronto Salon of Photography*, 1924, and *The International Exhibition of Pictorial Photography*, New Westminster, British Columbia, 1925. See also "Jaromír Funke: A Biography," in *Jaromír Funke: Pioneering Avant-Garde Photography (1896–1945)*, p. 171.

3   *Jaromír Funke: Pioneering Avant-Garde Photography (1896–1945)*, p. 202.

Cat. 30

1   Lili Corbus Bezner, *Photography and Politics in America: From the New Deal into the Cold War* (Baltimore: Johns Hopkins University Press, 1999), pp. 91–92.

2   For biographical information on Grossman, see *The International Center of Photography Encyclopedia of Photography* (New York: Crown, 1984), p. 234.

Cat. 31

1   *As I Saw It: Photographs by John Gutmann* (San Francisco: San Francisco Museum of Modern Art, 1976), p. 31.

Cat. 32

1   J.A. Schmoll gen. Eisenwerth, "Objective and Subjective Photography," in *Subjektive Fotografie*, ed. Otto Steinert (Munich: Brüder Auer, 1925), p. 31.

2   Peter Sager, "Hajek-Halke, Heinz," in *Contemporary Photographers*, ed. George Walsh, Colin Naylor, and Michael Held (New York: St. Martin's Press, 1982), p. 311.

Cat. 33

1   *Arbeiter Illustrierte Zeitung* XI:29 (17 July 1932), p. 675.

2   David Evans, *John Heartfield, AIZ: Arbeiter-Illustrierte Zeitung, Volks Illustrierte, 1930–1938* (New York: Kent, 1992), p. 20.

3   Ibid.

Cat. 34

1   Translation by Charles Isaac Gallery, curatorial files, National Gallery of Canada.

2   Emilio Bertonati, *Das experimentelle Photo in Deutschland, 1918–1940*, trans. Linde Birk (Munich: Galleria del Levante, 1978), p. 51.

Cat. 35

1   Martin Kazmaier et al., *Horst: Sixty Years of Photography* (New York: Rizzoli, 1991), p. 12.

Cat. 36

1   Christopher Wilk, "The Healthy Body Culture," in *Modernism: Designing a New World: 1914–1939*, ed. Christopher Wilk (London: Victoria and Albert Museum; New York: Abrams, 2006), p. 250.

2   Alexander Lavrentiev, "Boris Ignatovitch: Biography," http://www.redart.kharkiv.net/ignatovich/biographye.html

3   Ibid. The author quotes from W.F. Stepanova's handwritten notes for 1927–1939 in the Rodchenko and Stepanova archives.

4   Anne-Laure Oberson, "Chronology," in *Aleksandr Rodchenko*, ed. Magdalena Dabrowski et al. (New York: Museum of Modern Art, 1998), p. 309.

Cat. 37

1   Kelly Wise, *Lotte Jacobi* (Danbury, N.H.: Addison House, 1978), p. 12.

2   After her husband's death in 1953 she studied drypoint and etching with Katz.

3   Wise, *Lotte Jacobi*, p. 8.

Cat. 38

1   For biographical information, see Karin Anhold, *Grit Kallin Fischer: Bauhaus and Other Works* (New Brunswick, N.J.: Jane Voorhees Zimmerli Art Museum, Rutgers, State University of New Jersey, 1986), and Monika Faber and Janos Frecot, ed., *Portraits of an Age: Photography in Germany and Austria 1900–1938* (Ostfildern: Hatje Cantz, 2005), p. 164.

Cat. 40

1   "Parmi les natures mortes, il faut surtout admirer une fourchette d'André Kertész, oui, tout simplement une fourchette, qui est presque émouvante de pureté et de tons. C'est peut-être là la seule image qui m'ait donné l'impression d'une oeuvre d'art réelle." Pierre Bost, "Spectacles et promenades," *La Revue hebdomadaire*, 16 June 1928, p. 338.

Cat. 42

1   Gustav Klutsis, "Photomontage as a New Kind of Agitational Art," quoted in Margarita Tupitsyn, "Gustav Klutsis: Between Art and Politics," *Art in America* LXXIX:1 (January 1991), p. 43. Originally from *Izofront: Klasovaya borba na fronte prostranstvennykh iskusstv* (Moscow, 1931).

2   Similarly, on a visit to Soviet coal fields in the early 1930s Klutsis had himself photographed as a miner, and the resulting image was incorporated in the poster *Towards a Struggle for Heat and Metal* (1933).

Cat. 43

1   Dorothea Lange, *The Making of a Documentary Photographer: An Interview Conducted by Suzanne Riess* (Berkeley: Bancroft Library, University of California; Regional Oral History Office, 1968), p. 144.

2   Therese Heyman, "Future Evidence: The Photographs of Dorothea Lange," in *Dorothea Lange: Photographs from the J. Paul Getty Museum*, by Judith Keller (Los Angeles: J. Paul Getty Museum, 2002), p. 102.

Cat. 44

1   Dorothea Lange, "The Assignment I'll Never Forget: Migrant Mother," *Popular Photography*, February 1961, pp. 42–43, 128, quoted in Milton Meltzer, *Dorothea Lange: A Photographer's Life* (New York: Farrar, Straus and Giroux, 1978), p. 133.

Cat. 45

1   Quoted in Ute Eskildsen, *Helmar Lerski: Verwandlungen durch Licht / Metamorphosis through Light* (Freren: Luca, 1982), p. 110.

2   Ibid., p. 108.

3   Andor Kraszna-Krausz, "Preface," in Eskildsen, *Helmar Lerski*, p. 12.

4   Ute Eskildsen and Jan-Christopher Horak, "Introduction," in *Helmar Lerski, Lichtbildner: Fotografien und Filme, 1920–1947* (Essen: Museum Folkwang, 1983), p. 26.

5   Ibid., pp. 23–27.

Cat. 46

1   Letter from Man Ray to Howald, 5 April 1922, University Libraries, Ohio State University, Columbus, Ohio, quoted in Francis F. Naumann, *Conversion to Modernism: The Early Work of Man Ray* (New Brunswick, N.J.: Rutgers University Press; Montclair, N.J.: Montclair Art Museum, 2003), p. 215.

2   Man Ray, *Self Portrait* (Boston: Little, Brown, 1963), p. 106.

3   Ibid.

4   Giulio Carlo Argan, *Rayograph* (Turin: Martano, 1970), p. 120, quoted in Arturo Schwarz, *Man Ray: The Rigour of Imagination* (London: Thames and Hudson, 1977).

Cat. 47

1   Man Ray, "A Note on the Shakespearean Equations," in *To Be Continued Unnoticed* (Beverley Hills: Copley Galleries, 1948), cited in *Man Ray*, ed. Jules Langsner (Los Angeles: Los Angeles County Museum of Art), p. 22.

2   Man Ray, *Self Portrait* (Boston: Little, Brown, 1963), p. 291.

3   William S. Rubin, *Dada and Surrealist Art* (New York: Abrams, 1969), p. 467.

4   Man Ray, *Self Portrait*, p. 291.

5   Man Ray, "A Note on the Shakespearean Equations."

6   Isabelle Fortuné, "Man Ray et les objets mathématiques," *Études photographiques*, no. 6 (May 1999), p. 102.

Cat. 48

1   "Mariën, Marcel," in *The Dictionary of Art*, ed. Jane Turner (New York: Macmillan, 1996), vol. 20, p. 414.

2   Winifred Schiffman, "Marcel Mariën," in Rosalind Krauss et al., *L'Amour fou: Photography & Surrealism* (Washington, D.C.: Corcoran Gallery of Art, 1985), p. 219.

3   Michel Baudson, "Marcel Mariën," in *Confrontations: 111 Contemporary Artists, Belgium and Luxemburg*, ed. Marcel van Jole (Tielt: Lannoo, 1993), p. 287.

Cat. 50

1   Eleanor M. Hight, *Picturing Modernism* (Cambridge, Mass.: MIT Press, 1995), p. 131.

Cat. 51

1   László Moholy-Nagy, *Vision in Motion* (Chicago: Paul Theobald, 1947), p. 188.

Cat. 52

1   Lucia Moholy, *Marginalien zu Moholy-Nagy / Moholy-Nagy, Marginal Notes* (Krefeld: Scherpe, 1972), p. 82.

2   Ibid. The film is currently viewable on the Moholy-Nagy Foundation website, http://www.moholy-nagy.org/Films_Lichtspiel.html

Cat. 54

1   Hugo Sieker, "Absolute Realistik: Zu Photographien von Albert Renger-Patzsch," *Der Kreis* (Hamburg), March 1928, pp. 144–148, translated as "Absolute Realism: On the Photographs of Albert Renger-Patzsch," in *Photography in the Modern Era: European Documents and Critical Writings, 1913–1940*, ed. Christopher Phillips (New York: Metropolitan Museum of Art, 1989), p. 112.

2   "Die Freude am Gegenstand," *Das Kunstblatt* (Berlin), no. 1 (1928), p. 19, translated as "Joy before the Object," in Phillips, *Photography in the Modern Era*, p. 109.

Cat. 55

1   Peter Galassi, "Rodchenko and Photography's Revolution," in *Aleksandr Rodchenko*, ed. Magdalena Dabrowski et al. (New York: Museum of Modern Art, 1998), p. 136.

2   Anne-Laure Oberson, "Chronology," in *Aleksandr Rodchenko*, ed. Dabrowski et al., p. 300.

Cat. 56

1   Information kindly provided by twentieth-century Russian photography scholar Steve Yates.

2   S.O. Khan-Magomedov, *Rodchenko: The Complete Work* (Cambridge, Mass.: MIT Press, 1986), p. 219.

3   Alexander Rodchenko, "The Paths of Modern Photography," *Novyi Lef*, no. 9 (1928), pp. 31–39, quoted in Khan-Magomedov, *Rodchenko*, p. 222.

Cat. 57

1   Franz Roh, *L. Moholy-Nagy: 60 Fotos* (Berlin: Klinkhardt & Biermann, 1930), p. 7.

2   Emilio Bertonati, *Das Experimentelle Photo in Deutschland: 1918–1940* (Berlin: E. Bertonati, 1978).

Cat. 58

1   Ferdinand Brüggemann, "Die Fotografie von Werner Rohde," *Werner Rohde: Fotografien, 1925–37* (Berlin: Nishen, 1992), p. 18.

Cat. 59

1   Antonín Dufek, "Devětsil and Photography," in *Devětsil: Czech Avant-Garde Art of the 1920s and 30s* (Oxford: Museum of Modern Art; London: Design Museum, 1990), p. 62.

2   Karel Srp, *Jindřich Štyrský* (Prague: Torst, 2001), p. 5.

3   Antonín Dufek, "Funke, Rössler and Modern European Photography," in *Czechoslovakian Photography: Jaromír Funke / Jaroslav Rössler* (London: Photographers' Gallery, 1985), p. 4. Dufek reports that these early photograms measured 40 by 60 centimetres, that they were probably first shown at the *Rote Fahne* exhibition in Berlin in 1926, and that unfortunately, like the rest of Rössler's works that were in the hands of Karel Teige, they have disappeared.

4   It was titled *Opus 1*. Dufek, "Funke, Rössler and Modern European Photography," p. 4.

5   *Czechoslovakian Photography: Jaromír Funke / Jaroslav Rössler*, p. 21.

6   Vladimir Birgus, *Jaroslav Rössler* (Prague: Torst, 2001), p. 21.

Cat. 60

1   Robert Kramer, "Historical Commentary," in *August Sander: Photographs of an Epoch, 1904–1959* (Millerton, N.Y.: Aperture, 1980), p. 19.

Cat. 61

1   Gilles Mora, "Charles Sheeler: A Radical Modernism," in *The Photography of Charles Sheeler, American Modernist* (Boston: Bulfinch Press, 2002), p. 89.

2   Theodore E. Stebbins, Jr., and Norman Keyes, Jr., *Charles Sheeler: The Photographs* (Boston: Little, Brown, 1987), p. 11. The letter to Newhall is cited by Stebbins and Keyes from *Germany: The New Photography, 1927–33*, ed. David Mellor (London, 1978).

3   Stebbins and Keyes, *Charles Sheeler: The Photographs*, p. 11. One image in particular is annotated on the mount: "best one."

Cat. 62

1   Quoted in Kotaro Iizawa, "'A Place Where the Light Is Just Right': Shinzo and Roso Fukuhara," in *The Light with Its Harmony: Shinzo Fukuhara / Roso Fukuhara Photographs 1913–1941* (Tokyo: Watari-Um, 1992), p. 23.

2   Information provided by Yuri Mitsuda, Curator, Shoto Museum of Art (correspondence, 1 April 1999). According to Ms. Mitsuda, Shimamura was also prominent as a member in the Mokkoku in Wakayama, and an important member of the Nihon Shashin-Kai (Japan Photographic Society) in Tokyo. Nihon Shashin-Kai was founded by members of the Shashin Geijyutsu-sha. Shimamura never practised as a professional photographer.

3   Anne Wilkes Tucker et al., *The History of Japanese Photography* (New Haven and London: Yale University Press in association with the Museum of Fine Arts, Houston, 2003), p. 359.

4   *Japan Photographic Annual* (Tokyo and Osaka: Asahi Shimbun, 1926), p. 56. The photograph, undated, was titled *Entrance to the Grounds*.

5   Tokyo Metropolitan Museum of Photography, *The Founding and Development of Modern Photography in Japan* (Tokyo: Tokyo-to Bunka Shinkokai; Tokyo-to Shashin Bijutsukan, 1995), p. 21.

6   "Japanese camera magazines were filled with articles on how to compose and shoot still lifes as well as portraits and landscapes. Still-life photographs by amateur photographers filled these magazines as interest in this genre rose." Noriyoshi Sawamoto et al., *The Age of Modernism* (Tokyo: Tokyo Metropolitan Museum of Photography, 1995), p. 114.

Cat. 63

1   Carl Chiarenza, *Aaron Siskind: Pleasures and Terrors* (Boston: Little, Brown, in association with the Center for Creative Photography, 1982), p. 27.

2   Ibid., p. 48.

Cat. 64

1   Keith F. Davis, "Living Art: The Sources of Frederick Sommer's Work," in *The Art of Frederick Sommer: Photography, Drawing, Collage* (New Haven and London: Yale University Press, 2005), p. 13.

2   Rosalind Krauss, "Corpus Delicti," in *L'Amour fou: Photography & Surrealism* (Washington, D.C.: Corcoran Gallery of Art, 1985), p. 65.

3   Davis, "Living Art," p. 13.

Cat. 65

1   Communication from Howard Greenberg, based on his conversation with Joanna Steichen.

2   Edward Steichen, *A Life in Photography* (Garden City: Doubleday, 1963), p. 41.

3   Ibid.

Cat. 66

1   In a letter of 15 January 1980 to James Borcoman, former Curator of Photographs at the National Gallery of Canada, Steiner wrote that at Dartmouth he took "Modern Art I and II," a course that began with the Flemish Renaissance painters Jan and Hubert van Eyck. "Although the Nude had already Descended the Stairs, we never heard one word of *even* the Impressionists – don't know if the professor approved." Curatorial files, National Gallery of Canada.

2   Photocopy of a letter from Steiner to Margaret Bourke-White, 24 April [1930], curatorial files, National Gallery of Canada (provided by Eugene Prakapas). My thanks to photographic historian Carol Payne for bringing this item to my attention.

3   Photocopy of a letter from Steiner to Eugene Prakapas, probably 1985, curatorial files, National Gallery of Canada (provided by Eugene Prakapas).

Cat. 67

1   Alfred Stieglitz, "How I Came to Photograph Clouds," *The Amateur Photographer & Photography*, 19 September 1923, p. 255.

2   See Sarah Greenough, *Alfred Stieglitz: The Key Set*, vol. 2 (Washington, D.C.: National Gallery of Art; New York: Abrams, 2002), p. XLIV.

3   In April 1929 O'Keeffe left for New Mexico; in September Stieglitz had his first major angina attack. See Sarah Greenough, "Alfred Stieglitz's Photographs of Clouds" (Ph.D. diss., University of New Mexico, 1984), p. 169.

4   Greenough, *Alfred Stieglitz: The Key Set*, vol. 2, p. XLII.

Cat. 68

1   Stieglitz was quick to point out to him that working with a soft-focus lens generalized rather than individuated forms.

2   Letter from Strand to Peter Bunnell, 9 July 1968, quoted in Calvin Tomkins, *Paul Strand: Sixty Years of Photographs* (Millerton, N.Y.: Aperture, 1976), p. 146.

Cat. 69

1   The other print was in the collection of Chuck Henningsen in 1989.

2   Strictly speaking, it is unclear whether his 1929 visit was in summer or fall.

3   Quoted in Calvin Tomkins, *Paul Strand: Sixty Years of Photographs* (Millerton, N.Y.: Aperture, 1976), p. 164.

Cat. 70

1   Franz Roh, "Der Wert der Photographie, Hand und Maschine," *Mittelungsblatt der Pfälzischen Landesgewerbeanstalt*, 1 February 1930, translated as "The Value of Photography," in *Photography in the Modern Era: European Documents and Critical Writings, 1913–1940*, ed. Christopher Phillips (New York: Metropolitan Museum of Art, 1989), p. 161.

Cat. 71

1   Karel Srp, *Jindřich Štyrský*, trans. Derek Paton (Prague: Torst, 2001), pp. 24–25.

2   Jindřich Štyrský, "L'artificialisme" (1927), in *Štyrský Toyen Heisler* (Paris: Centre Georges Pompidou: 1982), originally published in *ReD* (*Revue Devitsilu*), no. 1 (1927–1928), p. 82.

3   Srp, *Jindřich Štyrský*, p. 6.

4   Ibid., pp. 24–25.

5   Ibid., p. 5.

6   Ibid., p. 162. See also Antonín Dufek, "The Marvelous in the Everyday: The Surrealist Photography of Jindřich Štyrský," in *On the Needles of These Days: Photographs 1934–1935* (New York: Ubu Gallery, 1994), n.p.

7   "Artists' Biographies," in Jaroslav Anděl et al., *Czech Modernism, 1900–1945* (Boston: Bulfinch Press, 1989), p. 253.

Cat. 72

1   Karel Teige, "The Poetist Manifesto" (1924); see http://home.sprynet.com/~awhit/pmanifes.htm

Cat. 73

1   Rosalind Krauss has explored this thesis in her essay "À propos de Maurice Tabard," in *Maurice Tabard* (Paris: Contrejour, 1987), pp. 5–7.

Cat. 74

1   D'Arcy Wentworth Thompson, *On Growth and Form*, abridged ed. (Cambridge: Cambridge University Press, 1961), p. 48.

2   Published by the K.K. Lehr- und Versuchs-Anstalt für Photographie und Reproductions-Verfahren in Wien (Vienna, 1896).

3   Ernö Kallai, "Bildhafte Photographie," *Das Neue Frankfurt* (Frankfurt), no. 3 (1928), pp. 42–49, translated as "Pictorial Photography," in *Photography in the Modern Era: European Documents and Critical Writings, 1913–1940*, ed. Christopher Phillips (New York: Metropolitan Museum of Art; Aperture, 1989), p. 119.

Cat. 75

1   Sandra Shaul, *The Modern Image: Cubism and the Realist Tradition* (Edmonton: The Gallery, 1982), p. 38.

2   For biographical information on Vanderpant, see Charles C. Hill, *John Vanderpant: Photographs* (Ottawa: National Gallery of Canada, 1976).

3   Ibid., p. 19.

4   Ibid., p. 22.

5   In 1931 Vanderpant invited Weston and Cunningham to show work at the Vanderpant Galleries. Hill, *John Vanderpant*, p. 23.

Cat. 77

1   Beatrice Wood, "The Richard Mutt Case," *The Blind Man* (New York), no. 2 (May 1917), p. 5.

2   Margaret Watkins, "Advertising and Photography," *Pictorial Photography in America*, no. 4 (1926), n.p.

Cat. 78

1   Information on Gang's life is based on two autobiographical sketches that are now in the Gallery's Archives.

2   *The Daybooks of Edward Weston: Volume II. California*, ed. Nancy Newhall (New York: Horizon Press, in collaboration with the George Eastman House, Rochester, 1966), p. 3.

Cat. 79

1   Edward Weston, "From My Day Book," *Creative Art* III:2 (August 1928), p. xxxvi.

2   *The Daybooks of Edward Weston: Volume I. Mexico*, ed. Nancy Newhall (Rochester: George Eastman House, 1961), p. 132.

3   *The Daybooks of Edward Weston: Volume II. California*, ed. Nancy Newhall (New York: Horizon Press, in collaboration with the George Eastman House, Rochester, 1966), p. 140.

4   Ibid.